虚实之界

REAL AND IMAGINARY LANDS

上海图书馆 —— 编

上海书画出版社

CHINA AND MARCO POLO
A TALE OF BOOKS

奇迹之书
《马可·波罗游记》
主题文献图录

虚实之界：奇迹之书
《马可·波罗游记》主题文献图录

REAL AND IMAGINARY LANDS.
China and Marco Polo: A Tale of Books

主办 Organizer	上海图书馆 Shanghai Library		
支持 Supporters	意大利驻沪总领事馆 Consulate General of Italy in Shanghai 意大利驻沪总领事馆文化处 Italian Cultural Institute in Shanghai 意大利特雷卡尼百科全书研究院 Istituto della Enciclopedia Italiana Treccani 意大利威尼斯马尔恰纳国立图书馆 Biblioteca Nazionale Marciana, Venice 意大利佛罗伦萨老楞佐图书馆 Biblioteca Medicea Laurenziana, Florence 意大利佛罗伦萨里卡迪纳图书馆 Biblioteca Riccardiana, Florence		
策展 Curators	陈超 Chen Chao		达仁利 Francesco D'Arelli
设计 Designers	西比克工作室 Cibic Workshop （乔久园 Joseph Dejardin		安多·西比克 Aldo Cibic）

编委会（按姓名拼音顺序）
Editorial Committee

主编 Editors in Chief	陈超 Chen Chao		达仁利 Francesco D'Arelli
撰稿 Textual Contributors	邓岚 Deng Lan 陆丹妮 Lu Danni 杨明明 Yang Mingming		雷舒宁 Lei Shuning 徐锦华 Xu Jinhua 周仁伟 Zhou Renwei
翻译 Translators and Proofreaders	褚蕊蕊 Chu Ruirui 西西 Kendra Fiddler		罗马克 Marco Lovisetto 岳琦凌 Yue Qiling

目录
CONTENTS

004　总领事致辞　/　安缇雅
　　　Consul General's Message　/　Tiziana D'Angelo

006　序　/　陈超
　　　Preface　/　Chen Chao

008　前言　/　马西莫·布雷
　　　Foreword　/　Massimo Bray

010　文字是"别处"　/　陈恒
　　　The Text is the Otherness　/　Chen Heng

012　书页无言　/　达仁利
　　　The Silence of Books　/　Francesco D'Arelli

018　跟随马可·波罗的脚步　/　董少新
　　　Following Marco Polo　/　Dong Shaoxin

021　第一部分　奇迹之书
　　　Section 1　The Book of Wonders

029　第二部分　沙舟海帆
　　　Section 2　Across Seas and Deserts

073　第三部分　日月有常
　　　Section 3　Through the Tide of Time

193　第四部分　烂然星陈
　　　Section 4　Bright Interconnections

总领事致辞

Consul General's Message

安缇雅
意大利驻沪总领事

Tiziana D'Angelo
Consul General of Italy in Shanghai

"其所行之路，必经此数处。"1254年，马可·波罗（1254—1324）出生于一个威尼斯商人家庭，后来在中国生活了十七年（1274—1291）。他与但丁是同时代的人物。13世纪至14世纪，威尼斯无比富庶，是东西方颇具影响力的贸易中心，货物与商人在此云集，并带来了各自的习惯、风俗和语言。马可·波罗是商人之子，他抵达了元朝时期（1279—1368）的中国。那时的中国是一个令人惊叹的国际十字路口，几十年来一直是知识交流的中心。在西方人看来，中国是一个强大的文明古国，一个充满奇迹的迷人国度。

"虚实之界：奇迹之书《马可·波罗游记》主题文献展"是马可·波罗逝世700周年（1324—2024）纪念活动的重要组成部分，该展览由意大利驻沪总领事馆文化处与上海图书馆共同策划，得益于意大利威尼斯马尔恰纳国立图书馆、意大利佛罗伦萨老楞佐图书馆、意大利佛罗伦萨里卡迪纳图书馆与上海图书馆的通力合作。展览由意大利特雷卡尼百科全书研究院负责协调，并获得了意大利驻沪总领事馆的支持。

书籍是这一纪念项目当之无愧的主角。事实上，该展览的愿景兼具了特殊性和普遍性。特殊性在于纪念马可·波罗这一重要人物，其著作的意大利语名为"百万"，法语名为"寰宇记"，在英语中常被译为"游记"。普遍性则在于展览在第24届世界意大利语言周后开幕，今年语言周的主题正是"意大利语与书籍：字里行间的世界"。意大利和中国是伟大的文明古国，除诸多共同点外，二者都拥有源远流长的手工艺制作技艺与书籍印刷传统。因此，展览"虚实之界"将核心版块聚焦于来自意大利图书馆的珍贵《游记》抄本，并凸显马可·波罗在中国文献中的形象与影响，展览的中文文献主要来自上海图书馆的馆藏。中国文明之成就令马可·波罗印象深刻，其中包括寺庙和宫殿的建造，以及艺术品和装饰品的制作，展览以这位威尼斯商人的经历为原点，一段中意文化交流史通过相

总领事致辞

关文献如画卷般徐徐展开。

最后,正如马可·波罗所言,"已清清楚楚、有条有理且毫无差错地尽述一切"。我们也可以将"虚实之界"视为进一步拓展意大利机构与上海图书馆文化交流之路的当代里程碑。对于那些拥有如此价值的书籍,我们期望进一步促进富有成效的对话和建设性的交流,以保持那份珍贵的好奇,从而"悉心留意一切奇闻逸事"。

"[He] made his passage through the[se places], for his way was directed thither..." Marco Polo was born in 1254 to a family of Venetian merchants and, midway along the journey of his life (Dante and Marco were contemporaries), came to live in China for 17 years (1274-1291). Between the 13th and 14th centuries, Venice was incredibly rich and was the influential emporium of the East and the West, where goods and merchants met, bringing along their own habits, customs, and languages. Born into a merchant family, Marco Polo reached Yuan-dynasty China (1279-1368): an astonishing international crossroads, which had been for decades the largest area of exchange of knowledge. China appeared to Westerners to be a powerful civilization featuring an enchanting land of wonders.

An exhibition project of the events scheduled for the celebrations of the 700th anniversary of the death of Marco Polo (1324-2024), *Real and Imaginary Lands. China and Marco Polo: A Tale of Books* is conceived by the Italian Cultural Institute in Shanghai and Shanghai Library, achieved thanks to the cooperation between Biblioteca Nazionale Marciana (Venice), Biblioteca Medicea Laurenziana (Florence), Biblioteca Riccardiana (Florence), and Shanghai Library, coordinated by the Istituto della Enciclopedia Italiana Treccani (Rome), and supported by the Consulate General of Italy in Shanghai.

This is a celebrative project, of which the book, in general, is protagonist. The aim, in fact, is both particular–in the sense that we celebrate Marco Polo as the author of the travelogue on his experience entitled *Milione in Italian, Devisement dou monde* in French, and often translated into English with the title The Travels and general, as the exhibition follows the 24th annual session of the Week of the Italian Language in the World, which topic for this year is *L'italiano e il libro: il mondo fra le righe (The Italian and the Book: The World between Lines)*. Both Italy and China are great civilizations featuring, among many commonalities, a profound tradition of handicraft production and the printing of books. *Real and Imaginary Lands* thus sets its core on the precious manuscripts of the *Devisement* conserved in Italian libraries and highlights the tradition of Marco Polo's presence in the Chinese sources, primarily conserved in the Shanghai Library. As Marco Polo was impressed by the achievements of the Chinese civilization, including its construction of temples and palaces, along with the production of works of art and ornaments, the exhibition begins from the experience of the Venetian merchant and unfolds documents related to the history of Sino-Italian cultural exchanges.

Finally, *Real and Imaginary Lands* is a contemporary milestone for further developing the road of cultural exchanges between Italian institutions and the Shanghai Library, because we claim to "have told generally and in particular orderly enough, ...as our book tells you of them all clearly and in the right order and one after the other and without mistake," but with books that are elevated to this point, we can only wish to further promote fruitful dialogue and constructive exchanges, maintaining that precious "attention [to] all the novelties and all the strange things."

序
Preface

陈　超

上海图书馆馆长

Chen Chao

Director of Shanghai Library

2024年1月8日是马可·波罗去世700周年的日子。这位在700多年前就将中华文明介绍给西方的意大利人，不仅被中国人所熟知，在意大利也享有盛名。据媒体报道，从2024年1月开始，他的故乡威尼斯市就以盛大的嘉年华开启为期一年的纪念活动。在威尼斯嘉年华开幕式上，大约600名身着古装的划船手举桨致敬，并高喊"我们都是马可·波罗"，他们沿着大运河从圣马可广场划船前往里亚尔托桥。这样的主题纪念活动，旨在让今天的人们重新了解这位伟大的威尼斯商人和旅行家的事迹，以及他的《马可·波罗游记》。这本游记被认为是对东方世界第一个可靠而完整的记录，对亚欧相互了解做出了历史性的贡献。因此，在这样一个充满历史意义的年份内，上海图书馆也在意大利驻沪领事馆和中意两国相关文化和收藏机构的大力支持协助下，在上海图书馆（本书简称"上图"）东馆接续举办了"马可·波罗奇迹之旅：探索与求知主题数字沉浸互动体验展"和"虚实之界：奇迹之书《马可·波罗游记》主题文献展"。

虽然自古以来有不少推动东西方文化交流的知名使者，但马可·波罗几乎可以算是最早为西方社会揭开东方神秘面纱的探险家之一。13至14世纪，正是欧洲文艺复兴的前夜，马可·波罗口述、鲁斯蒂谦笔录的《马可·波罗游记》一经问世，便成为前往东方"取经"的"旅行攻略"，点燃了欧洲人内心对东方的向往，中华文明的种种元素，也由此以一种积极的形象在欧洲留下印记。

图书典籍，作为文化与文明交流的重要媒介，在这漫长的历史进程中扮演了关键角色，记录了一段段绚烂多彩的佳话。七百多年来，关于这本"奇迹之书"的研究已经成为世界中国学范畴内的一门显学，留存至今的145件《马可·波罗游记》早期手抄本分属20个"抄本系统"，从中生发出大量的研究成果。我国现代图书馆、博物馆事业的奠基人，曾任国立北平图书馆（今中国国家图书馆）馆长的袁同礼先生（1895—1965）曾为我们留下了一份国人研究马可·波罗的书单。这份书单清晰地显示，从清

序

末民初到1940年前后这三十多年时间里，我国知识界对马可·波罗这个课题非常重视。书单所列出的著作、文章的作者中，有洪钧、柯绍忞、丁谦等清朝博学之士，有张星烺、冯承钧、姚从吾、李思纯、向达等有海外游学经历的一流历史学家，也有朱杰勤和杨志玖等新一代学者。

在那段极为困难的时期，我国学界在马可·波罗研究方面取得了许多重要成果。冯承钧先生1936年翻译的沙海昂（A. J. H. Charignon）《马可·波罗行纪》法文注释本，以其文字雅驯而流传至今。1941年杨志玖先生发表的论文《关于马可·波罗离华的一段汉文记载》，虽然只是一篇短文，且也已过去了八十多年，至今我国学术界仍引以为傲，在马可·波罗研究这个领域，其他任何一篇论文可能都不能与之相提并论。历史的诡异（神奇）之处在于——马可·波罗来到13世纪的中国，回去又写了书，在欧洲流传了几百年，对欧洲乃至世界历史产生了重要影响，但他在中国历史上却没有留下"任何痕迹"，直到数百年后的19世纪，他的故事再由欧洲人传回中国。这些典籍和事实是非同寻常的，很少有哪个学术领域会出现类似情况，这一切都足以说明马可·波罗这个课题的不同寻常。我们的文献展只能非常简略地把这样的历史过程勾勒呈现给普通读者，希望能够激发更多读者通过书籍和阅读去探索这一人类文明史上的奇迹之旅和奇迹之书。

文明的交流总是相互的，文化的传播总是双向的。"东方"与"西方"之间跨越各种界限的文化交流苍黄翻覆、绵延不绝，古老的传说总是在被不断地重新阐释中，产生新的交融和影响。西学东渐和东学西传总是同步并行的，西学汉籍和西译汉籍就是记录这段人类文明历史的最好注脚。马可·波罗是商人也是旅行家，更是文化的使者、传播者和文明的感召者、先行者，今天和未来的人类依然在这个宇宙中不断行走、不断冒险、不断探索新的世界文明。我们图书馆人期待通过这样展览帮助人们正确地阅读历史、理解历史，从而更好地传承人类文明、走向美好未来。

Abstract

Commemorating the 700th death anniversary of Marco Polo, Venice has initiated a series of commemorative activities covering the whole year, starting with a grand carnival in January 2024. With the support of the Consulate General of the Republic of Italy in Shanghai and relevant institutions from both China and Italy, the Shanghai Library has also presented a digital immersive interactive exhibition as well as a documentary exhibition on the same themes. Marco Polo was one of the earliest explorers to introduce Chinese civilization to the West. His Travels, serving at that time as a guide book for Europeans who were eager for eastern knowledge, has made a historic contribution to mutual understanding between two continents. In the past 700 years, the study of *The Travels of Marco Polo* has become a prominent part of Sinology worldwide, and scholars from both China and abroad have achieved significant progress in this field. The communication between civilizations and the dissemination of culture is always being rejuvenated over time through bidirectional interaction. Marco Polo, as an ambassador and disseminator of culture, and as a beacon and pioneer of civilizations, has left a profound mark on past cultural exchanges between the East and the West through his legendary experiences and writings. In the future, his works may continue to inspire new cultural resonances and facilitate mutual learning and appreciation. We hope that this special documentary exhibition will not only promote a correct and deep understanding both of the history and of the significance of Marco Polo in his era, but also serve as a bridge to the inheritance of the essence of human civilizations, to the advance of a harmonious integration of Eastern and Western world, and to a brighter future of all parts.

前言

Foreword

马西莫·布雷
意大利特雷卡尼百科全书研究院总干事

Massimo Bray

Director General of the Istituto della Enciclopedia Italiana Treccani

---

"虚实之界：奇迹之书《马可·波罗游记》主题文献展"由上海图书馆和意大利驻沪总领事馆文化处（意大利外交与国际合作部）共同策划，并得到意大利驻沪总领事馆的大力支持。在意大利特雷卡尼百科全书研究院的协调下，展览的实现还要感谢意大利威尼斯马尔恰纳国立图书馆、意大利佛罗伦萨老楞佐图书馆和意大利佛罗伦萨里卡迪纳图书馆的宝贵协作。

作为马可·波罗逝世700周年（1324—2024）和诞辰770周年（1254—2024）纪念活动的重要项目之一，这场在图书馆举办的展览旨在将人们的目光聚焦于《马可·波罗游记》（又名《百万》）之上，该书最早以其法文名"寰宇记"而为人熟知，在英语中则常被译为"游记"。得益于乔久园与安多·西比克在展陈设计领域的创新先锋思想，展览"虚实之界"通过抄本、印刷本以及数字化图书等多种形态呈现，不仅凸显了书籍作为获取知识的宝贵工具，还将其作为人类文明进步的象征加以颂扬。因此，展览呈现的是一段关于书的故事，带领着观众们步入一场时序之旅，从14世纪的意大利漫游至之后几个世纪的中国。

今年世界意大利语言周的主题是"意大利语与书籍：字里行间的世界"，展览"虚实之界"也致敬了马可·波罗所描述的世界，这种描述不仅体现于字里行间，更是跨越了不同的文化。

同时，在此展出的部分作品还彰显了与马可·波罗相关传统的历史延续，比如其叔父老马可·波罗的遗嘱，该档案由威尼斯马尔恰纳国立图书馆珍藏并特别借展，是波罗家族活跃于威尼斯与东方之间的有力见证。展览聚焦于《马可·波罗游记》早期抄本，其中展出了两个托斯卡纳语版本（佛罗伦萨老楞佐图书馆的 TA 和 TB 版本）、一个威尼斯语本以及一个拉丁语版本（二者均来自佛罗伦萨里卡迪纳图书馆），体现了《游记》的受欢迎程度。通过但丁·阿利吉耶里的《神曲》抄本，观众还能看到一个意大利语和蒙古语之间语言接触的例证：在《地狱篇》第七首的开头中（在此展示了里卡迪纳图书馆藏的14世纪下

前言

半叶早期抄本），但丁——这位与马可·波罗同时代的人物——使用了一个源自蒙古语的词汇。

在此之后的单元围绕着马可·波罗及其《游记》在中国的影响而展开：上海图书馆馆藏中的大量文献呈现了与这位威尼斯商人《游记》相关的反响、翻译以及学术研究，另外还有可考证马可·波罗曾在中国活动的地方文献。展览的最后讲述了自马可·波罗以来中意两国的交流历程，这部分展品主要来自上海图书馆馆藏，尤其是其中一个对中意文化交流具有重要意义的机构——徐家汇藏书楼。

今年我们纪念和致敬马可·波罗，同时我也由衷希望，这位威尼斯商人所留下的传统，能够成为人类历史上两大书籍文明之间进一步开展丰富活动和文化项目的序章。

Real and Imaginary Lands. China and Marco Polo: A Tale of Books is an exhibition project conceived by the Shanghai Library and the Italian Cultural Institute in Shanghai (Ministry of Foreign Affairs and International Cooperation), supported by the Consulate General of Italy in Shanghai. With the coordination of the Istituto della Enciclopedia Italiana Treccani, the project was achieved thanks to the precious contributions of Biblioteca Nazionale Marciana (Venice), Biblioteca Medicea Laurenziana (Florence), and Biblioteca Riccardiana (Florence).

As a major project included in the celebrations of the 7th centenary of Marco Polo's death (1324-2024) and the 770th anniversary of his birth (1254-2024), the exhibition takes place in a library, with the intention to draw the focus on Marco Polo's book–*Milione*, primarily known by its French title *Devisement dou monde*, and often translated into English with the title *The Travels*. Thanks to the innovative and pioneering ideas of Joseph Dejardin and Aldo Cibic applied to the field of exhibition design, *Real and Imaginary Lands* presents the book in its various forms–manuscript, printed, and digital–elevates it to precious tool for knowledge, and celebrates it as the evolutionary symbol of human civilization. Therefore, the exhibition presents a tale of books which leads the visitor through a chronotopical journey, starting from 14th-century Italy and moving to the China of the following centuries.

In line with the theme of this year's Week of the Italian Language in the World–*L'italiano e il libro: il mondo fra le righe* (The Italian and the Book: The World between Lines), *Real and Imaginary Lands* pays tribute to Marco Polo's description of the world, a description which not only is illustrated between lines, but also spans among cultures. As a matter of fact, the selection of works here on display presents a historical continuum in the tradition related to Marco Polo, originating from an archive document-*the Will of Marco Polo Senior*, conserved in and exceptionally bestowed by the Biblioteca Nazionale Marciana of Venice-that is unconfutable evidence of the existence and activity of the Polo family between Venice and the Orient. The exhibition focuses on the *Milione's* manuscripts, putting on display two major examples of the Tuscan versions (TA and TB conserved in the Biblioteca Medicea Laurenziana), of the Venetian version, and of the Latin version (both conserved in the Biblioteca Riccardiana), and indicating the degree of popularity of Marco Polo's travelogue. With a manuscript of Dante Alighieri's *Divine Comedy*, the exhibition brings an example of linguistic contact between the Italian and Mongol languages: in the incipit of *Inferno's* Canto VII (here on display is a manuscript of the early second half of the 14th century, conserved in the Biblioteca Riccardiana), Dante-a contemporary of Marco-uses a word of Mongol origins. *Real and Imaginary Lands* then opens to the chapter dedicated to the influence and impact of Marco Polo and his *Milione* in China: a comprehensive selection of documents and books from the archives of Shanghai Library itself tells the tale of the reception, translations, and academic research related to the travelogue of the Venetian merchant, as well as the studies of local documents as pieces of evidence of Marco Polo's activity in China. Finally, the exhibition presents a section dedicated to the history of Sino-Italian interactions from Marco Polo onward as documented in the collections of Shanghai Library, particularly one of its sections, the Zikawei Library, an institution of crucial meaning for the cultural exchanges between China and Italy.

Our gratitude goes to Marco Polo, whom we celebrate this year, and my personal wish is that the tradition left behind by the Venetian merchant is the preface of further chapters rich in initiatives and cultural projects between two of the greatest civilizations of the book in human history.

文字是"别处"

The Text is the Otherness

陈 恒

上海师范大学世界史系教授

Chen Heng

Professor of Department of World History, Shanghai Normal University

---

"在所有的世纪里，有一些诗人和作家从马可·波罗的游记中获得启发，就像从一个幻想性的异域情调的舞台背景获得启发一样：柯勒律治在他的一首著名的诗中，卡夫卡在《皇帝的圣旨》中，布扎第在《鞑靼人的沙漠》中……这部书变得就像是一些想象出来的大陆，在这里，另一些文学作品找到它们的空间；这是些'别处'的大陆……"[1] 在卡尔维诺看来，《马可·波罗游记》不仅是故事的宝库，也是其他创作者借鉴其丰富异域风情构建自己想象力的平台。这就是文字与书籍的力量！它们跨越时空，促进理解，激发创新，从《吉尔伽美什史诗》《荷马史诗》到《物种起源》《资本论》，等等，哪一本名著不是照亮人类发现自我、打破陈见、促进共鸣的灵感之源？

《马可·波罗游记》这样一本"奇迹之书"，记录了那个时代的中国与世界，它改变了欧洲，亦改变了世界。作者是探险与发现的世界级偶像人物马可·波罗（Marco Polo, 1254—1324），他是欧洲"发现文化"的一个重要象征，他把巨额财富、异域传说、先进技术、复杂文明和世界上最强大的统治者忽必烈的故事带到了西方，成为连接东西方两个不同文化领域的桥梁。

马可·波罗将生动的故事和对中世纪欧亚大陆的洞察力结合在一起，用目击者的智慧，为惊叹的观众讲述了远东的迷人空间。他讲述了纸币、煤炭和其他在欧洲几乎闻所未闻的东西，揭示了大量的跨文化交流。他所描述的陌生宗教、新奇风俗、珍贵宝石、城市与人、东方香料和丝绸、奇异植物和野兽等，无不激活了欧洲人的想象力。"几个月后，这本书就传遍了整个意大利"，在其生前就被翻译成拉丁文和多种方言。

马可·波罗的描述为欧洲探险家提供了重要的信息，在亚洲研究和地理大发现史上发挥了巨大作用。他所描述的文化多样性及其知识发酵帮助欧洲走出黑暗时代。"马可·波罗之行和他的归来标志着欧洲扩张史上的一个阶段，从十字军东征开始，这一阶段在15世纪愈演愈烈……直到1497年，葡萄牙人终于绕过好望角，到达

---

1 [意] 伊塔洛·卡尔维诺，张宓译：《看不见的城市》，译林出版社，2006年，第5页。
2 Cynthia Clark Northrup, eds., *Encyclopedia of World Trade: From Ancient Times to the Present*, Routledge, 2015, pp.746-747.
3 "Marco Polo", in *The New Encyclopædia Britannica*, vol.9, 15 ed., p.4.

远东，从而与马可·波罗记录的世界建立了新的联系。马可·波罗之行清楚地标志着欧洲历史进入了一个新阶段，欧洲不仅在政治上，而且在经济上开始扩张，从而加强了与世界其他地区的交流。"[2] 无知和隔绝的障碍开始消解，预示着一个重塑历史的交流时代的到来。

马可·波罗所描绘的那个遥远且色彩斑斓的世界，改变了西方人对当时未知东方的看法，重塑了欧洲对这个此前一直笼罩在神秘中的世界的认识。马可·波罗让欧洲人认识到，与他们自己的社会相比，中国是一个幅员辽阔的、富裕得多的国家，技术、兵法和政府也先进得多，统治者拥有无与伦比的权力，激发了他们对中国文化的钦佩之情。这种传统随着一代又一代耶稣会传教士、百科全书编纂者、启蒙运动思想家所建立的思想体系而丰满起来，将中国理想化为理性治理、任人唯贤与和谐的象征，以至于在18世纪的欧洲出现了"中国热"，对中国的迷恋达到了顶峰。

可以说《马可·波罗游记》是旅行指南、商人手册、传教宝典，亦可以说是混合浪漫主义叙事手法的地理学与人种志学著作，甚至可以被视为殖民话语的先驱，因此有人称马可·波罗为"中世纪的希罗多德"。也许马可·波罗忽略了现代读者所期待的话题，因为没有描写中国的文字、茶叶、长城和裹脚的习俗，而受到怀疑。但他所写的大部分内容已被证明是非常准确的。该书作为沟通东西方文化的奠基之作，它依然是改变历史和塑造文化的永恒见证。

其实《马可·波罗游记》永恒意义超越了其准确性的问题，它的魅力在于不断激发人们对更广阔世界的探索与好奇。诚如《不列颠百科全书》所描述的："无论如何，波罗的描述为欧洲人的思想开辟了新的视野，随着西方视野的扩大，波罗的影响也在增长。他对日本的描述为克里斯托弗·哥伦布1492年的旅程设定了明确的目标，而他对香料的详细定位则鼓励西方商人寻找这些地区，打破阿拉伯人长期以来的贸易垄断。15世纪末和16世纪，在欧洲伟大的发现和征服航行时代，波罗记录的大量新地理信息被广泛使用。"[3]

这就是上海图书馆所策划的"虚实之界：奇迹之书《马可·波罗游记》主题文献展"所带来的价值与意义，它所点燃的好奇心和探险精神，在几个世纪后仍在继续产生共鸣。这场经过精心策划的展览不仅是对历史文献的颂扬，还让参观者现场体会到文化交流在理解过去和塑造未来方面的价值。众多展品以丰富的色彩和直接的方式唤起读者对遥远世界的想象。独特的布置将参观者与历史、思想、文化和想象联系起来，生成新的意义，并构建自己的世界。阅读这些展品就是重新认识世界，重新"发现"一个许多文化彼此陌生的时代。

Abstract

The Travels of Marco Polo, known as a book of wonders, recorded China and the world of that era. It has transformed Europe, and indeed, the world. It also serves as a bridge connecting the two distinct cultural entities of the East and the West. Marco Polo's narration of his adventure passed various messages that had scarcely been heard of before in Europe at the time, revealing a wealth of cross-cultural encounters. By sparking the imagination of Europeans and providing crucial information for European explorers, his *Travels* played a significant role in the Age of Discovery and thus facilitated Asian studies. The rich connotations of *The Travels* transcend the issue of its accuracy: its charm lies in its continuous stimulation of curiosity and exploration in a broader world. The exhibition, *Real and Imaginary Lands. China and Marco Polo: A Tale of Books*, curated by the Shanghai Library not only celebrates the historical documents, but also allows visitors on-site to experience the value of cultural exchange in terms of understanding the past and shaping the future. We hope that the numerous exhibits would make visitors feel closely connected with history and culture, and therefore help enrich their spiritual world.

书页无言

The Silence of Books

达仁利

意大利驻沪总领事馆文化处处长

Francesco D'Arelli

Director of Italian Cultural Institute in Shanghai

在《马可·波罗游记》（又名《百万》《寰宇记》，下简称"《游记》"）的序言中，作者敦劝读者取此书阅之，因其"准确而真实"，征引内容"所见者著明所见"和"所闻者著明所闻"。的确，《游记》应当被视作一本真相之书："有聆是书或读是书者，应信其真。"[1]然而，并非所有人都认同这一观点。自14世纪以来，一些人对《游记》的内容产生了强烈质疑，来自托斯卡纳小镇的镇长阿梅利奥·博纳圭西便是其中之一。为了消磨时间，他开始誊抄《游记》，并于1392年11月12日写道："在我看来，他所讲述的那些不可思议之事不是谎言，更像是奇迹。这些故事或许是真实的，但令我难以置信。"[2]另一方面，我们从彼得·达巴诺（卒于1316年）的口中得到了不同意见，这位颇负盛名的哲学家和科学家曾与马可·波罗有过一面之缘，并毫不犹豫地声称后者是"宇宙最伟大的旅行家和最勤勉的探索者"。关于马可·波罗游记的真伪之辩一直存在，这一点体现在吴芳思[3]的著作中，后来罗依果[4]与傅汉思[5]对其论点进行了回驳。

正如贝内代托在九十多年前指出，马可·波罗是一座"东方财富之宝库"。这是一个包罗万象的百宝箱，里面盛满了华丽的地毯等织物，形态各异的金银、青金石，珍贵的木材、香料、果实、异兽，甚至前所未见的人、宗教传统和日常习俗。总之，人们可以在其中阅尽世间万物，甚至是城市和地方的地形细节。事实上，这些信息成了中世纪晚期乃至现代地图的重要来源，比如制图学史上的杰作——《世界地图》便是最好的体现。该地图由威尼斯穆拉诺圣米歇尔修道院的毛罗修士于1450年前后绘制，自1924年以来一直在威尼斯马尔恰纳国立图书馆展出。

然而，在《游记》中我们却发现了一处明显的缺失：随着纸张和印刷术的发明，中国可谓在人类文明史

---

1. 参见 [法] 沙海昂注，冯承钧译，《马可波罗行纪》，上海古籍出版社，2014年。
2. Marco Polo, *Il Milione*, first complete edition by L.F. Benedetto, Firenze 1928, p. LXXXIV.
3. F. Wood, *Did Marco Polo Go to China*, London 1995.
4. I. de Rachewiltz, "Marco Polo Went to China", *Zentralasiatische Studien*, 27, 1997, pp. 34-92.
5. H.U. Vogel, *Marco Polo was in China: new evidence from curriencies, salts and revenues*, Leiden-Boston 2013.
6. L. Olschki, *Marco Polo's Asia*, Berkeley-Los Angeles 1960, p. 119.
7. Olschki, *Marco Polo's Asia*, pp. 119-120.
8. Olschki, *Marco Polo's Asia*, pp. 120-121.
9. Polo, *Il libro di Messer Marco Polo*, p. 2.
10. F. Cigni, "Il fantasma 'Rustichello'", in *Marco Polo. Storia e mito di un viaggio e di un libro*, edited by S. Simion and E. Burgio, Roma 2024, pp. 127-128.

上留下了浓墨重彩的一笔，而该书却并未提到任何形式的书籍，也没有谈及中国的文字传统。马可·波罗在元朝时期（1279—1368）的中国生活多年，时常往来于宫廷，这里洋溢着世界大都会的氛围，文字的传播与流通在此蓬勃发展，且充满了意想不到的效果。例如14世纪初，在著名学者和执政官拉施德·丁（1247—1318）的慷慨资助下，一些关于法律和国家学说的中国著作被译成波斯文。诸多其他的例子不胜枚举：一份于1273年编纂的清单报告称，在忽必烈（1260—1294）统治期间，观象台与御书房相连，收藏着琳琅满目的伊斯兰科学著作，涵盖了天文学、占星术、制图学、历法和年代学等领域，这些书籍没有被翻译成中文，很可能为穆斯林学者所用。尽管如此，马可·波罗未曾提及书籍的事实并不会令人诧异，因为这只是体现了其作为威尼斯商人的特定态度。他出生于商贾之家，自幼耳濡目染，在活跃的贸易往来中自发形成了敏锐的商业嗅觉，并熟练掌握了将一切事物转化为商品的技能。奥勒斯吉[6]曾简练评价道，马可·波罗是一位"缺少文学抱负之人"，他"将自己未曾探索的世界，视作一场光影交替的奇观，这里奇迹与传闻并存，自然现象与人类命运交织。而在这变幻莫测的图景背后，作者几乎完全隐匿，置身于一种中立的客观性之中，这种客观性有时虽显得平淡无奇，但又并非僵化的科学主义或枯燥的教条主义。其文化素养仅限于写出吟游诗人般的回忆录，这些人在讲述亚历山大大帝的丰功伟业时，会穿插一些粗浅的民间通俗教义"[7]。在热那亚身陷囹圄期间，马可·波罗偶遇了来自比萨的鲁斯蒂谦，后者"帮助我们这位不识字的作者将冗长杂乱的回忆整合为条理清晰的记述。游记的文字用法意混合语写就，由于缺乏更合适的语言，在当时的热那亚和威尼斯之间，这种语言为文人雅士广泛使用"[8]。《游记》创作于"公元1298年的热那亚监狱"[9]，鲁斯蒂谦作为"写手"的工作并非仅是简单辅助，事实上，不少学者坚持认为该书是"马可·波罗与比萨的鲁斯蒂谦"的合著。奇尼在最新发表的文章中明确阐述了对《游记》作者身份的看法："总的来说，我们可以认为马可为本书提供了地理、人文、历史、贸易相关的数据，鲁斯蒂谦则负责框架结构和写作风格的选择，不过二者在对方领域的介入是不可避免的。在这种持续的对话过程中，我们难以界定本书的唯一著作人，但不可否认的是，就文本的整体风格及其严密的结构而言，让人很容易联想到鲁斯蒂谦（以及来自热那亚－比萨抄写室的效仿者们）在1298年之前就曾运用过的精湛手法。"[10]

目前仅存两种法意混合语版本的《寰宇记》（《马可·波罗游记》），其中一份残缺不全，另一份完整的抄本（BnF, ms. français 1116）保存在法国国家图书馆。该抄本很可能保留了此书的原名，即《寰宇记》，《马可·波罗游记》在意大利以"百万"而广为人知，根据贝内代托的说法，这一书名似乎源自波罗家族的绰号。此外，法图版抄本保留了原作的章节划分。1928年，贝内代托首次出版了该抄本的校勘本，这也是迄今为止唯一的版本。法图版ms. français 1116是诸多抄本系统的其中之一，贝内代托首次采用字母"F"来进行标注。马可·波罗的游记之所以广泛流传，主要因为它曾被多次翻译成13至15世纪欧洲的通俗语和拉丁文。现存最早的法语本可追溯至14世纪初，其中流传下来的FG或Fr版抄本共计17种，包括一份绘有华丽插图的ms. français 2810抄本（仿真件见展品9）。在加泰罗尼亚语K本中，现存三种抄本，可追溯至14世纪下半叶，其中发现了法语本的文本元素。

托斯卡纳语TA本可追溯至14世纪上半叶，主要在托斯卡纳大区，尤其是佛罗伦萨的商人间传阅，共包含五种抄本：其中三份保存在佛罗伦萨国立中央图书馆（Ⅱ.Ⅱ.61、Ⅱ.Ⅳ.88〔原Magliab. XIII.104〕和Ⅱ.Ⅳ.136〔原Magliab. XIII.69〕），一份保存在佛罗伦萨老楞佐图书馆（ms. Ashburnham 525），后者在本次展览中展出（见展品1）。威尼托－艾米利亚语VA本现存五种抄本，最古老的一种可追溯至14世纪早期，展览中呈现了该抄本系统的经典见证：一份来自伦巴第大区东部的14世纪抄本，现珍藏于佛罗伦萨里卡迪纳图书馆（Ricc. 1924，见展品3）。此外，VA本还衍生出了两种拉丁语抄本系统：LB本于14世纪上半叶在伦巴第大区完成，目前仅存两种抄本；P本由多明我会教士弗朗切斯科·皮皮诺在14世纪初译成，该版抄本数量众多，如今保存在欧洲各图书馆的抄本高达69种。皮皮诺的译本题为"东方风土记"，它为《游记》在14世纪欧洲教会和学术界的声誉与传播奠定了基础。在人文主义和文艺复兴时期，尤其是中欧地区，皮皮诺译本作为官方权威版本一直流传至18世纪。此次展出的是保存在佛罗伦萨里卡迪纳图书馆的P本（Ricc. 983，见展品4）。1483至1484年间，在荷兰印刷商杰拉德·勒乌的推动下，皮皮诺的拉丁语译本首次在豪达印刷，后来该印本甚至来到克里斯托弗·哥伦布手中，他在第三次新大陆航行（1498－1500）之前对其进行了批注，原件至今保存在塞维利亚哥伦比亚图书馆（仿真件见展品7）。威尼托－艾米利亚语VA本还演化出了另一个抄本系统，即托斯卡纳语TB本，可追溯至14世纪下半叶。这一版本由7种抄本组成，其中来自佛罗伦老楞佐图书馆的Ashburnham 534抄本在展览中展出（见展品2）。

意大利学者贝内代托对《马可·波罗游记》抄本进行了最系统的研究，并于1928年将其作为《游记》校勘本的全面导论进行发表。[11]现存《游记》抄本数量超过140种，为便于分类，它们被归类于不同的抄本系统，并收录在西密奥与布尔乔所编著的《马可·波罗：一段旅程与一本书的历史与神话》一书中。文艺复兴时期，《马可·波罗游记》最具权威性的译本出自人文学家剌木学（1485－1557）之手，在他百年后，该版本于1559年在威尼斯出版，题为《航海与旅行（第二卷）》（见展品10）。正如贝内代托所证，剌木学以皮皮诺的拉丁语版本为底本，将作品分为三卷，并采用了对应章节的划分方式，同时还融合了其他版本的内容进行补充。

尽管《马可·波罗游记》中没有提到"书"或其他与文字相关的传统，但在这七百多年间，它早已成为后世文学作品取之不尽、用之不竭的灵感源泉，以至于杰出的法国东方学者伯希和在1904年提出、最近又被安德烈欧塞[12]再次重申的观点依然适用："在未来很长一段时间内，马可·波罗之书仍将是一个硕果累累的研究领域。人们会不时将自己和他人的研究成果汇聚成册，这是件益事。"[13]

---

11 Polo, *Il Milione*, pp. IX-CCXXI.
12 A. Andreose, "Il lungo viaggio del *Devisement dou monde* di Marco Polo", in *I mondi di Marco Polo. Il viaggio di un mercante veneziano del Duecento*, edited by G. Curatola and C. Squarcina, Arezzo 2024, p. 50.
13 P. Pelliot, "Sir Henry Yule, *The Book of Ser Marco Polo the Venetian concerning the kingdoms and marvels of the East*", Bulletin de l'Ecole française d'Extrême-Orient, 4, 1904, p. 772.

In the prologue of the *Milione* or *Devisement dou Monde*, the readers are exhorted to have the book read to them, because it is a "right and truthful" one originating from "things seen... and... heard." The *Milione* purports to be telling strictly the truth: "Chiunque legga od ascolti questo libro gli creda, poiché tutto vi è vero" (Each one who shall read or hear this book must believe it fully, because all are most truthful things).[1] Not everyone, however, took this exhortation into consideration, and since the 14th century, some have strongly doubted the contents of the *Milione*. Among the large number of skeptics was Amelio Buonaguisi, chief magistrate of Cerreto Guidi, a small town in Tuscany. To find enjoyment against the slow passing of time and melancholy, Buonaguisi began to transcribe the *Milione* and, on November 12, 1392, noted: "It seems to me that these are incredible things, and the way they are told make me think of miracles rather than lies. And well it might be true what he [Marco Polo] tells, but I do not believe it."[2] On the other hand, we have a different opinion from Pietro d'Abano (d. 1316), a philosopher and scientist of great fame who personally knew Marco Polo. D'Abano considered Polo to be "orbis maior circuitor et diligens indagator" (the greatest traveler and diligent investigator of the universe). The authenticity of Marco Polo's work is a dilemma that has lasted to the present day, as appears evident in the book by F. Wood,[3] successively disavowed first by I. de Rachewiltz,[4] and by H.U. Vogel[5] more recently.

Marco Polo is an "inventory of oriental riches," as L.F. Benedetto noted over 90 years ago. The *Milione* is a treasure chest overflowing with magnificent carpets, fabrics, silk, gems of all kinds and shapes, gold, silver, lapis lazuli, precious woods, spices and fruits, skins, animals of all kinds, peoples never known before, religious traditions, and customs and practices of daily life. In this book, one can read about everything, even the topographical details of cities and places. In fact, it is an exclusive and primary source of cartographic representations connecting the late Middle Ages and modernity, as expressed in the masterpiece of cartography, the *World Map*, drawn around 1450 by Fra Mauro, a Camaldolese lay brother of the monastery of San Michele di Murano (Venice), and showcased in the Biblioteca Nazionale Marciana of Venice since 1924.

Yet, in the pages of the *Milione* there is a glaring shortcoming: neither reference to books in any forms appears, nor does the *Milione* register mention of the Chinese textual tradition – which, to say the least, has made a distinctive impact on human

---

1 Marco Polo, *Il libro di Messer Marco Polo cittadino di Venezia detto* Milione *dove si raccontano Le Meraviglie del Mondo*, edited by L.F. Benedetto, Milano-Roma 1932, p. 1.
2 Marco Polo, *Il Milione*, first complete edition by L.F. Benedetto, Firenze 1928, p. LXXXIV.
3 F. Wood, *Did Marco Polo Go to China*, London 1995.
4 I. de Rachewiltz, "Marco Polo Went to China", *Zentralasiatische Studien*, 27, 1997, pp. 34-92.
5 H.U. Vogel, *Marco Polo was in China: new evidence from curriencies, salts and revenues*, Leiden-Boston 2013.

civilization with the invention of paper and printing. Yuan-dynasty China (1279-1368), where Marco Polo lived and interacted with the imperial court, shone with a cosmopolitan atmosphere, featuring the transmission and circulation of textual traditions that led to astonishing results. For instance, a selection of Chinese works on law and state doctrine were translated into Persian at the beginning of the fourteenth century, thanks to the generosity of Rashīd al-Din (1247-1318), a renowned scholar and first-rate government official. There are certainly numerous other examples, as an inventory compiled in 1273 shows that the astronomical observatory, which was directly connected to the Imperial Library during the reign of Qubilai Khān (1260-1294), collected a large number of scientific works on Islamic science – including books on astronomy, astrology and cartography, calendars and chronologies – without translation into Chinese and very likely for the use of Muslim scholars. The lack of references to "books" is not surprising, since it could be the result of the specific attitude of Marco Polo, as *mercator Venetiarum* (Venetian merchant), who, since childhood, had been learning by necessity rather than by choice. He became familiar with the dynamic and industrious life of trade, learned how to grasp the most propitious business opportunities, and acquired the skill of turning everything into a commodity. To use a laconic expression of L. Olschki,[6] Marco Polo was a "man without literary pretensions," a man who considered "his unexplored world as a spectacle in which light and shade alternate, together with miracles and reported events, natural phenomena and human fortunes. And behind this moving, varied scene the author so far disappears as to lose himself in a neutral objectivity, which is colorless at times without being dispassionately scientific or unadornedly doctrinal. His culture is limited to reminiscences of the minstrels, who would punctuate their recital of the feats of Alexander the Great with some rudimentary treatise of popular doctrine."[7] As chance would have it, Marco Polo shared his jail in Genoa with Rustichello da Pisa, a professional author who "helped our illiterate author to transform the ponderous mass of his recollections into an orderly account, written in that Italianized French or Gallicized Italian which, for want of a better idiom, was then, between Genoa and Venice, the literary language of the most cultured readers."[8] Rustichello's work of *scriptor* (writer) was not marginal or simply instrumental in the composition of the *Milione*, which took place "in the prisons of Genoa ..., in the years of Christ 1298."[9] As a matter of fact, several scholars claim insistently that the *Devisement* is a work by both Marco Polo and Rustichello da Pisa.

A position on the authorship of the *Milione* is clearly illustrated in a recent work by F. Cigni: "In general, we can say that Marco is responsible for the data (geographical, ethnographic, historical, commodity, etc.), while Rustichello was in charge of strategic and stylistic choices. The intrusions of both into the other's respective areas of relevance are inevitable. In this continuous dialogic work, it is impossible to establish a single authorship of the work: it is undeniable that the stylistic and structural integrity of the text must be traced back to a series of expedients that Rustichello (and his emulates of the Genoese-Pisan *scriptorium*) already enacted with great expertise by 1298."[10]

Only two copies, one of which is fragmentary, are still conserved of the Franco-Italian version of the *Devisement dou monde*, and the manuscript with the complete text is preserved in the Bibliothèque Nationale de France (BnF, ms. *français* 1116). It is very likely that this codex presents the authentic title of Marco Polo's work, namely *Devisement dou monde* (Description of the World), since the title *Milione*–more commonly used in Italy – seems to derive, according to L.F. Benedetto, from a nickname of the Polo family. In addition, the Parisian codex shows the division into chapters as supposedly presented in the original work. The first and so far only critical edition of the manuscript BnF, *français* 1116 was published in 1928 by L.F. Benedetto. In his publication, Benedetto adopted for the first time the letter "F" to indicate the manuscript BnF, *français* 1116, as part of the numerous and varied versions of the manuscript tradition. The impressive spread of Marco Polo's work is primarily due to the numerous translations appearing in the vernacular languages of thirteenth-and fifteenth-century Europe, as well as the Latin version. The French version, of which the oldest manuscript dates back to the beginning of the fourteenth century, is now represented by 17 manuscripts marked with the letters "FG" or "Fr," including the astonishingly illuminated codex BnF, ms. *français* 2810 (see *infra* facsimile edition, n. 9). In the Catalan version, marked "K" and represented by three manuscripts dating back to the second half of the fourteenth century, textual elements of the French family appear.

The Tuscan version, marked "TA," dates back to the first half of the fourteenth century and was originally meant for and quite common among the mercantile readership of Tuscany, particularly Florence. Represented by five manuscripts, the Tuscan family conserves three manuscripts in the Biblioteca Nazionale Centrale of Florence (Ⅱ.Ⅱ.61, Ⅱ.Ⅳ.88 [formerly Magliab. ⅩⅢ.104], and Ⅱ.Ⅳ.136 [formerly Magliab. ⅩⅢ.69]), and one in the Biblioteca

Medicea Laurenziana in Florence (ms. Ashburnham 525), on display in this exhibition (see *infra*, n. 1). The Venetian-Emilian version, marked "VA," is represented by five manuscripts, the oldest of which dates back to the beginning of the fourteenth century. Here on display is a fourteenth-century codex of this family originally coming from eastern Lombardy and now preserved in the Biblioteca Riccardiana in Florence (Ricc. 1924, see *infra*, n. 3). In addition, the Latin translations included in two families of manuscripts were derived from this version: one is marked "LB," originating in Lombardy in the first half of the fourteenth century and containing only two examples; the other is the numerous "P" family, originating from the work of the Dominican friar Francesco Pipino da Bologna and completed within the first quarter of the fourteenth century. The "P" family is represented by 69 manuscripts preserved in various European libraries. Known by the title *Liber de condicionibus et consuetudinibus orientalium regionum*, Francesco Pipino's translation brought fame to Marco Polo's work and spread it throughout fourteenth-century Europe, especially within ecclesiastical circles and among scholars. Particularly in central Europe, it became the official and authoritative version of the *Milione* widespread during the humanistic and Renaissance ages, and maintained such status until the eighteenth century. Of the "P" family, the exhibition showcases a manuscript preserved in the Biblioteca Riccardiana in Florence (Ricc. 983, see *infra*, n. 4). In 1483-84 in Gouda, thanks to the Dutch printer Gerard Leeu, the Latin translation of Francesco Pipino was printed for the first time. A copy fell into the hands of Christopher Columbus, who made his own notes on the incunabulum before his third voyage to the New World (1498-1500). The original is still preserved in the Biblioteca Colombina in Seville (see *infra*, facsimile edition, n. 7). From the Venetian-Emilian version ("VA") originated a further family of manuscripts, the so-called Tuscan version, which is marked "TB" and dates back to the second half of the fourteenth century. This family is represented by seven manuscripts, including the codex Ashburnham 534 of the Biblioteca Medicea Laurenziana in Florence here on display (see *infra*, n. 2).

The most systematic study of the manuscript tradition of the *Devisement* is due to L.F. Benedetto, who published it in 1928 as a comprehensive introduction[11] to his critical edition of Marco Polo's work. At present, the total number of preserved manuscript codices, divided into different families for ease of classification, exceeds 140 examples. These manuscripts are included and presented in the recently-published *Marco Polo. Storia e mito di un viaggio e di un libro*, edited by S. Simion and E. Burgio (Rome 2024, pp. 131-163, 181-200, 435-444). The most authoritative translation of Marco Polo's work is by the Trevigian-born humanist Giovanni Battista Ramusio (1485-1557), published posthumously in Venice in 1559 by Giunti. Included in *Secondo volume delle Navigationi et viaggi*, the work is titled *De i viaggi di messer Marco Polo gentil'huomo venetiano* (see *infra*, n. 10). Ramusio's version is based on the Latin version by Francesco Pipino da Bologna, and thus adopts the subdivision of the work into three books and the corresponding division into chapters. As demonstrated by L.F. Benedetto, Ramusio made use of various other sources to integrate the contents of his work.

Despite the lack of references to the "book" or to any textual tradition in Marco Polo's *Devisement dou monde*, the travelogue itself has become, in the course of over seven centuries, an inexhaustible and endless source of inspiration for books and related literature, to the point that the claim advanced in 1904 by illustrious French orientalist P. Pelliot, and lately recalled by A. Andreose,[12] is still valid: "Marco Polo's book will be a fruitful field of study for a long time to come. It is good that from time to time someone takes it upon himself to bring together the results of his own research and those of others."[13]

6   L. Olschki, *Marco Polo's Asia*, Berkeley-Los Angeles 1960, p. 119.

7   Olschki, *Marco Polo's Asia*, pp. 119-120.

8   Olschki, *Marco Polo's Asia*, pp. 120-121.

9   Polo, *Il libro di Messer Marco Polo*, p. 2.

10   F. Cigni, "Il fantasma 'Rustichello'", in *Marco Polo. Storia e mito di un viaggio e di un libro*, edited by S. Simion and E. Burgio, Roma 2024, pp. 127-128.

11   Polo, *Il Milione*, pp. IX-CCXXI.

12   A. Andreose, "Il lungo viaggio del *Devisement dou monde* di Marco Polo", in *I mondi di Marco Polo. Il viaggio di un mercante veneziano del Duecento*, edited by G. Curatola and C. Squarcina, Arezzo 2024, p. 50.

13   "Le livre de Marco Polo sera encore pendant longtemps un fructueux champ d'études. Il est bon que de temps en temps quelqu'un se charge de réunir le résultat de ses propres recherches et de celles des autres." P. Pelliot, "Sir Henry Yule, *The Book of Ser Marco Polo the Venetian concerning the kingdoms and marvels of the East*", Bulletin de l'Ecole française d'Extrême-Orient, 4, 1904, p. 772.

跟随马可·波罗的脚步

Following Marco Polo

董少新

复旦大学文史研究院研究员

Dong Shaoxin

Professor of National Institute for Advanced Humanistic Studies, Fudan University

---

1. Zhang Zhishan(张至善), "Columbus and China," in *Monumenta Serica* (41, 1993), pp. 178-179.
2. Christiaan J. A. Jorg, "The Portuguese and the trade in Chinese porcelain: from the beginning until the end of the Ming dynasty," in A. Varela Santos (ed.), *Portugal in Porcelain from China: 500 years of Trade*, Lisbon: Artemagica, 2007, volume 1, p. 54.
3. 荣振华、耿昇译,《在华耶稣会士列传与书目补编》,中华书局,1995年,第957—997页。
4. 康熙四十六年(1707),罗马教廷使节多罗(Carlo Tommaso Maillard de Tournon, 1668—1710)在南京发布了关于中国礼仪的禁令,激怒了皇帝,康熙帝降旨:"众西洋人,自今以后,若不遵利玛窦规矩,断不准在中国住,必逐回去。""利玛窦规矩"是康熙皇帝对利玛窦践行的调试策略的概括,体现了中国皇帝对耶稣会士尊重中国文化的认可。
5. 参见梅谦立、王慧宇:《耶稣会士罗明坚与儒家经典在欧洲的首次译介》,载《中国哲学史》2018年第1期,第118-124页。
6. [比]柏应理等著,《中国哲学家孔夫子》,大象出版社,2021年。
7. 参见聂崇正主编:《郎世宁全集》,天津人民美术出版社,2015年。

在本次展览中,有一部哥伦布批注过的1484年拉丁文版《马可·波罗游记》复制件(展品序号7),它不仅确凿地证明了哥伦布研读过《马可·波罗游记》,[1]而且将13世纪马可·波罗的东方旅行及其对中国的描述与15世纪后期开启的欧洲大航海时代联系在一起。特别指出的是,马可·波罗和哥伦布都是意大利人,前者来自威尼斯,后者来自热那亚。1291年,马可·波罗在结束了长达十七年的中国之旅后,从泉州乘船返回欧洲;1492年,哥伦布在西班牙王室的资助下横穿大西洋,抵达美洲。这是两场由两位意大利人开启的间隔两个世纪的全球旅行,他们都有一个共同的目的——去到中国,认识中国,与中国贸易。

尽管哥伦布最终没能到达中国,但仅过了六年,从伊比利亚半岛开往东方的新航路便由葡萄牙航海家达·伽马(Vasco da Gama, 1469—1524)完成开辟了。目前还没有明确的证据表明达·伽马读过《马可·波罗游记》,但以《马可·波罗游记》在欧洲的风靡程度推之,他没读过的可能性很小。1499年,达·伽马返回里斯本,在其献给葡萄牙国王曼努埃尔一世(Manuel I)的东方礼物中,从卡里库特(Calicut)获得的十余件中国瓷器深受国王的喜爱。[2]新航路不仅是一条从西方到东方的商贸之路,也是一条东西方文化深入交流的通道。此后的两个世纪中,天主教传教士(尤其是1540年正式获教宗批准成立的耶稣会的传教士)成为东西方文化交流的主要媒介。贸易和传教虽属两个不同的领域,但在近现代以前,二者可谓如影随形、密不可分。就像意大利方济各会士孟高维诺(Giovanni da Montecorvino, 1247—1328)几乎在马可·波罗离开中国的同时抵达泉州并最终在元大都建立教区一样,1582年意大利耶稣会士利玛窦(Matteo Ricci, 1552—1610)乘坐葡萄牙商船抵达澳门,并于1601年进入北京,建立了耶稣会在北京的首个驻院。从此,中西文化交流进入了一个全新的时代。

利玛窦之所以能在中国站稳脚跟,主要得益于"调适策略"（accommodation policy），即在传播天主教的过程中尝试融会天主教与儒家思想，平等对待中国文化，尊重中国礼俗，并重视利用知识和科技传教。"调适策略"在本质上是对异文化的包容。16世纪70年代，面对无法进入中国内地传教的困境，担任耶稣会日本—中国传教区巡按使（visitor）的意大利耶稣会士范礼安（Alessandro Valignano, 1539—1606）便为传教士制定了学习中国语言和文化、尊重中国风俗习惯的传教策略，正是在这一策略的指导下，意大利耶稣会士罗明坚（Michele Ruggieri, 1543—1607）和利玛窦才最终得以进入中国内地，并在肇庆建立了传教驻院。利玛窦进一步将这一策略发展为"合儒"策略，并在传教过程中贯彻，他的《天主实义》是将西方宗教思想与中国儒家思想相融合的最早尝试，更通过《乾坤体义》《坤舆万国全图》《几何原本》等一系列中文著作，将西方的天文学、地理学和数学知识介绍到中国。不仅如此，利玛窦的意大利文著作《中国札记》经金尼阁（Nicolas Trigault, 1577—1628）翻译成拉丁文在欧洲出版后，更是成为《马可·波罗游记》之后欧洲认识中国的最重要书籍，且因为其内容的真实性和时效性而在欧洲人获取中国信息方面迅速取代了前者。1610年，利玛窦在北京去世，获万历皇帝赐葬地，成为继孟高维诺之后第二位长眠于此的意大利人。

跟随利玛窦的脚步，在晚明至清中前期有数百位欧洲传教士来到中国，其中意大利耶稣会士有百余位。[3]更为重要的是，意大利来华耶稣会士在这个群体中表现得尤为突出，包括一批践行"利玛窦规矩"[4]、在沟通中西文化方面做出杰出贡献的重要人物。与利玛窦同时代的郭居静（Lazzaro Cattaneo, 1560—1640）是上海开教的先驱，而他的同胞潘国光（Francesco Brancati, 1607—1671）则长期经营上海教务，建立教友会多达120个，使上海成为明末清初天主教最为繁盛之地。熊三拔（Sabatino de Ursis, 1575—1620）用中文撰写了《泰西水法》，其部分内容被徐光启（1562—1633）收入《农政全书》之中。被誉为"西来孔子"的艾儒略（Giulio Aleni, 1582—1649）不仅著有《职方外纪》《西学凡》《西方问答》《性学粗述》等重要西学著作，而且将天主教带入福建，并长期与当地文人群体保持密切交流。罗雅谷（Giacomo Rho, 1593—1638）1631年与德国耶稣会士汤若望（Johann Adam Schall von Bell, 1591—1666）一同被招入北京历局，参与修历工作，对《崇祯历书》的修成有其重要贡献，可惜他于1638年英年早逝。高一志（Alfonso Vagnone, 1568—1640）来华后专研中国经典，著述甚丰，包括《教要解略》《空际格致》《寰宇始末》《斐录汇答》《童幼教育》《修身西学》等宗教、哲学、教育和政治方面的著作，这些西学著作在明末清初产生了广泛的影响。利玛窦去世同年来华的毕方济（Francesco Sambiasi, 1582—1649）不仅著有《灵言蠡勺》，将亚里士多德的学说介绍到中国，而且效力于崇祯、弘光、隆武、永历四朝，为抵御清军进攻而奔走南北。

入清以后，意大利来华传教士无论在西学东渐还是在中学西传方面，继续表现出色。利类思（Ludovic Bugli, 1606—1682）耗时二十余年译成《超性学要》26卷，这是托马斯·阿奎那《神学大全》第一个中译本（节译）。1651年返回欧洲的卫匡国（Martino Martini, 1614—1661）是17世纪中叶最重要的传教士汉学家，他的《中国地图新志》《中国历史》《鞑靼战纪》《中国文法》等书在欧洲出版后引起巨大反响，助推了欧洲"中国热"的形成。殷铎泽（Prospero Intorcetta, 1626—1696）继承了罗明坚、利玛窦的未竟之业，[5]与葡萄牙耶稣会士郭纳爵（Ignacio da Costa, 1599—1666）一同将《大学》和《论语》前十章翻译成拉丁文，在江西建昌出版，取名"中国智慧"（*Sapientia Sinica*，展品序号118），又将《中庸》译为拉丁文在广州和果阿出版，取名《中国政治道德学说》（*Sinarum Scientia Politico-Moralis*，展品序号119），此二书构成了比利时耶稣会士柏应理（Philippe Couplet, 1623—1693）在巴黎出版的拉丁文《中国哲学家孔子》（*Confucius Sinarum Philosophus*）的主体内容。[6]

康熙时期宫廷中有一批西洋传教士为其效力，其中包括在宫中行医的意大利耶稣会士鲍仲义（Giuseppe Baudino, 1657—1718）和罗怀中（Giovanni Giuseppe da Costa, 1679—1747），以及从事艺术和工艺工作的意大利传教士马国贤（Matteo Ripa, 1682—1746）。马国贤在清宫效力十三年后，携一批中国儿童返回那不勒斯，并于1732年为他们创立中国学院（Collegio dei Cinesi），教授他们拉丁文和神学，这批中国儿童也成为最早的中国留学生。在清宫艺术上更具造诣和影响力的是意大利耶稣会士郎世宁（Giuseppe Castiglione, 1688—1766），他在宫廷服务长达五十一年，效力过康熙、雍正、乾隆三位皇帝，传来了画珐琅技术和焦点透视法，参与圆明园的设计和建造，创作了至少百余幅绘画作品，[7]培养了焦秉贞、丁观鹏等一批中国画师，在清宫中开创了一种中西合璧的全新艺术风格。1771年来华的意大利耶稣会士潘廷璋（Giuseppe Panzi, 1734—1812）则是最后的两位宫廷西洋画家之一，曾与法国耶稣会士画家贺清泰（Louis Antoine de Poirot, 1735—1813）合绘《贡象马图》。

叙述到这里，我们不禁要问，中西文化交流的开辟者为什么是马可·波罗、利玛窦这样的意大利人？在中西文化交流史上为什么会有这么多杰出的意大利人？我想，其中的关键之一就是，这些意大利人是怀着平等和包容的心态来到中国的，他们尊重中国文化，有强烈的与中国开展文化交流的愿望，热衷于以自己所拥有的知识和文化换取中国的文化并将其介绍到欧洲，在必要的时候甚至愿意对自己的观念、习俗乃至宗教做适当的调适。在明朝后期至清代中前期来华的欧洲人中，意大利人可能是最没有民族主义观念和排他性意识的一群人。考虑到作为一个民族国家的意大利王国直到1861年才建立，这一现象也就不难理解了。同一时期来华的葡萄牙人、西班牙人和法国人，无论是传教士还是商人、使节或旅行者，整体而言，其所表现出的民族主义和排他性意识要比意大利人强烈得多，而后来的英国则有着更强的殖民帝国意识、傲慢心态和侵略野心。平等、包容和对异文化的尊重是以和平方式开展文化交流的前提，也是全球化时代不同国家、民族和宗教能够和平共处的必要条件。这是早期来华意大利人带给我们的启发，也是"利玛窦规矩"留下来的宝贵遗产。在当前世界"孤立主义""去全球化"盛行、地区冲突乃至战争频发的时代，纪念马可·波罗和利玛窦更具意义。

Abstract

Italian explorers such as Marco Polo and Matteo Ricci hold a significant place in history for fostering mutual understanding between China and the West. Their achievements stemmed from their approach of fairness, openness, and respect toward Chinese culture. They were curious about Chinese traditions and eager to share their own knowledge and customs in return. Through their efforts, they also introduced Chinese culture to Europe, bridging two distant worlds. When necessary, they demonstrated remarkable adaptablity, even modifying their own beliefs, habits, and perspectives to enhance communication and foster mutual understanding.

In today's interconnected world, the principles of treating all cultures equally, maintaining an open mind, and respecting differences are not only essential for cultural exchange but also for promoting peace among nations, ethnic groups, and religions. This is the enduring legacy left by these early Italian travelers, particularly Matteo Ricci. At a time when isolationism, deglobalization and regional conflicts are on the rise, commemorating figures like Marco Polo and Matteo Ricci is more relevant than ever. Their example serves as a powerful reminder of the importance of building more inclusive and understanding world, one that values dialogue and cooperation over division and conflict.

SECTION 1

奇迹之书

The Book of Wonders

　　七百余年前，意大利人马可·波罗（1254—1324）踏上了一场通往中国的"东方之旅"。这段独特旅程不仅铸造了他的个人传奇，更催生出一部传世之作——《马可·波罗游记》。这部作品以详尽且引人入胜的东方叙述，在彼时的西方世界产生了广泛而深远的影响。它不仅极大地拓宽了欧洲人的地理视野与文化认知边界，更激发了欧洲人对东方的浓厚兴趣和无限遐想，还为欧洲"文艺复兴"提供了思想火花与灵感源泉。

　　时至今日，我们虽已无法回到马可·波罗的时代，但仍能通过诸如马可·波罗的叔叔老马可的遗嘱、《马可·波罗游记》早期不同语种的手抄本，以及马可·波罗同时代人物但丁（1265—1321）所著的《神曲》抄本等珍稀文献，捕捉到马可·波罗及其著作的历史印记。这些原始档案、手稿和抄本，不仅细腻地勾勒出马可·波罗家族的过往，而且清晰地展现了《马可·波罗游记》的早期面貌与流传轨迹。更重要的是，它们还揭示了《马可·波罗游记》对欧洲文艺复兴所起到的推动与启迪作用，彰显了其在历史长河中的独特价值与重要地位。

Over 700 years ago, Marco Polo (1254-1324) embarked from Venice on a journey to China and the East. The unique journey made him a legend and led him to create a fabulous masterpiece, initially known by the French title *Devisement dou monde* (*The Travels of Marco Polo*, in English). This work presents detailed and fascinating aspects of the Orient, which had a widespread impact on the European world at that time. It not only greatly broadened the geographical horizons and cultural cognitive boundaries of Europeans, but also inspired their strong interest and infinite reverie in the East. Furthermore, the *Devisement* served as a source of intellectual spark and inspiration for the Renaissance.

Unable to physically return to the era of Marco Polo, we can still capture the historical traces of Marco Polo and his travelogue thanks to rare and unique documents such as the *Will of Marco Polo Senior*, the early manuscripts of the *Devisement dou monde* in various languages, and a manuscript of *Divine Comedy* by Dante Alighieri (1265-1321), who was a contemporary of Marco Polo. The collection of these original pieces precisely outline the tradition of Marco Polo's family and clearly show the early influence and circulation of his travelogue. The manuscripts here on display also reveal the enlightening role that the *Devisement* played in the Renaissance, demonstrating its unique value and important status in the course of history.

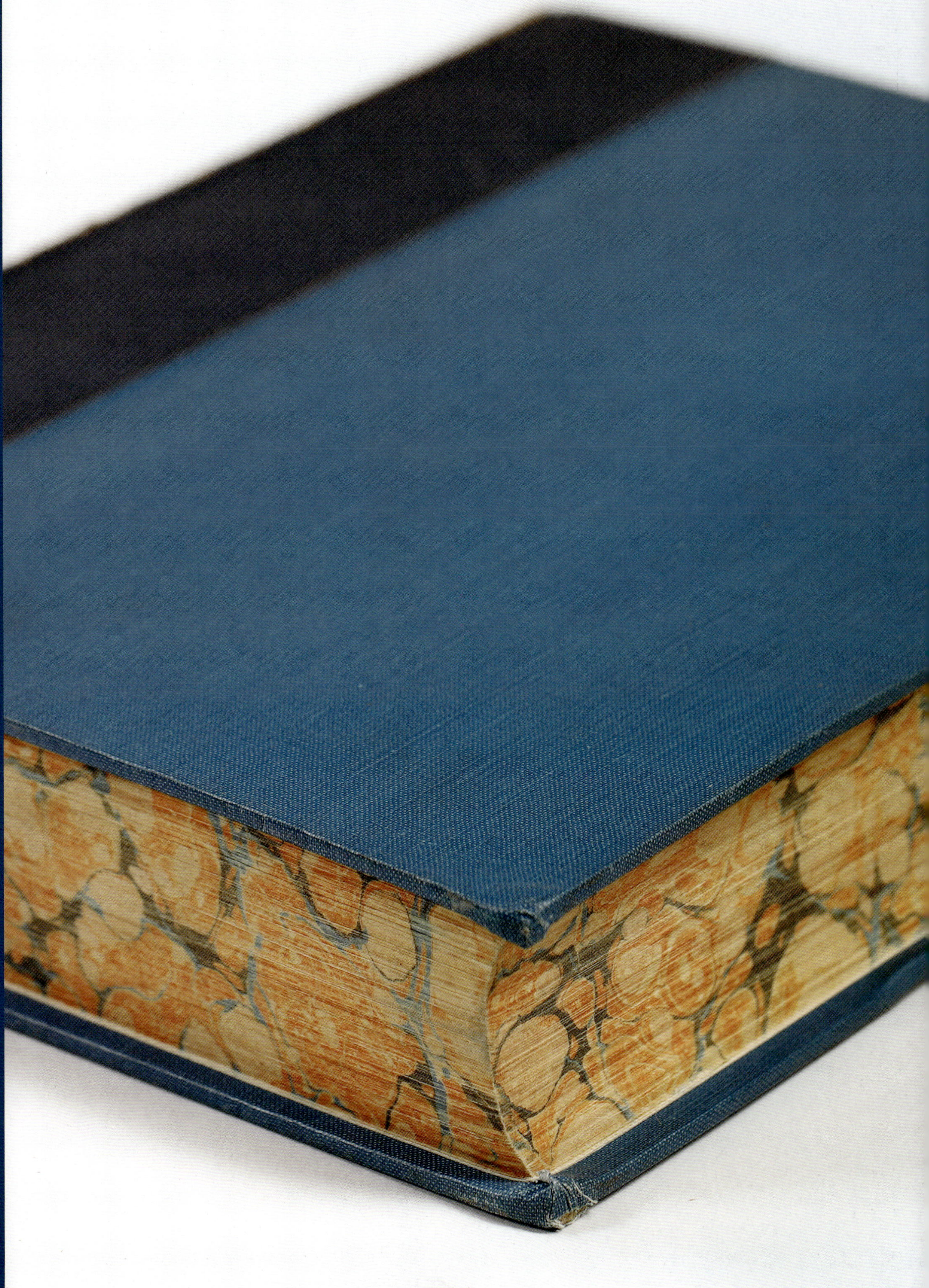

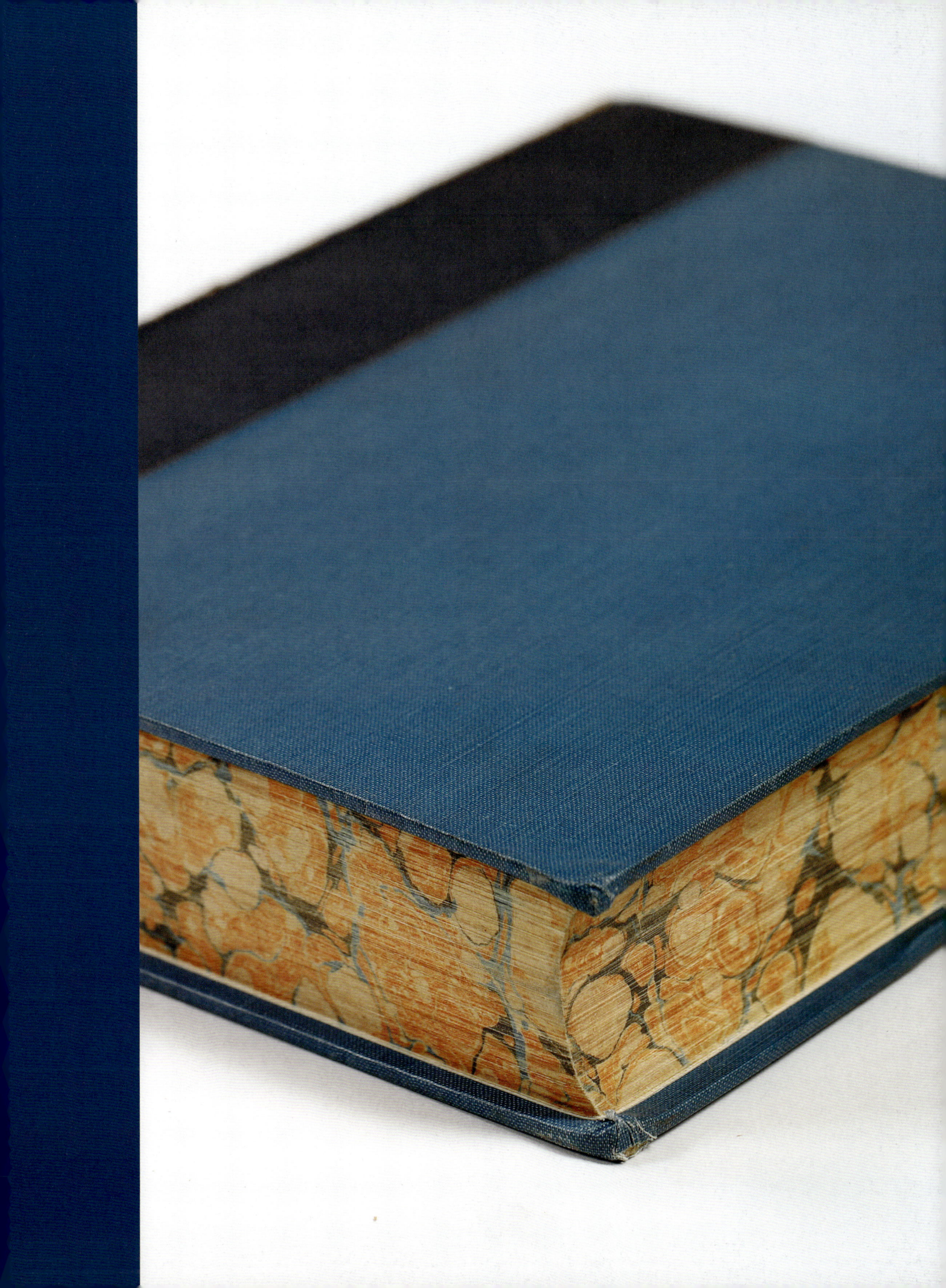

1

《马可·波罗游记》
1391

抄本，托斯卡纳语（TA）
羊皮纸，30.5×23×2.7 cm
佛罗伦萨老楞佐图书馆

Devisement dou monde (*Milione*), 1391
Manuscript, Tuscan version (TA)
Parchment, 30.5×23×2.7 cm
Biblioteca Medicea Laurenziana, Florence
Ms. Ashburnham, 525

2

《马可·波罗游记》
14世纪

抄本，译自威尼斯语版本的托斯卡纳语（TB）
羊皮纸，29.2×21×1.5 cm
佛罗伦萨老楞佐图书馆

Devisement dou monde (*Milione*), 14th century
Manuscript, Tuscan version descending from the Venetian version (TB)
Parchment, 29.2×21×1.5 cm
Biblioteca Medicea Laurenziana, Florence
Ms. Ashburnham, 534

第一部分
奇 迹 之 书

虚实之界：奇迹之书
《马可·波罗游记》主题文献图录

3

《马可·波罗游记》
14世纪

抄本，威尼斯语（VA）
纸，32.5×25.5×3 cm
佛罗伦萨里卡迪纳图书馆

Devisement dou monde (*Milione*), 14th century
Manuscript, Venetian version (VA)
Paper, 32.5×25.5×3 cm
Biblioteca Riccardiana, Florence
Ricc. 1924

4

《马可·波罗游记》
14世纪

［意］皮皮诺（译），抄本，拉丁文（P）
纸，22×15.8×3 cm
佛罗伦萨里卡迪纳图书馆

Devisement dou monde (*Milione*), 14th century
Francesco Pipino da Bologna O.P. (tr.),
manuscript, Latin version (P)
Paper, 22×15.8×3 cm
Biblioteca Riccardiana, Florence
Ricc. 983

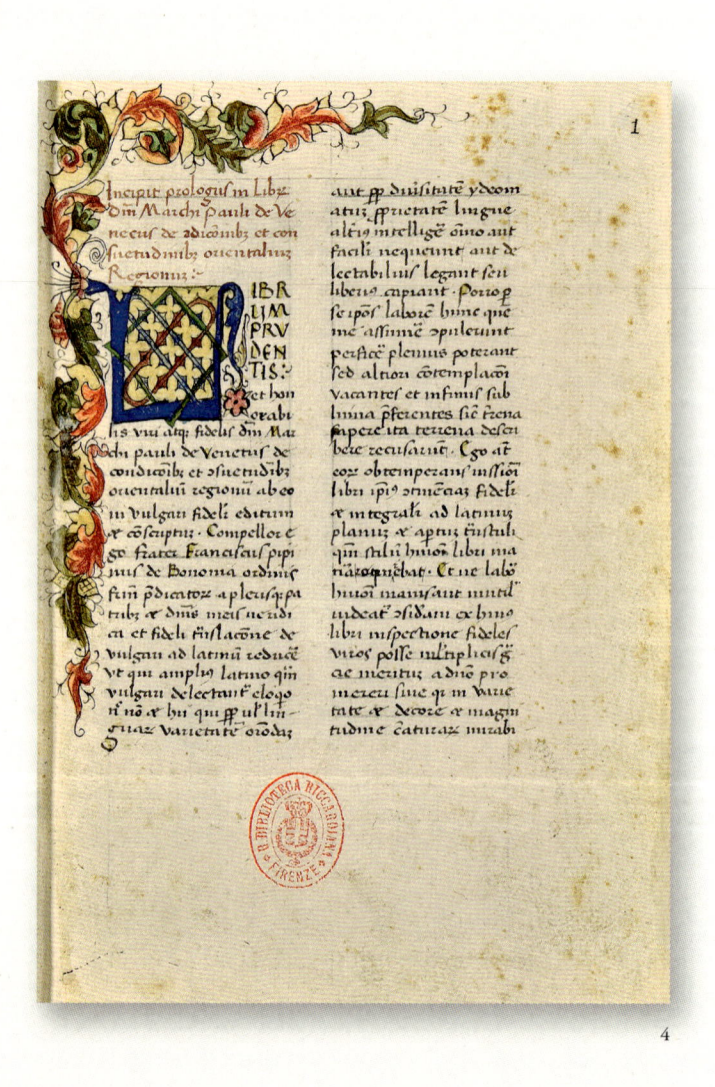

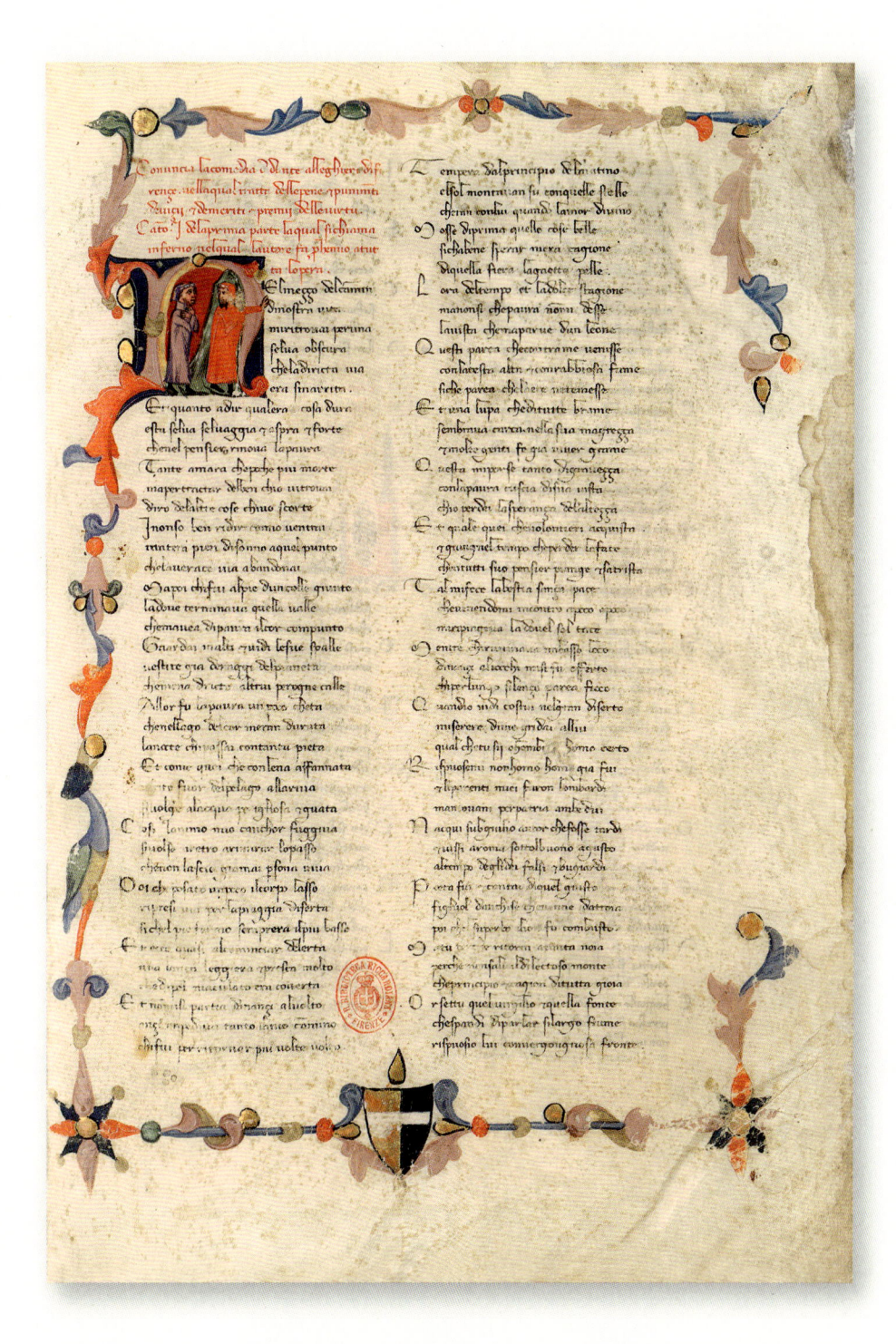

第一部分
奇 迹 之 书

5

《神曲》
1346—1365

[意]但丁（撰），抄本，意大利文
羊皮纸，41.5×29.5×4 cm
佛罗伦萨里卡迪纳图书馆

Divina Commedia (*Divine Comedy*),
1346-1365
Dante Alighieri (au.), manuscript, Italian
Parchment, 41.5×29.5×4 cm
Biblioteca Riccardiana, Florence
Ricc. 1010

6
《老马可·波罗遗嘱》
1280

［意］老马可·波罗（撰），抄本，拉丁文
羊皮纸，57×23 cm
威尼斯马尔恰纳国立图书馆

Testamento di Marco Polo il Vecchio (*Will of Marco Polo Senior*), 1280
Marco Polo Senior (au.), manuscript, Latin
Parchment, 57×23 cm
Biblioteca Nazionale Marciana, Venice
Lat. V, 58 (2437), n.31

SECTION 2

沙舟海帆

Across Seas and Deserts

如同马可笔下的驼队翻越戈壁、帆船横绝大洋，《马可·波罗游记》的翻译和传播同样是一段充满冒险与惊奇的旅程。

哥伦布（1451—1506）航行时携带的拉丁文本《马可·波罗游记》，剌木学（1485—1557）悉心会校的意大利文《马可·波罗游记》，颇节（1801—1873）翻译的法文本《马可·波罗游记》，亨利·玉尔（1820—1889）的英文评注版，张星烺（约1888—1951）的中译本……我们在这里看到的不同年代、语言的《马可·波罗游记》，都是这本"奇迹之书"在印刷、翻译过程中的代表性节点版本。

我们在这里见证一部脍炙人口的经典著作，是如何跨越语言障碍流传开去的；也见证人类文明的记载是如何渡过时间之沙与空间之海。同时，也看到了700年间的翻译与研究，为《马可·波罗游记》增添的不同魅力。

Like the camel caravans that traveled the Gobi and the sailing ships that crossed the oceans in Marco Polo's writing, the translation and dissemination of the *Devisement dou monde* was also a journey full of adventures and surprises.

From the copy of the *Devisement* carried by Columbus (1451-1506) during his voyage to the *Delle navigationi et viaggi* carefully proofread by Ramusio (1485-1557) to the *Le livre de Marco Polo* translated by Pauthier (1801-1873); from the English commentary edition by Henry Yule (1820-1889) to the Chinese edition by Zhang Xinglang (c. 1888-1951)... These editions of the *Devisement* here on display are from different times and in different languages, representing prominent milestones in the journey of translation and dissemination of Marco Polo's travelogue.

This section shows how a popular classic work has spread across linguistic barriers, becoming an everlasting record of human civilization. We will also see how the translations and researches accomplished in the past seven centuries have added attractiveness and scientific value to the *Devisement*.

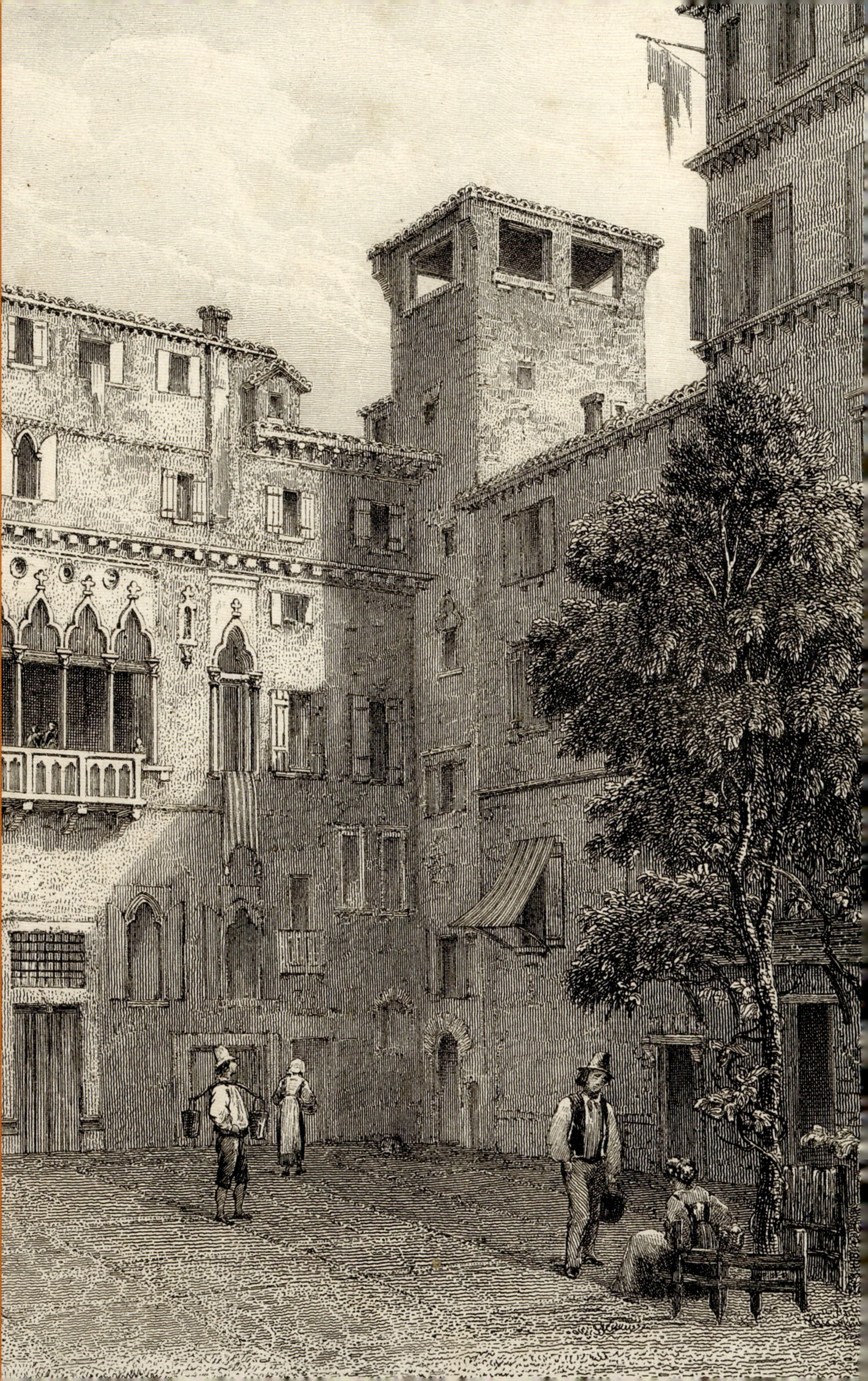

Liber de condicionibus, Incipit   *Liber de condicionibus, Liber primus*

第二部分
沙舟海帆

7
《马可·波罗游记》
（仿真复制件）
1484/1992

[意] 马可·波罗，豪达 / 马德里，拉丁文
20.5×28 cm
西班牙塞维利亚哥伦布图书馆 / 私人收藏

De consuetudinibus et condicionibus orientalium regionum (facsimile edition), 1484/1992
Marco Polo, Gouda / Madrid, Latin
20.5×28 cm
Biblioteca Capitular y Colombina del Cabildo Catedral de Sevilla, Sevilla / Private collection

Liber de condicionibus, Explicit

8
《马可·波罗游记》
（仿真复制件）
1480—1500/2024

抄本，巴黎，法文
47×31.5 cm
法国阿森纳图书馆 / 意大利特雷卡尼百科全书研究院

Devisement du monde (facsimile edition, Istituto della Enciclopedia Italiana Treccani), 1480-1500/2024
manuscript, Paris, French
47×31.5 cm
Bibliothèque de l'Arsenal de Paris
MS 5219

第二部分
沙舟海帆

9
《马可·波罗游记》
（仿真复制件）
1410—1412/1995

抄本，巴黎，法文
44×31 cm
法国国家图书馆 / 上海图书馆

Le livre des merveilles (facsimile edition, Shanghai Library),
1410-1412/1995
manuscript, Paris, French
44×31 cm
Bibliothèque Nationale de France / Shanghai Library
fr. 2810

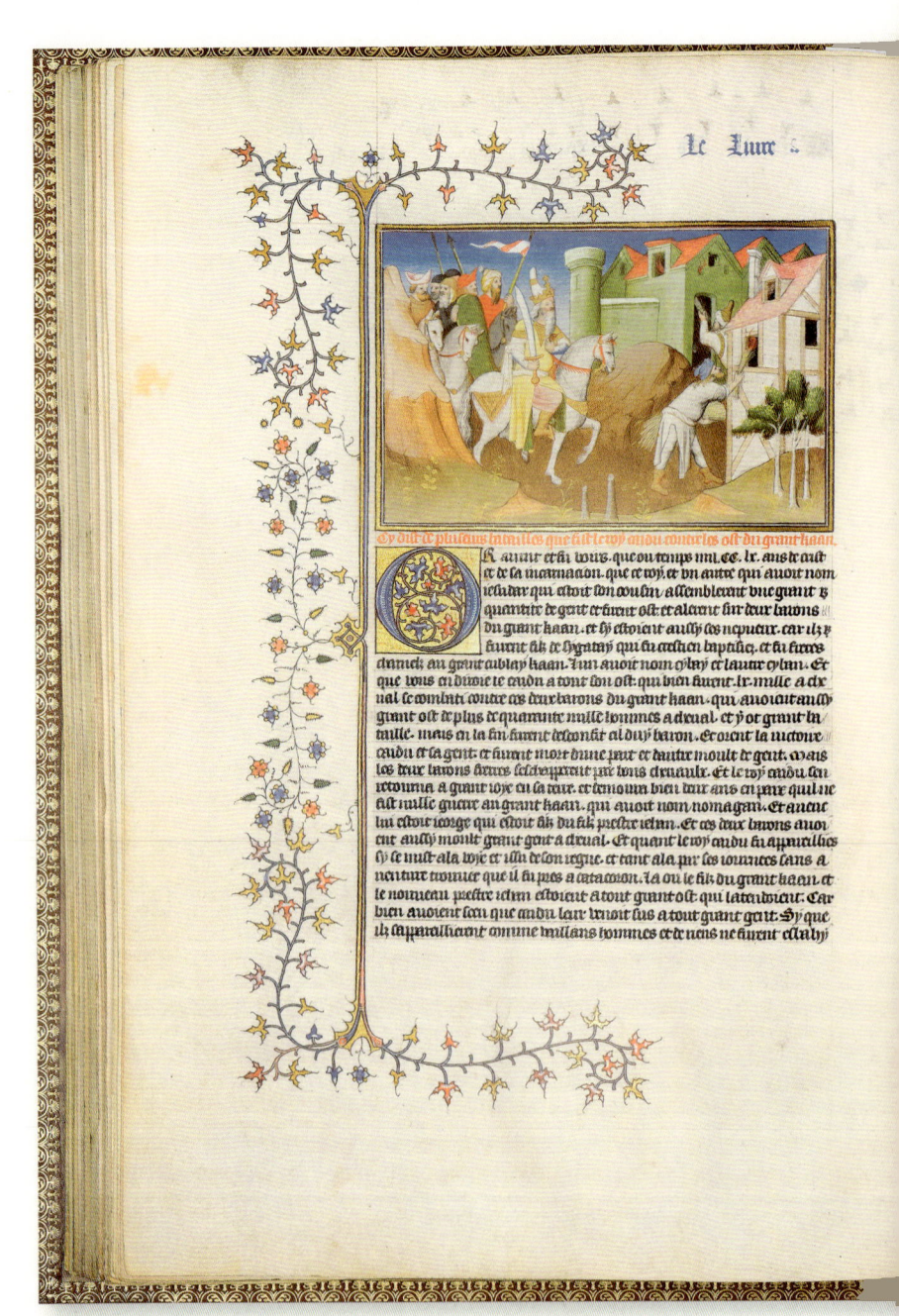

第二部分
沙舟海帆

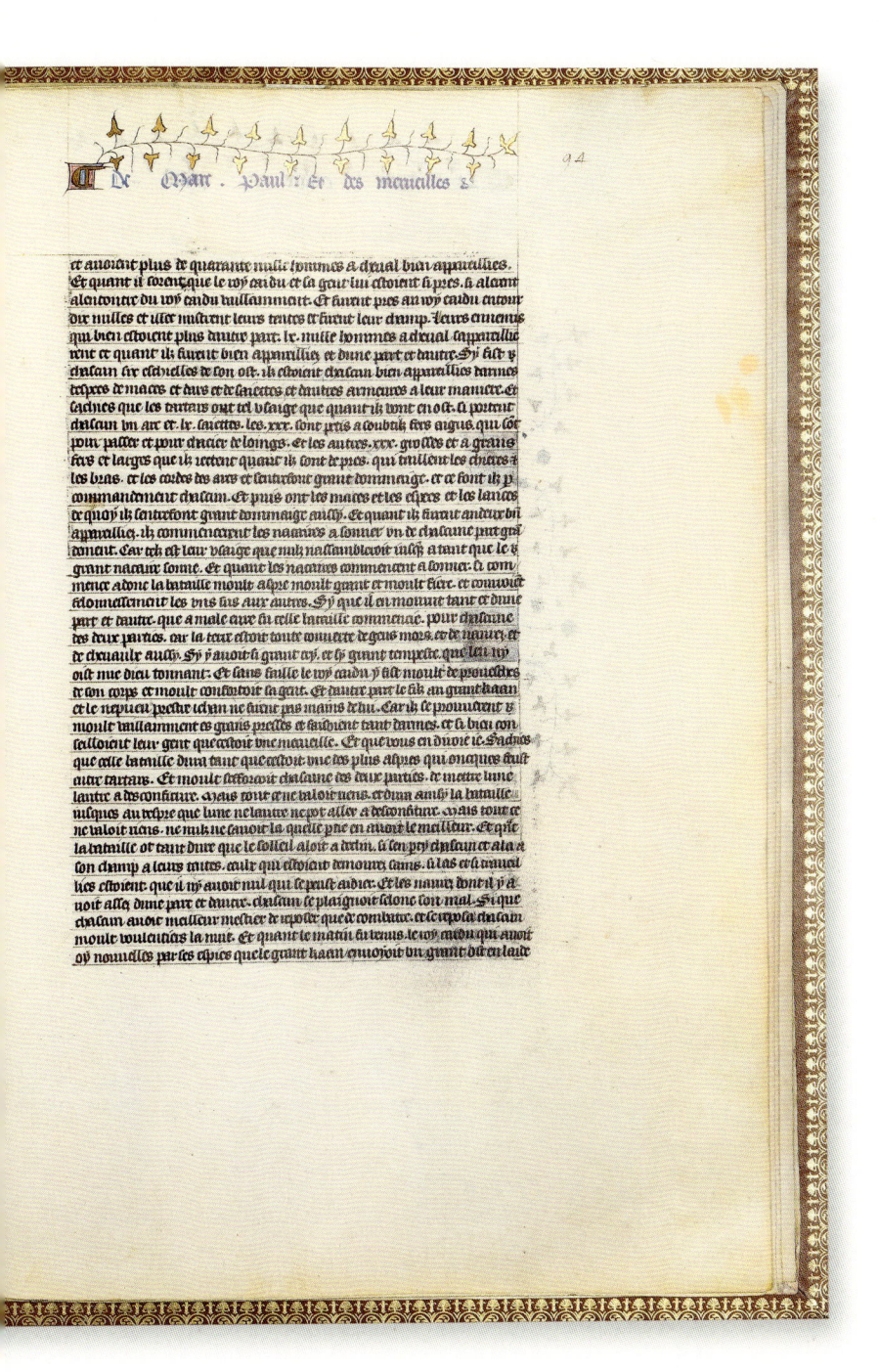

虚实之界：奇迹之书
《马可·波罗游记》主题文献图录

第二部分
沙舟海帆

10
《航海与旅行（第二卷）》
1559

[意]剌木学（撰），威尼斯，意大利文
30×21.5 cm
上海图书馆

Delle navigationi et viaggi (secondo volume),
1559
Giovanni Battista Ramusio (au.), Venice, Italian
30×21.5 cm
Shanghai Library

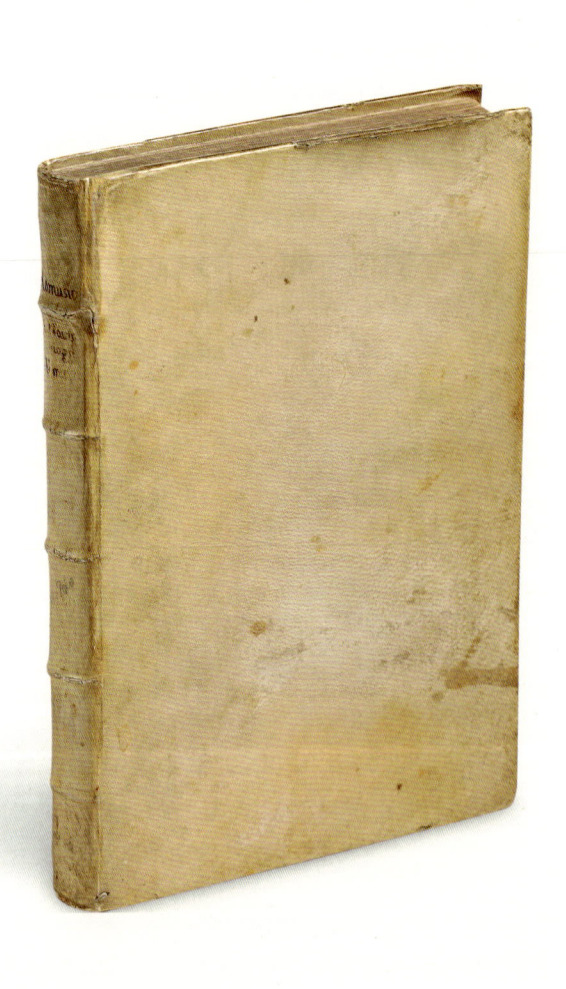

DI M. GIO. BATTISTA RAMVSIO
PREFATIONE
SOPRA IL PRINCIPIO DEL LIBRO DEL MAG.co M. MARCO POLO
ALL'ECCELLENTE M. HIERONIMO FRACASTORO.

IN quanta stima fusse appresso gli antichi, Eccellente messer Hieronimo, la scientia che tratta di questo mirabil globo della terra, che si chiama Geographia, da questo si puo comprendere, che essendoui bisogno di gran dottrina, & contemplatione, per venir alla cognitione di quella, tutti i piu letterati huomini ne volsero scriuere. & il primo fu Homero, qual non seppe con altra forma di parole esprimer vn'huomo perfetto, & pieno di sapientia, che dicendo, ch'egli era andato in diuerse parti del mondo, & haueua vedute molte citta & costumi de popoli. tanto la cognition della geographia gli parea atta a far vn'huomo sauio & prudente. ne scrissero dopo lui molti altri auttori Greci, & fra gli altri Aristotele ad Alessandro, & Polibio maestro di Scipione, & Strabone molto copiosamente. il libro del quale, & di Tolomeo Alessandrino, son peruenuti all'eta nostra: Appresso de Latini, Agrippa genero d'Augusto, Iuba Re di Mauritania, & molti altri: le fatiche de quali si sono smarrite col tempo. ne si sà altro di loro, se non quanto si legge ne i libri di Plinio: che anchor egli ne scrisse. Di tutti i sopranominati, Tolomeo, per esser posteriore, n'hebbe maggior cognitione. percioche, verso di tramontana, trapassa il mar Caspio, & sà che glie come vn lago serrato d'intorno. la qual cosa al tempo di Strabone, & Plinio, quando i Romani eran Signori del mondo, non si sapeua. pur anchora con questa cognitione oltra il detto mare per gradi quindici di latitudine, mette terra incognita, & il medesimo fa verso il polo Antartico, oltra l'equinottiale.

Viaggi vol. 2°.   i ij   Delle

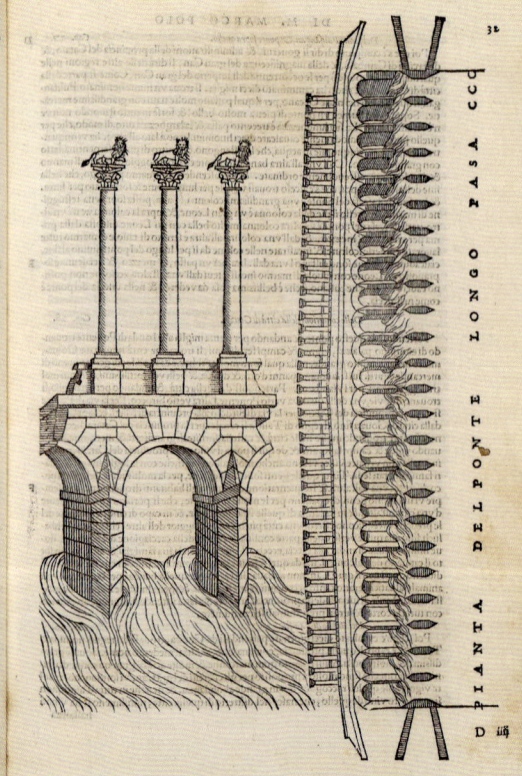

虚实之界：奇迹之书
《马可·波罗游记》主题文献图录

Ramusio Navig...

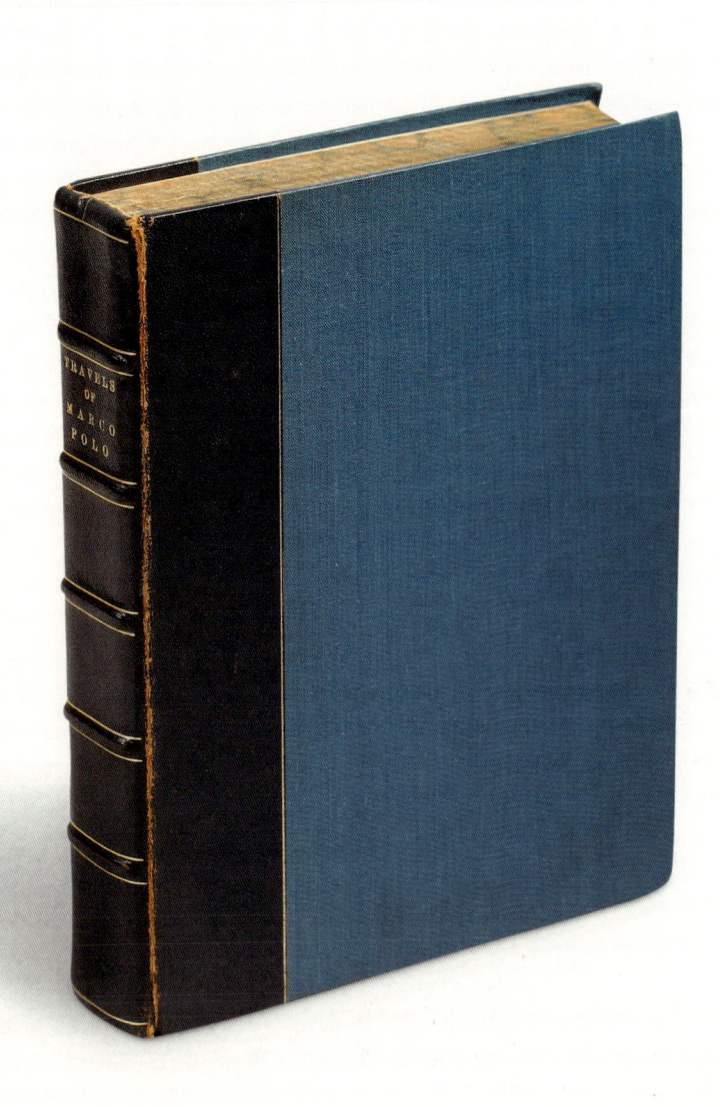

虚实之界：奇迹之书
《马可·波罗游记》主题文献图录

11
《马可·波罗游记》
1818

[英] 威廉·马斯登（译），伦敦，英文
27×22.5 cm
上海图书馆

The Travels of Marco Polo, 1818
William Marsden (tr.), London, English
27×22.5 cm
Shanghai Library

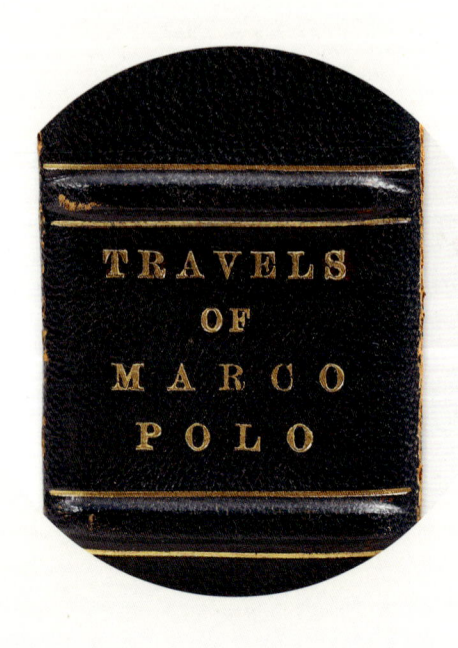

THE
TRAVELS
OF
MARCO POLO,
A VENETIAN,
IN THE THIRTEENTH CENTURY:

BEING A

DESCRIPTION, BY THAT EARLY TRAVELLER,

OF

REMARKABLE PLACES AND THINGS,

IN

THE EASTERN PARTS OF THE WORLD.

TRANSLATED FROM THE ITALIAN,

WITH

NOTES,

BY WILLIAM MARSDEN, F.R.S. &c.

WITH A MAP.

LONDON:
PRINTED FOR THE AUTHOR,
BY COX AND BAYLIS, GREAT QUEEN-STREET, LINCOLN'S-INN-FIELDS,
AND SOLD BY LONGMAN, HURST, REES, ORME, AND BROWN, PATERNOSTER ROW;
AND BLACK, KINGSBURY, PARBURY, AND ALLEN,
LEADENHALL STREET.

MDCCCXVIII.

INTRODUCTION.

Previously to entering upon a consideration of the particular motives that have led to the publication of a new English version of the Travels of Marco Polo, it may prove satisfactory to the reader that he should be furnished with such information as the existing materials will allow, of the distinguished person by whom, and the circumstances under which they were achieved and afterwards communicated to the world. It is true that for the most interesting portion of his life, or that which passed abroad, in the service of the Tartar conqueror of China, reference might be made to the account which he himself has given of it, in the preliminary chapter of his work ; but as some few facts have been recorded of him and his family, subsequent to his return to his own country, and as the travels themselves, by separating them from the descriptions of places and narrative of public events, may be rendered more properly the subject of biography, the whole of what is known to us respecting the house of Polo shall here be succinctly stated in that form.

We are told that Andrea Polo da S. Felice, a patrician or nobleman of Venice,* but of Dalmatian extraction, had three sons, who were named Marco, Maffio, and Nicolo ; of whom the second, who was the uncle,

---

* The members of this family are repeatedly styled "nobiles viri," which might be understood to mean "eminent persons," rather than as belonging to the class of hereditary nobility ; but in the Annotazioni of Apostolo Zeno (t. ii, p. 166) I find mention of a manuscript work by Marco Barbaro, intitled "Alberi delle Famiglie patritie Venetiane," which includes the Polo family.

---

558   TRAVELS OF MARCO POLO.

NOTES.

BOOK II. CHAP. LXXVI. Notes.

1106. It cannot be doubted that the word *Kan-giu* is here intended for *Kuang-cheu* or *Quang-cheu*, the name of the city improperly termed by Europeans, Canton, being a corruption of *Kuang-tong*, which belongs to the province of which it is the capital ; but however clear the identity of the name may be, its application to the place is attended with insuperable difficulty ; for not only the distances stated could not have led us beyond the province of *Fo-kien*, but the circumstance of the river being said to discharge itself not far from the port of *Zai-tun* or *Zarten* (afterwards described) obliges us to consider our author as again speaking of the city of *Fu-cheu*, which he had before incidentally mentioned as the capital of that province. The inference here drawn is also strengthened by the texts of the Basle and the early Italian editions, both of which speak of the latter city as that which was distant fifteen miles from *Un-guen*, *Un-guen*, or *U-guen*, without noticing the name of *Kan-giu* or *Kuang-cheu*. Yet it must be allowed that the latter could not have been introduced in Ramusio's version, unless it had been found in some of the manuscripts which he consulted, nor is it likely that a place of its great commercial importance should be passed entirely unnoticed in our author's original account. It seems therefore most probable that as there are in this south-eastern part of China at least three considerable ports frequented by foreign traders (although not by ships from Europe), it may have appeared to persons ignorant of and indifferent about the geography, that there was too much sameness in the descriptions, and that one or other of them might be conveniently omitted. Upon any other supposition it will not be an easy matter to account for the same chapter, containing substantially the same facts, being said in some editions to treat of *Fu-gui*, answering to *Fu-cheu* the capital of *Fo-kien*, and in another, to treat of *Kan-giu*, answering to *Kuang-cheu* (Canton) the capital of *Kuang-tong* : neither of which were known to Europeans through any other channel, for two centuries after the date of these travels.

1107. "On fait dans toute l'étendue de son ressort" says Du Halde, speaking of *Fu-cheu* "du sucre extrêmement blanc." T. i, p. 155.

1108. "Mesme les plus grands vaisseaux de la Chine" says P. Martini speaking of the same city "peuvent, sortans de la mer, monter jusqu'aux murailles qui sont vers le midy, par une grande embouchure, où est le fauxbourg de *Nantai*." P. 153. These qualities may be thought to apply equally to Canton, which lies more directly open to the trade from India, and was certainly the *Can-su* of the early Arabian travellers, but by some well-informed persons the port of *Fu-cheu* is considered, under all its circumstances as the best adapted to foreign trade of any in China.

CHAPTER

TRAVELS OF MARCO POLO.   559

CHAPTER LXXVII.

Of the city and port of Zai-tun, and the city of Tin-gui.

Upon leaving the city of *Kan-giu* and crossing the river to proceed in a south-easterly direction, you travel during five days through a well inhabited country, passing towns, castles and substantial dwellings, plentifully supplied with all kinds of provisions. The road lies over hills, across plains, and through woods, in which are found many of those shrubs from whence the camphor is procured.[1109] The country abounds also with game. The inhabitants are idolaters. They are the subjects of the Grand *khan*, and within the jurisdiction of *Kan-giu*. At the end of five days journey you arrive at the noble and handsome city of *Zai-tun*, which has a port on the sea-coast celebrated for the resort of shipping, loaded with merchandize that is afterwards distributed through every part of the province of *Manji*.[1110] The quantity of pepper imported there is so considerable, that what is carried to Alexandria, to supply the demand of the western parts of the world, is trifling in comparison, perhaps not more than the hundredth part. It is indeed impossible to convey an idea of the concourse of merchants and the accumulation of goods, in this which is held to be one of the largest and most commodious ports in the world.[1111] The Grand *khan* derives a vast revenue from this place, as every merchant is obliged to pay ten per cent. upon the amount of his investment. The ships are freighted by them at the rate of thirty per cent. for fine goods, forty-four for pepper, and for lignum aloes, sandal-wood, and other drugs, as well as articles of trade in general, forty per cent. : so that it is computed by the merchants, that their charges, including customs and freight, amount to half the value of the cargo ; and yet upon the half that remains to them, their profit is so considerable, that they are always disposed to return to the same market with a further stock of merchandise. The country is delightful, the people are idolaters, and have all the necessaries of life in plenty. Their disposition is peaceable, and they are fond of ease and indulgence.[1112] Many persons arrive in this city from the interior parts

of

12
《元代客卿马哥博罗游记》
1913

（清）魏易（译），北京，中文
23×16 cm
上海图书馆

The Travels of Marco Polo, 1913
Wei Yi (tr.), Beijing, Chinese
23×16 cm
Shanghai Library

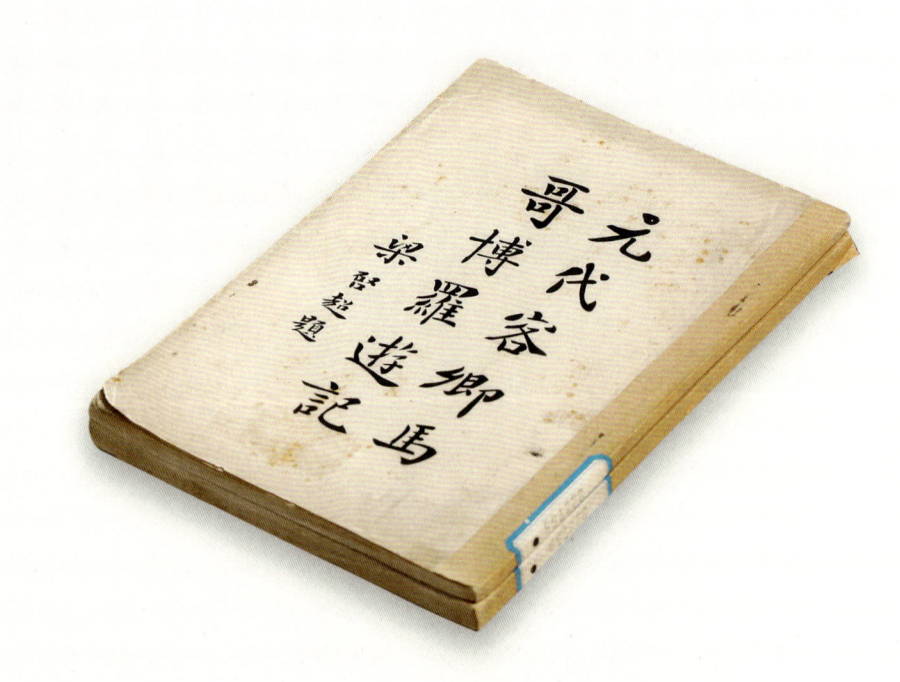

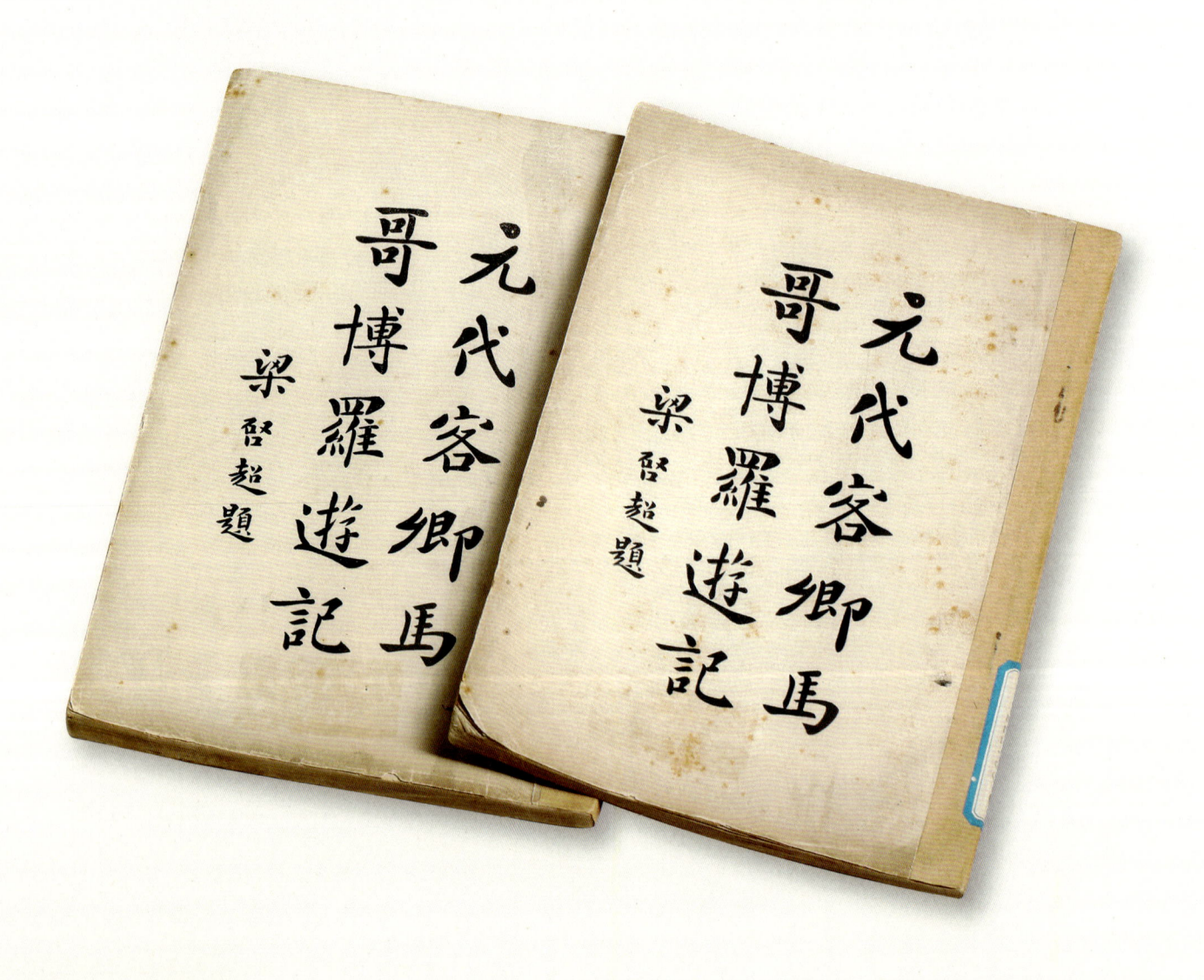

第二部分
沙舟海帆

序

元世祖時有伊大利威尼斯人名馬哥博囉者隨其父尼古羅博囉來東亞服官於元代十餘年一使安南再赴西域又爲江南路行中書省樞密副使凡中國風土人情知之最悉馬哥博學多才極爲世祖所信任他大臣頗有忌之者馬哥父子亦知世祖春秋漸高異時必不能安其位故託護逸公主下嫁藩王之名歸伊大利以終馬哥後著有遊記一卷此實爲歐羅巴人對於我國有著作之始出版以後風行一時至今文明各國均競相逐譯數年前嘗有西友訊易此書中國曾有譯本否易答以未詳西友似甚駭異謂日此書歐美各國重若經典中國爲書中最有關係之國奈何不急加逐譯易報然無以答諸徐當譯之後汪君康年設日報於北京名日京報後人輾轉重譯譯人名地報末顧原書爲十三世紀之古著又經人輾轉重譯譯人名地訛舛脫漏當里方向與今世與圖所載當不相符當時明知其誤然無以改正之心殊勿悒

也京報出版未及一歲以觸怒親貴停止發行而余書亦因之中輟前年武昌起義京師紛擾余挈眷居津門鎮日開居無所事事乃發篋取西友所贈之中西地名對照表觀之內有馬哥遊記中之今昔地名考問之喜甚去年七月間金君仍珠約余入京佐辦西報得暇輒取馬哥遊記與今昔地名考悉心比照日譯數篇詳加註釋至陰曆年終全書告竣視前登錄於京報者較爲正確惜乎汪君嘉木已拱不得起而一就正之可憾也夫抑易更有言者元史雖無馬哥博囉列傳惟其名嘗一見於奸臣阿合馬傳及本紀中之今昔地名考之至於礦改襄陽城一事元史謂製礮取馬替亞 今廠今國氏 之祖金君人考之元史記馬替亞 今廠今國氏 之祖亦與有力馬余書既脫稿嘗謂同邑孫君仲華閱之孫君謂此書可以補正史之脫漏並可於此得當日社會之消息爲果爾考古家或亦將有取於斯歟
江杭縣魏易序
民國二年二月

元代客卿馬哥博羅遊記原序

中古時代伊大利威尼斯人馬哥博羅東方遊記一書重譯至十餘種文字其所記載皆屬信史已不煩申論顧讀者往往疑其書而不詳其人之家世遺憾何如據伊大利史家言博羅氏系出華族先世來自達而馬替亞 今與國氏 之祖爲安特里亞博羅生三子伯馬仲馬非倭叔馬皆爲威尼斯商人合資而營業焉西歷一千二百五十四年或五十五年間仲叔皆挾貨行賈於君士但丁蓋其時威尼斯與君士但丁互商正在極盛之時也當達爾丁亞細亞內地也各君其土而受節制於蒙古大帝故諸王之治亞細亞內地路不梗商旅稱便歐洲客商輻湊因購珍寶渡黑海至開里米亞 戰與土夾 之某埠自此復水陸兼程終乃得達爾喀什百爾喀什朝巴爾喀者拔都之弟成吉師之孫也時方建都於亞撒拉及布爾噶拉兩處仲叔至其地居一

222758

虚实之界：奇迹之书
《马可·波罗游记》主题文献图录

序

元世祖時有伊大利威尼斯人名馬哥博羅者隨其父尼古羅博羅叔馬非倭東亞服官於元代者十餘年一使安南再使西域父為江南路行中書省樞密副使凡中國風土人情知之甚悉馬哥博學多才楷為世祖所信任他大小事務必委任之至元乙酉春秋間高麗時必不能失其位故託謀送父于下嫁藩王之名豁爾脫後有遊記一卷此書發於歐羅巴人對於我國有總作之名豁爾脫譯本謂讀相符以未詳西友似茲加譯異國均諤加譯本昔有譯日志此書歐美各國重譯之後出版以後汪君康年前曾為西友詢易昔中國曾有譯本今不論加查譯本亦有難日等但口報此書中翻譯之後汪君康年馳馬哥以是等著又經憲人懷榛軍譯人名豁譯異國所藏者常不相容當時明知其譯義無以改正之心殊勿惺里束順原書于十三世紀之古著又經發入懷榛軍譯人名豁

第一章

卷二

第一章 印度及其諸島之構造法

上卷所紀者為堅丹海諸名有之構造之舟及大可汗海原各地泰然皆於遠海軍紀必先蔣印度尚大可汗海原各地泰然皆於印度印度舟板大可汗海諸各之構造有異人所居一層中板用木釘合下層分為十三艙分隔甚密蓋底有板有機設數千一對於之急則以麻魚油及石水滴其中使非本板雜及新及新破設設一可引此者均用油灰護接接後施之以製陶器骨身皆有嗞檀內外皆用油灰護接然皆繼有水不值

卷首

第一章 記馬哥博羅父若叔之經歷

千二百五十年東羅馬皇帝包德溫 Baldwin 在位之時伊大利亞威尼斯望族尼古羅博羅(即馬哥博羅之父)偕其兄馬非倭(即馬非)携貨物安抵君士坦丁計貿易獲利無過於黑海沿岸一帶於是決意前往意購珍貴寶石珠玉買舟渡黑海至蘇而代亞埠 Soldaia 由今舍舟登陸策馬行數日至蒙古外落大酋巴爾喀駐節之地 巴爾喀當時駐節之地凡二處一為布而喀拉 Bolgara 在烏達克之南都一為薩拉 Sarai 亞俄拉河東 亞苒巴拉之支流 今俄國窩瓦河東岸今俄羅斯喀山之子為 Tushi 之地為Tushi 幹半島今保加利國都 巴爾喀之孫彼拔即都拔都拔巴 Tushi 之第二子為巴爾喀素有賢名為蒙古藩王中之最修文事者尼古羅等之來王厚遇之尼古羅等感念王之知遇將所携珍寶悉陳王前王顧而愛之尼古羅顧將所有悉以奉王王重其義倍價予之值實

小引

小引 此小引為馬斯登拉丁文本所無僅巴黎世上諸帝王牧伯俠之大夫欲知東方人種之駁雜土地之廣袤宗教之派別則不可不讀此書係威尼斯聞人馬哥博羅氏親見親聞之事實經其友人耳聽手錄所傳之紀載凡亞米尼亞波斯印度韃靼大原諸土之政教風俗無不列入全書皆屬可信之事其中有傳聞而錄之者亦非作者本意彼虛身死以後一生事蹟無以遺之後世故於千二百九十五年在日奴亞獄中與同在因中之勒斯鐵星二人共成之馬哥口授勒氏筆述全書都為三卷洵過方之寶冊考古之良書也

十七 十六

第二部分
沙舟海帆

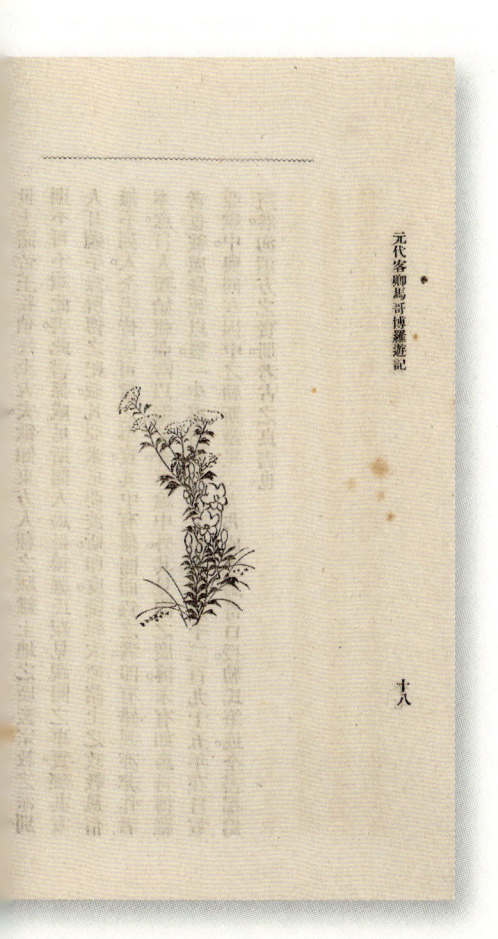

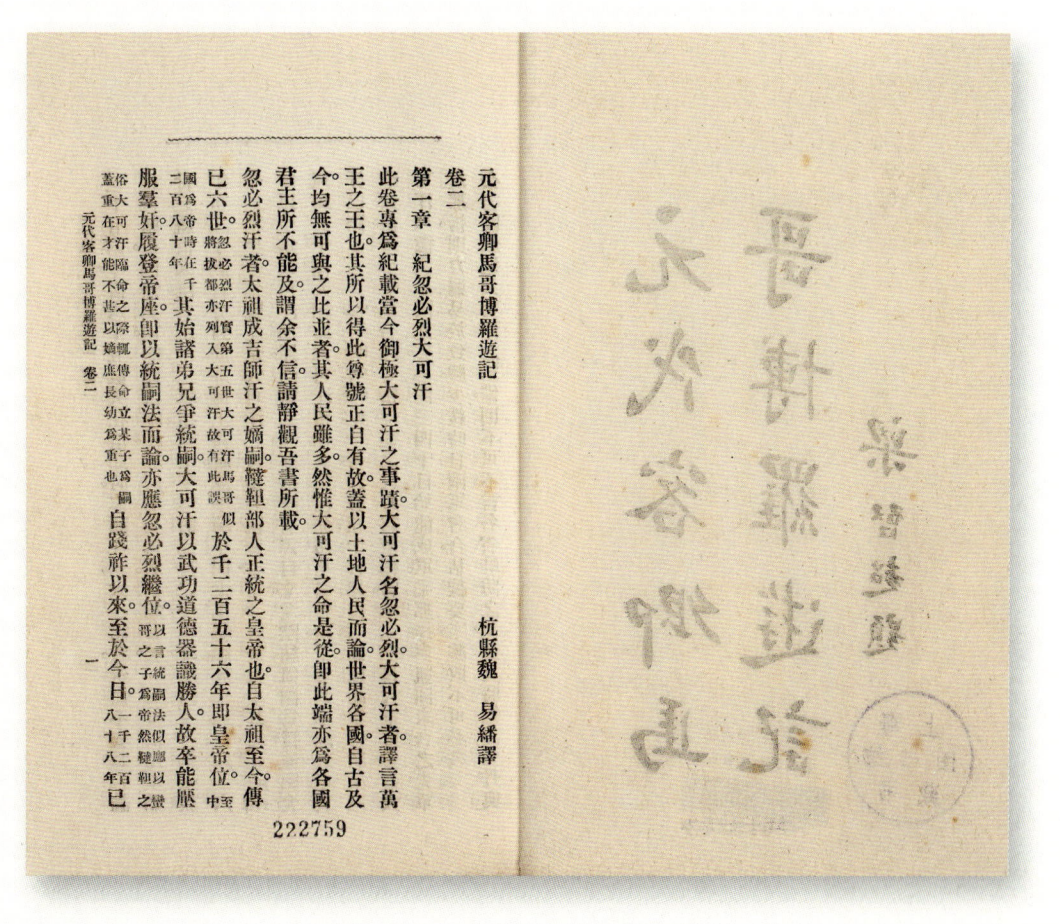

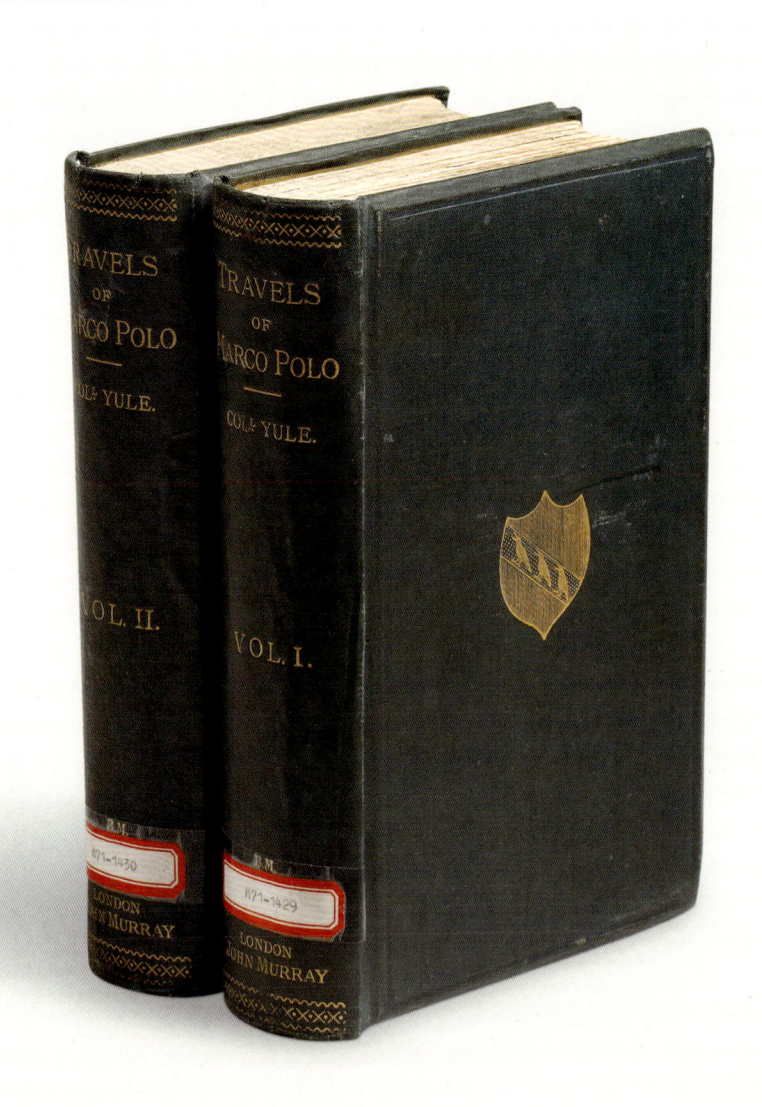

13
《马可·波罗游记》
1874

[英]亨利·玉尔（编译），伦敦，英文
24×15.5 cm
上海图书馆

The Book of Ser Marco Polo, 1874
Henry Yule (ed. & tr.), London, English
24×15.5 cm
Shanghai Library

第二部分
沙舟海帆

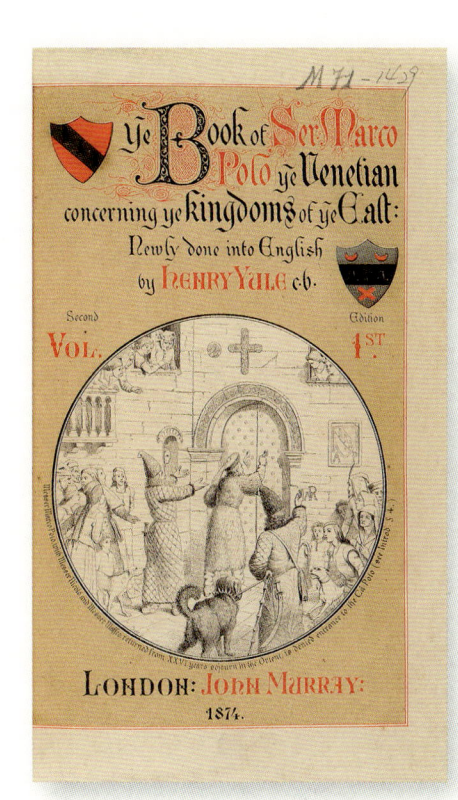

虚实之界：奇迹之书

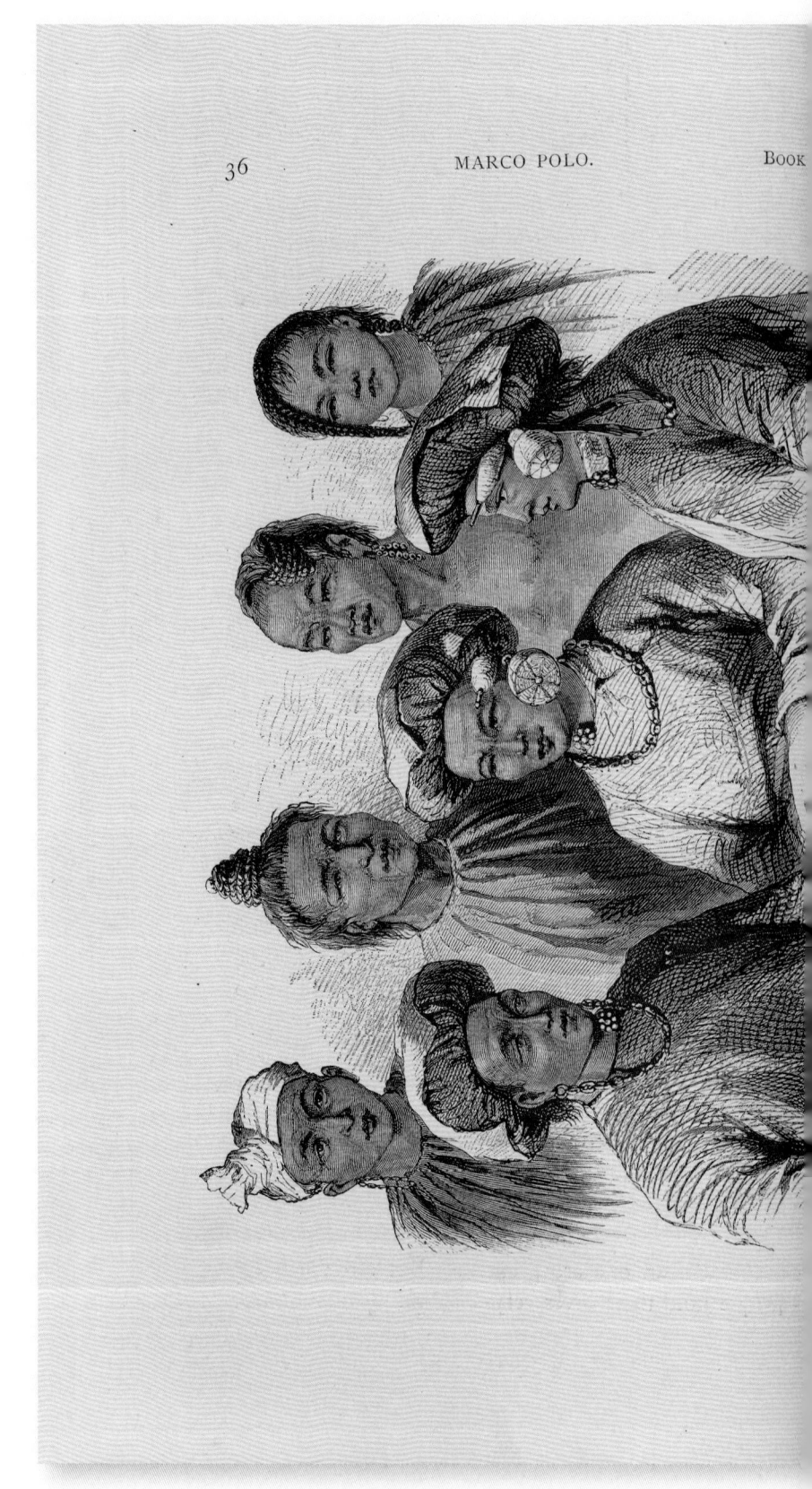

《马可·波罗游记》主题文献图录

052

第二部分
沙舟海帆

CHAP. XLV. PEOPLE OF TEBET. 37

it a great villainy for a man to meddle with another's wife; and thus though the wives have before marriage acted as you have heard, they are kept with great care from light conduct afterwards.

Now I have related to you this marriage custom as a good story to tell, and to show what a fine country that is for young fellows to go to!

The people are Idolaters and an evil generation, holding it no sin to rob and maltreat: in fact, they are the greatest brigands on earth. They live by the chase, as well as on their cattle and the fruits of the earth.

I should tell you also that in this country there are many of the animals that produce musk, which are called in the Tartar language *Gudderi*. Those rascals have great numbers of large and fine dogs, which are of great service in catching the musk-beasts, and so they procure great abundance of musk. They have none of the Great Kaan's paper money, but use salt instead of money. They are very poorly clad, for their clothes are only of the skins of beasts, and of canvas, and of buckram.[5] They have a language of their own, and they are called Tebet. And this country of TEBET forms a very great province, of which I will give you a brief account.

NOTE 1.—The mountains that bound the splendid plain of Chingtufu on the west rise rapidly to a height of 12,000 feet and upwards. Just at the skirt of this mountain region, where the great road to Lhása enters it, lies the large and bustling city of Yachaufu, forming the key of the hill country, and the great entrepôt of trade between Szechwan on the one side, and Tibet and Western Yunnan on the other. The present political boundary between China Proper and Tibet is to the west of Bathang and the Kinsha Kiang, but till the beginning of last century it lay much further east, near *Tat'sianlu*, or, as the Tibetans appear to call it, *Tartsédo* or *Tachindo*, which a Chinese Itinerary given by Ritter makes to be 920 *li*, or 11 marches, from Chingtufu. In Marco's time we must suppose that Tibet was considered to extend several marches further east still, or to the vicinity of Yachau.* Mr. Cooper's Journal

* Indeed Richthofen says that the boundary lay a few (German) miles west of Yachau. I see that Martini's map puts it (in the 17th century) 10 German geographical miles, or about 46 statute miles, west of that city.

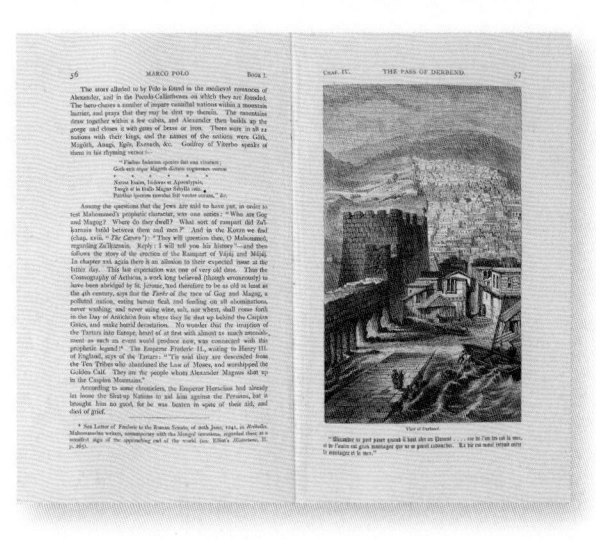

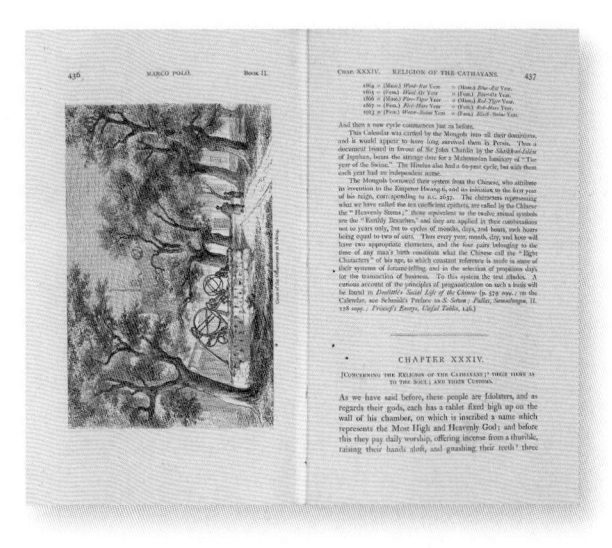

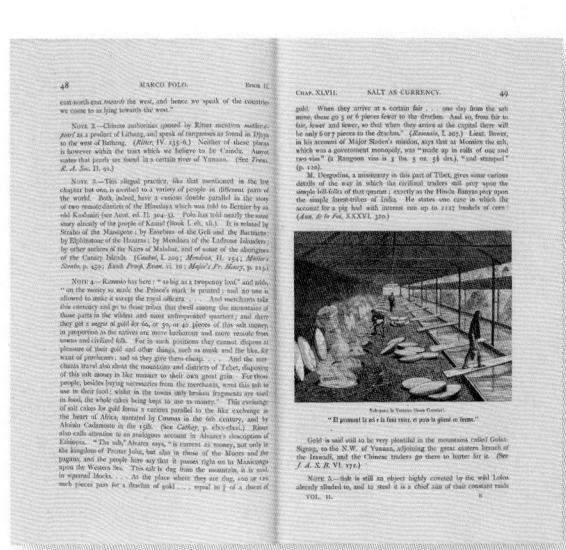

053

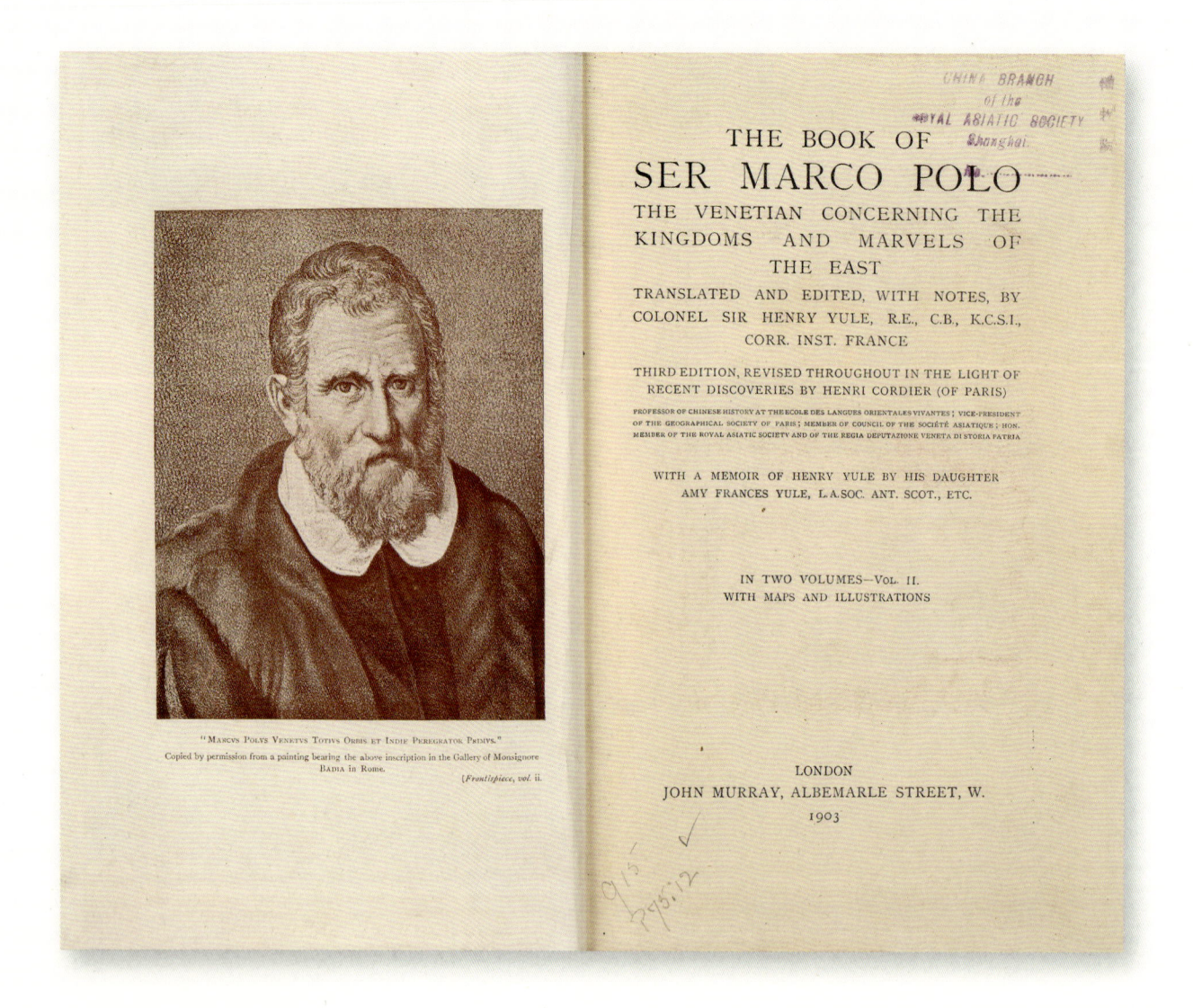

虚实之界：奇迹之书
《马可·波罗游记》主题文献图录

14
《马可·波罗游记》
1903

[英]亨利·玉尔（译注）、[法]亨利·考狄（补注），
伦敦，英文
24×15.5 cm
上海图书馆

The Book of Ser Marco Polo, 1903
Henry Yule (ed. & tr.), Henri Cordier (revised),
London, English
24×15.5 cm
Shanghai Library

054

第二部分
沙 舟 海 帆

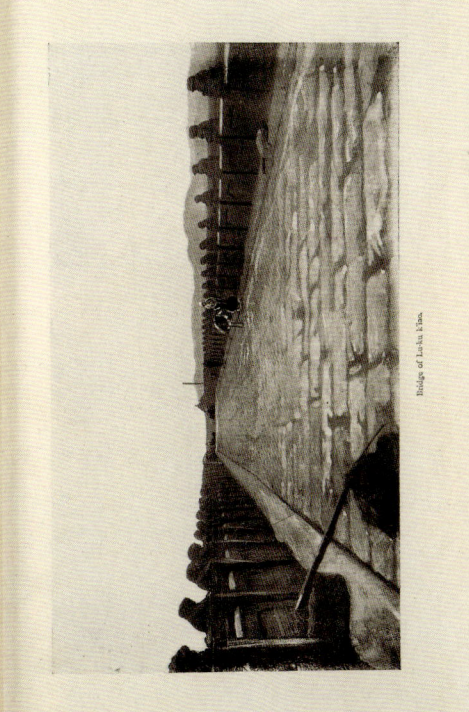

15

《马哥孛罗游记》
1936

张星烺（译），上海，中文
23.5×15 cm
上海图书馆

The Book of Ser Marco Polo, 1936
Zhang Xinglang (tr.), Shanghai, Chinese
23.5×15 cm
Shanghai Library

第二部分
沙舟海帆

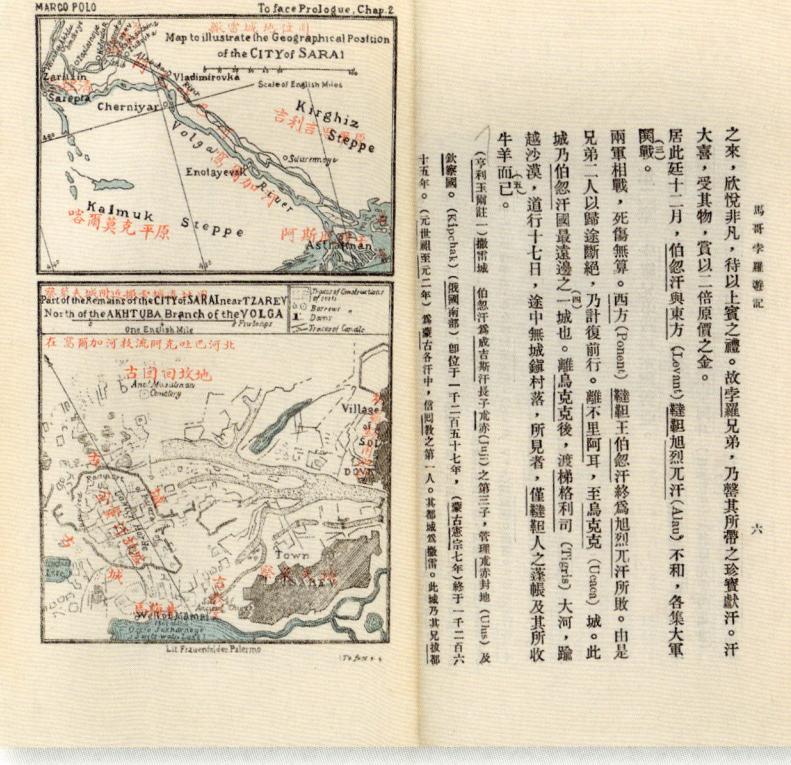

馬哥孛羅遊記本書卷一第一冊目錄

章數	面數
序言	一
羅斯梯謅奴序文	二
第一章 孛羅氏兄弟二人離君士旦丁堡週遊世界	
註一 「大海」	
註二 「年代攷」	
第二章 孛羅兄弟跋涉索爾對亞	五
註一 欽察汗部域撒爾地及忽顯攷	
註二 古代布爾加利城攷	
註三 東方韃靼王阿老汗 (即旭烈兀)	
註四 富爾加河畔烏克城攷	
註五 佛格利司大河攷	

馬哥孛羅遊記本書卷一目錄

馬哥孛羅遊記

英國 亨利玉爾 英譯兼註
法國 亨利致狄 修訂兼補註
中國 張星烺 漢譯兼補註

序言

尊貴之皇帝、國王、親王、公爵、侯爵、伯爵、勇士、議員，及各色人民，欲知世界人種與各國情形者，必須讀此書，因書中記種種奇事及大黑梅尼亞，波斯，韃靼，印度，曁其餘諸國之歷史，均依次言之，盡皆威尼斯貴人馬哥孛羅所目覩者也。若非彼親見，而得諸確實可信之人者，間亦有之，故書中將其所親見者，與所傳聞者，皆標出之，俾不致細微不實之事，害全書之眞誠。讀者卽當信全書內容之可悖矣。自上帝造亞當以來，迄於今日，無論其信基督，信異端，韃靼人，印度人，或他國人，知世界奇事之多，遊歷地面之廣，未有如馬哥孛羅者也。孛羅以

馬哥孛羅遊記 一

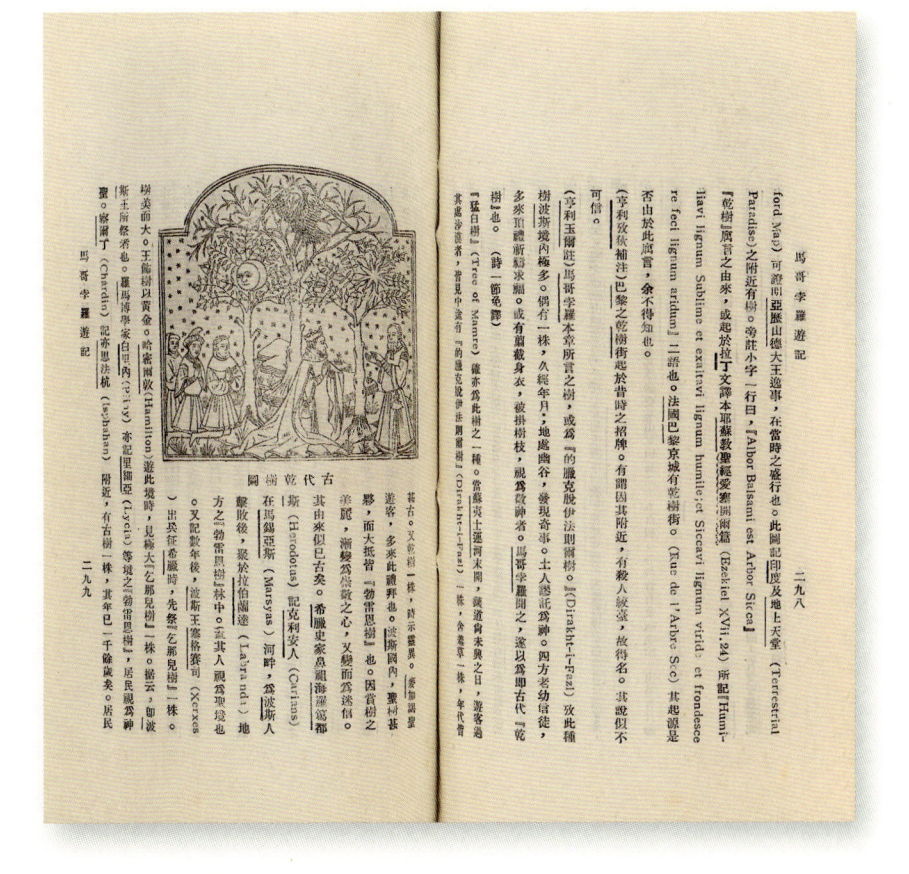

之來，欣悅非凡，待以上賓之禮。故孛羅兄弟大喜，受其物，賞以二倍原價之金。居此廷十二月，伯忽汗與東方 (Levant) 韃靼王旭烈兀汗 (Alau) 不和，各集大軍關戰。〔亨利玉爾註〕伯忽汗爲成吉斯汗長子朮赤 (Juji) 第三子，管理廉索封地，十五年。〔元世祖至元二年〕即位于一千二百五十七年。其都城爲撒萊，此城乃其所在都城。欽察國 (Kipchak) 撒萊城 〔俄國南部〕

兩軍相戰，死傷無算，伯忽汗終爲旭烈兀汗所敗。由是兄弟二人以歸途斷絕，乃計復前行。離不里阿耳，至烏克利司 (Ucaca) 大河，城乃伯忽汗國最遠邊之一城也。離烏克後，渡梯格利司 (Tigris) 大河，踰越沙漠，道行十七日，途中無城鎭村落，所見者，僅韃靼人之營帳及其所收牛羊而已。

馬哥孛羅遊記 六

(fod, Nut) 可證卽「亞歷山德大王遊記」在當時之流行也，此圖記印度及地上天堂 (Paradise) 之附近有樹，寄註小字「行目」Albor Balsani est Arbor Sicca」「乾樹」廣言之由來，或起於拉丁文譯本耶穌教舊經塞開爾篇 (Ezekiel XVII, 24) 所記「Humilavi lignum Sublime et exaltavi lignum humile; et Siccavi lignum viride et frondescere feci lignum aridum」二語也。法國巴黎京城有乾樹街。〔Rue de l'Arbre Sec〕其起源是否由於此處乾樹起於昔時之招牌。有謂因巴格達附近，有殺八級壺，故得名。其說似不可信。
〔亨利玉爾補註〕巴黎之乾樹街。余不得知也。
〔亨利玉爾境新綠多極多〕偶有一株，久經年月，地底幽谷，雪根脚奇高，土大器粗。彼拜樹徒，多來頂禮新綠多極多。或有圖殺身炎，彼拜樹枝，親爲敬禱，馬哥孛羅卽之，遂以爲古代「乾」樹也。「詩」之爲名「詩」。

古代乾闥樹圖

崤美亦大。王陵掃以黃金。哈密國奴 (Hamilton) 記波斯於羅馬掃學家白里內 (Pliny) 帝記里亞 (Ischaban) 附記，有行山一株，一千徐年。
蔣古人舍讀都
斯 (Herodotus) 記馬斯雅斯 (Marsyas) 河畔，爲波斯人地。 (Chardin) 記希臘史家鮑海蘭都。土耳其斯坦 (Tycia) 帝城中，茄果拉伯蘭德 (Laranda) 地方，宗廟恩惠中之心，又鬱節而雲誌也。「勃雷因樹」也。因舊樹之大抵，先祭「勃雷因樹」 (Dirakht-i-Fuzl) 地出炭任氣。
「猛日樹」 (Tree of Manners)，當時有一株，在某年已「千餘載」。
樹。「詩」「街名樹」。

馬哥孛羅遊記 二九八
馬哥孛羅遊記 二九九

16
《马可·波罗游记》
1865

[法]颇节（译），巴黎，法文
26×18 cm
上海图书馆

Le livre de Marco Polo, 1865
Guillaume Pauthier (tr.), Paris, French
26×18 cm
Shanghai Library

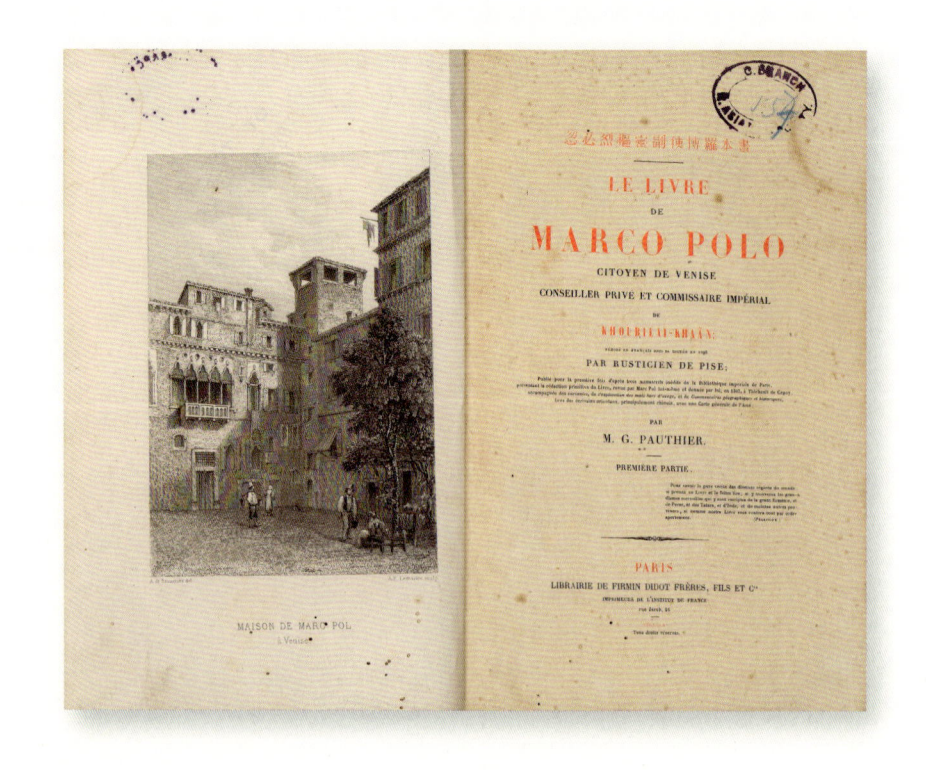

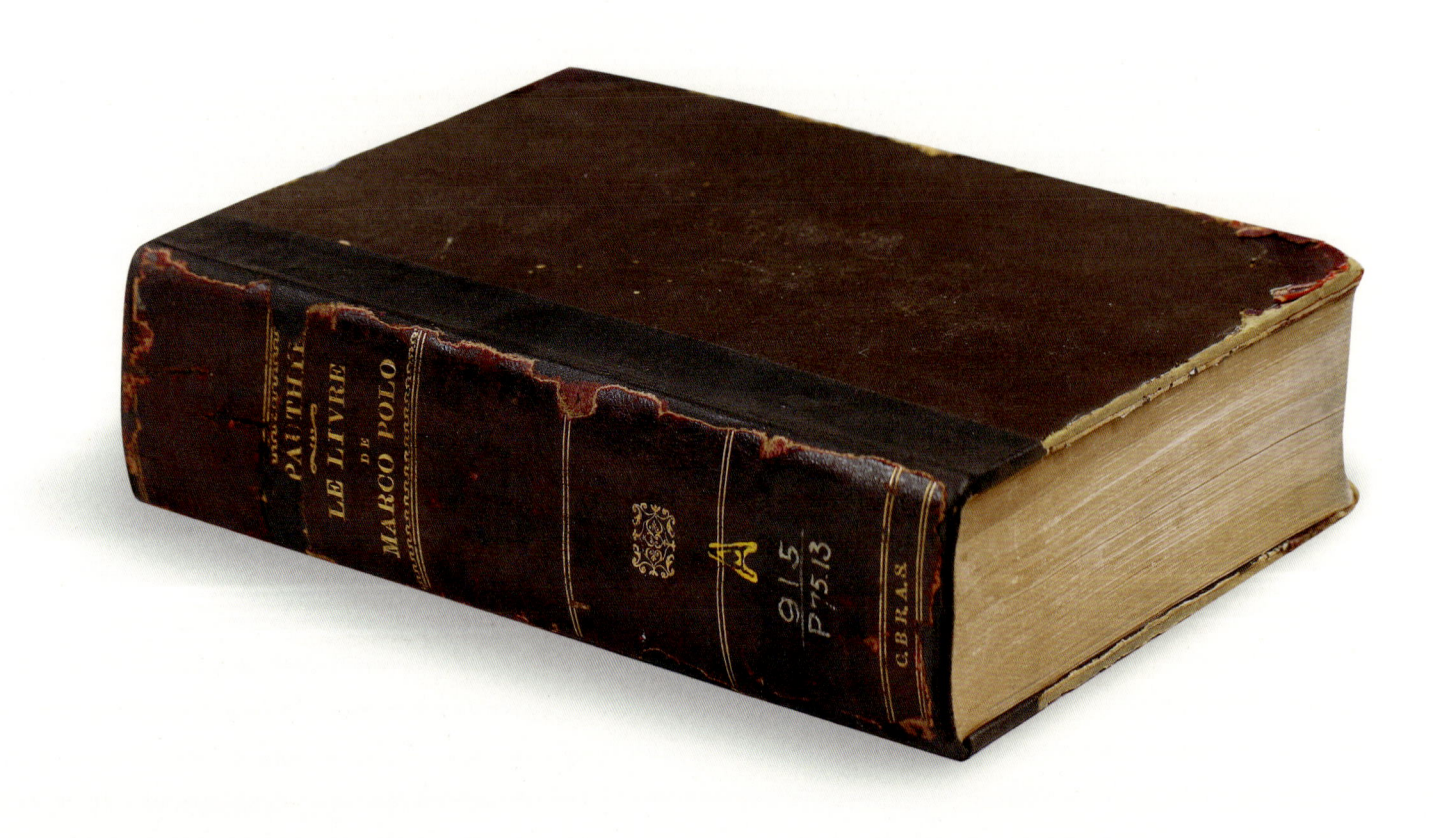

第二部分
沙舟海帆

17

《马可·波罗游记》
1924—1928

[法]沙海昂（译），北京，法文
19.6×26.3 cm
上海图书馆

Le livre de Marco Polo, 1924—1928
Antoine Joseph Henri Charignon (tr.), Beijing, French
19.6×26.3 cm
Shanghai Library

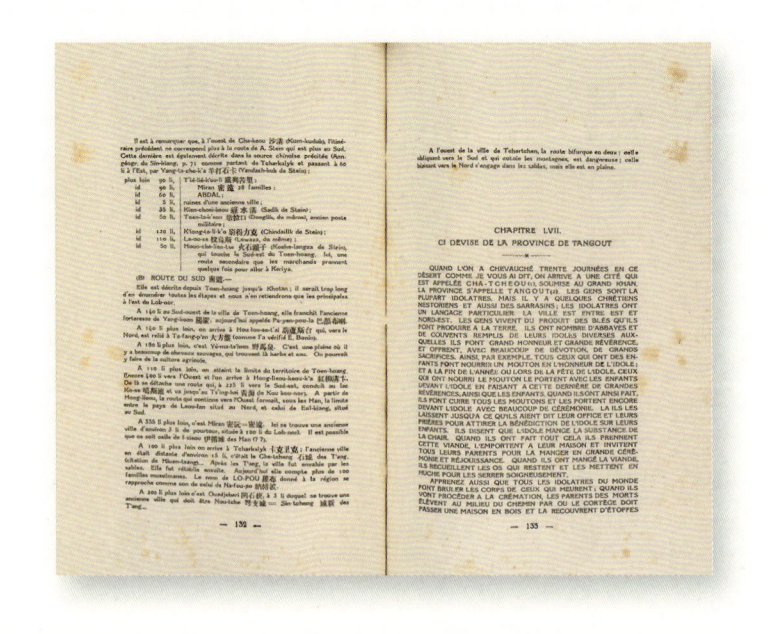

第二部分
沙舟海帆

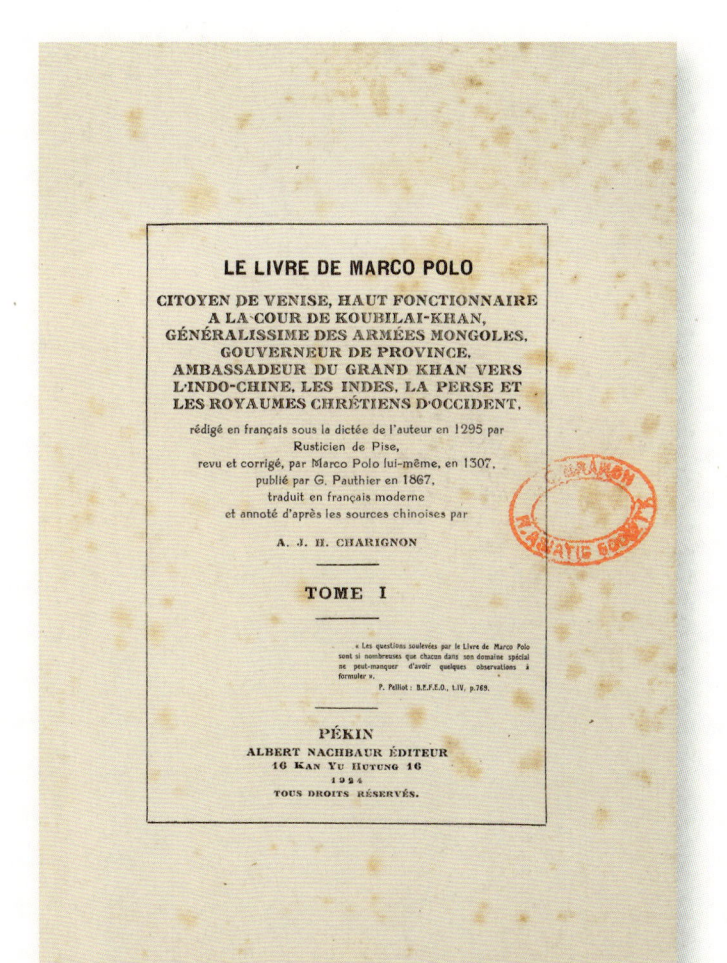

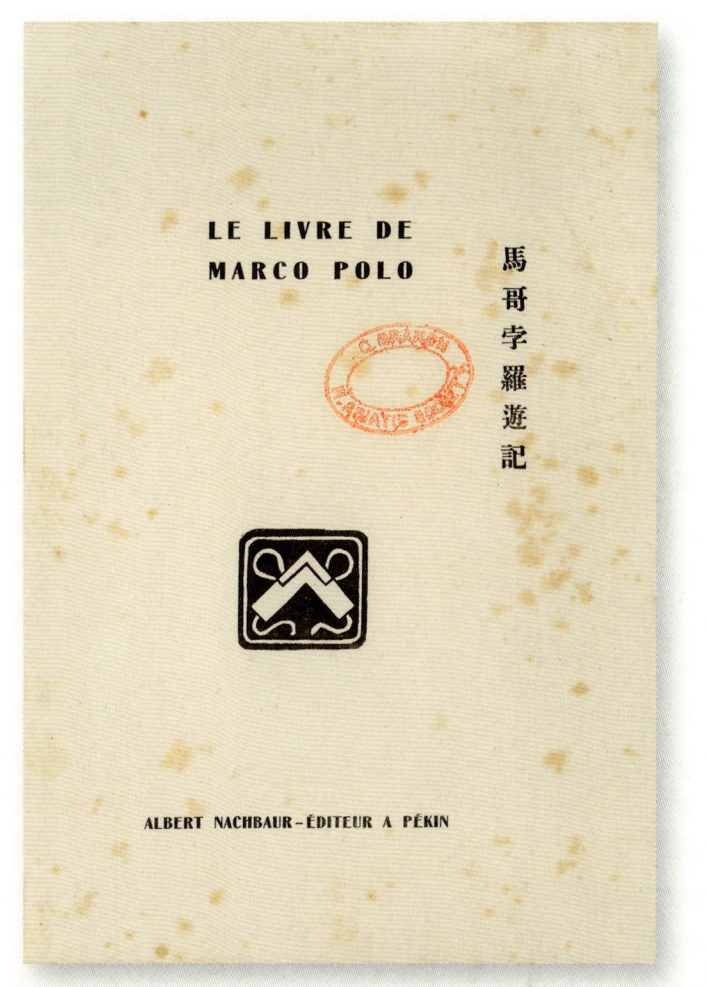

18
《马可波罗行纪》
1936

[法]沙海昂（译注），冯承钧（译），上海，
中文
22×16 cm
上海图书馆

Le livre de Marco Polo, 1936
Antoine Joseph Henri Charignon (tr. & ed.),
Feng Chengjun (tr.), Shanghai, Chinese
22×16 cm
Shanghai Library

第二部分
沙舟海帆

【書影頁】

馬可波羅行紀 上冊

A. J. H. Charignon 註
馮承鈞 譯

中華教育文化基金董事會編譯委員會編輯
商務印書館發行

序

馬可波羅書的中文譯本，我所見的有兩本。初譯本是馬兒斯登（Marsden）本，審其譯文可以說是一種翻譯匠的事業而不是一種考據家的成績。後譯本是玉耳戈爾迭（H. Yule-H. Cordier）本，此譯文雖然小有舛誤譯人補註亦頗多附會牽合，然而比較舊譯可以說是後來居上。惟原書凡四卷此本僅譯第一卷之強半，迄今尚未續成全帙。

馬可波羅書各種文字的版本，無慮數十種，戈爾迭在他的「馬可波羅紀念書」中業已詳細臚列，大致可以分爲三類：一類合訂本，如頗節本之類是；一類改訂本，如刺木學（Ramusio）本之類是；一類原寫本，如玉耳本之類是。版本旣多，各有短長，很難於中加以取捨，不過我以爲能將各重要版本的寫法裒輯校勘詳加註釋其餘似可不成問題。

我近來很想縮小研究範圍專在元史一方面搜集材料，所以大膽地譯了一部

多桑書。馬可波羅書也是參證元史的一部重要載籍舊譯本中旣無完本善本，我也想將其轉爲華言相傳此本是初用法文寫成而現存之諸法文本所用的文體幾盡是舊文體很難暢讀。本書註者沙海昂旣將頗節（Pauthier）本轉爲新文體，而出版時又在民國十三年至十七年間（亦在民國十七年出版）可以說是一部比較新的版本。除開別奈代脫（Benedetto）本晚出（亦在民國十七年出版）沙氏未能參考外他參考的版本爲數不少，這是我續譯此本的重要理由。

沙海昂原法國籍清末國籍法頒佈首先歸化中國人民國任交通部技正有年，是一鐵道專家於公餘之暇從事考據這部註釋可以說是一種好事者（amateur）的成績也不是一種純粹考據家的作品所以也免不了若干舛誤，而於材料亦昧於鑑別。可是現在的漢學名家是決不肯犧牲許多年的光陰來做這種吃力而不討好的事業的。本書敘言開始引證烈繆薩（A. Remusat）的一段話，就是使人望而却步的一箇大原因。旣然不能求各方面的專門家通力合作，一箇人學識無論如何淵博終歸要出漏洞的。伯希和對於此書雖然頗多指摘（參看西域南海史地考證譯叢）。

然而要知道，蜀中無大將，廖化作先鋒，兒且沙氏的成績不能說毫無優點，他將原文譯文有十二萬字，後經我刪削的大致以第五十九章以後爲多。我原來計算第一卷的譯文有十二萬字，後經我刪削僅存六分之一，但僅限於不得不刪的文字此外我仍前譯多桑書的譯法凡地名人名有舊譯者盧先探用，考訂未審者則錄其對音。

沙氏沿襲頗節的錯誤，仍以馬可波羅爲元代樞密副使孛羅，致使華文譯本有以孛羅爲本書標題者，伯希和對此辯之甚詳。我以爲不用多說僅據元史本紀之文，已足明此種考訂之爲考。元史至元七年以御史中丞孛羅兼大司農卿；至元十二年以大司農御史中丞孛羅兼大司農卿宣慰使兼領侍儀司事孛羅爲樞密副使；記載此孛羅拜官始末甚詳，則不得爲至元九年初至上

都之波羅彰明矣。又考程鉅夫雪樓集拂林忠獻王神道碑，及剌失德丁書，至元二十一年偕愛薛奉使至宗王阿魯渾所後留波斯不歸中國者，應亦為同一孛羅，亦與此波羅毫不相涉。所以我名其人曰馬可波羅，而不名之曰馬哥孛羅。

現在馬可波羅書的威權當首數伯希和戈爾迭從前撰玉耳本補註時曾大得伯希和之助。沙氏註此本時可惜有若干篇伯希和的考訂文字未曾見著讀此書者必須取伯希和諸文參看第一卷校勘既畢特誌數語於端民國二十四年二月二十日馮承鈞命兒子先恕筆受訖。

敍言

「校勘一部馬可波羅 (Marco Polo) 書，不是一件容易的事業要作這種事業必須確知中世紀的地理東方的歷史此時代旅行家的行記當時同現在韃靼人 (Tartares) 印度人同其他亞細亞民族使用的語言以及他們的風俗同世人不大認識的出產既確知矣，尚須加以適當的批評細密的鑑別這些事無論一箇人學識如何博洽用力如何勤摯很難兼而有之。」——見烈繆薩 (Abel Rémusat) 撰「亞洲雜纂新編」第一冊三八二頁。

這些話絕對不錯我們作此事時業已有這種感想，必須一箇博學的人才能夠註釋馬可波羅書這是我們所欠缺的從前有幾箇朋友勸我們將這部「世界奇異書」刊行一種新版本我們頗受這種事業的誘惑。可是我們所認識的馬可波羅同眾人所認識的一樣我們曾經讀過讚賞過並承認過頗節 (G. Pauthier) 玉耳 (H. Yule) 戈爾迭 (H. Cordier) 同其他學者對於他們所研究的不少問題所刊

第二部分
沙舟海帆

馬可波羅行紀

人探知世界各地及其偉大奇蹟者，無有如馬可波羅君所知之其廣也，故欲以爲，若不將其實在見聞各地及其偉大事筆之於書，使他人未嘗聞見者獲知之，其事誠爲不幸。余更有言者，凡此諸事皆彼居留各國垂二十六年之所見聞，或造其禁錮之時乃求其同獄者皮撒(Pise)城人魯思梯謙(Rusticien)詮次之，時在基督降生後之一二九八年云（註一）

（註一）馬可波羅書最初編纂之時代及處所，由是可以確定，惟其書所用之語言，在此文中尚懸而未決。第今業已證明其所用之語言即是當時歐洲流行最廣之法蘭西語。

此小引即吾人後此書中所謂「改訂原文」與最初小引不同處，此文最初小引前有一冒語，歷述閱覽此書之語皇帝國王公爵侯爵伯爵騎尉男爵此冒頭在其他諸本中多載有之。

（註二）法文本名此海曰 Mer-maïour 日 Mar-mor，Mar-magium 曾為古代 Pont-Euxin 之後稱，普丁文本名此海曰 Mare magnum 或日 Mare majus, Nigrum，此言「大海」，曾為古代 Pont-Euxin 之後稱，普丁文本名此海曰 Maurum, vz. Nigrum，此言「黑海」，催此名或適用於今之黑海，非專有所指也。剖壁(Arabe)史家阿不菲答(Aboulféda)說此名在當時很普通。

格(Michel Paléologue)所廢，此帕烈幹羅格朝，於一四五三年為突厥朝之摩訶末二世(Mahomet II)所滅。

（註三）其名亦作速達墨(Sondaq)城名也，在克里米亞(Chinée)半島之南，今尚存在蒙古人侵略半島以後。是黑海中重要港也。馬可波羅同時，盧布魯思(Rubruquis)曾有記云「凡由土耳其(Turquie)運往北方諸地之商貨皆集於此，而由俄羅思(Russe)運往土耳其之商貨亦然。」

蒙古人攻取此地以後，曾在克里木(Krim)城廣為貿易，支里木即東方人名克里米亞半島之全地或此城之一城也。——頗節書六頁註二

第一章 波羅弟兄二人自孔士坦丁堡往遊世界

馬可君之父尼古剌(Nicolas)同尼古剌之弟瑪竇(Matteo)，自物搦齊亞城負販商貨而至孔士坦丁堡茲二人乃華胄謹慎而賢明。基督降生後之一二六〇年，（註一）此兄弟二人自物搦齊亞出發以後，實在博丹(Baudoin)爲孔士坦丁堡皇帝之時，此兄弟二人商議後決定赴黑海（註二）營商，於是購買珍寶，自孔士坦丁堡出發逢海而抵速達克(Soudaï)（註三）

（註一）據後此第九章云：此兩弟兄在一二六九年歸物搦齊亞見馬可已有十五歲。如再據剌木學本馬可之出生在此兄弟二人自物搦齊亞出發以後，則可出生於一二五四年，二人之出發應在一二五三至一二五四年之間，文考後本註三他們行抵斧爾動伽(Volga)河畔之時，出發時間在一二五三至一二六一年之間他們必在孔士坦丁堡出發無疑。——玉耳書第一冊三頁

（註二）博丹二世君臨孔士坦丁堡之富浪(France)帝國始一二二八迄一二六一年後為帕烈幹羅第一卷　第一章　波羅弟兄二人自孔士坦丁堡往遊世界

此城造於一二〇四年孔士坦丁堡富浪人之侵略時臣屬於一二六一年。

九年蒙古人兩次侵略以後終脫離富浪帝國蓋屬在十三世紀中葉時物搦齊亞設一商館於此一二八七年改爲領事館一二三三年敎皇壁二十二世(Jean XXII)因基督敎徒被逐於速達克域外改基督敎堂爲回敎禮拜寺等事有人訴之於撒萊(Saraï)汗(Khan Uzbek)所一三四五年時吉那哇人奪據速達克始設壁壘其遺跡今尚可見有若干剌壁人所撰之地誌名阿卓夫(Azof)，海日速達克海馬可波羅之伯父亦名馬可(Maro)亦在此居此一二八〇年波羅兄二人經過此城時會贈今尚可見有若干剌壁人之遺贈中曾遂速克域下之房屋一所給於濟各會(Franciscain)敎士惟限以其牧益付其尚居此屋之子女。一二六〇年波羅兄已屬之。——頗節書六頁註二

（註四）營商於是購買珍寶，自孔士坦丁堡出發逢海而抵速達克(Soudaï) 位在其出發時間，在一二五三至一二六一年後從孔士坦丁堡出發，其說或者不誤一二五四年至一二六〇年之間，則若干寫本說他們在一二五四年從孔士坦丁堡出發以其說或者不誤。——玉耳書第一冊三頁

星或者馬已屬之。——頗節書六頁註二

屋或者馬已屬之。細亞(Asie)八四二頁。

第一卷　第一章　波羅弟兄二人自孔士坦丁堡往遊世界

虚实之界：奇迹之书
《马可·波罗游记》主题文献图录

第二部分
沙舟海帆

目錄

序

敘言

馬可波羅贈謝波哇藩主迪博鈔本原序

第一卷 馬可波羅自地中海岸赴大汗忽必烈駐夏之上都沿途所經之地及傳聞之地

引言

第一章 波羅弟兄二人自君士坦丁堡往遊世界

第二章 波羅弟兄二人之離速達克

第三章 波羅弟兄二人經過沙漠而抵不花剌城

第四章 波羅弟兄二人從使臣言往朝大于

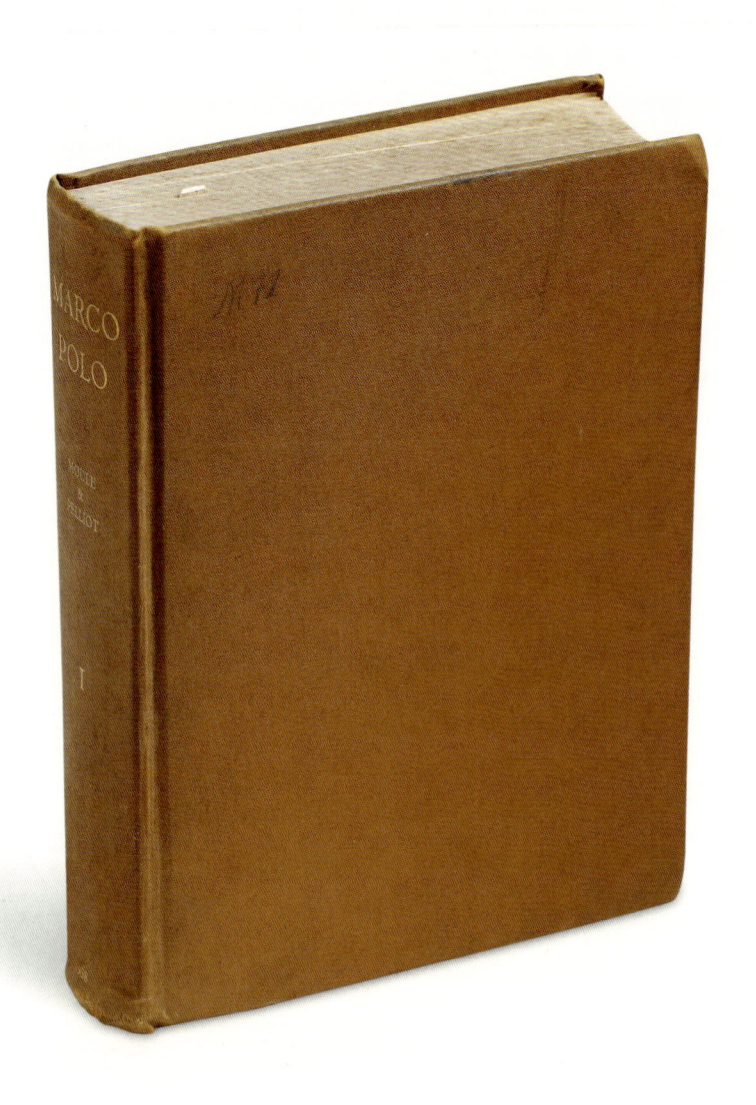

虚实之界：奇迹之书
《马可·波罗游记》主题文献图录

19
《马可·波罗寰宇记》
1938

[英]慕阿德、[法]伯希和（译），伦敦，英文
23×28.9 cm
上海图书馆

Marco Polo: The Description of the World, 1938
Arthur Christopher Moule & Paul Pelliot (tr.),
London, English
23×28.9 cm
Shanghai Library

068

第二部分
沙舟海帆

虚实之界：奇迹之书
《马可·波罗游记》主题文献图录

Page of Z 6

Page of Z 7

turcomani sunt qui retinent legem Macometi

a leuante & greco est turchia chayseria & seuastio & multe alie ciuitates. que omnia subdita sunt tartaris versus occidentem est mare per quod nauigatur ad partes xpistianorum dicto de armenia parua subsequenter dicamus de turcomania //hic naratur de prouincia turcomanie//

Jn turchomania sunt tria genera gentium. videlicet turcomani qui macometum adorant & retinent suam legem/ & est gens simplex & habent turpe loquinium & permanent in montaneis & in uijs ubi sciunt esse bonum pasculum quia uiuunt sollummodo de bestijs/ & nascuntur ibi boni equi & muli magni ualoris. Et

hic sunt armenij & greci

alie gentes sunt armenij & greci qui cum ipsis mixsti sunt in ciuitatibus & castris & uiuunt de mercimonijs & artibus/ & ibi laborantur drappi de syrico crimisi sunt similiter in ea regione multe alie ciuitates &castra que longum foret describere omnes subditi sunt regi tartarorum orientalium qui eis potestates & rectores mitit// hic naratur de continentijs armenie maioris//

Armenia maior est quedam magna prouincia que incipit a quadam ciuitate nomine arcinga in qua laborantur meliores bucheranj de mundo & multe alie artes fiunt ibi que narari non possunt & habent pulcriores & meliores balnea aquarum scaturientium que in mundo reperiantur. in ea sunt multe ciuitates & castra & nobilior ciuitas est Arcinga que habet archiepiscopum & hic bestie male permanent propter inmensum frigus & niuem quam ultra modum ningit deus. & in quadam castro] quod uocatur paperth est maxima argentera & 3ª* inuenitur hoc castrum eundo de trapesunda in thauris. & in medio armenie

mons ubi arca noe dicitur astitisse

maioris est quedam maximus & altissimus mons ad modum unius cube super quem arca Noe dicitur astitisse & ex hoc mons ille appelatur mons arche noe & est tam latus & longus quod in duobus diebus circui non posset & in sumitate montis continue tanta multitudo niuis habundat quod nullus potest ascendere sumitatem quia nix nunquam in totum liquescit in confinibus uero armenie uersus meridie sunt iste prouincie musulmo. & meridin in quibus infra dicetur & multe alie sunt. quas longum esset narare. versus uero tramontanam est Jorgia de qua infra

nota quod nascitur hic oleum ex quadam fonte.

dicemus. & in confinibus Jorgie quidam fons est de quo scaturit oleum in tanta quantitate quod mile camelis simul & semel illo honerari & honerantur pro nichil in comestione ualet set bonum est ad ungendum homines & quelibet animalia propter scabiem. & homines de longi[n]quis partibus ueniunt pro oleo isto & omnes contracte circumstantes non comburunt aliud oleum quam istud. & ualet ad multos langores.// hic naratur de rege Jorgensj & eius esse/

Jn jorgia est quidam rex qui dauid melic totis temporibus nuncupatur quod in lingua galica dicitur rex dauid. pars una cuius prouincie subdita est tartareo regi reliqua uero pars propter fortilicias quas habet non set subdita ei set regi dauid & in istis fortilicijs & montibus sunt eorum nemora in quibus non est aliud

lignum quam busus & predicta prouincia duo equora prospicit quorum unum uocatur mare maius quod est a latere tramontane alterum uero abaco./ uersus

4ª* orientem quod durat] in suo circuitu per duo milia viij' miliarium & est tanquam stagnum quia non miscetur cum aliquo mari. & in eo sunt multe insule bene habitate in quibus sunt pulcre ciuitates. & habitate sunt iste insule a gentibus que fugerant a facie magni tartari quando ibat conquirendo per regnum siue prouinciam persie/ cuius ciuitates & terre regebantur a comuni que quidem gentes fugiendo reduxerunt se ad istas insulas & ad montes ubi tutiores esse credebant. & sic habitate sunt insule ille. Jtem dictum mare multos pisces producit & precipue storiones salmones & alios magnos pisces. Antiquitus quidem omnes reges illius prouincie nascebantur cum quodam signo aquile super spatulam dexteram. & sunt in ea pulcre gentes & ualentes ad arma sunt boni arceri & pugnatores in bello. Jpsi sunt xpistiani & obseruant legem grecorum more *xristiani qui obseruant* clericorum paruos portantes capilos. hec est prouincia quam rex alexander *legem grecorum* preterire non potuit   item est quidam passus ibi qui porta ferea nuncupatur/ *nota quod porta ferea hic* Alexander inter duos montes dicitur tartaros inclusisse/ set quod tartari fuerint *est* non est uerum quia tunc temporis non erant ymo gens quedam fuit nomine cumani & aurei laborantur de mercimonijs & laboribus uitam ducunt. In ea est quoddam monasterium titulo beati leonardi descriptum/ iuxta quod huiusmodi *sanctus leonardus* habetur miraculum. Nam fons quidam iuxta ecclesiam de quodam monte *aqua quedam est que*

4ª* desendit in cuius aqua per totum anum] nuli pisces apparent nisi sollummodo a *solummodo in quadrage-* die prima quadragesime usque ad uigiliam pascatis videlicet resurectionis dominj *sima producit pisces.* ipsorum abundantia maxima reperitur & facto de pascatis amplius non apparent/ mare quidam montem superius nominatum/ mare geluchelam & mare abacco appelatur/ in quod finiunt/ Tigris gyon/ Et eufrates & alia flumina multa/ penes istam prouinciam quedam ciuitas est nomine pulcra & magna ualde nomen cuius *xristiani scilicet armeni* Tyflis circa quam multa sunt castra & burgi/ que isti ciuitati obedient. in qua *& iorgienses & saraceni &* habitant xpistiani scilicet armenij & Jorgienses & aliqui saraceni & iudei set pauci: / *iudei set pauci*

Moxul est quedam prouincia in qua habitant plura gentium genera. vna *hic adorant macometum* quidem gens est que macometum adorat & arabi appelantur. Jtem sunt etiam aliqui xristiani alia gens est que fidem xristianam obseruat non tamen secundum quod *ane set non obseruant* mandat ecclesia. quia in pluribus falit. Nam nestorini/ capiti/ & armeni sunt/ & *fidem secundum ecclesiam* patriarcam habent/ qui archiepiscopos episcopos & abbates statuit & blebanos. romanam nam nestorini ipsos per omnes partes Jndye. & Alochayray & in baldach ac per universas partes *capiti & armeni sunt* quibus habitant xpistiani transmittens quemadmodum papa romanus Et noueritis quod omnes xpistiani illis partibus comorantes nestorinj sunt & Jacopiti/ Jn sunt omnes nestorini &

第二部分
沙 舟 海 帆

20
《马可·波罗游记》
1936

李季（译），上海，中文
19×13 cm
上海图书馆

The Travels of Marco Polo, 1936
Li Ji (tr.), Shanghai, Chinese
19×13 cm
Shanghai Library

《马可·波罗游记》主题文献图录

目錄

譯者序言

序言

馬可波羅到中國去
亞細亞的皇帝
忽必烈汗的鼙鼓
遊記草成的經過
這是『馬可波羅』
本版的計畫
馬可波羅的爲人

譯者序言

遊記(The Travels of Marco Polo)在萬人叢書(Everyman's Library)出版的馬可波羅遊歷家之一』(見原書序言一二頁)威爾士(H. G. Wells)在他的世界史綱(The Outline of History)中更說『馬可波羅遊記爲大歷史書之一，牠對着我們的想像打開了十三世紀……的世界，這不是單純的作史者的編年史所能做到的。』(見原書第三版六七八頁)然這不過是就西十一般人的自我中國人看來此人與此書實具有一種更重要和更親切的意義因爲馬可波羅是元世祖的客卿居任中國十七年，曾任樞密副使並做揚州都督三年，極得世祖的信任(阿哈瑪特的罪狀是由他舉發的見瀆通志六一九卷二頁)；而他的書中的紀述有五分之二以上是描寫梅斯菲德(John Masefield)序言中稱馬可氏爲世界史上看過奇蹟的五個唯一

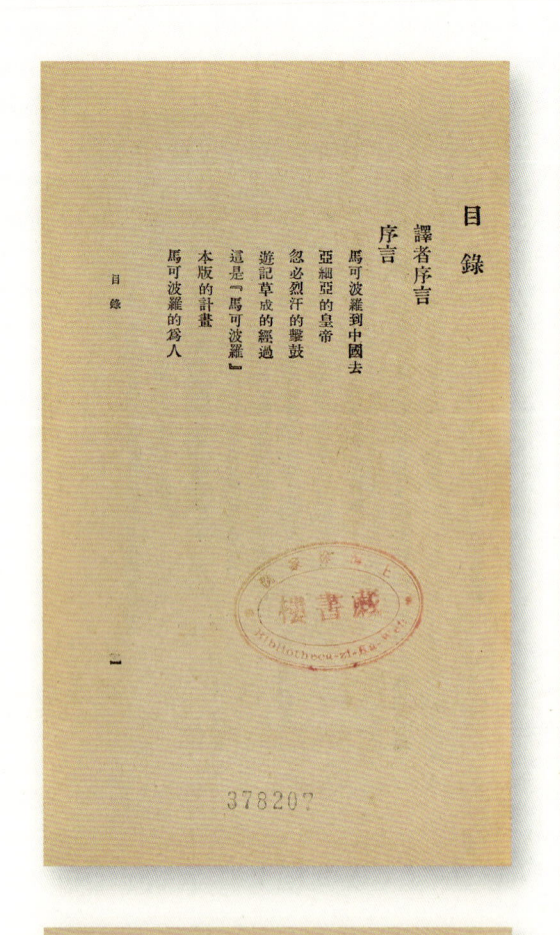

馬可波羅遊記

馬可波羅述
李季 譯

小引

皇帝國王公侯伯騎士和其他一切人民，如果想要知道世界人種的差異和東方各國的人民其最大的和最奇異的特點，都分別紀載於馬可波羅這部書中，波羅係威尼斯一個聰明而有學識的市民，曾在書中明白說出何者爲他所觀見何者爲他所覽聞因爲此書是一部眞實的紀錄。

大家必須知道，自上帝創造亞當(Adam)以來，一直到現在，無論是異教徒威拉森人(Saracen)基督教徒無論屬何族類居何時代從沒有人看見過或考察過馬可波羅這些省及一切地方的不同可一讀此書凡人民特別是亞美尼亞(Armenia)波斯印度和韃靼

第一卷 從小亞美尼亞到大汗上都帝廷的行程 中各地的見聞錄

第一章 小亞美尼亞 來亞蘇斯港埠 省區的邊界

我們于開始描寫馬可波羅在亞洲所到的各國和所考察的值得注意的事件之時，注意小亞美尼亞和大亞美尼亞的分別。小亞美尼亞王居塞巴斯拖慈(Sabasta)城，統治區以嚴守法律爲正鵠，武裝防地和城堡爲數甚多，凡生活必需品和享樂的物品都很豐富。鳥獸這種獵物也很多。不過我們必須說明這個國內的空氣不甚適于衛生當從前的時代牠的紳耆們都是可敬的熟練勇敢的戰士但此時變成精神沮喪和沒有價值的大醉漢。

海濱有一城市叫做亞蘇斯，牠的港埠爲鉅額貿易之地，牠的交易品爲各種香料藥材絲毛製品和其他珍貴的商品那多地方的商人麇集之所他們的交易品爲各種香料藥材絲毛製品和其他珍貴的商品那

SECTION 3

日月有常

Through the Tide of Time

在文化和历史的长河中，关于《马可·波罗游记》的讨论与研究如繁星点点般闪烁着万千流光，过往学者们的心力与智慧在此凝聚。其中，国内围绕《马可·波罗游记》真实性问题展开的历史考证，以《至顺镇江志》（成书于1333年）和《永乐大典》（成书于1407年）中与《游记》能互相验证的史料记载为核心，辅以其他史料佐证，产生了诸多学术著作与论文，《游记》构成了中文世界对《马可·波罗游记》研究的基础。同时，以《马可·波罗游记》为史料，对元代世界和社会以及中西交流史的考察构成了研究的另一翼。

在产生巨大学术影响力之前，《马可·波罗游记》在中国经历了从早期零星介绍到逐渐被大众读者熟知的过程，其中始自19世纪中叶前后的书报等媒介中对马可·波罗事迹的刊载，对其在国内的早期传播起到了至关重要的作用。这些提及《马可·波罗游记》的文献，无论是晚清的新学著作，还是好莱坞电影的中文海报宣传，都承载着中文世界从初识到逐步形塑马可·波罗其人其书印象的集体记忆。

自《马可·波罗游记》于13世纪末诞生至今，数百年间针对其文本真实性的质疑就一直没有间断过，正是在这种压力驱使下，国内外学者锲而不舍地进行史料的挖掘和考证，使得马可·波罗之学在多学科领域取得了多视角的丰硕成功。

作为力证马可·波罗到过中国的先锋，杨志玖（1915—2002）先生在明《永乐大典》残本中的一条重大发现（即三位波斯使臣护送阔阔真公主远嫁伊利汗国）为其论断提供了确凿证据；此外，又有学者发现《马可·波罗游记》中对江苏镇江天主教教堂的记载，与元朝人俞希鲁（生卒年不详）编写的《至顺镇江志》中的相关内容相吻合。基于此两条史料的发现，国内外学者在进一步研究马可·波罗与中国关系时信心倍增，如近年来试图将《马可·波罗游记》中的内容，同元朝社会的文化、经济与习俗等诸方面史料记载相互验证的研究也相继涌现。随着此类研究的深入，马可·波罗学有望取得进一步突破。

马可·波罗进入中国普通民众的视野，并不晚于受到国内学术界关注的时间。19世纪上半叶，西方传教士通过办中文杂志力图打开中国传教之路，这位旅行家的名字已经在早期的中文刊物上出现。1874年，《申报》上一篇署名"求知子"的《询意国马君事》被认为是国内媒体上最早出现的对马可·波罗的介绍。1906年传教士李佳白（1857—1927）在上海作关于马可·波罗的专题讲座，同样因《申报》的报道而引起热潮。在民国时期日新月异的社会发展过程中，出现了供不同年龄层阅读的马可·波罗传记，他的事迹也被写入历史教科书，各类大众刊物也从各自的角度挖掘他和他游记的价值。文艺领域更不会放过这样一位传奇人物，诗歌、小说甚至电影，让一部数百年前的古书和它的作者迅速变得家喻户晓。

Throughout history, debates and research on the *Devisement dou monde* reflected the achievements and wisdom of scholars. Among them, this section puts on display Chinese textual-historical research on the authenticity of the *Devisement*, including the historical records in the *Yongle Canon* (1407) and the *Chronicles of Zhishun Zhenjiang*. Integrated with other historical materials, these documents led to the production of numerous academic publications, which now constitute the basis for studies on the *Devisement* in the Chinese-speaking world. At the same time, the *Devisement* represents a historical source on which studies of the world and society during the Yuan Dynasty are based. In addition, Marco Polo's *Devisement* is a powerful instrument for research on the history of Sino-Western exchanges.

Before achieving significant scientific influence in China, the *Devisement* had to go through a process that upgraded it from sporadic mentions and reviews to becoming widely known among the general public. Reports about Marco Polo's story in newspapers and other media since around the mid-19th century have played a crucial role in its initial dissemination. These references to the *Devisement*, whether from scholarly publications of the late Qing Dynasty or Chinese-language posters for Hollywood films, embody the collective memory of Marco Polo and his book in the Chinese-speaking world.

Since its appearance in the late 13th century, the *Devisement dou monde* has been greeted with persistent skepticism regarding the authenticity of its contents. Such diffidence has driven scholars to tirelessly excavate and verify historical materials on a global scale, leading to fruitful results in Marco Polo studies, approached from multiple perspectives and disciplines.

As a pioneer in proving Marco Polo's presence in China, Yang Zhijiu (1915-2002) made a significant discovery in the incomplete version of the *Yongle Canon* (the records of three Persian envoys escorting Princess Cocachin to marry the Ilkhanate King). Additionally, scholars found that the *Devisement's* account of Christian chapels in Zhenjiang, Jiangsu, aligns with the content in the *Chronicles of Zhishun Zhenjiang* compiled contemporaneously by Yu Xilu. These findings from the two historical texts have greatly bolstered scholars' confidence in further exploring the relationship between Marco Polo and China. In recent years, studies attempting to cross-validate the content of the *Devisement* with historical records of the culture, economy, and customs of the Yuan Dynasty have emerged. With the deepening of such research, Marco Polo studies are promising to achieve further breakthroughs.

The figure of the Venetian merchant became quite popular among the Chinese people no later than when the Chinese academia started to focus on Marco Polo studies. In early 19th century, when Western missionaries paved the road of regular publications in Chinese language to spread their faith, the name of the Venetian began to be mentioned in Chinese periodicals. An article by a pen named author Qiuzhizi (lit. Knowledge seeker) titled "Inquiries about Ser Ma from Italy" was published in *Shun Pao* in 1874; this is believed to be the first essay mentioning and debating over Marco Polo in the domestic press. In 1906, American missionary Gilbert Reid (1857-1927) delivered a lecture in Shanghai on Marco Polo, which aroused a wide interest in the public also thanks to the article of *Shun Pao*. Within the increasingly rapid modernization of the Chinese society, the story of Marco Polo inspired the creativity of various cultural products, including biographies for audience of different levels, history text books, as well as a wide range of popular magazines that focused on illustrating and interpreting Marco Polo's experience and works. Marco Polo had then already become a prominent figure under the attention of the circles of art and literature: works of poetry, narrative, as well as movies depicted the figure of the Venetian merchant elevating him to a character of modern popularity thanks to a manuscript of centuries ago.

Das ist der edel Ritter Marcho polo von Venedig der groß lanttfarer der vns beschreibt die grossen wunder der welt die er selbs gesehen hat. Von ein aufgang bis zu den nidergang der sunne. Der gleychen vor nicht meer gehort seyn

21

《永乐大典》
（影印本）
1960

（明）解缙、姚广孝（编），北京，中文
30×23 cm
上海图书馆

Yongle Canon (reproduction), 1960
Xie Jin & Yao Guangxiao (eds.),
Beijing, Chinese
30×23 cm
Shanghai Library

第三部分
日月有常

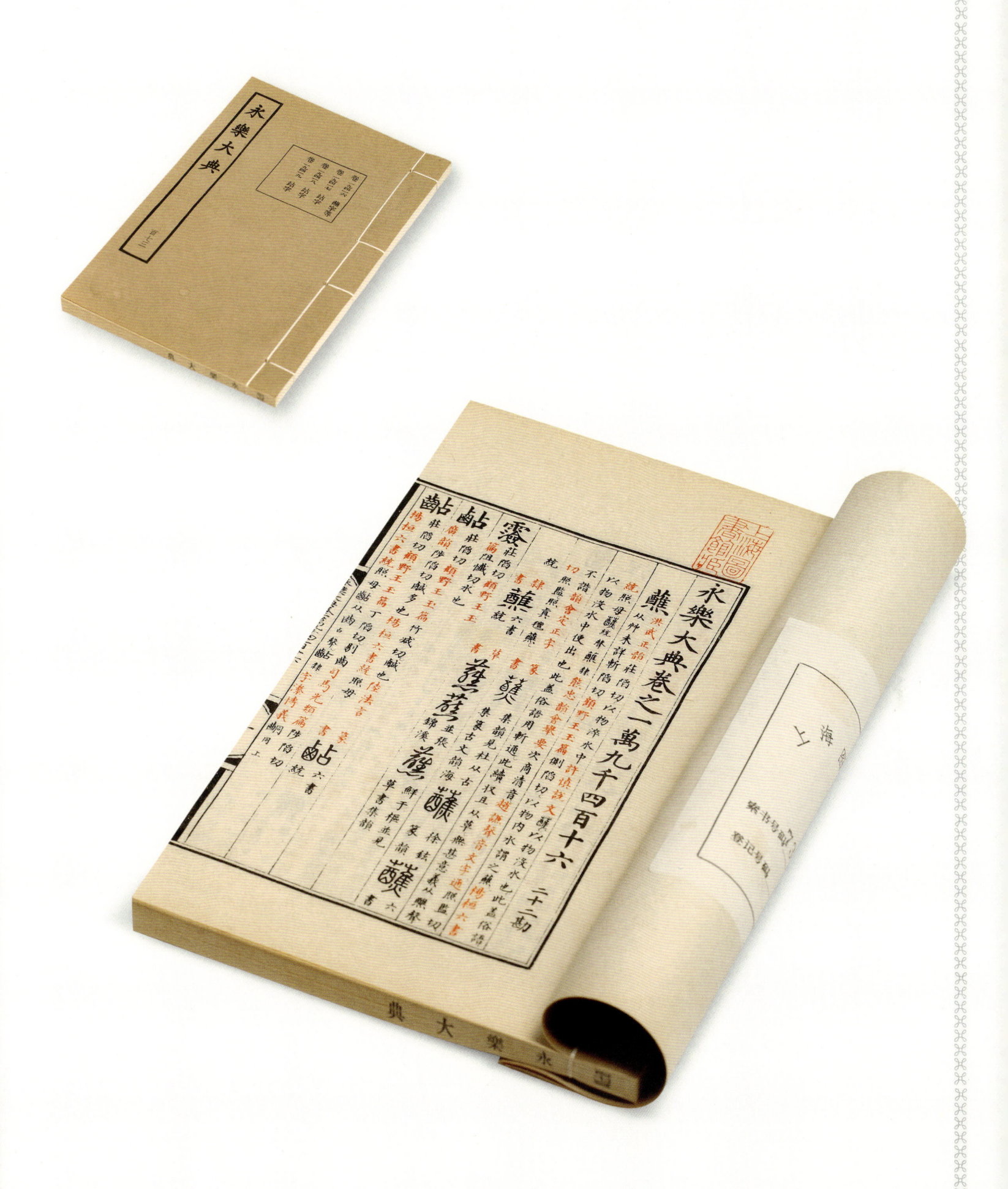

22
关于马可波罗离华的一段汉文记载
《文史杂志》
1941

杨志玖（撰），重庆，中文
21×15 cm
上海图书馆

A passage in Chinese relating to Marco Polo's departure from China,
Journal of Literature and History, 1941
Yang Zhijiu (au.), Chongqing, Chinese
21×15 cm
Shanghai Library

第三部分　日月有常

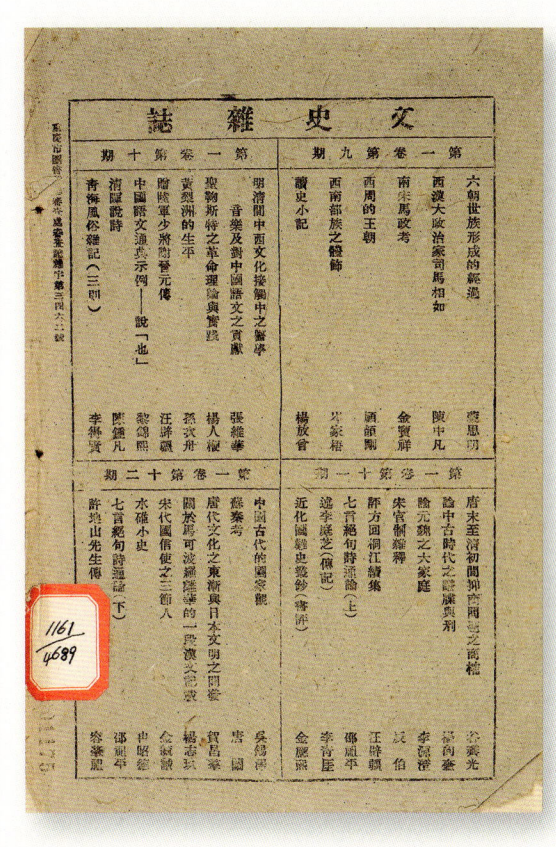

23

马可波罗与马可波罗游记
《旅行家》
1956

向达，北京，中文
25.5×18 cm
上海图书馆

Marco Polo and *The Travels of Marco Polo*,
Traveler Magazine, 1956
Xiang Da (au.), Beijing, Chinese
25.5×18 cm
Shanghai Library

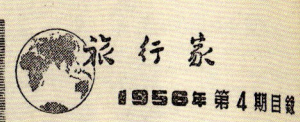

馬可波罗与馬可波罗游記

向达

一 馬可波罗前后东方和西方的旅行家

一二一九年，蒙古成吉思汗西征花剌子模，其后又经过一二三七年的拔都和一二五三年的旭烈兀的兩次西征，是东自中国，西抵欧洲，东西交通暢行無阻。这是过去歷史上所未曾有的一件大事。从十三世紀初期到十四世紀中叶一百多年的时候，中国人到欧洲的，欧洲各处人到中国的，眞是"道路相望，不絕于途"。这些旅行家們往往留下了記載，述說他們的所見所行，对于中古时代的歷史以及地理知識，是很寶貴的材料。他們中間最有名的首推意大利人馬可波罗，本文所謂就是馬可波罗旅行东方和他的游記的大概。在叙述馬可波罗之先，我先簡单的說說在东西交通的大道上来往的另外几个有名的旅行家。先从中國的旅行家講起。

第一个要說的就是元代有名的政治家 耶律楚材(1190—1244)。一二一九年耶律楚材随成吉思汗西征，参贊戎幕。跟随成吉思汗在西域走了不少地方，并在撒馬兒干、巴尔克等处住过，一二二七年回到北京。他在西域前后九年，著有《西游录》一書。比耶律楚材稍晚一点到西域的还有丘处机(1148—1229)。丘处机是道教中的一个有名的祖师，法号長春眞人，于一二二一年奉成吉思汗之召赴西域。他經过阿尔泰山，取道今天山北麓，经伊犁，渡伊犁河，从今阿拉木图轉巴尔克，在那里見着成吉思汗，追随至撒馬尔干，稍后于一二二三年东归，住在今北京城西的白云观。他的学生李志常随他往返，因寫長春眞人西游記一書，記述西游經过，路途見聞，收入道藏。此后又三十六年，游歷西域而留下記録的，是为常德。常德在一二五三年旭烈兀第三次西征之后，他的行踪則为报达。听人說到埃及，那时称为密失兒，并知埃及之西为海，海西即富浪或。这里的海指的地中海，富浪即法蘭克，即中古时代的法蘭克帝国。一二六三年有一位刘郁，寫了一部西使記，就是专記常德这一次的出使的。西游錄、西使記二書都是今天研究十三世紀西域史地的重要史料。

一二七七年，又有兩位中國旅行家远赴西域。这兩位都是维吾尔族，一位生長于今北京，名为扫馬，一位生長于今内蒙古的托忽忒，名为馬可；他們都是基督教的聶斯脱里教徒。他們到达波斯后，馬可被任为景教法主，法名雅八·阿羅呵。一二八七年扫馬受当时波斯的伊兒汗主阿魯渾之命出使羅馬。扫馬經过君士坦丁堡、拿波里，七月到达羅馬；九月到巴黎，暢見美腓立王，参观过巴黎大学；十月又会見英國国王愛德華一世；一二八八年归波斯向阿魯渾报命。扫馬于一二九四年逝世于报达，一三一七年馬可亦亡。馬可亡后，大约是景教徒为二人用波斯文寫了一本傳記，后来又从叙利亚文譯成叙利亚文。現在通行的法文和英文譯本都是从叙利亚文翻譯出来的。日本文譯本又是翻自英文本。十三世紀时中國旅行家到过西欧而下記録的，大約以扫馬为第一人了。

以上是中國到西方去的旅行家，以下說一說西方到中國来的旅行家。

一二三七年拔都率領蒙古大軍第二次西征，歐洲國家大为震動。西方听說中國有長老約翰的故事，于是羅馬教皇想用宗教的力量来阻止蒙古人的侵略。一二四五年教皇諾森第四派了方濟会修士意大利人柏朗嘉賓出使蒙古，一二四六年七月柏朗嘉賓到达和林，同年十一月归國，一二四七年初回到法國報告。一二四八年法國路易九世派遣了多明我会修士魯如奠和林修好。一二五二年路易又派出了方濟会修士魯伯魯等三人从陆路到和林，那时元憲宗蒙哥大汗剛即位一年。魯伯魯等在和林住了八个月，仍遵原路回國，其时旭烈兀已發动第三次西征了。旭烈兀西征的第二年，小亚美尼亚國王海屯自到和林来朝貢。一二六一年以后至一二九五年，波羅諸人在中国和东方。一二九一年，敎皇尼古老四世又派方濟会修士意大利人孟高未諾等到中国。孟高未諾取的海路。其时元朝已在北京建都，漢名大都，蒙古名汗八里，即京城之意。孟高未諾在北京傳教，并在今西什庫附近建立教堂。一三二二年孟高未諾死于北京。一三一四年，时孟高未諾尚未死，方濟会修士和多理由海道来中国，經游山西、陝西、四川、西藏諸地，其后于一三三〇年取陸路回國。一三四二年小弟会教士馬黎諾里曾親受敎皇命來中国，一三四六年由泉州归国。馬黎諾里曾帶过西方廢馬，因此拂菻國獻天馬的故事盛傳一时，一直到明朝初年还称道不衰。

柏朗嘉賓、羅伯魯、海屯、孟高未諾、和多理、馬黎諾里諸人游歷东方，都留下自己或他們的侍从寫下的游記、書信之类，其中記載很多的見聞，大部分确实可信，为研究当时东方和东西交通絕好的史料。

24

马可波罗离开中国在1291年的根据是什么?
《历史教学》
1983

杨志玖(撰),天津,中文
25×18 cm
上海图书馆

What's the proof of Marco Polo's departure from China in 1291?,
History Teaching, 1983
Yang Zhijiu (au.), Tianjin, Chinese
25×18 cm
Shanghai Library

歷史教學 (月刊)

History Teaching (Monthly)

一九八三年第二期（总第230期）　№2 1983 General Number 230

目　录

洪水问题真象的探索	刘蕙孙 (2)
近代爱国的外交家黄遵宪	葛玉岗 (7)
福建事变期间十九路军与红军的几次谈判	王顺生 (10)
察哈尔民众抗日同盟军的崛起和失败	郑全备　薛谋成 (14)
意大利杰出的革命家加里波迪	佘士雄 (20)
英国社会民主联盟在工会问题上的立场	刘克华 (23)
历代度量衡亩制度的演变和数值换算（续一）	黄盛璋 (28)
天津师范大学中文系教授朱星同志逝世	本刊编辑部 (32)
《历史教学》月刊编委	
·人物介绍·	(33)
成吉思汗（匡裕彻）　路易丝·密歇尔（[苏]Н·П·叶弗列莫娃）	

教学问题
初中《中国历史》第二册修订本答问（隋唐部分）	王宏志 (39)
高中《世界历史》下册修订本答问	严志梁 (43)
《贞观之治和唐朝社会经济的繁荣》一节教材分析	郭英斌 (48)
《唐朝的衰落》教材分析	韦唐 (53)
在中国历史教学中搜集和运用乡土教材的体会	
北京市大兴县教师进修学校	马玖斌 (57)

·图书评介·
通俗性和科学性的统一——评白寿彝主编《中国通史纲要》	瞿林东　朱尔澄 (62)

问题解答
马可波罗离开中国在1291年的根据是什么？	杨志玖 (6)
古代埃及金字塔和古代美洲印第安人金字塔有何区别？	陈志强 (22)

学术动态
中国现代史学会第三次学术与教学讨论会在厦门举行	傅菲刚 (36)
中国非洲史研究会召开第二届学术讨论会	谌忠人 (37)
河北省历史教学研究会成立大会在保定召开	窦惠汾 (61)
中国世界现代研究会中南地区首届学术讨论会在长沙举行	湘史

图片
世界历史参考图片（十三）	齐文颖
十七——十八世纪的英国（封二）　十七——十八世纪的法国（封三）	
封底图片——唐代人物花鸟螺钿铜镜（说明见31页）	吕树芝

25

试论马可波罗在中国
《中国社会科学》
1992

蔡美彪（撰），北京，中文
25×18 cm
上海图书馆

On Marco Polo in China, *Social Sciences in China*, 1992
Cai Meibiao (au.), Beijing, Chinese
25×18 cm
Shanghai Library

第三部分
日月有常

试论马可波罗在中国

蔡美彪

本文依据元代中国的历史环境与《马可波罗游记》的记事,对马可波罗在中国期间的语言与观点、地位与身分及仕宦记的特征等,作了探索和讨论。认为马可波罗在中国期间习用波斯语文,他的国家观念与政治观点和波斯人或回回人相近或相同。马可波罗既不是作为旅行家或传教士,也不是作为元朝的色目官员留在中国,据基作为一名色目商人在中国各地以至沿海诸国从事商业贸易;深入社会乃广涉谐录是《游记》的最为显著的两个特点。

作者蔡美彪,1928年生,中国社会科学院近代史研究所研究员、学术委员。

1271年马可波罗(Marco Polo)随从他的父亲尼哥罗(Nicholo)与叔父玛菲(Maffeo)自威尼斯启程来华,到1991年已是七百二十年。1291年他们离开中国回国也已七百年了。马可波罗回国后,在1298年的海上战争中被俘入狱,狱中口述他在中国和东方诸国的见闻,由同狱的意大利文学家鲁思惕谦诺(Rusticiano,又名Rusticheilo)笔录成书,即是举世闻名的《马可波罗游记》(又名《见闻录》、《寰宇记》、《行纪》)。此书先后在法国、意大利以至欧洲诸国流传,极大地丰富了欧洲人对中国和东方的认识,并在15世纪激起航海家对东方的向往,从而产生了深远的影响。19世纪以来,本书又作为历史学和地理学的文献,受到欧洲东方学家的注意。关于本书版本的校勘、翻译、注释以及对行路线和有关史事的考订,历来为学者普为研究的课题。我国自本世纪初始有本书的译文刊行,八十年来,几种版本的翻译、注释和有关专题的研究,都取得了新的成果。

五十年前,业师杨志玖先生在《永乐大典》所收《经世大典·站赤》中发现了1290年(至元二十七年)波斯使臣火者(Coja)等护送阔阔真(Cocachin)公主返回波斯的记事,从而证实了马可波罗自述的随从波斯使臣离华的事实与年代[1]。这是迄今为止在汉文

[1] 杨志玖,《关于马可波罗离华的一段汉文记载》,原刊《文史杂志》第1卷第12期,1941年。又见《元史三论》,人民出版社1985年版,第89页。

· 177 ·

在中国时期经历的最重大的政治事件,即是1282年(至元十九年)王著杀阿合马案。据马可自述,此事发生时,他正在大都城里,因而致详地记录了见闻。这一事件包含着蒙古皇室、汉人官员与当时被称为回回的官员们之间的错综复杂的矛盾,包含着蒙汉法与回回法两种文化的冲突。所以,对这一事件的反映,也反映着不同的观念。在汉人官员士大夫看来,王著杀阿合马,乃是"为天下除害"的义举,王著虽被处死,仍被称为"义侠"。时任南台侍御史的著名文士王挥,曾为王著作乐府《义侠行》,自呼说:"著大奸大恶,凡民罔不憝,又以奉秋法论,乱臣贼子,人人得而诛之,不以义与之可乎?"又说王著"正以义激于忠,而奋捐一身之轻,为天下除害为重。"[1]马可波罗则采取了另一种观点,视之为大都城里的汉人造反或叛乱,甚至是谙谋诛除伊斯兰教与基督教徒等一包色目人。对此事的记述,也与王挥不同,而与拉施特《史集》的观点相近[2]。马可波罗记录了阿合马的罪行后,又说忽必烈因此而嫌恶伊斯兰教徒,禁止教徒遵依教规行事。其实,忽必烈是处置了与阿合马案有关的回回官吏,但并无限制所有依伊斯兰教徒。至于《游记》中所说禁止用斯塔法杀牲之事,据《史集》记载,系发生于哥不卒相时期,也与阿合马案无涉[3]。马可波罗视此案为汉人造反排斥色目,又指责忽必烈因而迫害信仰伊斯兰教的回回人,是反映了波斯人或回回人的政治观点。

依据以上的考察,似可得出这样的结论:马可波罗在中国期间习用波斯语文,他的国家观念与政治观点,也与波斯人或回回人相近或相同。

二、地位与身分

马可波罗作为一名来自欧洲的基督教徒,为什么会与信奉伊斯兰教的波斯人或回回人,在国家观念和政治观点上达到一致?这当然不能仅仅以他懂得波斯语来解释,而和他在中国的地位与身分,有更密切的关系。

中国文献中至今尚未发现有关马可波罗的直接记载,但依据元代的惯例,他应被称为也里可温。也里可温一词来自波斯语,源于希腊语。它在中国文献里有两种含义,一是由专指景教徒即基督教徒聂里脱里派"Nestorians",进而泛指基督教徒各派的教徒,一是泛指来自信奉基督教国家的各国人户。在元代,被免差役赋税的文书里,也里可温与僧(道人)、道(先生)、答失蛮并列,是泛指基督教徒。在有签户籍和旅藉的文书里,它和畏兀、河西、回回人并列,是概称来自信奉基督教各国人们的国籍或族

[1] 吾天爵,《国朝文类》卷四,王挥,《秋润先生大全文集》卷九。
[2] 拉施特《史集》第2卷,中译本,商务印书馆1985年版,第341—345页。
[3] 同上,第346—347页。
[4] 参看陈垣《也里可温考》,《陈垣学术论文集》第1集,蔡美彪《元代白话碑集录》,科学出版社1955年版。

· 180 ·

藉[1]。马可波罗既是基督教徒,又来自欧洲的威尼斯,他被称为也里可温,是没有疑问的。

元代社会中,蒙古、色目、汉人、南人曾被划分为四等,享有不同的待遇。这当然是形成于元世祖末年至成宗时期。马可波罗来华时,还没有这样明确的制度。但是,来自中亚和欧洲的各族人,在这个群体中,当以回回人,即来自中亚各地信奉伊斯兰教的各族人为其主体,也里可温,作为一种教藉,也就包括在色目之中,被称为色目人。所以,钱大昕著《元史氏族表》、屠寄著《蒙兀儿史记·氏族表》,都把也里可温列为色目氏族之一。这是很有道理的。在色目这个群体中,既然包含有不同来源教徒的各族人,彼此之间自然难免发生各种矛盾,但由于他们是独立于蒙古、汉人之外的群体,在许多方面具有共同的利益,所以,在对待蒙、汉事物时,又往往持有相同的观点。马可波罗在述及基督教与伊斯兰教的冲突时,十分明确地站在反对回回人的立场。《游记》中详据记述报达(Baudas)基督教徒的移山大事,对伊斯兰教嘲讽至深,便是一例,但在对待回回人与汉人的冲突时,又明显地站在回回人一边。前举有关阿合马的记事,便是显著的例证。马可波罗多次指责佛教徒崇祭偶像,也与他对待伊斯兰教徒的态度,是有不同的。

马可波罗在华的17年间,蒙古人与汉人当然是把他作为色目人看待,他自己大概也以色目自处。元军灭宋襄阳时,曾使用回回人亦思马因率献的投石炮,被称为回回炮。马可波罗自叙是他的贡献,当然并不可信,但也说明,直到他回国前见闻时,仍然自觉或不自觉地把自己与回回人、回回炮联在一起。

元代中国色目群体中的各族人,有多种途径在官府任职,但是商业活动的回回商人仍是这个群体中的主体,在人数上大概也占多数。在官府任职的色目官员,是人民的统治者和压迫者,并多恃权逐利,因而遭到广大人民,特别是汉族人民的厌恶和歧视。《马可波罗游记》在记述阿合马事件时说,"你们必须知道,所有契丹人(汉人)全都痛恨大可汗的统治权,因为他们鞑靼人和许多委回回使他们统治他们,这叫他们看起来,是象他们当作奴隶。"又说忽必烈"对这件(汉地)人民有信任心,但只相信自己的鞑靼人、回回教徒和基督教徒,而他们对回回人和回回都没有,所以时他们去治理这地。"[2]马可波罗敏感地看到了色目官员与汉地人民之间的矛盾,所论也大体上符合当时的实际。这种矛盾,由于阿合马一党的横行而更加加深化。马可波罗在中国的社会身分,我以为并不是这类色目官员,而是往来各地,在民间经营商业贸易的色目商人。我之所以做出这样的判断,是基于对以下事实的考察。

(一)马可波罗在中国期间是否担任过元朝的行政官员或奉使官员即使臣,历来研究者多有异议。《游记》中的有关记述,很为模糊含混,难以置信。书中只说马可波罗

[1] 参看《至顺镇江志》卷三"户口"。
[2] 张星烺译Z本《马哥孛罗游记》卷164页,又见科本学术,参见冯译《行纪》。

· 181 ·

26

《永乐大典》与《马可波罗游记》
《津图学刊》
1997

杨志玖（撰），天津，中文
20×13.5 cm
上海图书馆

Yongle Canon and *The Travels of Marco Polo*,
Tianjin Library Journal, 1997
Yang Zhijiu (au.), Tianjin, Chinese
20×13.5 cm
Shanghai Library

第三部分
日月有常

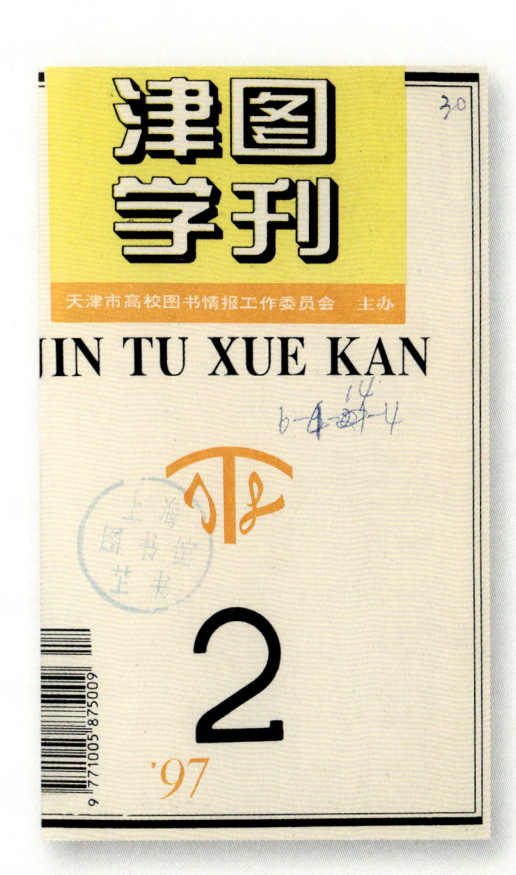

虚实之界：奇迹之书
《马可·波罗游记》主题文献图录

第三部分
日月有常

27

马可波罗行迹扬州方志考
《扬州大学学报（人文社会科学版）》
2012

余志群（撰），江苏扬州，中文
28×20.5 cm
上海图书馆

A study on Marco Polo's trace in the chronicle of Yangzhou,
Journal of Yangzhou University (Humanities & Social Sciences), 2012
Yu Zhiqun (au.), Yangzhou, Jiangsu, Chinese
28×20.5 cm
Shanghai Library

28

关于马可波罗离华的汉文资料
及其到达波斯的波斯文资料
《哈佛亚洲学报》
1976

[美] 柯立夫（撰），坎布里奇，英文
23.5×16 cm
上海图书馆

A Chinese source bearing on Marco Polo's departure
from China and a Persian source on his arrival in Persia,
Harvard Journal of Asiatic Studies, 1976
Francis Woodman Cleaves (au.), Cambridge, English
23.5×16 cm
Shanghai Library

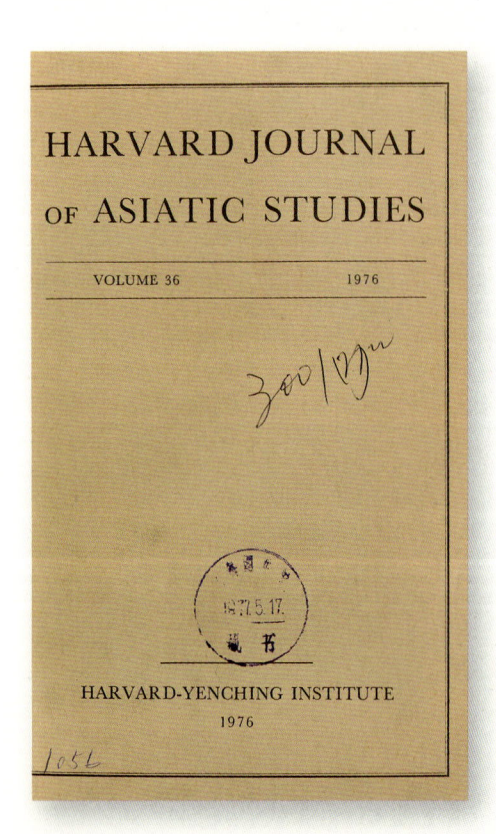

第三部分
日月有常

HARVARD JOURNAL OF ASIATIC STUDIES

EDITED BY

DONALD H. SHIVELY

EDITORIAL BOARD

GLEN W. BAXTER	EDWIN O. REISCHAUER
PATRICK D. HANAN	BENJAMIN I. SCHWARTZ
HOWARD S. HIBBETT	EDWARD W. WAGNER
JAMES R. HIGHTOWER	LIEN-SHENG YANG
MASATOSHI NAGATOMI	YING-SHIH YÜ

This journal is published under the auspices of the Harvard-Yenching Institute. Manuscripts, books for review, subscription orders, and inquiries should be addressed to The Editor, *Harvard Journal of Asiatic Studies*, 2 Divinity Avenue, Cambridge, Mass. 02138, U.S.A. Checks should be drawn payable to the Harvard-Yenching Institute.

Subscription, $12.50, U.S. currency, per volume.

CONTENTS

MINEAR, Richard H., Ogyū Sorai's *Instructions for Students*: A Translation and Commentary	5
GRAHAM, William T., Jr., Yü Hsin and "The Lament for the South"	82
McCANN, David R., The Structure of the Korean *Sijo*	114
EGAN, Ronald, On the Origin of the *Yu hsien k'u* Commentary	135
RUBIN, Jay, *Sanshirō* and Sōseki	147
CLEAVES, Francis Woodman, A Chinese Source Bearing on Marco Polo's Departure from China and a Persian Source on His Arrival in Persia	181
TERASAKI, Etsuko, *Hatsushigure*: A Linked Verse Series by Bashō and His Disciples	204

REVIEW ARTICLE:

TOTMAN, Conrad, The State of the Art, the Art of Statecraft, and Where Do We Go from Here: Reflections on Hall's *Tanuma* and Ooms's *Sadanobu*	240

REVIEWS:

Leo Ou-fan Lee, *The Romantic Generation of Modern Chinese Writers* (CYRIL BIRCH)	256
Herrlee G. Creel, *Shen Pu-hai: A Chinese Political Philosopher of the Fourth Century B.C.* (DERK BODDE)	258
Thomas A. Metzger, *The Internal Organization of Ch'ing Bureaucracy* (S. N. EISENSTADT)	270

---

180 JAY RUBIN

Tose was his brother's wife, a woman whom he was forbidden to view as a woman, an ordinary human being who, for him, had to be placed into a separate category. If in fact Sōseki did have an affair with this sister-in-law for whom he expressed great admiration and respect, (Etō, 1: 194–96) then the joy of it must have been accompanied by a profound disillusionment of the sort that Hirota experienced and that Sanshirō is destined to experience. People cannot be stereotyped; "A human being placed in particular circumstances has the ability and the right to do just the opposite of what the circumstances dictate."

In any case, biography aside, the parallels between Sanshirō and Hirota are clear. As early as chapter 4, a hint appears that Sanshirō and Mineko are meant to have the same poem-and-picture (changing, moving; unchanging, still) relationship as Hirota and the girl in his dream forest: "Sanshirō began to flip through a book of poems. Mineko opened a large picture book on her lap."³⁸ (101) And when Hirota has recounted his dream, Sanshirō asks, "What happened after that?" to which Hirota replies with an indication of what lies in store for him, "After that, you came." (11: 282) Sanshirō's "Girl in the Forest," like Hirota's, is not simply one idealized woman, but his last.

To the very end, however, Sanshirō does not see that he must "go on changing, moving," that—as Kenzō would put it—"Hardly anything in this life is settled." (102: 592; McClellan, 169) He wants to remain a stray sheep with his unreal image of Mineko in a picture-like world that never changes. At the gallery, Yojirō asks him,

"How do you like 'The Girl in the Forest'?"

"The title is no good."

"What should it be, then?"

Sanshirō did not answer him, but to himself he muttered over and over, "Stray sheep. Stray sheep." (13: 309)

---

³⁸ In "Bungei no tetsugakuteki kiso," Sōseki distinguishes between literature as a temporal art emphasizing movement (*dō*) of consciousness, and painting as a spatial art emphasizing stillness (*sei*). (92) Sōseki was a close—and critical—reader of Lessing's *Laocoön*. (16: 239–42)

A CHINESE SOURCE BEARING ON MARCO POLO'S DEPARTURE FROM CHINA AND A PERSIAN SOURCE ON HIS ARRIVAL IN PERSIA

FRANCIS WOODMAN CLEAVES

HARVARD UNIVERSITY

UNTIL recently the date of Marco Polo's departure from China and that of his arrival in Persia were a matter of speculation. Thanks to the work of three scholars—Chinese, French, and English—dealing independently with different facets of the same problem a more accurate chronology for his voyage from China to Persia has been established.

Marco's account of how the Mongolian Princess Kökejin was escorted from China to Persia by a party of which he, his father Nicolò, and his uncle Maffeo, were members may be read in the beautiful translation by the late A. C. Moule:[1]

Now it happened after a certain time that the great queen Bolgana who was wife of Argon, the lord at that time of the Tartars of the sunrising, died. And that queen at the point of death asks favour of the king, and so leaves by her last will that no lady might sit on her throne nor be wife of Argon if she were not of her line, which was found in Catai. So then Argon took three of his wise barons who had names like this, the first Oulatai, the second Apusca, and the third Coja. And he sends them very grandly as his messengers to the great Kaan with a very great [and] fair company in order to ask that he should send him a lady who was of the line of the queen Bolgana his wife who was dead, to marry him; because she had so ordained, as was said above. And when the three barons were come to the great Kaan then they told him their message and the reason why they were come from Argon. The great Kaan

---

[1] A. C. Moule and Paul Pelliot, *Marco Polo: The Description of the World* (London: George Routledge, 1938), I, 88–93. (I have omitted Moule's footnotes and indications of sources, but have retained his use of italic letters which, as he stated on page 6, are used to distinguish "all the important and a multitude of less important passages and words from other texts.")

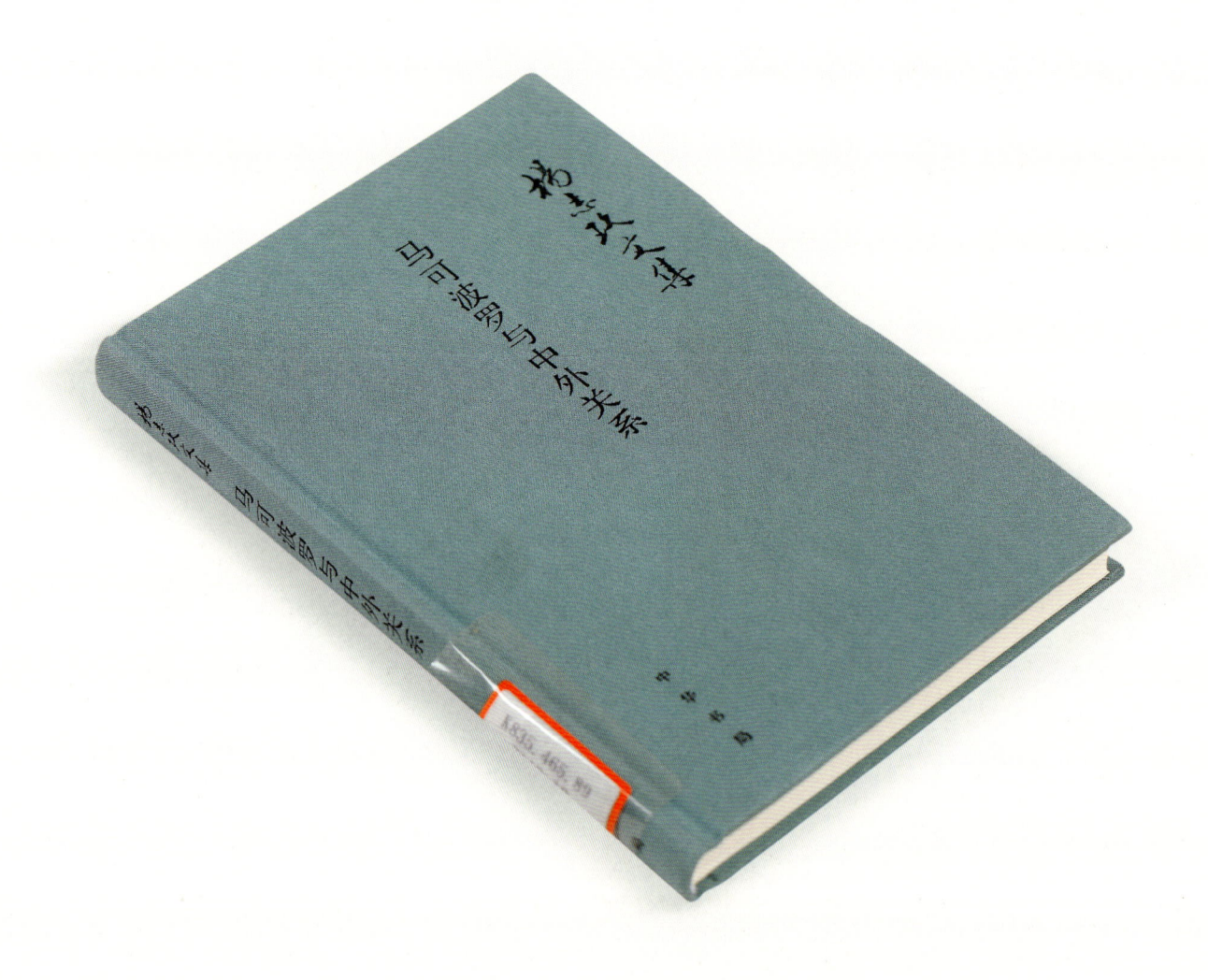

29
《马可波罗与中外关系》
2015

杨志玖（著），北京，中文
22×15 cm
上海图书馆

Marco Polo and Sino-Western relations, 2015
Yang Zhijiu (au.), Beijing, Chinese
22×15 cm
Shanghai Library

第三部分
日月有常

导言：马可波罗其人及在中国的游历

马可波罗（1254—1324年）是中世纪大旅行家，是使西方人了解中国的重要人物之一。他的《游记》（应称《寰宇记》）不仅在西方世界产生了重大影响，也是中国和西方，特别是中国和意大利人民友好关系的历史见证。

马可波罗出生在意大利威尼斯城一个商人家庭。公元1275年，他随他父亲和叔父到达中国，居留了十七年。1291年，他们伴随波斯出使元朝的使臣离开中国，1295年返回故乡。不久，马可波罗参加了对热那亚城的海战，兵败被俘入狱。在狱中口述其在东方的见闻，由同狱难友为之笔录，这就是举世闻名的《马可波罗游记》。这部书在意大利和世界其他各国广为传播，为学者潜心研究和世人阅读欣赏。然而，直到20世纪90年代中期，仍有人怀疑其真实性，认为他没有到过中国。为了验证其真实性，有必要把此书所记和元代汉文有关资料两相对比，才能得出恰当的结论。本书的几篇论著主要即围绕此题而展开研讨。本文是开宗明义第一篇，除简述马可波罗的时代和生平外，主要就马可波罗书中有关中国的记事与中国载籍相互印证。以下诸篇则重点阐述有关问题及对怀疑论者的答辩。西方马可波罗研究专家学者在注释、出版马可波罗的书时，都有极具学术价值的长篇《导言》，如亨利·玉尔（Henry Yule）编译、亨利·考狄埃（Henri Cordier）修订的《马可波罗游记》，穆尔（A.C.Moule，或译牟里、摩勒、穆阿德）与伯希和（P.Pelliot）整理出版的《马可波罗寰宇记》的《导言》。本文不敢效颦前贤，只着力于马可波罗中国记事的简要疏证，可说是有中国特色的《导言》吧。一笑！

1957年与夫人、子女合影

1983年在庐山与中国元史研究会同仁合影

1983年和南开大学滕维藻校长（右五）访问日本京都大学留影

1991年在北京马可波罗国际学术讨论会上与马可波罗后裔波罗·帕多莱基亚合影

前　言

杨志玖先生（1915—2002年），山东省淄博市周村区人。著名历史学家。回族。1934年同时考取北京大学和清华大学。是年9月，入北京大学史学系。卢沟桥事变后，随校南迁，在西南联合大学继续学习。1938年8月大学毕业，被推荐到中央研究院历史语言研究所作所外研究生。1939年9月，考取北京大学文科研究所研究生，师从姚从吾、向达教授研究蒙元史。1941年北京大学文科研究所研究生毕业，留西南联合大学暨南开大学历史系任教。1944年3月，应傅斯年先生邀请，借调到四川南溪县李庄中央研究院历史语言研究所任助理研究员，编写中国边疆史清代部分。1946年10月，应南开大学文学院长冯文潜先生之聘，到南开历史系任教。新中国建立后，杨先生历任南开大学副教授、教授、中国古代史专业博士生导师，《中国历史大辞典》主编，《历史教学》编委会主任，中国元史研究会名誉会长，中国海外交通史学会顾问，中国民族史学会顾问，中国唐史学会顾问等。还是中国人民政治协商会议天津市第六、第七、第八届委员会委员和常务委员。著有《隋唐五代史纲要》、《元史三论》、《马可波罗在中国》、《元代回族史稿》、《陋室文存》等专著，发表论文近两百篇，主编《中国封建社会土地所有制形式问题讨论集》等。他坚持"少而精"的著述原则，在蒙元史、隋唐史、回族史、中西交通史等诸多领域内学术贡献卓著，受到海内外学界的尊重和赞赏。

杨先生对蒙元史的研究，主要集中在马可波罗来华、回回人和探马赤军等国内外高度关注的三个热点问题。

马可波罗来华及其所撰《游记》，是中西交通史上的重大事件。1941年，杨先生利用《永乐大典》卷一九四一八《经世大典·站赤》一段

关于马可波罗在中国的几个问题

一、懂不懂汉语？

马可波罗说，他到达忽必烈汗（元世祖）的朝廷后不久，"已经知道四种语言，同他们的字母，他们的写法"①。这四种语言是什么，他没有一一指明，因而引起后人的揣测。

法国学者颇节（G. Pauthier）在 1865 刊行和注释的《忽必烈枢密副使博罗本书》(Le Livre de Marco Polo) 上首先认为，马可波罗所学会的四种语言是蒙古文、阿拉伯文、维吾尔文和亢文（即汉语）②。我国此说在我国也相当流行。

但是，著名的《马可波罗游记》注释家，英国的玉耳（H. Yule）和法国的戈耳迭（H. Cordier）却反对马可波罗懂汉语一说。他们的理由归纳起来有三条：(1) 马可把苏州解释为"地"而称杭州 (Kinsay 即行在译音) 为"天"，说明他不懂汉语苏、杭的意义，而是爱听俗谚"上有天堂，下有苏杭"后的误解③。(2) 汉字的书法很特殊，马可却一点没有提到④。(3) 马可在书中提到的许多地名，如

《关于马可波罗在中国的几个问题》手稿

第三部分
日月有常

一 时代与生平

马可波罗一家到达和旅居中国时，正是元朝的皇帝忽必烈（元世祖）统治时期（1260—1294 年）。元朝是我国以蒙古族为主建立的国家。公元 1206 年，成吉思汗统一了漠北的蒙古诸部，建立了大蒙古国，五传至忽必烈至元八年（1271 年），改国号为元。成吉思汗及其继承者不断地向外扩张。向南，消灭了金朝和南宋；向西，曾发动了三次西征，灭亡了西夏、西辽和在中亚及西亚建立的花剌子模王朝、阿拉伯人建立的阿拔斯哈里发帝国，征服了阿速、钦察、斡罗思诸部，建立了钦察汗国（1243—1502 年）：疆域东起也儿的石河，西至斡罗思，南起巴尔喀什湖、里海、黑海，北至北极圈附近，国都萨莱（今俄国阿斯特拉罕北）。伊利汗国（1258—1355 年，又译伊儿汗）：疆域东起中亚的阿姆河，西至小亚细亚，南起波斯湾，北至高加索山，国都桃里寺（今伊朗大不里士）。察合台汗国：疆域东起吐鲁番，西至阿姆河，南越兴都库什山，北至塔尔巴哈台山，国都阿力麻里（今新疆霍城附近）。三次西征使被征服的地区和人民遭到很大的破坏和伤亡，但其结果是使亚洲大陆北部和中、西部都在蒙古成吉思汗家族统治之下，在客观上打通了中西交通的路线，便利了中西经济、文化的交流。虽然各汗国之间有时也发生矛盾和斗争，一度影响了道路的畅通，但总起来看，元代的中西交往较之前代是更为便利和频繁了。

应该特别指出的是，由于蒙古势力的向西扩张，引起西欧基督教世界的教皇、国王等各界人士的震惊和好奇心。他们一方面害怕蒙古铁骑的再深入，一方面又为蒙古人消灭了他们的对头穆斯林诸王朝而幸灾乐祸，于是不断派遣一些教士作为使臣到东方来探听情报，要与蒙古修好并劝蒙古人皈依基督教。他们的一厢情愿虽然落空，但使他们写出的报告，如意大利人方济各会教士普兰诺·加宾尼（一译柏朗嘉宾，约 1182—1252 年）写的《蒙古史》，法国人方济各会教士卢布鲁克（约 1215—1270 年）写的《东游记》，都对蒙古人的军事、政治、人民生活、宗教信仰、风俗习惯等有翔实的报告。但他们只到蒙古地区，对我国中原一带情况则无所记载。另外，一些西方商人也有来的，但他们却没想到写书。在这些方面，马可波罗的《游记》可谓独树一帜，异常珍贵。

马可波罗的诞生地威尼斯，是意大利东北部的一个商业城市，地滨亚得里亚海，原属东罗马帝国，公元 10 世纪末建为一个独立的共和国。由于交通便利，成为西欧与东方贸易的中心之一。13 世纪初，在威尼斯人的怂恿下，西欧的十字军发动了第四次东侵（1202—1204 年），威尼斯乘机在地中海沿岸的一些城市取得商业特权，并占有爱琴海上许多岛屿，夺取了东罗马帝国的国际贸易地位。但此时在其西南部、地滨利古里亚海的城市热那亚共和国早已崛起。她嫉视威尼斯的霸权，两城常有冲突。1261 年，她支持被第四次十字军颠覆的东罗马帝国，取得黑海进出口控制权，从此两城积怨更深，战争规模也日益扩大。马可波罗就是在一次与热那亚的海战中战败被俘的。

马可波罗出自威尼斯波罗氏商人家族。他祖父名安得利亚·波罗，生三子：长名马可，次名尼柯罗，季名马菲奥。马可波罗是尼柯罗·波罗之子，他的名字与他伯父的一样，是有意纪念其伯父的。三人俱以经商为业，老马可先在君士坦丁堡（今伊斯坦布尔）开业，其后又向东在黑海北岸克里米亚半岛东南岸的索尔得亚设立货栈。他的两个兄弟也步其后尘，向东方发展其事业。

公元 1260 年，尼柯罗和马菲奥携带货物自威尼斯出发到达君士坦丁堡，在那里买了许多珍宝，又渡海至索尔得亚，再由陆路前行至钦察汗国的国都萨莱，受到汗国国王别儿哥（1257—1266 年在位）的欢迎。他们留居一年之后想回故乡，恰逢别儿哥为争夺伊利汗国的阿塞拜疆地区与该国君主旭烈兀发生战争，回乡原路不通，听人建议折向东行，到达察合台汗国的不花剌城（今乌兹别克斯坦的布哈拉），停留的三年，直到旭烈兀汗派往元朝的使臣路经不花剌时，他们又随同东行，约于 1265 年，到达元朝的都城上都（又名开平府，今内蒙古正蓝旗东五一牧场，为元帝夏季驻地），受到元世祖忽必烈的接见，并受命出使罗马教廷，请教皇选派精通教义的教士百人来华，并从耶稣圣墓的长明灯上带点圣油来。经过许多曲折（由于教皇去世和新教皇未选出）时日，他们才于 1271 年夏季，会同两名教士和尼柯罗的小儿子马可波罗起程东来。途中，二教士畏难退回，波罗一家则继续前进，终于在 1275 年（元世祖至元十二年）夏季抵达元朝皇帝避暑、议政的上都开平府（Chemeinfu）。

据马可波罗自述，由于他聪明谨慎，并学会几种文字（可能是蒙古、突厥、波斯等），甚受大汗宠爱，命他出使各地，都使大汗满意，因此他们在中国住了十七年。

波罗一家久居异国，思回故乡而不得允许。直到最后，由于伊利汗国王阿鲁浑（Argon）的皇后卜鲁罕去世，遗嘱必须其同族女子继其后位。阿鲁浑派三位使臣到元廷求婚，忽必烈选一位十七岁少女阔阔真（Cocacin）出嫁，波罗一家以护送三使及该女由海道得准许，于 1291 年初从泉州出发，航行两年多时间，完成使命。1295 年他们回到威尼斯。

阿鲁浑所派三使臣名字是 Ulatai, Apusca, Coja，这三个名字在《永乐大典》卷一九四一八引元修《经世大典·站赤》中一道公文内能找到，他们是兀鲁䚟（音歹）、阿必失呵、火者，在至元二十七年（1290 年）奉旨 "取道马八儿，往阿鲁浑大王位下的"。经笔者考释，这道公文中讲的即是马可书中所述他们得以离开中国的原委。由于是泉州行省向中央请示出使随员的口粮供给问题，不仅未提马可之名，连被护送的主角阔阔真也未提及，因无必要。但联系《游记》所述，则恰是一回事。足证马可波罗确曾到过中国。

据传他们回家时，其房舍已被其亲戚占住，因为他们早已死于外域了。同时，他们衣衫褴褛，口音和举止颇有蒙古人风味，也引起故乡人的怀疑。他们设计请亲友赴宴，在宴会中，换了三次所穿的华贵衣服，并将衣服撕开分送侍者，使来宾不胜惊讶。最后，马将初到家时三人所穿破衣取出，割开边缝，露出各种珍宝石头，亲友们才相信他们真的属于波罗家族，对他们亲敬有加。威尼斯少年争来与马可订交，询问其东方见闻，马可辄以百万为单位夸述中国皇帝（忽必烈大汗）的财富收入或其他地方之富有，听者于惊叹之余遂以百万君称之，其居室则称为百万之宅。这些传说似不可信，但并非毫无根据。如几次换衣是蒙古皇帝赐宴群臣的礼俗，普兰诺·加宾尼《蒙古》第九章中即有记载；意大利文版的马可波罗《游记》即称为《百万》，其宅至今仍称为百万宅第，都可以说明，虽然也有不同说法①。

他们回家的第二年（1296 年），热那亚城的舰队来犯。马可乘一舰参战被俘，在狱中口述其在东方的见闻，引起热那亚人的兴趣，因而受到优待。同狱中有一比萨（Pisa）市人鲁思蒂谦诺（Rustichello 或 Rusticiano），是一善于撰写骑士传奇小说的文人，将其口述内容记录下来，马可也托人把他在东方任所时的有关札记弄来作为补充，1298 年书稿完成，

---

① 《马可波罗寰宇记》英译者穆尔在其《导言》中对马可的评名"百万"提出怀疑。他统计马可死后遗产，算出其财产值 1924 年币值不过 3000 英镑，与百万相差甚远（《导言》p.31）。澳洲国立大学教授罗依果博士（Dr. Igor de Rachewiltz）研究波罗家族语者的考察，指出"百万"浑号乃指马一波罗家族，这一家的祖孙三代。马菲奥一老尼柯罗和名字相同，后人遂误认这是马可波罗的称号（或马可里诺）都有"百万"的浑号。详于世系和名字相同，后人遂误认这是马可波罗的称号（或马可里诺）都有"百万"的浑号。[见其《马可波罗到过中国》（Marco Polo Went to China），刊于波恩大学《中亚研究》1997 年第 27 期，pp.68—69]。

30

马可波罗到过中国——
对《马可波罗到过中国吗？》的回答
《历史研究》
1997

杨志玖（撰），北京，中文
25×18 cm
上海图书馆

Marco Polo was in China, a reply to Frances Wood's "Did Marco Polo Go to China?",
Historical Research, 1997
Yang Zhijiu (au.), Beijing, Chinese
25×18 cm
Shanghai Library

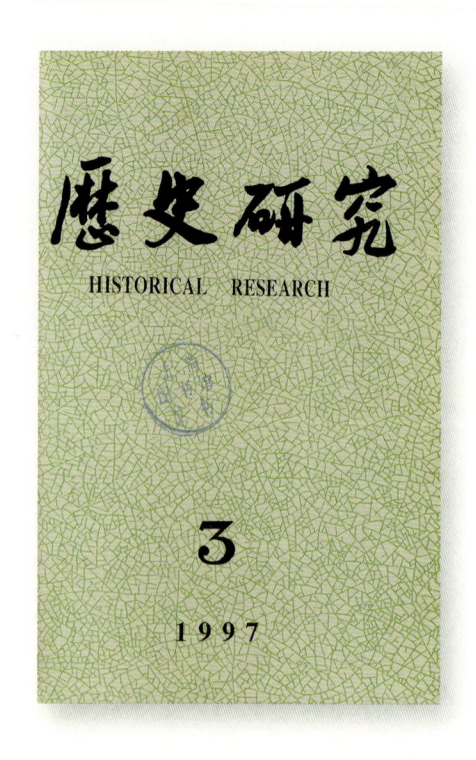

马可波罗到过中国
——对《马可波罗到过中国吗?》的回答

杨志玖

英国不列颠图书馆中国部主任弗兰西丝·伍德博士(汉名吴芳思)1995年所著《马可波罗到过中国吗?》一书的出版,引起了国内外有关学者的关注和议论。此前,怀疑和否定马可波罗到过中国的学者也有几位,但只是写些短文或附带提及。这次她却是以182页专著的形式进行论证,所引论著97种,包括我国学者余士雄主编的《马可波罗介绍与研究》中的论文。除《导言》和《结语》外,还用了15章阐发她的宏论,集此前怀疑和否定论者之大成。这部著作值得我们认真研究和评论。限于篇幅,暂将某些观点提出来与之商榷。

一、旧话重提

在《导言》中,伍德博士说,她是从克雷格·克鲁纳斯那里得知德国著名蒙古学者傅海波(Herbert Franke,一译福赫伯)有一篇怀疑马可波罗到过中国的文章[①]。傅氏认为,波罗一家是否到过中国,还是个没有解决的问题。他举出波罗书中一些可疑之点,如在扬州做官、献投石机攻陷襄阳等虚夸之辞以及书中未提中国的茶叶和汉字书法等问题。他说:"这些事倒使人们对波罗一家长期住在中国一说发生怀疑。"伍德

[①] 傅文题为 Sino-Western Contacts under the Mongol Empire(《蒙古帝国时期的中西接触》),刊于 Journal of the Royal Asiatic Society, Hong Kong Branch, 6. 1966. Hong Kong, pp. 49—72. 其中指摘马可波罗的文字不过一页。克雷格·克鲁纳斯(Craig Clunas)在英国泰晤士报(The Times) 1982 年 4 月 14 日《中国增刊》(China Supplement)上发表 The explorer's tracks(《探险者的足迹》),文中引用了傅海波教授的文章,认为马可波罗曾见过某种波斯的《导游手册》,1982 年 7 月号《编译参考》有杨德璐译文,改题为《马可波罗到过中国吗的怀疑》。笔者在 1982 年第 10 期《环球》发表《马可波罗到过中国》一文,对克氏文提出质疑,收入《元史三论》,人民出版社 1985 年版,第 127—132 页;《马可波罗介绍与研究》,书目文献出版社 1983 年版,第 52—58 页。

一家甚为吃惊。据她统计,全书只有 18 处提到马可波罗或其一家。她说,这不是一本个人见闻录而更像一部地理或历史著作,一部味道浓厚的旅行指南。

按,马可波罗所述旅行路线确有迂迴之处,但大体上仍有线索可寻。亨利·玉尔所指难点只是从水路到缅甸缅国沿以及缅甸与老挝之间一段而已,其它地方并无大困难,有玉尔所制旅行路线图可证。所举只有 18 处提名更令人怀疑;书中不提名而用"我"或"我们"字样的地方不胜枚举,难道伍德博士所据的 Latham 版本《马可波罗》没有这些字样吗?

在《结语》中,作者除了简要指出书误导了一些追踪马可波罗的足迹者、不是游记只是一部《寰宇记》(description of the world)外,还从宏观方面提出:有些人可能有一种悬想,认为 13 世纪晚期和 14 世纪早期人们对地理学知识已逐渐需要,受此驱动,逐编写此类书籍。她举出了阿魁(Jacopo da Acqui)、万桑(Vincent of Beauvais)、曼德维尔(Sir John Mandeville)都编过世界历史和地理等书[①],拉施特(Rashid al-Din)也用阿拉伯文(按,应为波斯文——引者)写过世界史(即《史集》——引者)。她说,曼德维尔的书曾大受欢迎并译为多种欧洲语言,但终被揭露为赝品,乃剽窃 15 种以上资料而成。对比之下,马可波罗的《寰宇记》经鲁思蒂谦诺之修饰会充与此书译者的增添,虽为二手资料,却与曼氏命运不同而享誉后世至今不衰。将马可波罗与曼德维尔书相提并论,言外之意,不同可知。

伍德博士进一步指出,《寰宇记》中旅行路线之缺乏连贯,"可能"由于鲁思蒂谦诺之鼓励,使一旅游记扩大为世界历史、地理著作,因而加进了一些不相干的内容,如俄罗斯、日本等地区古代战争故事等。又说,作为一个职业传奇故事作家,鲁思蒂谦诺"也许"是想利用人们对记载猎奇异事物书籍的普遍需要,"可能"在听了马可波罗讲的奇异故事后,提请与他合作,遂撰此书。他说,鉴此书,他尚无印刷机和版权问题,写一部稿件很难反对,但鲁氏此前曾借英国王储之助来完成其文学创作[②],此次仍想借此书取得英王的恩惠也颇有"可能"。请注意,在这一段说明中,她连续用了"possible"、"may"、"may be"、"perhaps"等猜测性词语。

以下,伍德博士又就《寰宇记》的资料来源发表她的看法。她承认,这是一道难题,但仍提出了她的答案:(一)"假如"马可波罗从家中得到书面材料,他家中应该

[①] Jacopo da Acqui 为马可波罗的同时人,所著书名 Imago Mundi(《世界形象》),是地理书。其中记有马可波罗与其父、叔自蒙古归家,在与热那亚战争中被俘,在狱中口述其世界见闻事。Vincent of (de) Beauvais (1190—1264 年) 1244 年著名 Speculum Historiae (《历史通鉴》),是一部自开辟以来至 13 世纪的世界历史。Sir John Mandeville, 英国作家,自称于 1322—1356 年间游历世界后著书。

[②] 鲁氏曾与英国王子亨利处得见当时已罕见的抄本甚平见的《环航传奇》小说,节录新编为《梅柳杜斯》(Meliadus)一事,见亨利·玉尔书上册《导言》,第 59—60 页。

有到东方经商的资料,而且,"也许"有波斯文的商人指南一类书,"可能"还有波斯文历史著作,其中有关于古代战争以及他们从未经历过的俄罗斯和日本的描述。(二)唐代阿拉伯人对中国的记载,如存于公元 851 年的《中国印度见闻录》,14 世纪初期拉施特的《史集》、中期的白图泰(或译拔都他)游记[①],是《寰宇记》的另一史源,因其记载同以上三书有很多类似之处。她举出《寰宇记》和《史集》关于王著谋杀事件的叙述同样混乱不清作为证明。其实,如笔者前面所说,二者的记载并不相同,前书较后书更接近实情。她虽然知道《史集》和《白图泰游记》出书在后,可马可波罗不可能看到,却说,马可波罗与白图泰关于中国的某些记载的相似颇引人注意,以致傅海波教授认为,马可波罗"可能"或"也许"(might, perhaps)是参考一种波斯或阿拉伯的中国指南书,使他和白图泰的叙述趋于一致(第 146 页)(笔者未见傅教授论及白图泰的文章,伍德博士书中也常引用。但编集这里未指出处,令人纳闷。她又说,有人曾寻找这种指南书,不幸的是,13 世纪是"波斯通俗读物的黑暗时代",这类读物还没有找出来。

"虽然如此,"她接着说,"或许马可波罗之'可能'依靠阿拉伯或波斯史料,从他书中所用词汇上以及对中国东方比大体形之鸟的描述与拉施特、白图泰的记者相似而得知。"假如"(if) 他在狱中从其家中获得波斯文指南书或波斯文蒙古征服等记载,他也会取得原始资料。

伍德博士既然认定马可波罗所用的是二手资料而非其本身见闻,则其本人的未到中国自然是顺理成章的事了。那么,马可波罗这些年到哪里去了?请看伍德博士的答案。

她的第一句话是:不幸的是,假若马可波罗不在中国,在 1271 到 1295 年间他究竟在哪里却无可证明。随后,她提出自己的见解:在《序言》中所记马可波罗的父亲和叔父的第一次东行并遇到某些贵人事,是唯一具体的实证。他们家中的"金牌"(作为蒙哥给使臣的通行证——引者)可能作为与一蒙古贵族(虽然不一定是忽必烈本人)有过高级接触的实物见证。他家族中曾为金牌问题发生一次争论(在《寰宇记》完成后的 1310 年),"或许"(might) 是由于马可波罗并未到过中国而他却声称去过《国而要求一件金牌》;"或许"他父亲和叔父到东方作了一次冒险旅行,得到几个金牌回来,而马可波罗在狱中却窃取其名,写于书中,作为自己的荣耀。她又指出马可波罗的叔父马飞(Maffeo,一作 Matteo,汉译玛寨——引者)在 1310 年的遗嘱中暗示过马

[①] 白图泰(Ibn Battuta, 或译依班拔都、拔都他,全称伊本·白图泰,1304—1368 或 1369 年),非洲摩洛哥丹吉尔城人,1325 年起,历阿拉伯、波斯、中亚、印度等地,1342 年 (元顺帝至正二年) 到达中国,1354 年回国,1355 年口授成书,原名为阿拉伯文,有法、德、葡萄牙等国译本。汉译有张星烺节译其记中国部分 (参阅穆译和亨利·玉尔英译本《中西交通史料汇编》第二册,中华书局 1977 年版) 及马金鹏自阿拉伯文全译本《伊本·白图泰游记》,宁夏人民出版社 1985 年。

31
元代旅华的西方人——兼答马可波罗到过中国吗？
《历史研究》
2001

周良霄（撰），北京，中文
27.5×20 cm
上海图书馆

Westerners who traveled to China during the Yuan Dynasty, also answering whether Marco Polo visited China, *Historical Research*, 2001
Zhou Liangxiao (au.), Beijing, Chinese
27.5×20 cm
Shanghai Library

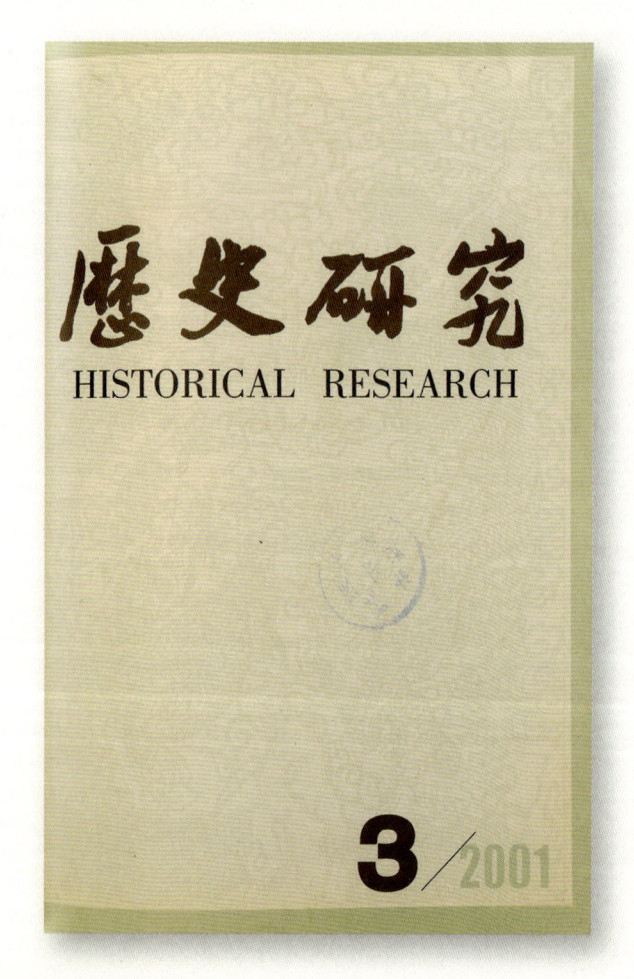

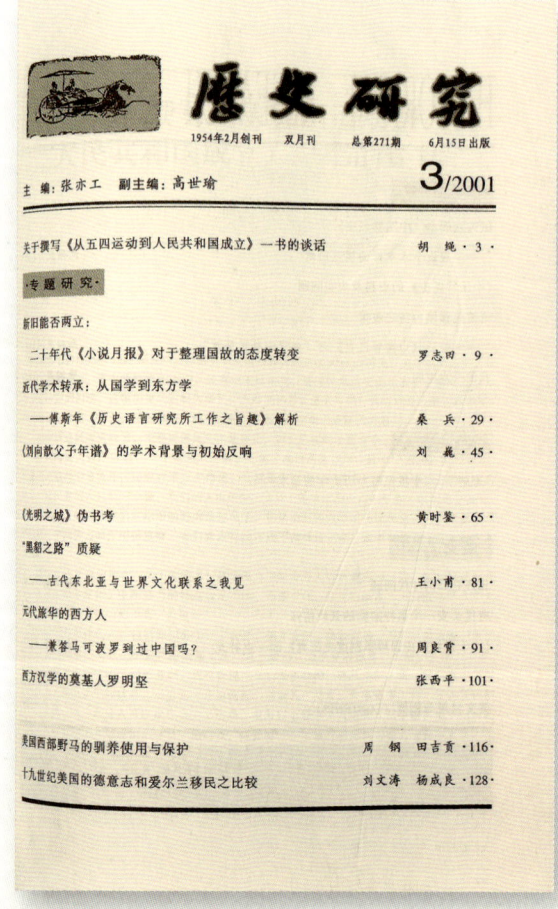

第三部分
日月有常

32

蒙元时期的中西文化交流
——《马可·波罗游记》史事探论
《社会科学辑刊》
2001

申友良（撰），辽宁沈阳，中文
25.5×18 cm
上海图书馆

Sino-Western cultural contacts during the Yuan period, discussions on the historical events in *The Travels of Marco Polo*,
Social Science Journal, 2001
Shen Youliang (au.), Shenyang, Liaoning, Chinese
25.5×18 cm
Shanghai Library

第三部分
日 月 有 常

33

元代居留江浙行省的西域人
《社会科学》
2006

马建春（撰），上海，中文
28×21 cm
上海图书馆

Xiyu People (People from Western Area) Who stayed in Jiangzhe Province in Yuan Dyansty,
Journal of Social Sciences, 2006
Ma Jianchun (au.), Shanghai, Chinese
28×21 cm
Shanghai Library

第三部分
日月有常

34

从《大兴国寺记》看元代江南景教的兴起
《中华文史论丛》
2006

殷小平（撰），上海，中文
20×13 cm
上海图书馆

Observations on the rise of Nestorian Christianity in Jiangnan area during the Yuan Dynasty from *The Inscription of Da Xingguo Temple*, *Journal of Chinese Literature and History*, 2006
Yin Xiaoping (au.), Shanghai, Chinese
20×13 cm
Shanghai Library

第三部分
日 月 有 常

那以後,這裏就有了教堂;然而此前,鎮城既無教堂也無教徒。①

儘管《馬可波羅行紀》的可信度學界還不無懷疑,但此段文字與《寺記》相互印證,說明所述應言之有據。馬可波羅作爲天主教徒,對基督教的流派理當熟悉,故特別指出其爲景教派信徒,從性質上將鎮江的教堂與拉丁派分別開來。這恰如鄂多立克途經揚州城時,特別留意揚州之基督教堂與方濟各派一樣,②均是西人對基督教在東方各地傳播之教派尤加留意之故。總而言之,元代鎮江有景教堂,中西方文獻均有記載,當屬不爭之事實,可補正史之闕載。

雖然撒馬爾干城在回曆93年(712)就被阿拉伯人占領,此後漸漸伊斯蘭化,但宗教的存留具有較長的歷史延續性,伊斯蘭教也一度對景教寬容。在阿拔斯帝國時代,巴格達還被列爲主教區,而帝國內的景教僧侶也據有各等公職;中亞景教的生存環境也一直維持到伊兒汗國的阿魯渾汗時代(Argun,1284—1291)。③當然,兩種宗教之間的爭鬥也一直未有間歇,這是由伊斯蘭教的教旨所決定的。《寺記》中所記撒馬爾干城內教堂石柱懸空之傳說,應當就是當地穆斯林傾軋景教徒這一歷史大背景下的產物,大概是作爲弱勢羣體的景教徒爲堅定其基督信仰而創造出來的"神迹",印

---
① 譯自 A. C. Moule, *Christians in China before the Year 1500*, pp. 139-140. 並參見馮承鈞譯《馬可波羅行紀》第一四八章,上海書店出版社,2000年,頁344;穆爾著,郝鎮華譯《一五五〇年前的中國基督教史》,頁160.
② 何高濟譯《鄂多立克東遊錄》,北京,中華書局,2002年,頁77.
③ 但當時的處境已十分困難,拉班·掃馬與馬可斯西行記中處處表明了中亞穆斯林與景教徒的水火不容之勢。在這裏,宗教的爭鬥和政治的關係顯得更爲息息相關.

了"奇迹是宗教的支柱"①這一歷史名言。較之中亞,元代中國的宗教環境顯然寬容很多,正如伯尼迪托(L. F. Benedetto)編《馬可波羅遊記》(*Marco Polo Il Milione*)提到的:"這些韃靼人並不關心他們的土地上是崇拜甚麼神。只要他們忠於大汗,十分恭順,並因此而繳納規定的貢物,公正得以維持,那麼,如何安慰靈魂,便悉聽其便了。"寬鬆的宗教環境自然吸引了不少景教徒前往。

馬可波羅稱在馬薛里吉思之前鎮江並無基督教徒,這未必符合歷史的真實。假設江南當時並無基督教徒,那麼馬薛里吉思無須大費周章修建教堂,且數以七計,可知此地當時教徒爲數不少。因爲,寺院是宗教徒從事宗教活動的場所和中心,其存在的重要條件,就是要有相當數量的信徒爲基礎。那麼,元代江南基督教的出現始於何時呢?

正史明確記載"江南"之也里可溫,是在距馬薛里吉思建寺十餘年後的大德(1297—1307)年間。《元典章·禮部六·禁也里可溫擾先祝讚》載:

大德八年(1304),江浙行省准中書省咨,禮部呈奉省判集賢院呈,江南諸路道教所呈,溫州路有也里可溫,創立掌教司衙門,招收民戶,充本教戶計;及行將法籙先生誘化,侵奪管領;及於祝聖嚴祈禱去處,必欲班立於先生之上,動致爭競,將先生人等毆打,深爲不便,申乞轉呈上司禁約事。得此,照得江南自前至今,止有僧道二教,各令管領,別無也里可溫教門。近年以來,因隨路有一等規避差役之人,投充本教戶計.

---
① 帕斯卡爾著,何兆武譯《思想錄》,北京,商務印書館,1997年,頁428.
② 轉引自劉南強(S. N. C. Lieu)著,林悟殊譯《華南沿海的景教徒和摩尼教徒》,附錄於克里木凱特著,林悟殊翻譯增訂《達·伽馬以前中亞和東亞的基督教》,頁163.

然是出於忽必烈汗對其恩寵有加,也與朝中有人扶持密切相關,當中代表首推丞相完澤①和崇福使愛薛。完澤丞相"奏聞璽書護持,仍撥賜江南官田三十頃,又益置浙西民田三十四頃,爲七寺常住";②愛薛則負責馬其傳旨、奏稟。愛薛乃元代著名的景教徒,而完澤本人,據劉迎勝先生考證,③乃出自克烈部。很可能也是一個景教徒。此二人在馬薛里吉思建寺的過程不時通風報信,提供實質性的援助,對也里可溫在江南的興起和發展,貢獻自不在言下。我們相信,雲山、聚明山二寺後來的厄運,恐與朝中愛薛和完澤的相繼去世不無關係。若然,則益證明宗教的發展與當權者的支持有着至爲密切的關係。

馬薛里吉思曾任鎮江路副達魯花赤一職。按達魯花赤乃元代官制所特有,蒙古語意爲"鎮守者",或譯"宣差",是蒙古人控制地方政權所設置的監管官員。葉子奇《草木子·雜制》記載:

元路州縣各立長官曰達魯花赤,掌印信,以一府一縣之治,判署則用正官,在府則總管,在縣則縣尹。達魯花猶華言荷包上壓口捺子也,亦猶古言總轄之比。④

達魯花赤一般僅限蒙古人擔任,但作爲特權階級的色目人,也有機會獲任。其職權上有民政和軍政官署之分,馬薛里吉思屬前者,欽

---
① 完澤於1291年出任中書省丞相,直到1303年5月去世。參看《元史》卷一三〇,頁3173—3174.
② 七寺不僅能占有官田,還獲得朝廷大量封地,對地上的人口、牲畜、房屋,都統統充人寺院的固定財產。可以推測,元代也里可溫應當形成有一定規模的寺院經濟,此乃其優於唐代景教的又一表現.
③ 上引劉迎勝《關於馬薛里吉思》,頁16—17.
④ [明]葉子奇《草木子》卷三,北京,中華書局,1997年,頁64. 對達魯花赤的相關任命,參蒙思明《元代社會階級制度》,北京,中華書局,1984年,頁39—41,45—46.

察之完者都拔都魯後者。馬薛里吉思正是借助達魯花赤道一職察,始能取得官地租子,作爲買地的資本。也因爲有這一層官方背景,雲山、聚明山立寺之初,佛教的反對勢力未能構成實質性的威脅。而且,也正因爲鎮江在其轄下,方成爲建寺的首選地點。

綜上所述,作爲統治階級的馬薛里吉思,身兼官僧兩種身份;其建寺不僅出於自身的宗教需要,也和當時江南景教的興起有關,在客觀上促進了該教在異質文明中的傳播。

五 結 語

本文圍繞《大興國寺記》之碑文記載,討論了元代江南也里可溫與唐代景教的關係,以及馬薛里吉思建立七寺的條件和背景等問題,認爲元代江南也里可溫初期乃以景教徒爲主,但並非唐代景教遺族,與唐代景教也無直接的繼承關係,而應來源於蒙古軍及隨軍遷徙而來的其他中亞民族(色目人)中的景教徒。因此,元代也里可溫的傳播,實表現爲以外來教徒爲主體的"移民傳播",這與唐代景教、明清天主教依靠傳教士進行傳教頗爲不同。值得注意的是,這些外來宗教移民占據了當時社會的統治地位,享有政治、經濟、軍事上的特權,致使也里可溫在短期內得以迅猛發展,亦宦亦僧的馬薛里吉思,便是其典型。"移民傳播"及其官方背景,也成爲我們理解元代也里可溫教傳播特點和興衰原因的兩個關鍵。

2006年4月14日

(本文作者係中山大學歷史系博士生)

35
《至顺镇江志》
清道光二十二年刻本

（元）俞希鲁（撰），江苏镇江，中文
29×18 cm
上海图书馆

Chronicles of Zhishun Zhenjiang, 1842
Yu Xilu (au.), Zhenjiang, Jiangsu, Chinese
29×18 cm
Shanghai Library

第三部分 日月有常

虚实之界：奇迹之书
《马可·波罗游记》主题文献图录

36

《元也里可温考》
1923

陈垣（撰），上海，中文
26×15 cm
上海图书馆

A Study on Erkehun in the Yuan Dynasty, 1923
Chen Yuan (au.), Shanghai, Chinese
26×15 cm
Shanghai Library

第十三章　關於也里可溫碑刻之留存
第十四章　也里可溫與景教之異同
第十五章　總論

此書之目的、在專以漢文史料證明元代基督教之情形、先認定元史之也里可溫為基督教、然後搜集關於也里可溫之史料、分類說明之、以為研究元代基督教史者之助、惜乎著者譾陋、得見元代著述至少、未能滿其志、冀博雅君子之教之也、

著　者　識

三版增訂元也里可溫考

新會陳　垣菴撰

第一章　也里可溫之解詁

元以前未聞有也里可溫之名也、讀元史則數數見也里可溫四字相聯屬矣、也里可溫之見於元代著述者不一、果為何等語耶

錢大昕元史氏族表曰也里可溫氏不知所自出、卷二

元史國語解曰也里可溫蒙古語 ᠡᠷᠺᠡᠦᠨ 應作伊嚕勒昆伊嚕勒福分也、昆、人也、部名、卷三又曰也里可溫有緣人也、卷十四

劉文淇至順鎮江志校勘記曰此志述僑寓之戶口、所謂也里可溫者、西洋人也、卷九大興國寺條載梁相記云薛迷思賢在中原西北十萬餘里、乃也里可溫行教之地、教以禮東方為主取像人身四方上下、以是為準、據此則薛迷思賢乃西洋之地、而也里可溫即天主教矣、卷上

謂也里可溫即天主教者、莫先於此、劉文淇道光間人、阮元門下士、其說並非附

會、較元史語解之解釋為確切矣、

洪鈞元史譯文證補元世各教名考曰也里可溫之為天主教有鎮江北固山下殘碑可證、自唐時景教入中國、支裔流傳、歷久未絕、也里可溫、當即景教之遺緒、卷十九

又曰、多桑譯著旭烈兀傳有蒙古人稱天主教為阿勒可溫、一語始不解所謂繼知阿剌比文回紇文、均有此阿二音、往往互混、阿勒可溫即也里可溫、非能臆撰、必本於拉施特諸人、卷同

多桑為有名之蒙古元史著者、元史譯文證補探之其言自可信據、惟鎮江北固山下殘碑、余未之見、洪書亦未舉其文是否即至順鎮江志之大興國寺碑不可知也、然余觀大興國寺記及元典章均有也里可溫之詞、則也里可溫之為教、而非部族、已可斷定、復有廉兒也里牙、及也里可溫十字寺等之名、即也里可溫之為基督教、而非他教、更無疑義、元史國語解所釋為福分人者、或指其為奉福音教人也、

魏源元史語解略於釋耶里可溫者、本紀免租稅、皆有此二等人在僧道之

外、蓋回教之師也、元典章章稱先生曰耶里可溫、蓋可溫即今之所謂阿渾也云云、史元

可謂勇於武斷者矣、元典章之所謂先生元人以稱道士也有時曰和尙先生也里可溫、有時曰僧道也里可溫先生、有時曰和尙先生也里可溫先生、日人田中萃一曰馬可孛羅之支那旅行記第一編第五十九章有稱為混生民族、古拉布羅多以是推定爲也里可溫、如斡寗監謂土耳其語日Argoum又亞爾美尼亞之希臘語Arkhoun之轉訛也、果然則長安景教碑之阿羅本、是也里可溫之古音乎巴拉超士既謂也里可溫是蒙古語之Erkeun是其初專指轟斯托爾派之僧侶、其後為基督教徒之總稱也、十六編第三號史學雜誌

又坪井九馬三曰元史屢見之也里可溫、布烈多士迭迷爾斷其為基督敎徒、然不說明其理由及語源、據元史之記載觀之、則蒙古人之知有也里可溫、自追放特多

white 不白 為Arghun、西藏地方亦稱混成民族為Argons、故也里可溫、也、又亞雷伊爾遷世界征服者之歷史、謂蒙古人呼基督教徒曰Ark'haioun、關於此語源始為Arkhon之希臘語、Arkhon比利安歷史亦稱曰Ark'haioun、關於此語源始

37
《中西文化交流先驱——马可·波罗》
1995

中国国际文化书院（编），北京，中文
20×14 cm
上海图书馆

Marco Polo: A pioneer in Sino-Western cultural exchange, 1995
China International Culture Academy (ed.), Beijing, Chinese
20×14 cm
Shanghai Library

第三部分
日月有常

序 言

1991年,是举世闻名的意大利旅行家马可·波罗离开中国泉州,回意大利威尼斯700周年。

马可·波罗于1271年开始从欧洲到东方的长征,1275年到达中国上都(今内蒙古多伦县境内),足迹遍及中国南北,历时17年之久。他回国后口述并出版了他的《游记》。《游记》畅销欧洲乃至全世界,被誉为"世界一大奇书",意大利"13世纪最宏伟的作品"。《游记》的问世,向欧洲人揭示了奇异的东方世界之谜,第一次比较全面地向欧洲人介绍了高度发达的中国物质文明和精神文明,从而更地大物博、多采多姿的高大中国形象展现在欧洲人面前,冲击了长期来欧洲流行的"欧洲中心"和"基督教文明至上"的偏见,开阔了中世纪欧洲人的视野,无疑对欧洲人走出中世纪、迈向近代文明有着重要影响。更重要的是,这部"奇书"尽管一度被许多欧洲人所误解,被保守派们斥之为"天方夜谭式"的神话,但随着时间的推移,绝大多数人便从怀疑而逐渐确信,并震动了欧洲朝野。探险家、航海家有之,他们欲寻求新航路,以窥探东方的古老文明;基督教士们有之,他们想到异教异地去传播基督教义,使那里的人们皈依基督;早期殖民者有之,他们野心勃勃,想以"火"与"剑"趁机掠夺东方世界的黄金和财宝。于是,善恶兼及的欧洲人从向往而奔赴东方世界,促使了世界形势的大变革。哥伦布"发现"了新大陆美洲,新航路迅即开通,西方殖民者开始积极的全球殖民活动,东西方文化交流亦随之展开,形成了近代世界的新格局。

不言而喻,马可·波罗虽然不是第一个到中国来的欧洲人,但我们完全可以这样说,如果马可·波罗之前来华的欧洲人能够在中西文化交流的长河中吹起轻澜微波,那么马可·波罗则在这条长河中激起了轩然狂涛。可以这样确切地说,是马可·波罗正式沟通了中西文化交流。所以,马可·波罗作为中西文化交流的先驱者,是当之无愧的。

在一般情况下,任何一个国家、一个民族要想取得长足的进步,站在世界的前列,就必须与其他国家、民族进行友好交往,取长补短,才能达到目的。如若不然,闭关自守,固步自封,夜郎自大,禁锢于一地一方,势必使这个国家或民族陷于贫困落后的境地。在当今国际间相互依存、竞争异常激烈的态势下,更会处于被动挨打的地位,产生难以预料的后果。世界各国的历史和中国历史都充分证明这一点。现在,当我们对改革、开放意义有新的共识之时,对马可·波罗及其《游记》的历史意义和现实意义倍感亲切和珍贵。

正是基于这个原因,为纪念马可·波罗离华回国700周年,推动对马可·波罗学的研究,繁荣科学文化,增进中外学者、专家之间的交流和友谊,中国国际文化书院,意中经济文化交流协会,北京对外文化交流协会和新疆维吾尔自治区社科联于1991年10月6—9日在北京联合举办马可·波罗国际学术讨论会。

这次学术讨论会,是马可·波罗的祖国意大利和他的第二故乡中国的学者第一次联合举办的马可·波罗的国际学术会议,也是中、意两国学者同来自世界其他国家学者共同研讨马可·波罗学的一个良好开端。

讨论会受到有关学者、专家的普遍重视。出席的代表达80余人。研究马可·波罗的中国著名学者大都参加了这次讨论会,其中有南开大学历史系教授杨志玖、中国社会科学院近代史研究所研究员蔡美彪、历史研究所研究员陈高华、南京大学历史系教授陈得芝、杭州大学历史系教授黄时鉴和中国意大利文学会会长、研究员吕同六等;意大利方面,有威尼托大区马可·波罗研究所所长马达罗博士、罗马大学东方学院院长阿莫莱蒂、马可·波罗后裔波罗·帕多莱基亚教授以及来自罗马、米兰、威尼斯和帕维亚等地的著名学者、专家。

会议开幕式于10月6日在北京劳动人民文化宫大殿隆重举行。我国政协副主席程思远、中国国际文化书院院长陈翰笙、中国社会科学院副院长汝信和顾问吴介民、北京市市委宣传部长李志坚以及意大利驻华大使罗西出席了会议。意大利总理安德雷奥蒂从意大利发来了贺信。

讨论会的中心议题是:马可·波罗与东西文化交流。代表们共向大会提供论文40余篇,围绕议题中心,进行了踊跃、热烈和深入的讨论,总结和交流了长期以来马可·波罗学研究的成果,在马可·波罗学研究的深度和广度上获得了新的拓展,从而使这次讨论会成为国际马可·波罗学研究的里程碑。

本书分为两个部分:第一部分包括开幕式会议上的开幕词,我国领导人和意大利大使的发言、马可·波罗后裔的讲话以及意大利总理的贺信等等;第二部分包括中外学者、教授给这次学术讨论会所提供的论文。

但要说明的是,由于各种原因:有些学者的论文经编辑组严格挑选、分类、编辑加工而被收进了这本书内;而有些学者的论文却没有被收集进来,在此我们对这些供稿者表示歉意。还需补充说明的是,为便于马可·波罗学的研究,我们把杨志玖教授早期发表的具有重要学术价值的论文,即《关于马可波罗离华的一段汉文记载》一文,经征得本人的同意,破例地收了进来。这本书,总计收集了32篇学术论文。

111

38

明宪宗成化十三年德国牛恩堡市刊印
德文译本马哥孛罗游记之书面及题辞
《地学杂志》
1922

张星烺（撰），北京，中文
25.5×19 cm
上海图书馆

Cover and title of the German version of *The Travels of Marco Polo* in the 13th year of the Ming Xianzong Chenghua period,
The Geographical Magazine, 1922
Zhang Xinglang (au.), Beijing, Chinese
25.5×19 cm
Shanghai Library

第三部分
日月有常

明憲宗成化十三年德國牛恩堡市刊印德文譯本
馬哥孛羅遊記之書面及題辭

首行

Das ist der edel Ritter. Marcho polo von

右行

Venedig der Grost landſtfarer. der uns beschreibt die grossen wunder ber welt

下行

die er selber gesehenn hat. Von dem auf gang

左行

is zu dem nydergag der sunne. der gleyche vor nicht meer gehort seyn.

此乃威尼斯大遊歷家馬哥孛羅貴人之像，彼曾將日出處以至日落處之世界奇事，為彼所親見者，記錄於書，以遺吾輩。書中所言，皆以前所未聞者也。

39

答束世澂君中国史书上之马哥孛罗质疑
《史地学报》
1924

张星烺（撰），上海，中文
25×18 cm
上海图书馆

A reply to Mr. S. C. Sou relating to the "questions" suggested in his "Marco Polo as found in Chinese history",
The Journal of The Historical & Geographical Society
1924
Zhang Xinglang (au.), Shanghai, Chinese
25×18 cm
Shanghai Library

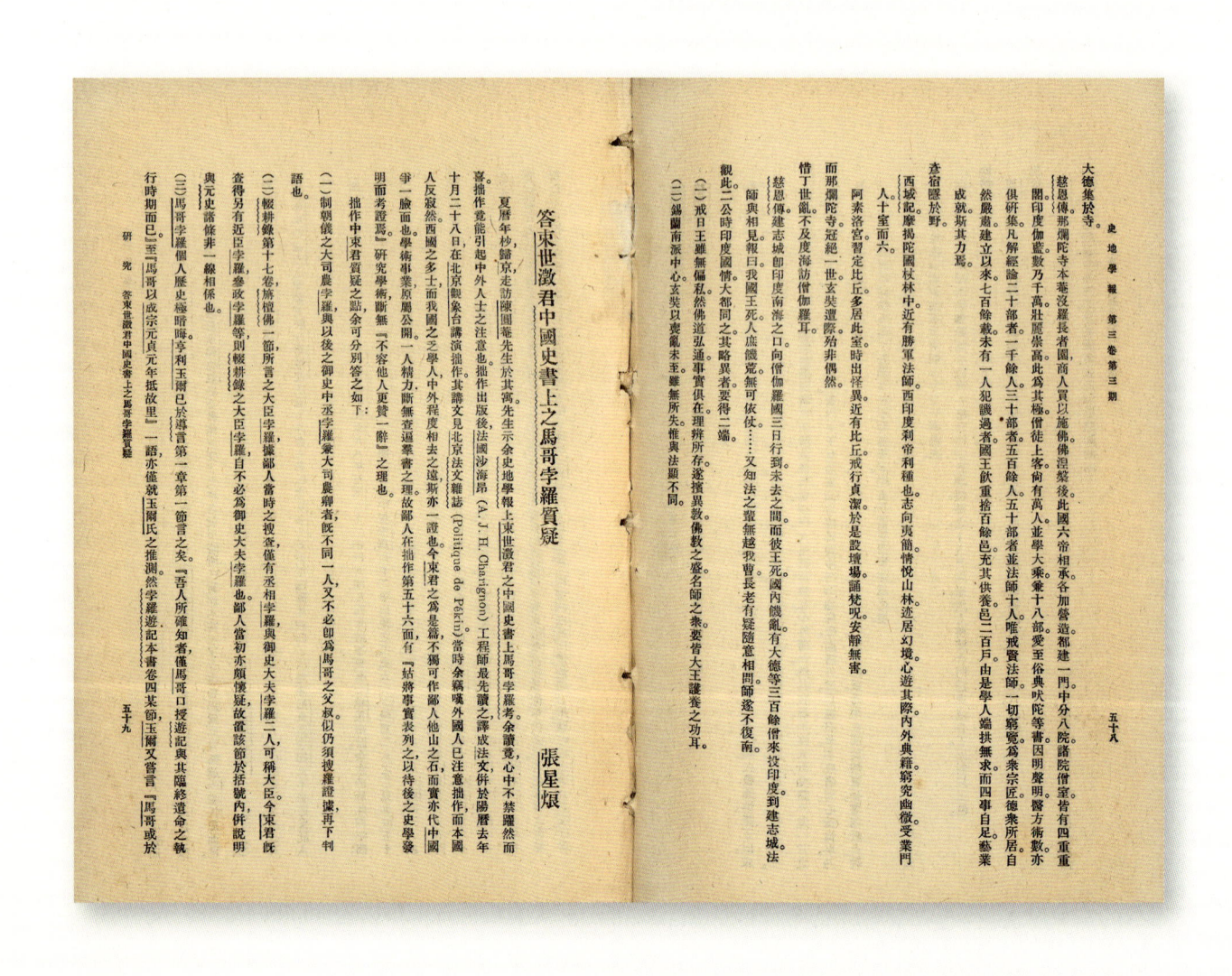

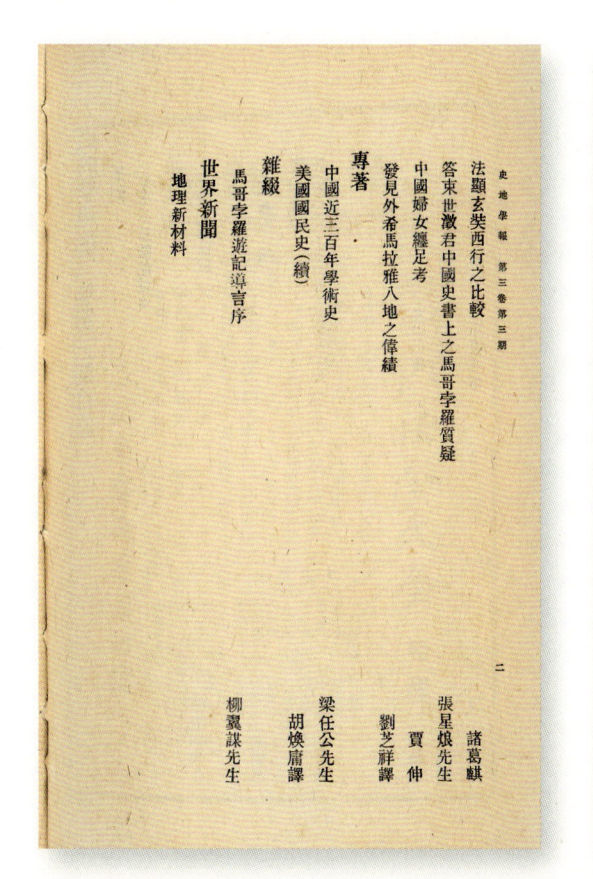

史地學報 第三卷第三期

專著

法顯玄奘西行之比較	諸葛麒
答束世澂君中國史書上之馬哥孛羅質疑	張星烺先生
中國婦女纏足考	賈 伸
發見外希馬拉雅八地之偉績	劉芝祥譯
中國近三百年學術史（續）	梁任公先生
美國國民史（續）	胡煥庸譯
雜綴	
馬哥孛羅遊記導言序	柳翼謀先生
世界新聞	
地理新材料	

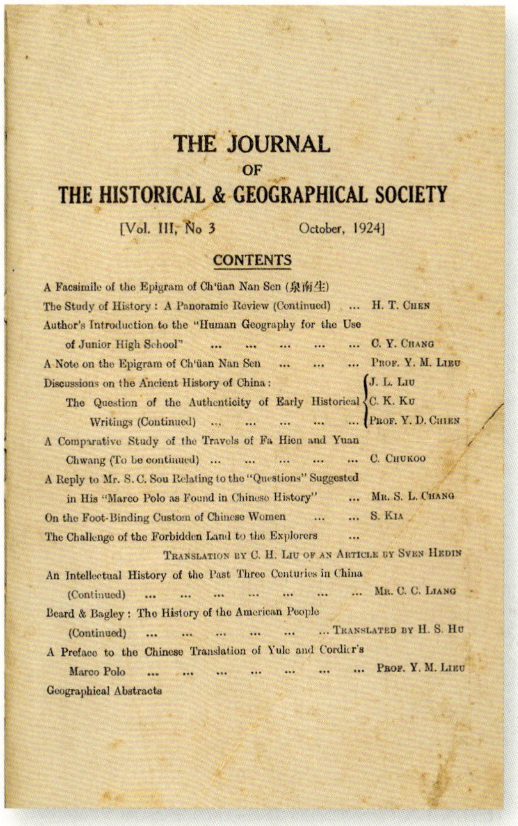

THE JOURNAL OF THE HISTORICAL & GEOGRAPHICAL SOCIETY

[Vol. III, No 3   October, 1924]

CONTENTS

A Facsimile of the Epigram of Ch'üan Nan Sen (泉南生)
The Study of History : A Panoramic Review (Continued) ... H. T. CHEN
Author's Introduction to the "Human Geography for the Use of Junior High School" ... C. Y. CHANG
A Note on the Epigram of Ch'üan Nan Sen ... PROF. Y. M. LIEU
Discussions on the Ancient History of China :
　The Question of the Authenticity of Early Historical Writings (Continued) ... J. L. LIU / C. K. KU / PROF. Y. D. CHIEN
A Comparative Study of the Travels of Fa Hien and Yuan Chwang (To be continued) ... C. CHUKOO
A Reply to Mr. S. C. Sou Relating to the "Questions" Suggested in His "Marco Polo as Found in Chinese History" ... MR. S. L. CHANG
On the Foot-Binding Custom of Chinese Women ... S. KIA
The Challenge of the Forbidden Land to the Explorers
　TRANSLATION BY C. H. LIU OF AN ARTICLE BY SVEN HEDIN
An Intellectual History of the Past Three Centuries in China (Continued) ... MR. C. C. LIANG
Beard & Bagley : The History of the American People (Continued) ... TRANSLATED BY H. S. HU
A Preface to the Chinese Translation of Yule and Cordier's Marco Polo ... PROF. Y. M. LIEU
Geographical Abstracts

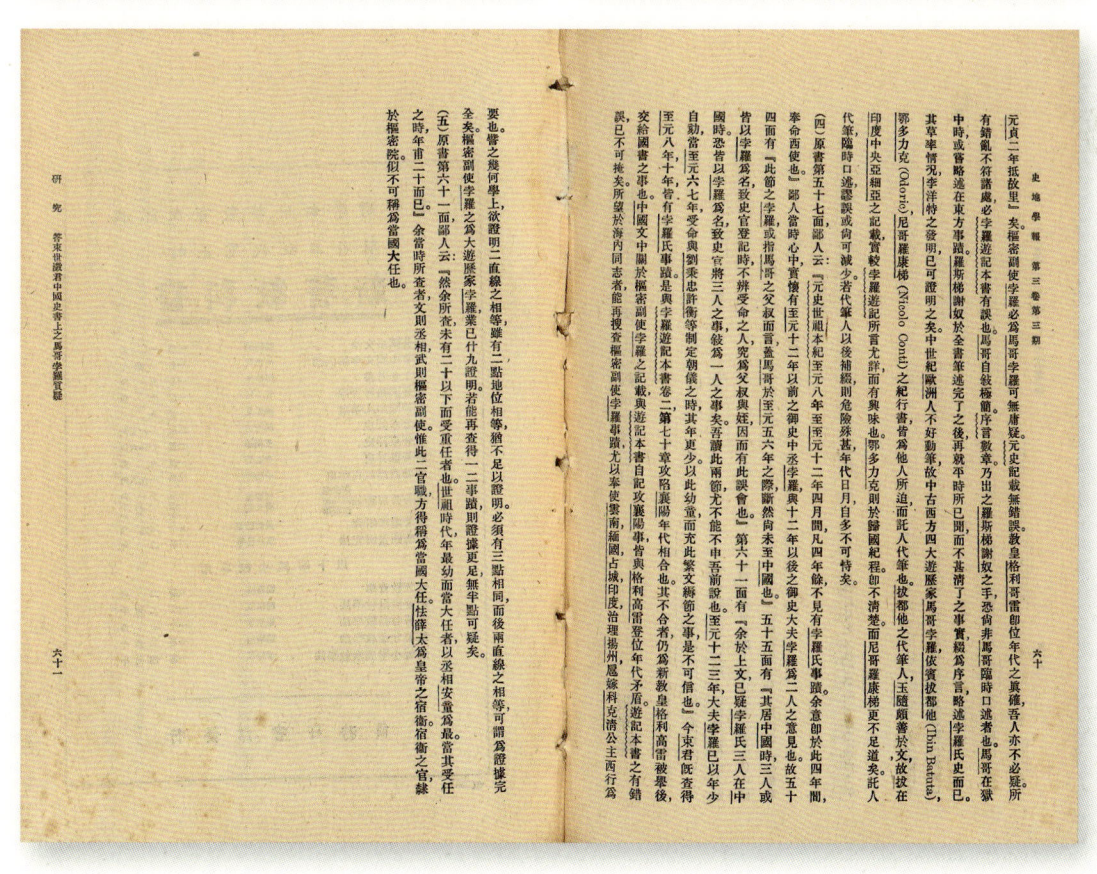

40

马可勃罗
《南开大学周刊》
1928

杨景才（撰），天津，中文
25×18 cm
上海图书馆

Marco Polo,
Nankai University Weekly, 1928
Yang Jingcai (au.), Tianjin, Chinese
25×18 cm
Shanghai Library

第三部分
日月有常

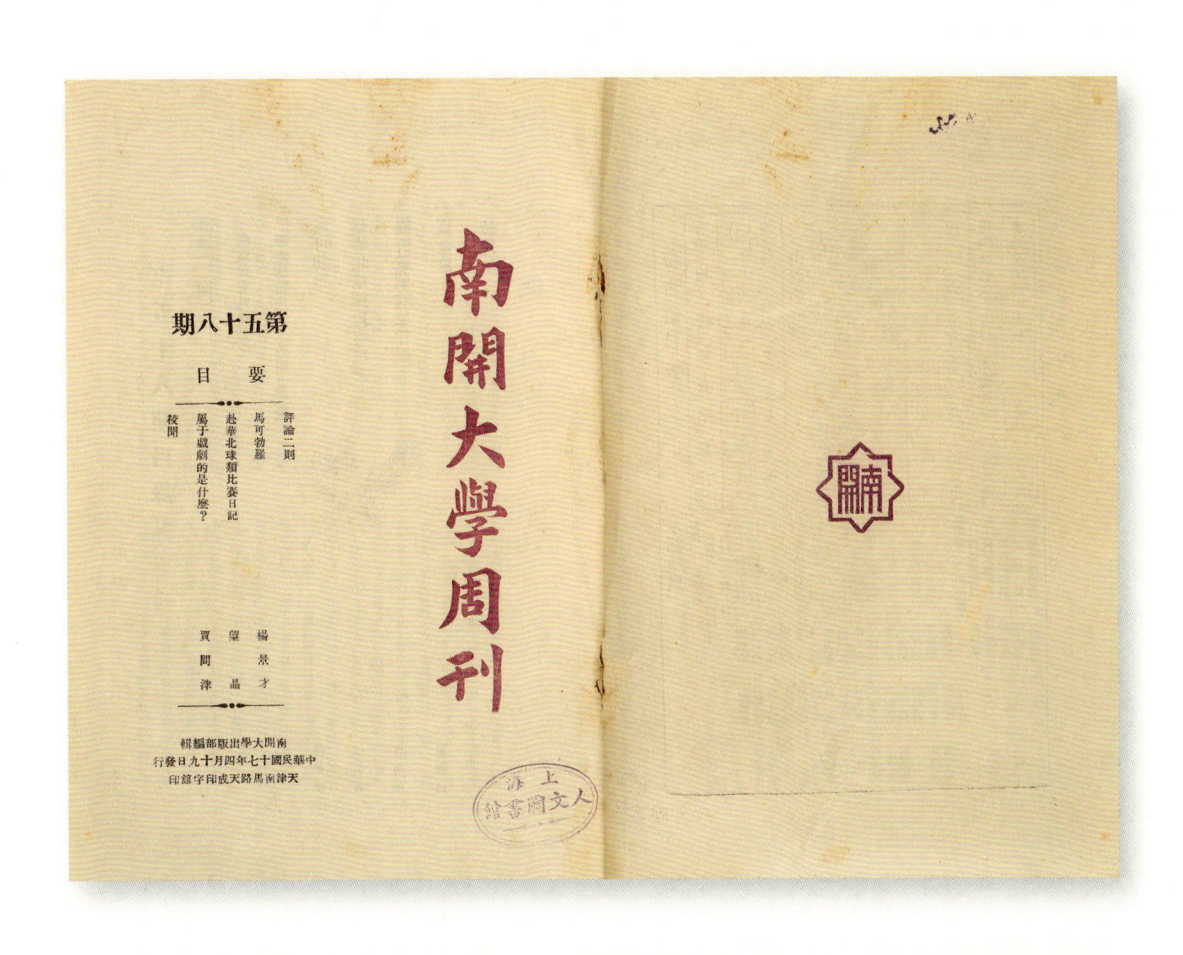

南開大學周刊

第五十八期

要目

評論二則
馬可勃羅
赴華北球類比賽日記
屬子歲劇的是什麼？
校聞

楊景才
買問津

南開大學出版部編輯
中華民國十七年四月九日發行
天津南馬路成文堂字館印

馬可勃羅

馬可勃羅 Marco Polo (一二五四──一三二四)

意大利之威尼斯產，中世紀最大遊歷家也。其族系自頭又最上，無可考。惟如十一世紀時，勃羅氏有為威城共和政府之議員者，祖父名安特拉 Andrea，有子三人：仲曰尼哥羅 Nicolo，馬可父也，勃羅氏世為巨商，尤以舊商著稱，其侄為君士坦丁西買，氏之父兄，均健於舊商營為。約當一二六○年時，勃羅氏第二次之自亞格出發也，嘗在一二七年冬，本意似欲出波斯灣而經海抵中國焉。因念艱巨歇，顏有減心。路北行再出波斯而東焉。意少年之馬可，曾輕藝附。途嘗艱辛苦，于是經始未舉，高原、轉歷戈壁沙漠，途過所經，首為此遊歷家所寡是。而數百年後有東西人士所經歷焉者，後探奇阻險，便此道相則于今世者。其世紀不到時，俄羅斯諸瑰奇之士之披荊斬棘。馬可意中尚無此，大悲絕矣。獨多歷所經六百歲前已契法師西行敘事故也。途威畿師人，再遠退而入坦率。大汗之召沿見此盛跡皆，均鑒費為馬可勃羅。能諸其能事。時氏年僅二十一歲，尤以言書文字之學，可評統治之民族，俄粗視民黨於方百能嫻習多種福言。伽楊氏勤敏和慧頗得寵，史中所敘一二七七年時有勃羅氏遺官為密使雲云，即指此威尼斯少年者也。其後歷官山西陝西四川

勃羅氏第二次之自亞格出發也，嘗在一二七年冬，本意似欲出波斯灣而經海抵中國焉。因念艱巨歇，顏有減心。路北行再出波斯而東焉。意少年之馬可，曾輕藝附。

教皇克來豪第四 (Clement IV) 已歿，繼位者未奢麗，遂諾商子勸皇派赴珠瑰及之大使，台途獨蘇eno。台達瑪帝惟勵以舊供教法。及歸尼哥拉之娣已沒於馬亞歸抵威城，則尼奔已故。馬可十五歲，他兒弟特為 Marco，年十五歲，惺時敦是大位久虛，遂一子曰馬可之二戰之久，面稿不能臨其堂卓。于是決童甘越選出。以証期厄以耳之故。為台得台特遞手事，lagva 海島，歐亞變是之要務，而台氏被稱為敦皇之登同遙。遙醫回直之歌，敢當，且當此顫庸矣。塗未盡。面己屬然退矣！

南大週刊　馬可勃羅

五

41
《欧化东渐史》
1933

张星烺（著），上海，中文
17.5×11.8 cm
上海图书馆

A history of Western civilization eastward, 1933
Zhang Xinglang (au.), Shanghai, Chinese
17.5×11.8 cm
Shanghai Library

歐化東漸史

第一章 歐化東傳之媒介

第一節 歐化界說

中國與歐洲文化有形上及無形上皆完全不同，上自政治組織，下至社會風俗飲食起居，各自其數千年之歷史展轉推演，而成今日之狀態。東西文化孰為高下，誠不易言。但自中歐交通以來，歐洲文化逐漸敷布東土，猶之長江黃河之水，朝宗於海，自西東流，晝夜不息，使東方固有文化日趨式微，而代以歐洲文化，則是西方文化高於東方文化也。尤以有形之物質文明，東西民族性不同，各國歷相去何啻千里之故。夫不效法他人，必致亡國滅種。至於無形之思想文明，則以東西民族性不同，各國歷史互為異，故勿行之西洋則有效，而行之中國則大亂。各種思想與主義，無非為解決民生問題而勉

第二節

第一章 歐化東傳之媒介

目次

歐化東漸史

第五節 教育事業

第三章 無形歐化卽歐洲思想文明之輸入 ……九八
第一節 宗教思想 ………………………………一〇五
第二節 倫理思想 ………………………………一〇八
第三節 政治思想 ………………………………一〇九
第四節 學術上各種思想 ………………………一二三
第五節 藝術思想 ………………………………一二四

人，非洲南端已窮盡，有新道可達東方。狄亞士發現好望角後十二年，而葡人竟得達其目的。一千四百九十七年（明孝宗弘治十年）七月，瓦斯柯達格瑪（Vasco da Gama）率小船三艘自葡京立斯本起航，繞過好望角後向東北航行，遠超以前狄亞士所至之地，直至桑西巴北二百邁耳。由是處作橫渡印度洋之壯舉。一千四百九十八年（弘治十一年）夏抵印度西海岸右里港（Calicut）。在此將帶來之歐洲貨物悉換作香料滿載而歸。一千四百九十九年（弘治十二年）夏三船安回立斯本原地。以前所久欲尋覓之歐亞新交通線，竟得成功矣。葡萄牙人急速利用此新發明貿易東方。一千五百年（弘治十三年）三月達格瑪歸回僅六月，派喀伯拉爾（Pedro a1vares cabral）率船十三艘，滿載貨物再往右里。至翌年七月歸立斯本。一千五百零二年（弘治十五年）二月，達格瑪率船二十艘再往印度洋上阿拉伯人之商業與勢力。獨霸東方海上。葡人利用其精良火器摧敗印度洋上阿拉伯人之商業與勢力。獨霸東方海上。葡人利用其精良火器摧敗印度。大宗流入歐洲，不久即成為歐洲最重要商埠之一，葡人利其精良火器摧敗印度，物大宗流入歐洲，不久即成為歐洲最重要商埠之一。一千五百十年（正德五年）攻陷印度西岸之臥亞府（Goa），作為根據地。次年又攻陷馬雷半島之麻六（Malacca）（明愛作滿刺加）道

使至印度支那各邦政府以通友好。白右（Pegu）遷羅、交趾支那及東京，皆有葡國使節之足跡。葡人待麻六甲之中國商人甚為優渥。此等商人回國以後，對於葡人有極佳之報告。一千五百十四年（明武宗正德九年）葡國總督佐治安達爾伯克喀（Jorge d'Alboquerque）遣婁斯特羅（Rafael Perestrello）往中國。葡人乘馬雷人海船，至一千五百十六年八月十二日無回音，乃復遣安特拉德（Perez d'Andade）再往，亦無功而返。葡國商人初至中國海岸貿易大獲利而歸次年（正德十年）麻六甲總督決意再遣安特拉德往中國船上滿載胡椒，於一千五百十七年六月十七日起碇同行者有皮來賓（Thomas Pirez），以葡萄牙大使名義往聘中國皮來賓素充藥劑師，然為人敏捷善於應對，使當外交官頗為相宜。八月十五日抵大門港（Tamang）（在後川島後川距上川不遠）距中國陸地尚有三海里外國尚有三海里外國的船至廣東省者，皆須寄泊於此。葡人欲往廣東省城中國官吏不許。葡人強駛入內河，放礮舉敬禮抵廣東後，國員登陸，中國人接待頗優擇安寓以舍之。葡人所載貨物，皆轉運上陸，姿為貯藏。皮來賓留廣州數年，以待明廷外文直至一千五百二十

虚实之界：奇迹之书
《马可·波罗游记》主题文献图录

42

《中西交通史》
1934

向达（编），上海，中文
19×13 cm
上海图书馆

A history of Sino-western communication, 1934
Xiang Da (ed.), Shanghai, Chinese
19×13 cm
Shanghai Library

第三部分 日月有常

中西交通史目錄

總序
小引
敍論
第一章　中國民族西來說 …… (一)
第二章　古代中西交通梗概 …… (九)
第三章　景教與也里可溫教 …… (三三)
第四章　元代之西征 …… (四五)
第五章　馬哥孛羅諸人之東來 …… (五五)
第六章　十五世紀以後中西交通之復興 …… (六八)
第七章　明清之際之天主教士與西學 …… (七五)

穫，就是西學的傳入，自明隆萬以至清乾隆二百年間，西洋的學術如曆算哲理、火器等等在中國植了一點清明的觀念。雖然因為宗教上的固執形勢一度惡化，但元明以來，才得了一點基礎，到了這一步已一發而不可遏。雖有壯夫莫之能挽鴉片一戰，中國同西洋的勢力見了一個高低，中國再不能閉關自守了，這又是一個劃分時代的戰爭。近百年來的中西交通真是洋洋大觀，這是一個時期一直到現在，還是在這一個大潮流中回環激盪之急劇真是洋洋大觀未有已日。

本書的目的只在探尋中西交通初步的史實，略略著其梗概，所以即以鴉片戰爭為全書的結末，近百年來中西交通的史實應該別有一部中國近代新史才可以著其涯略，非此區區短篇所能盡了。

人之東來，俱是為此，至於孛羅叔姪久留中國，乃藉貿易以東來，這俱別見下章，此處不能一一詳說。

參考書

關於蒙古西征，洪鈞元史譯文證補最為可看。太西征則有地理志補附西北地附錄譯地，同西域古地考，歐陽鈞譯河野元旭著元西征地理考，漢譯英國韋爾斯著世界史綱中有蒙古論述蒙古發凡，爲簡潔得要。總論蒙古全史簡單明瞭，也可參考。姚從吾譯德國柯勞斯著蒙古史發凡，爲簡潔得要。三的蒙古史力征經營的結果怎樣。

問題

一　十三世紀時亞洲北方有何偉大民族崛起，其威脅歐洲者何如？
二　蒙古族力征經營的結果怎樣？於中西交通上有何影響？
三　當時歐洲人對於蒙古民族的態度怎樣？

第五章　馬哥孛羅諸人之東來

元朝兵威及於西域，那時軍中各種民族都有朝廷上也是束西兼蓄如第三章所述的愛薛，係於西域，那時軍中各種民族都有朝廷上也是束西兼蓄如第三章所述的愛薛，係君士坦丁堡人為聖而公會會友，即是一例。那時西洋人入仕元朝的還不止此，拔都征匈牙利軍中即有不少的俄羅斯人在內，並且還有英國降人以為嚮導元定宗時，西洋奉基督教的如俄羅斯希臘匈牙利以及小亞細亞亞美尼亞敍利亞各處人因蒙古西征被擄東來的不少，有俄國人葛斯默(Cosmas)為大汗的工匠，即為基督教徒，而愛薛大約也是因為蒙古西征隨軍而來的時候，歐洲各國領過了他的教畏懼得了不得沒有辦法，只好於一二四五年由教皇懿諾增爵第四(Innocent IV)召集歐洲奉基督教的國家在法國里昂開一大會，是為有名的里昂會議。會議結果，決定派遣教

新大地發現

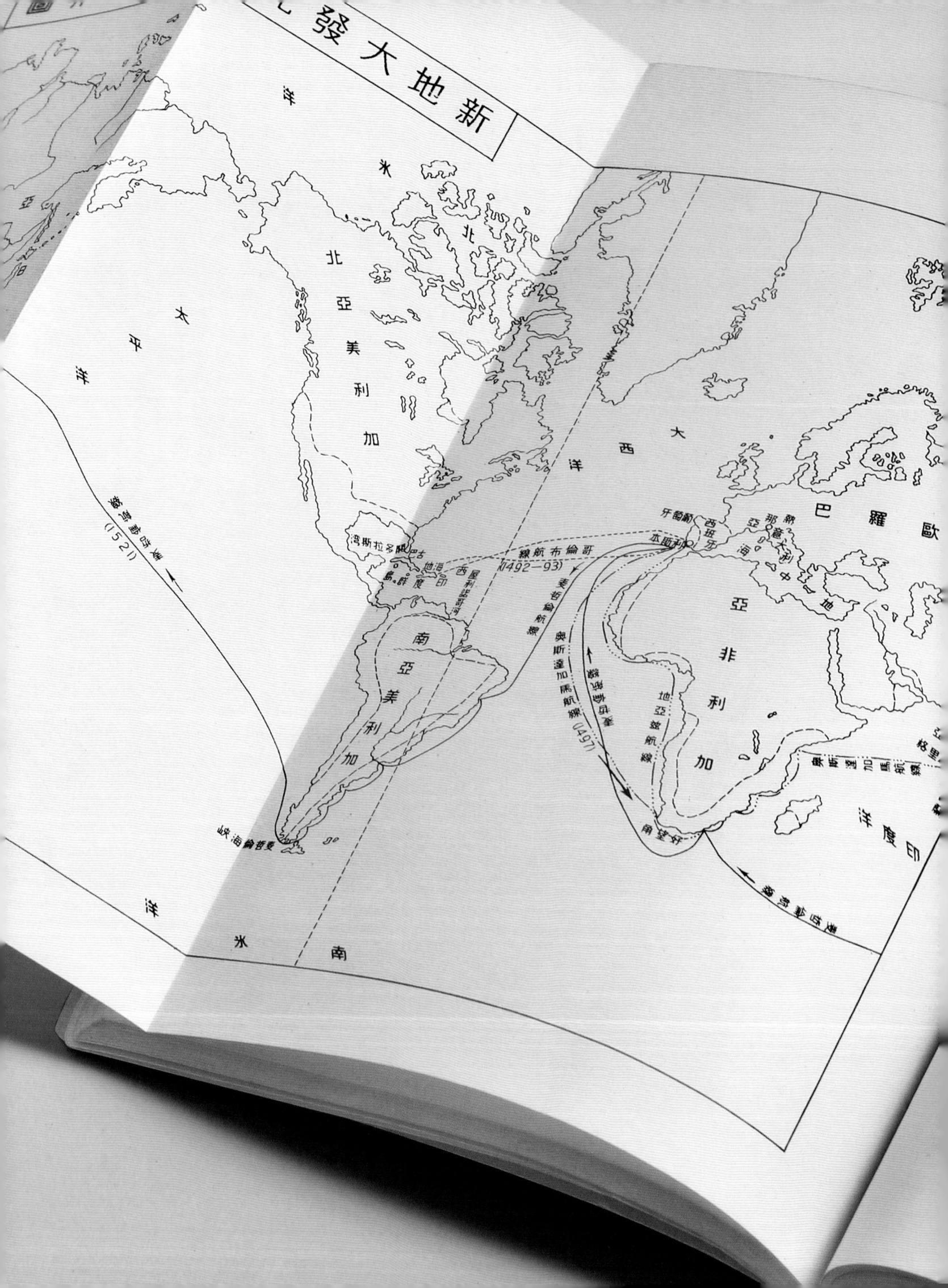

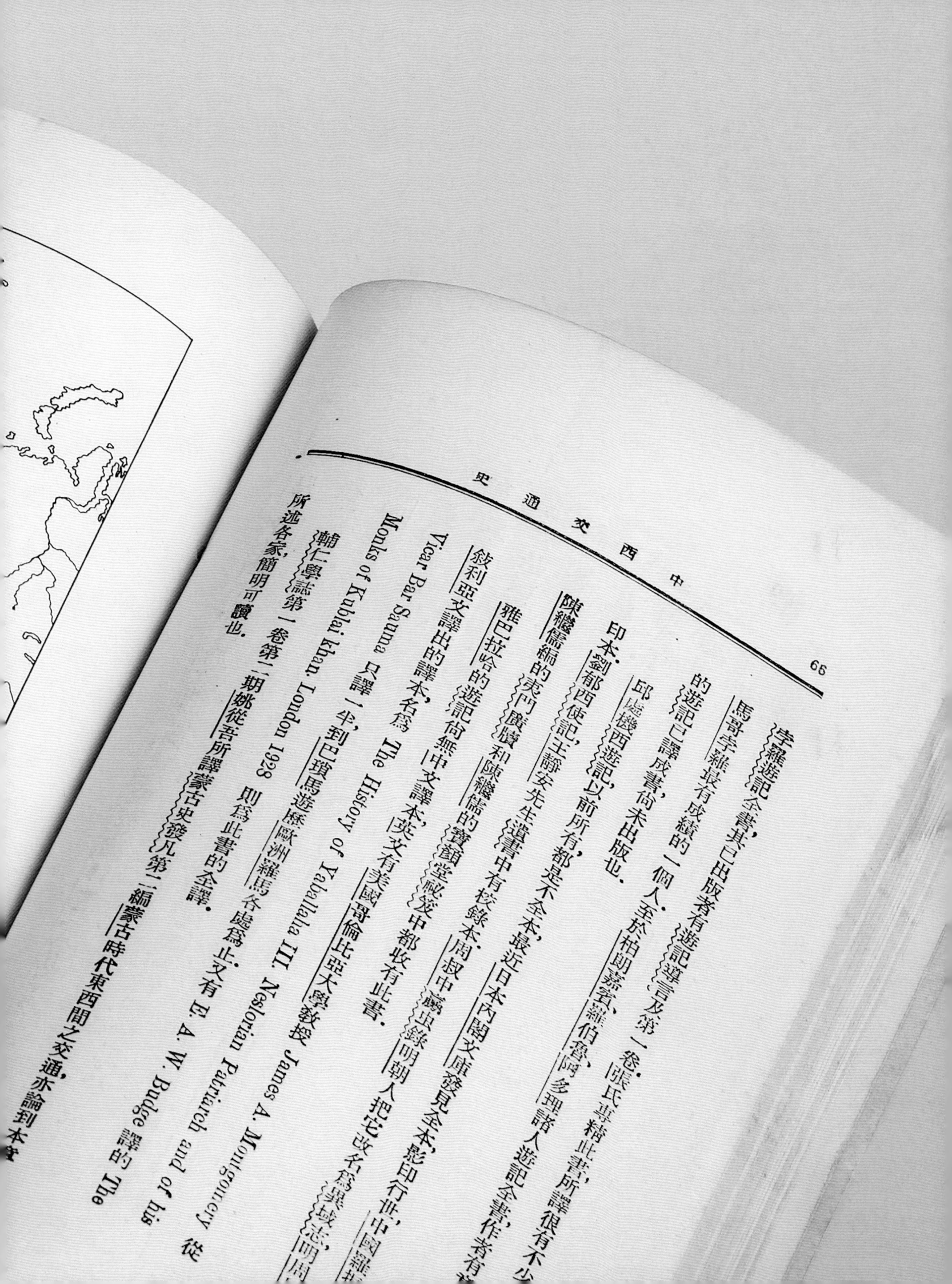

李羅遊記金書其已出版者有遊記導言及第一卷張氏專精此學,所譯很有不少的遊記已譯成書,尚未出版也。

印本劉郁西使記以前所有都是不全本,最近日本內閣文庫發見全本影印行世中國羅振玉邱處機西遊記,邱處機至於柏朗嘉賓、羅伯魯、多理諸人遊記

陳繼儒編的夷門廣牘和陳繼儒的寶顏堂祕笈中都收有此書。王靜安先生遺書中有校錄本,周叔彌巴拉哈的遊記尚無中文譯本周叔中有鐫虫錄明朝人把它改名為異域志明

敍利亞文譯出的譯本名為 The History of Yaballaha III. Nestorian Patriarch 從

Vicar Bar Sauma 只譯一半到巴瑣馬遊歷歐洲羅馬各處為止有美國哥倫比亞大學教授 James A. Montgomery 從

Monks of Kublai khan. London 1928 則為此書的金譯。

辅仁學誌第一卷第二期姚從吾所譯蒙古史發凡第二編蒙古時代東西間之交通亦論到本書

所述各家簡明可讀也。

43
《西域南海史地考证译丛》
1934

[法] 伯希和等（著），冯承钧（译），上海，中文
21×15 cm
上海图书馆

Historical and geographical studies on northwestern China and the South China Sea, 1934
Paul Pelliot et al.(au.), Feng Chengjun (tr.), Shanghai, Chinese
21×15 cm
Shanghai Library

第三部分
日月有常

叙

我從前介紹法國漢學家的著作，要以長篇研究居多，可是未經長篇研究的短篇考證尚有不少就嚴格說諸漢學家考證的精粹即在這些碎金片玉裏面我的這篇「西域南海史地考證譯叢」採集了十幾種短篇考證可是還有遺漏我現在搜集雖然輯了三編「史地叢考」內容與史地叢考譯本編所採之研究大致一樣前對於原文的附註多從省略，本編則盡量翻譯本編所採之研究大致一樣出於亞洲報者的這篇「西域南海史地考譯叢」者二篇都爲十二篇其中有十篇是伯希和的研究，二十五年紀念刊「亞洲研究」者一篇，出於河内遠東法國學校出於「梵衍那之佛教古跡」者一篇出於通報者八篇，有一篇是斯坦因的研究，有一篇是馬司帛洛的研究嗣後更有所得當輯續編。

民國二十一年九月二十五日　　馮承鈞識

西域南海史地考證譯叢

馮承鈞譯

中華教育文化基金董事會編譯委員會編輯
商務印書館發行

註二　第二冊止於玉耳戈節（Yule-Cordier）刊本第二冊【一三一】頁至者爭持未決的襄陽治問題、版今書三冊現已出全。

註三　蘇獻章寫作譯，誤甚，仝文未能標出，監改作攝轉。

同記述杭州的註釋沙海昂君著在第三冊裏面研究。

一八六五年時頗羯以爲馬可波羅就是一二七七年四月二日見諸任命的樞密副使孛羅（元史卷九）也就是一二八二年阿合馬（Ahmad）被殺後奉命討亂的樞密副使孛羅（元史卷二〇五）他以此爲起點遂將此人的漢文名字官位題在他的刊本封面，註三玉耳（玉耳戈節刊本第一冊二一頁及四二二頁）曾經採用頗羯的考訂可是巴克爾（Parker）在一九〇四年刊布的蒙古史的一段證明中國史書誌參加阿合馬案件的孛羅也不是馬可波羅，巴克爾同我的考證業由戈節轉載於他在一九二〇年刊布的馬可波羅行紀補考（Ser Marco Polo, Notes and Addenda）五頁至八頁之中。

雖然如此沙海昂君仍舊接用頗羯所稱，並且根據張星烺君的一篇研究加了不少，張君的研究在一羅誌裏面，而此羅誌在巴黎不能覓得一本，可是案照沙海昂君所引的那些條看起來，好像此君沒有使人信任的價值現在置此不言姑就沙海昂君本人的立論來看，取其緒說（三至四頁）的一段可以見其一班，據說「比方世人讀拉史烏丁一段說他修史之時，很得一箇名 Polo 的輔助此人來自中國，(Cathay) 曾作大元帥 (generalissime) 之時，曾留住波斯宮廷必曾見過拉史烏丁，祗取其所記東方韃靼歷史諸篇看起來，其細節同拉史烏丁所記很符他二人必曾相見無疑由承羅元朝祗有皇太子能作樞密副使的對稱自承參與此事的記載頗羯所考馬可波羅即是元史樞密副使孛羅之說、尤可證明其爲事實。」

馬可波羅行紀沙海昂原註正誤

44
元代马哥孛罗所见亚洲旧有之现代流行品
《现代史学》
1935

[美] 古杰尔（著），朱杰勤（译），上海，中文
26×19 cm
上海图书馆

Ancient Asian objects in Marco Polo's records, which are still in life today,
Modern Historical Studies, 1935
Eugene Willis Gudger (au.), Zhu Jieqin (tr.), Shanghai, Chinese
26×19 cm
Shanghai Library

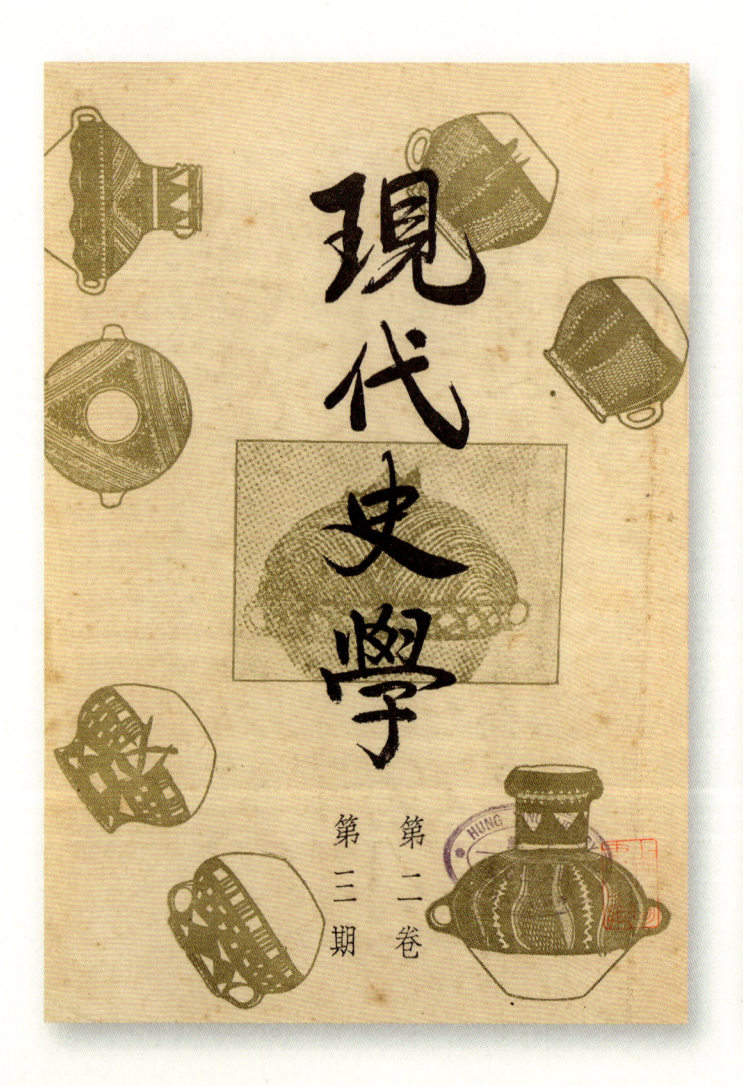

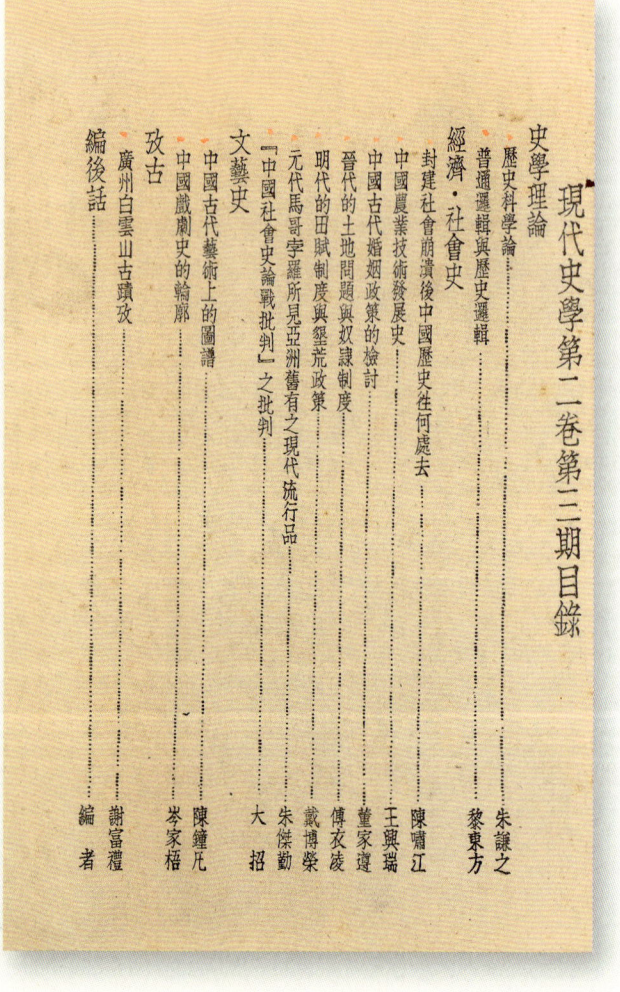

元代馬哥孛羅所見亞洲舊有之現代流行品

Dr. E. W. Gudger 著　朱傑勤 譯

1. 其人

馬哥孛羅(Marco pole 1254—1325或1326)適第一次東遊而返威尼斯(Venice)十五歲時，其父(Wioolo)及其叔(Maffeo pol)已不可考，惟於一二六○年則方在君士坦丁堡(Constantinople)從事商業，復由此地橫過中亞細亞而入蒙古族忽必烈大可汗之王庭。一二七一年離威尼斯，時馬哥孛羅隨行。一二七五年遠大皇帝之庭。第二次遊歷三年有半，卒於二十一歲之馬哥孛羅尤加位長者殷勤延接，敬禮有加，而於約二十青眼。馬哥乃殷勤於朝，預參樞密，又復奉使遠方，足遍全國。彼忽忽必烈特留意於管治事務，而對於民情風俗，各部之工商業及自然界事物等類亦感興趣。乃將其所見所聞之事或筆之於片楮（依刺木西奧Ramusio之說）或記之於備忘錄，彼上忽必烈之報告表殊可決其簡在帝心矣。考之，在馬哥孛羅書中卷言第十六章載忽必烈曾對於出使雲南而歸之青年威尼斯人加以評語。云：『倘

此少年長在，則必其為一大價值及大才幹之人矣。』日後孛羅之族殘緣乃燦然成世界最偉大之游記。

一二九二年忽必烈欲遣朝中科克淸公主(Lady Kiaochi)嫁於其姪阿魯汗(Arghon)即波斯之設涉义非也，而險狀亦至不可測，陸路之設涉义非十七歲之幼女所能當，意由海道而往。惟此隊專使並非海員，大可汗乃從波斯人之請，命威尼斯人導引。孛羅族人大加贊助，蓋括財帛，大可汗乃旋威尼斯也。最後忽必烈忽應承，蓋為祖餞送當，親為祖餞送當。海程不利，耗時甚久，一二九二年由刺桐（福建之泉州）出發，船十三艘，隨員六百人，船員不計。清公主卒達波斯漫之和爾木斯(Hormuz)三使團則失其二，其服裝器具燬盡失，宮主乃揮淚而別，入波斯太別士(Tebris)居之有頃，復由君士坦丁堡入威尼斯，其抵步時則在一二九五年或一二九六年也。

彼等｜去約二十四年(1271—1295或1296)，在王室者凡十七年(1275—1292)。此數十年間，威尼斯之變動大矣，數子亦不免有人事滄桑之感。按剌木西奧Ramusio之說，彼等認囘原籍，蓋甚艱難，惟最後卒達目的，孛羅族人擁巨資，施施然稱威尼斯之富民矣。

三人之中，馬哥最著。其述異之馬哥忽必烈之富，及中國全體之大，因其多財，人爭呼為百萬富翁(Marco milioui and IL million)。所居之家則呼為富翁之宮(Corte del milioue)。而馬哥孛羅或出口百萬之富人。中有一艦乃為茅名

2. 其書

才，乃比薩人拿氏丁斯安奴(Rusitianno of Pisa)是也。其筆乃注定作馬哥孛羅之書，而成為信史者。於是馬哥於長日漫漫之中偶逃其所見之奇事於拿氏丁斯安奴，而拿氏丁斯安奴乃勒之口授其遊記。然馬哥華日久，凡所記憶，必有賴於其零碎之日記，乃求於當事許其派人往威尼斯其父處討取。此事進行，甚為順利，一二九八年九月或十月入獄，復於一二九九年七月出獄，其囚威尼斯或在一二九九年也。消息於獄中者餘人矣氏之生活，由一二九四年或一三二五年中乃為安居樂業之市民。馬哥於一二九九年間威尼斯耋其殁於一三二四年。歿後葬於聖羅尼蘇教堂(San Lorenzo Church)從其顧也。當時同輩類都視其為野史稗官之流，不知其語實非鑿空也。聖羅尼蘇堂重建於一五九二年，斑斑古跡，蕩然無存氏之真容或畫本亦未傳於世。今之所見者，皆畫師憑自己之想像，而出之以白描，景仰前徽，迢乎遠矣！

其人之歿，距今已六○八年矣，而其書固長存天壤間而不可廢也。吾讀此語，事出有因，雅有文

南軍相接於達爾馬提亞island of Curzola)，此役威尼斯人大敗。馬哥孛羅亦卽派出一艦與聯合海口之軍以觀之。兵連禍結，兩爭不決，卒於一二九八年，日內瓦人大勝，乃大舉水師以伐威尼斯。旅行家馬哥孛羅所指揮者也。

降為囚，載往日內瓦，困於獄中。時獄中有一伴，雅有文

45

元代社会状况的研究——
介绍马可波罗游记对元代社会史的贡献
《中山文化教育馆季刊》
1935

季子（撰），上海，中文
26×19 cm
上海图书馆

A study on social conditions of the Yuan Dynasty: the contributions of *The Travels of Marco Polo* to the social history of the Yuan Dynasty,
Quarterly of the Sun Yat-Sen Institute for Advancement of Culture and Education,
1935
Ji Zi (au.), Shanghai, Chinese
26×19cm
Shanghai Library

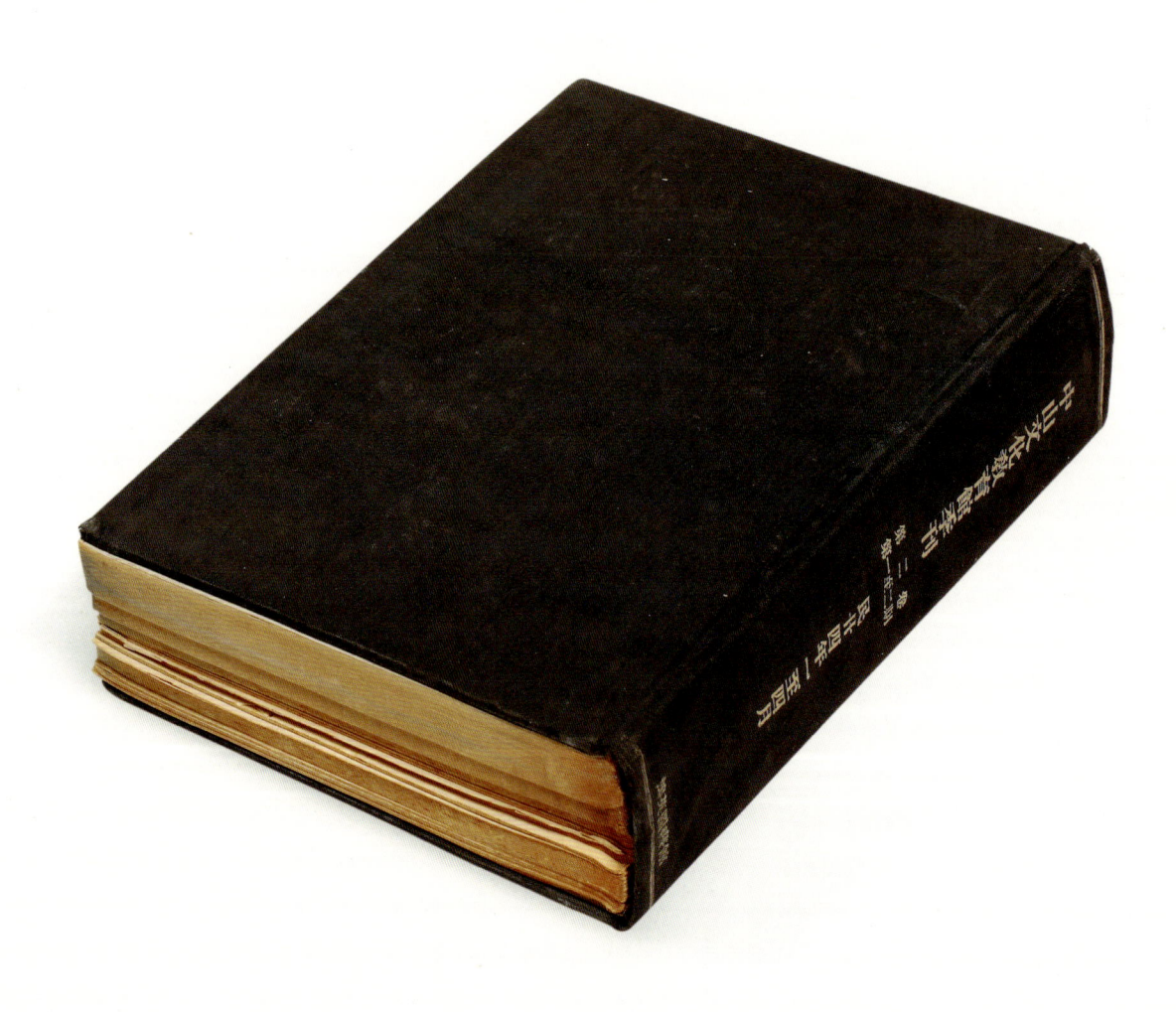

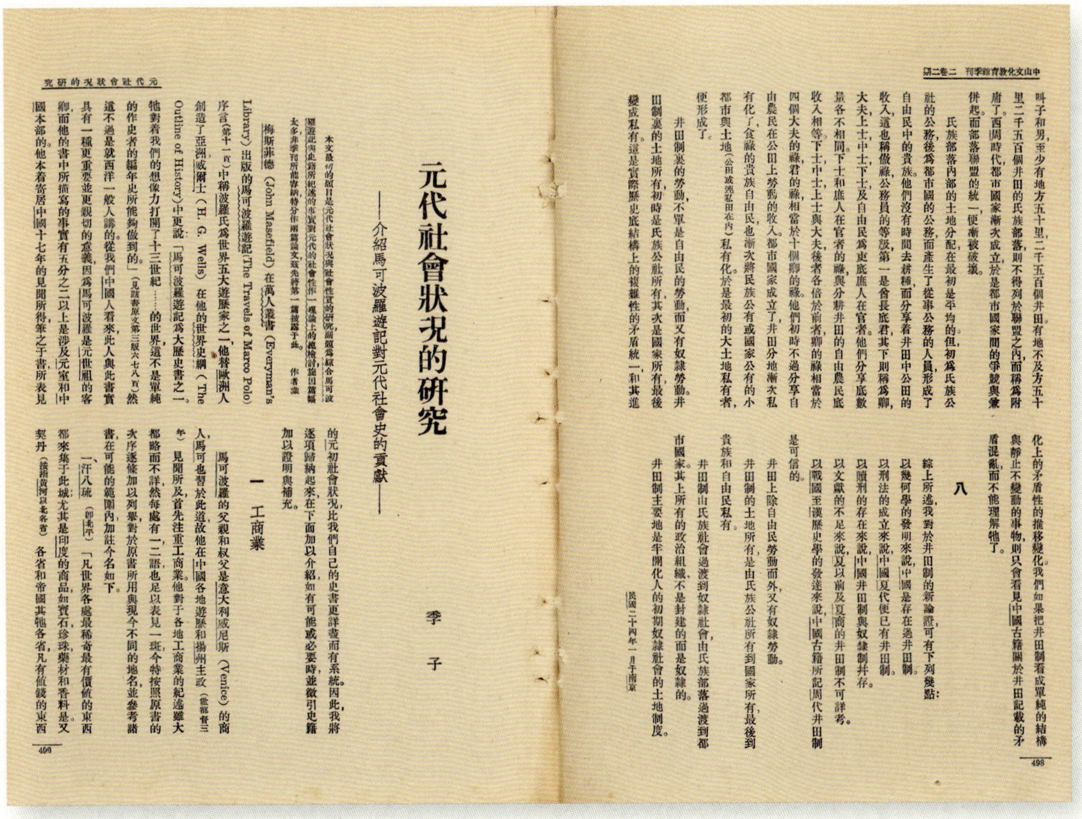

中山文化教育館季刊　二卷二期

叫子和男，至少有地方五十里，二千五百個井田。有地不及方五十里二千五百個井田的氏族部落，則不得列於聯盟之內，而稱爲附庸了。西周時代，都市國家漸次成立，於是都市國家間的爭競與兼併起。而部落聯盟的統一，便漸被破壞。

氏族部落內部的土地分配，在最初是平均的。但，初爲氏族公社的公務，後爲都市國的公務，而產生了從事公務的人員，形成了自由民中的貴族。他們沒有時間去耕種，而分享着井田中公田的收入，這也稱做祿，公務員的等級，第一是會長底君，其下則稱爲卿，大夫，上士，中士，下士，及自由民爲吏底庶人在官者。他們分享底數量各不相同。下士和庶人在官者的祿，與分耕井田的自由農民底收入相等。下士，中士，上士與大夫，後者各倍於前者，卿的祿相當於四個大夫的祿，君的祿，相當於十個卿的祿。他們初時不過分享自由農民在公田上勞動的收入。都市國家成立了，井田分地漸次私有化了，食祿的貴族自由民，也漸次將民族公有或國家公有的小都市與土地（公田減澳私田在內）私有化。於是最初的大土地私有者，便形成了。

井田制裏的勞動，不單是自由民的勞動，而又有奴隸勞動。井田制裏的土地所有，初時是氏族公社所有，其次是國家所有，最後變成私有。這是實際歷史底結構上的複雜性的矛盾統一，和其進化上的矛盾性的推移變化。我們如果把井田制看成單純的結構與靜止不變動的事物，則只會看見中國古籍關於井田記載的矛盾混亂，而不能理解牠了。

八

綜上所述，我對於井田制的新論證，可有下列幾點：

以幾何學的發明來說，中國是存在過井田制。

以刑法的成立來說，中國夏代便已有井田制。

以贖刑的存在來說，中國井田制與奴隸制并存。

以文獻的不足來說，夏以前及夏商的井田制不可詳考。

以戰國至漢歷史學的發達來說，中國古籍所記周代井田制是可信的。

井田上除自由民勞動而外，又有奴隸勞動。

井田制的土地所有，是由氏族公社所有到國家所有，最後到貴族和自由民私有。

井田制由氏族社會過渡到奴隸社會，由氏族部落過渡到都市國家。其上所有的政治組織，不是封建的而是奴隸的。

井田制主要地是半開化人的初期奴隸社會的土地制度。

民國二十四年一月于南京

498

元代社會狀況的研究

元代社會狀況的研究

——介紹馬可波羅遊記對元代社會史的貢獻——

季子

本文最初的題目是元代社會狀況與社會性質的研究，副題爲綜合馬可波羅遊記與史籍所紀述的事實，對元代的社會性作一理論上的總檢討。旋因篇幅太多，非季刊所能容納，特分作兩篇論文，茲先將第一篇披露于此。　作者識

梅斯菲德（John Masefield）在萬人叢書（Everyman's Library）出版的馬可波羅遊記(The Travels of Marco Polo)序言（第十一頁）中稱波羅氏爲世界五大遊歷家之一，他替歐洲人創造了亞洲。威爾士（H. G. Wells）在他的世界史綱（The Outline of History）中更說「馬可波羅遊記爲大歷史書之一。牠對着我們的想像力打開了十三世紀……的世界，這不是單純的作史者的編年史所能夠做到的。」（見該書原文第三版六七八頁）然這不過是就西洋一般人講的。從我們中國人看來，此人與此書實具有一種更重要並更親切的意義。因爲馬可波羅是元世祖的客卿，而他的書中所描寫的事實有五分之二以上是涉及元室和中國本部的。他本着寄居中國十七年的見聞所得，筆之于書，所表見的元初社會狀況，比我們自己的史書更詳盡而有系統。因此，我將逐項歸納起來，在下面加以介紹，如有可能或必要時，並徵引史籍加以證明與補充。

一　工商業

馬可波羅的父親和叔父是意大利威尼斯（Venice）的商人，馬可也習於此道，故他在中國各地遊歷和揚州主政（做都督三年）見聞所及，首先注重工商業。他對于各地工商業的紀述雖大都略而不詳，然每處有一二語，也足以表見一斑。今特按照原書的次序逐條加以列舉，對於原書所用與現今不同的地名，並參考諸書，在可能的範圍內，加註今名如下。

一、汗八琳（即北平）「凡世界各處最稀奇最有價値的東西都來集于此城，尤其是印度的商品，如寶石，珍珠，藥材和香料，是。又契丹（接指黃河以北各省）各省和帝國其牠各省，凡有値錢的東西

499

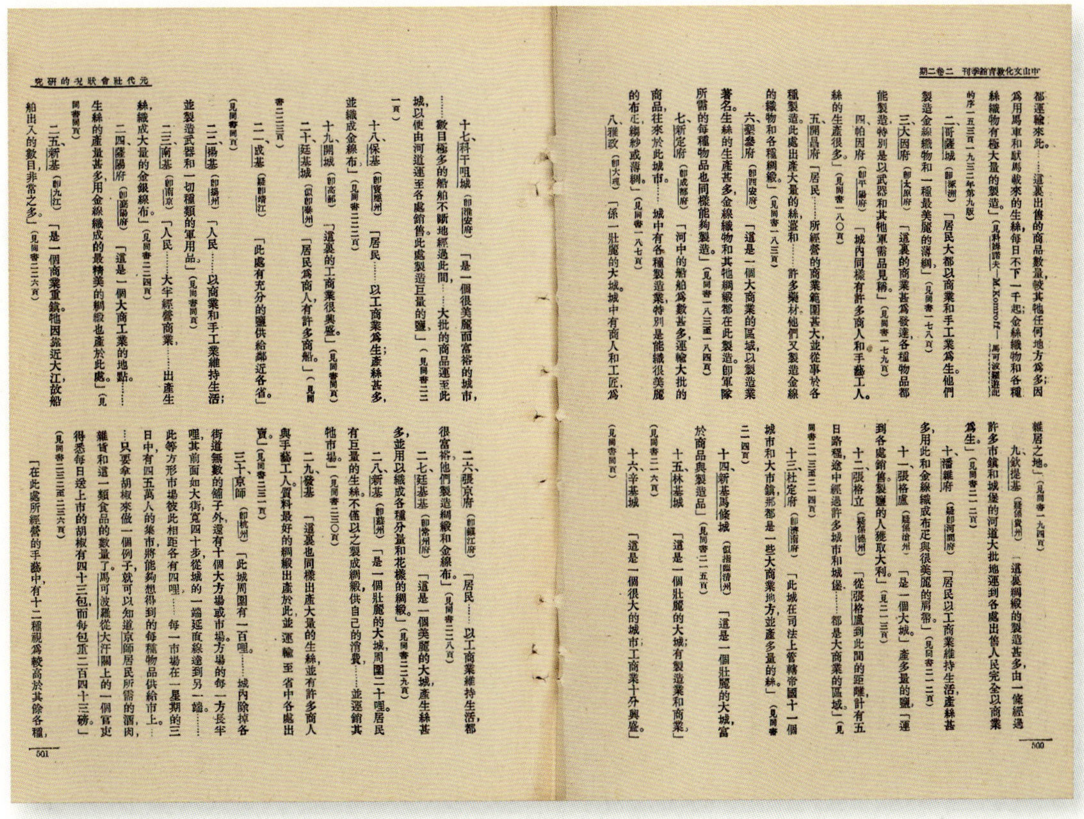

中山文化教育館季刊　二卷二期

都運輸來此。……這裏出售的商品數量，較其牠任何地方爲多；因爲用馬車和馱馬載來的生絲，每日不下一千起。金絲織物和各種絲織物有極大量的製造。」（見科姆諾夫—M. Komroff—馬可波羅遊記的序一五三頁一九三二年第九版）

二、哥薩城（即涿州）「居民大都以商業和手工業爲生。他們製造金線織物和一種最美麗的薄綢。」（見同書一七八頁）

三、大因府（即太原府）「這裏的商業甚爲發達，各種物品都能製造，特別是以武器和其牠軍需品見稱。」（見同書一七九頁）

四、帕因府（即平陽府）「城內同樣有許多商人和手藝工人。絲的生產很多。」（見同書一八〇頁）

五、開昌府「居民……所經營的商業範圍甚大，並從事於各種製造。此處出產大量的絲，蠶和……許多藥材。他們又製造金線的織物和各種綢緞。」（見同書一八三頁）

六、鑿參府（即西安府）「這是一個大商業的區域，以製造業著名。生絲的生產甚多，金線織物和其牠綢緞都在此製造。卽軍隊所需的每種物品也同樣能夠製造。」（見同書一八三至一八四頁）

七、新定府（即成都府）「河中的船舶爲數甚多，運輸大批的商品，往來於此城市。……城中有各種製造業，特別是能織很美麗的布疋，綢紗或薄綢。」（見同書一八七頁）

八、雅政（即大理）「係一壯麗的大城。城中有商人和工匠，爲雜居之地。」（見同書一九四頁）

九、欽提基（疑係貴州）「這裏綢緞的製造甚多，由一條經過許多市鎮和城堡的河道大批地運到各處出售。人民完全以商業爲生。」（見同書二一二頁）

十、潘維府（疑卽河間府）「居民以工商業維持生活，產絲甚多，用此和金線織成布疋與很美麗的肩帶。」（見同書二一二頁）

十一、張格盧（疑係滄州）「是一個大城。」產多量的鹽，「運到各處銷售，製鹽的人獲取大利。」（見二一三頁）

十二、張格立（疑係德州）「從張格盧到此間的距離，計有五日路程，途中經過許多城市和城堡……都是大商業的區域。」（見同書二一三至二一四頁）

十三、杜定府（即濟南府）「此城在司法上管轄帝國十一個城市和大市鎮，那都是一些大商業地方，並產多量的絲。」（見同書二一四頁）

十四、新基馬條城（似指臨清州）「這是一個壯麗的大城，富於商品與製造品」（見同書二一五頁）

十五、林基城「這是一個壯麗的大城；有製造業和商業」（見同書二一六頁）

十六、辛基城「這是一個很大的城市；工商業十分興盛。」（見同書同頁）

500

元代社會狀況的研究

十七、科干咀城（即淮安府）「是一個很美麗而富裕的城市，……數目極多的船舶不斷地經過此間，……大批的商品運至此城，以便由河道運至各處銷售。此處製造巨量的鹽。」（見同書二三一頁）

十八、保基（即寶應州）「居民……以工商業爲生；產絲甚多，並織成金線布。」（見同書二三二頁）

十九、開城（即高郵）「這裏的工商業很興盛。」（見同書同頁）

二十、廷基城（似即泰州）「居民爲商人，有許多商船。」（見同書二三三頁）

二一、成基（疑即靖江）「此處有充分的鹽供給鄰近各省。」（見同書同頁）

二二、揚基（即揚州）「人民……以商業和手工業維持生活；並製造武器和一切種類的軍用品。」（見同書同頁）

二三、南基（即南京）「人民……大半經營商業，……出產生絲，織成大量的金銀線布。」（見同書二三四頁）

二四、薩陽府（即襄陽府）「這是一個大商工業的地點。……生絲的產量甚多，用金線織成的最精美的綢緞也產於此處。」（見同書同頁）

二五、新基（即九江）「是一個商業重鎮。牠因靠近大江，故船舶出入的數目，非常之多。」（見同書二三六頁）

二六、張京府（即鎮江府）「居民……以工商業維持生活，都很富裕。他們製造綢緞和金線布。」（見同書二三八頁）

二七、廷基基（即常州府）「這是一個美麗的大城，產生絲甚多，並用以織成各種分量和花樣的綢緞。」（見同書二三九頁）

二八、新基（即蘇州）「是一個壯麗的大城，周圍二十哩。居民有巨量的生絲，不僅以之製成綢緞，供自己的消費，……並運銷其牠市場。」（見同書二三〇頁）

二九、發基「這裏也同樣出產大量的生絲，並有許多商人與手藝工人。質料最好的綢緞出產於此，並運輸至省中各處出賣。」（見同書二三一頁）

三十、京師（即杭州）「此城周圍有一百哩。……城內除掉各街道無數的舖子外，還有十個大方場或市場。方場的每一方長半哩，其前面如大街，寬四十步，從城的一端延直線達到另一端。……此等方形市場彼此相距各有四哩。……每一市場在一星期的三日中，有四五萬人的集市，將能夠想得到的每種物品供給市上。……只要拿胡椒來做一個例子，就可以知道京師居民所需的酒，肉，雜貨和這一類食品的數量了。馬可波羅從大汗關上的一個官吏得悉每日送上市的胡椒有四十三包，而每包重二百四十三磅。」（見同書二三三至二三六頁）

「在此處所經營的手藝中，有十二種視爲較高於其餘各種，

501

46
读马可孛罗（Marco Polo）游记证误
《学风》
1935

毛汶（撰），安庆，中文
26×19 cm
上海图书馆

Notes on *The Travels of Marco Polo*,
Academic Atomosphere, 1935
Mao Wen (au.), Anqing, Chinese
26×19 cm
Shanghai Library

第三部分
日月有常

47
《中国南海古代交通丛考》
1936

[日]藤田丰八（著），何建民（译），上海，中文
19×13 cm
上海图书馆

Study of The East-West Relations: The Nanhai Volume, 1936
Fujita Toyohachi (au.), He Jianmin (tr.), Shanghai, Chinese
19×13 cm
Shanghai Library

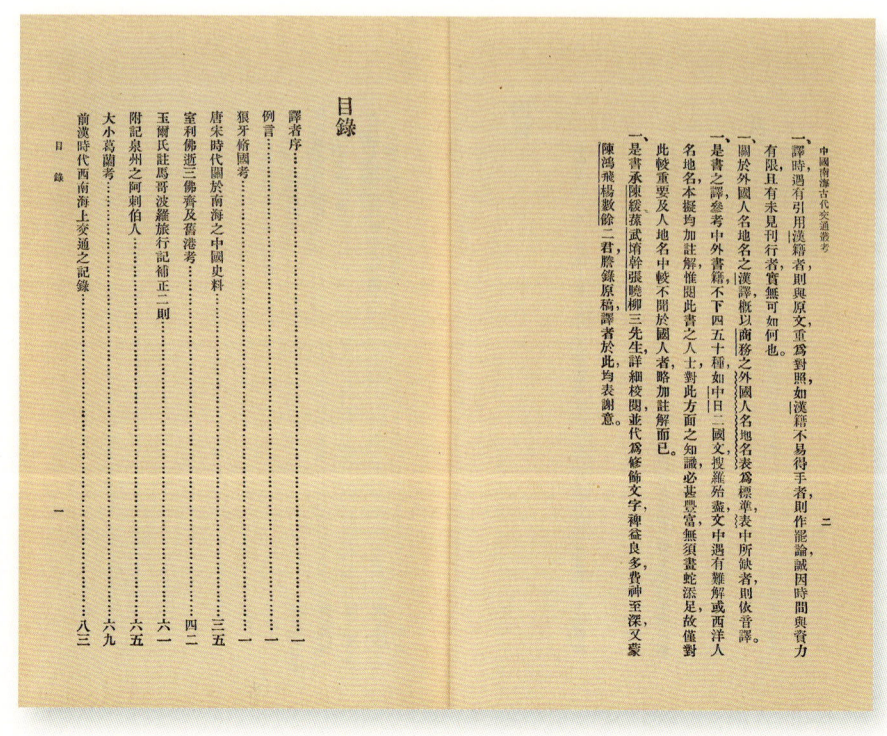

第三部分
日月有常

玉爾氏註馬哥波羅旅行記補正二則

一 Kinsay 非京師之對音

馬哥波羅旅行記中之 Suju 為蘇州，Kinsay 為杭州，固無懷疑之餘地然 Kinsay 對音為何，則無 Suju 之意瓦薩（Wessáf）氏關於此城亦有「天堂」或「天」之曖昧之敍述識如玉爾氏「天城」之意故也。（註一）然嘗有人將 Kinsay 作為杭州之旁證，但至考定其出自何語之對音則毫無價值固不待言。

玉爾氏云 Kinsay 為中國語之京師（Kingsze）實適確無遺憾為一千一百二十七年以後宋朝之都城，用於呼當時之隨安即今杭州。杭州確為南宋之都城，但當時忌京師之呼稱玉爾氏稱當時之京師實臨蘇耳當宋室南遷紹與八年奠都于杭州時為使君臣不忘恢復中原起見特稱為「行在」不呼京師此荷閱宋史或讀當時諸臣之奏議當可瞭然宋史本紀均作行在不呼京都而行在之名頗盛用於當時迄至元年間元史本紀卷九世祖至元十四年條始云：

『命中書省檄諭中外江南既平宋宜曰亡宋行在曰宋行在曰杭州。』

一見上文則可瞭然由上觀之知在南宋及元初時，如玉爾氏等所言杭州為行在迄至元十四年始檄諭中外改曰杭州，然已慣用一百五十多年之行在實不能一朝而消滅此名稱由是觀之予考馬哥波羅氏之 Kinsay 對音而為行在（Khang-zai）之對音。

馬氏之 Kinsay，鄂多列克（Odoric）氏謂係Caussy，馬里那利（Marignolli）氏考為 Kampsay，伊本巴圖塔（Ibn Batuta）氏呼為 Khan-sá。Kîn，Khîn，Can，Kanņ，Khan，等，一方固可為 Khian-sá Kîn，Khîn，Can，Kanņ，Khan 等之對音同時亦可為「京」之對音而 say，sai，sâ 等與其為「師」之對音毋寧謂為「在」之對音似覺適當此稱音字（phonetic）上之議論均不足輕重而宋元之史實斷不容以 Kinsay, Khinsai, Caussy, Kampsay, Khinsá 等為京師之對音。

二 Maabar 之 Chinese Pagoda

距 Negapatam 東北約一英里之地，有一著名之塔，俗稱（Chinese Pagoda，玉爾氏謂此塔可為中國商舶往來 Tanjore 諸港之證此塔不用水門汀而用磚築成與部式建築法根本不同，因無刻文與影像，故無由確知惟 Negapatam 地方為佛徒崇拜之靈地類為馳名故似彼等之手造而遺存者造一千八四六年，該塔仍為三層各層均為磚造牆頂花檐（Cornices）內部直通屋頂，離地約二十英尺處有抹板之痕跡至一千八百五十九年甚為毀壞殆無從修飾迄上面所遠乃當時對於此塔並無傳記至一千六百七十二年巴爾都斯（Baldens）氏始載其名其完成惟波羅及元時對此塔並無傳記特（Sir W. Elliot）氏所考之 Chinese Pagoda 之大略玉爾氏註馬哥波羅旅行記所引愛略特（Sir W. Elliot）氏所考之 Chinese Pagoda 之大略

48
《世界航海家与探险家历史》
1936

[美] 布兰敦（著），曾宗巩（译），江苏南京，中文
22×15 cm
上海图书馆

History of sailors and adventurers of the world, 1936
Brandon (au.), Zeng Zonggong (tr.), Nanjing, Jiangsu,
Chinese
22×15 cm
Shanghai Library

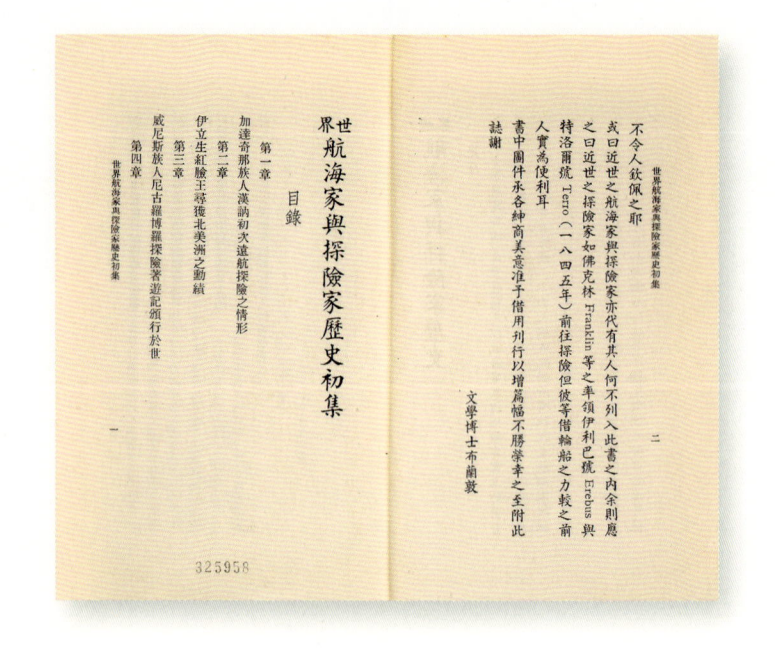

士。其外號族人稱之爲兆人魁。The man of millions 蓋因馬哥博羅學問優長。家財充裕。爲族中之矯矯者。故被敵人俘虜而去，

馬哥博羅未遇難之前。曾在遠東遊歷有年。其所經歷之地。多半爲當時歐州人士所未知悉。所以馬哥博羅回國後。將其遊歷所窺見他方之市鎮村落。如在中國 China 印度 India 緬甸 Burma 等處之各種景緻。人民之住屋花園公所。以及廟堂寺觀。並民間田園場圃。國內所出產綢緞紗羅。豐富而且美麗。馬哥博羅言詞美妙。叙述時。描摹盡致。幾使人。如入五里霧中。莫知其究竟。馬哥博羅識見高深。口才伶俐。國人以兆人魁之號加之。不亦宜乎。

馬哥博羅將其遊歷所窺見之事實。宣告其同族之人。而同族之人、未能盡信。殊以爲憾。但渠不願其所閱歷之事蹟。歷久煙沒無存。所以渠被敵人俘虜。囚於日奴亞牢獄。苦慘之時。請求其獄中同伴。拉斯持新奴 Rusticiano （西印度族人）引用

第七圖

上圖爲馬哥博羅Marco Polo之肖像

法語。編成一書。名曰馬哥博羅旅行遊記。The Travels of Marco Polo 實爲遊記中最特色之書。亦爲歷史中最有價值之書。（此書經杭縣魏易繙譯漢文發行於世）所述多關於亞細亞人類之風土人情。以及其他習慣。可稱之爲人類學。ethnographuy是書出版之後。其效果竟有尋獲美洲之事。則其效力之偉大可知矣。但尋獲美洲。爲後來之事。不具論。今先叙述馬哥博羅海外遊歷探險之緣起。一二六〇年。威尼斯商人尼古羅博羅 Nicolo Polo 與其第馬

其伙伴。竟肯遠涉重洋。冒昧探險。且無政治作用。或地盤觀念。此節稱爲航海家歷史中。最有興趣。不亦宜乎。

北歐人民當時所用航海探險之船舶。前數年。在腦威 Norway 阿西伯 Oseberg 地方出土。現保存於腦威阿斯羅博物院。Oslo Museum.

北歐人民當時所造之船。名曰格斯達式。Gokstad 此船之模型。現保存於南根斯敦。South Kensington（在坎拿大） 因是項船舶和藍色泥土。埋沒於格斯達區域。保存極爲得法。因由該處出土。故獲此名。是種船舶。卽於尋獲北美洲時期所創造者。且爲當時較小之戰鬥艦。亦稱之爲蛇形式。Serpent Class 艦體以橡木用打釘式製造之。艦內之縫。引用牛毛辮成小繩打鑿。所以堅實穩固。能經海浪之洶湧。較之西班牙哥倫布時代所製之船。尤爲出色。且航行速率。亦較哥倫布所製者。尤爲捷快。

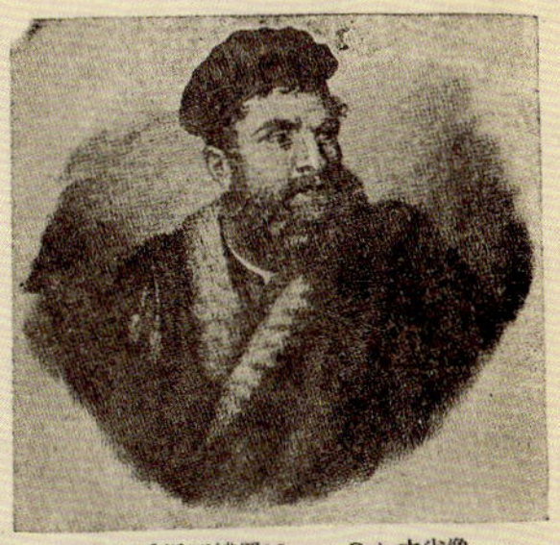

北歐人民。對於遠涉重洋之時。特造一種之船。名曰龍形式。Dragon Class 至於格斯達式。卽蛇形式之船。（見圖）船舷兩旁。有各六槳搖盪之。另有一方帆。懸掛於船之中部。如龍形式之船。（見圖）船舷兩旁各配木槳三十箇。國王賈奴特 Canute （腦威丹麥國王生於九九四年卒於一〇三五年） 所乘坐特等龍船。船舷兩旁。各配槳六十箇云。

第三章 威尼斯族人馬可博羅探險著遊記頒行於世

馬哥博羅 Marco Polo（生於一二四五年卒於一三二三年）

一二九八年。庫爾淑拉海島 Island of Curzola 對岸達馬西 Dalmatian （北緯四二、三五四度東經一六、三〇度現墺地利之皇地橫衝東北海） 之海濱。威尼斯 Venice 之海軍。與日奴亞 Genoa 之海軍。作一猛烈戰鬥。威尼斯海軍敗績。以致其境內居民等。被敵方俘虜而去者。七千餘人之多。彼時馬哥博羅爲本地著名紳

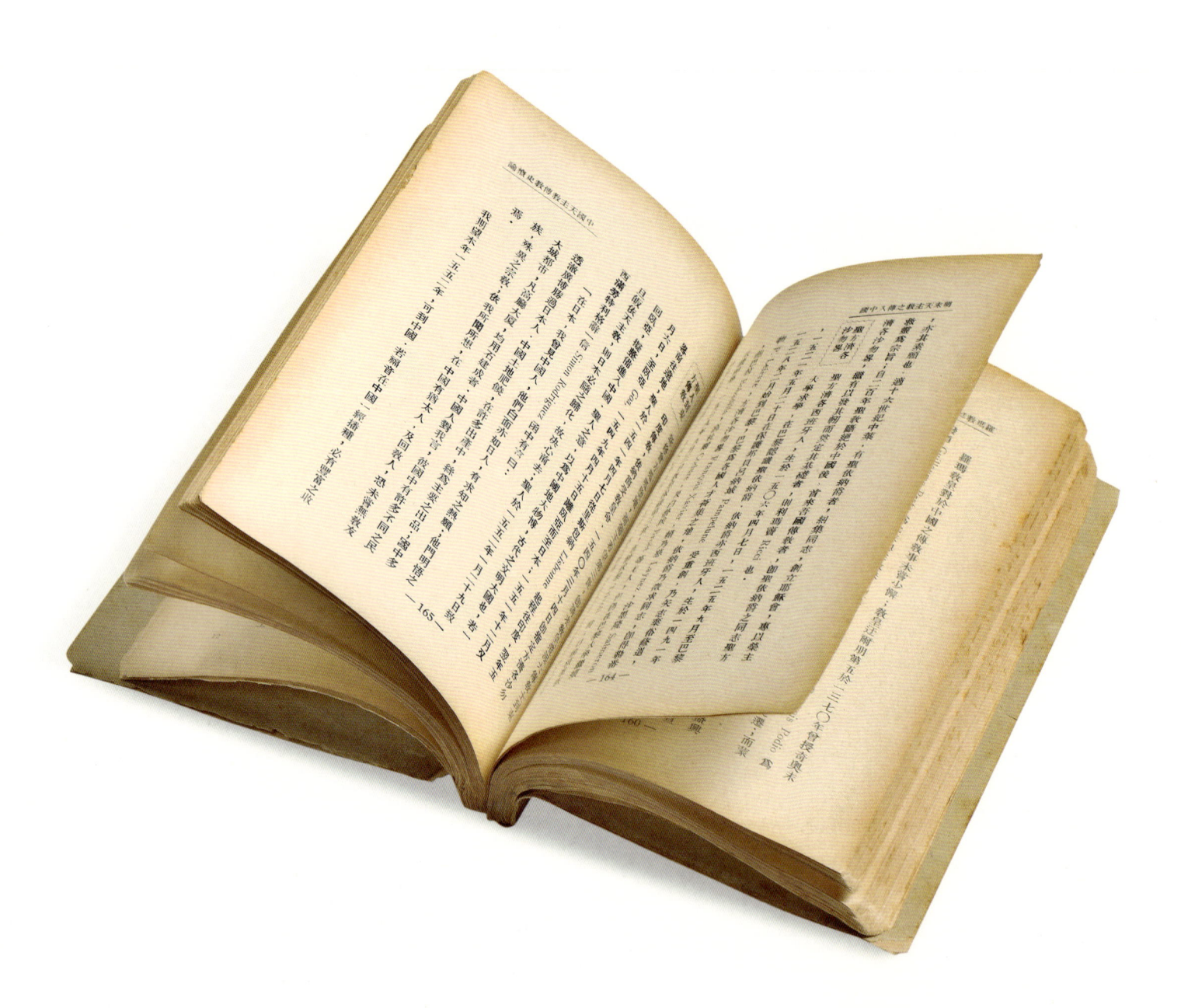

49
《中国天主教传教史概论》
1938

徐宗泽（著），上海，中文
19×13 cm
上海图书馆

Outline of the history of Catholic mission in China, 1938
Xu Zongze (au.), Shanghai, Chinese
19×13 cm
Shanghai Library

第三部分
日月有常

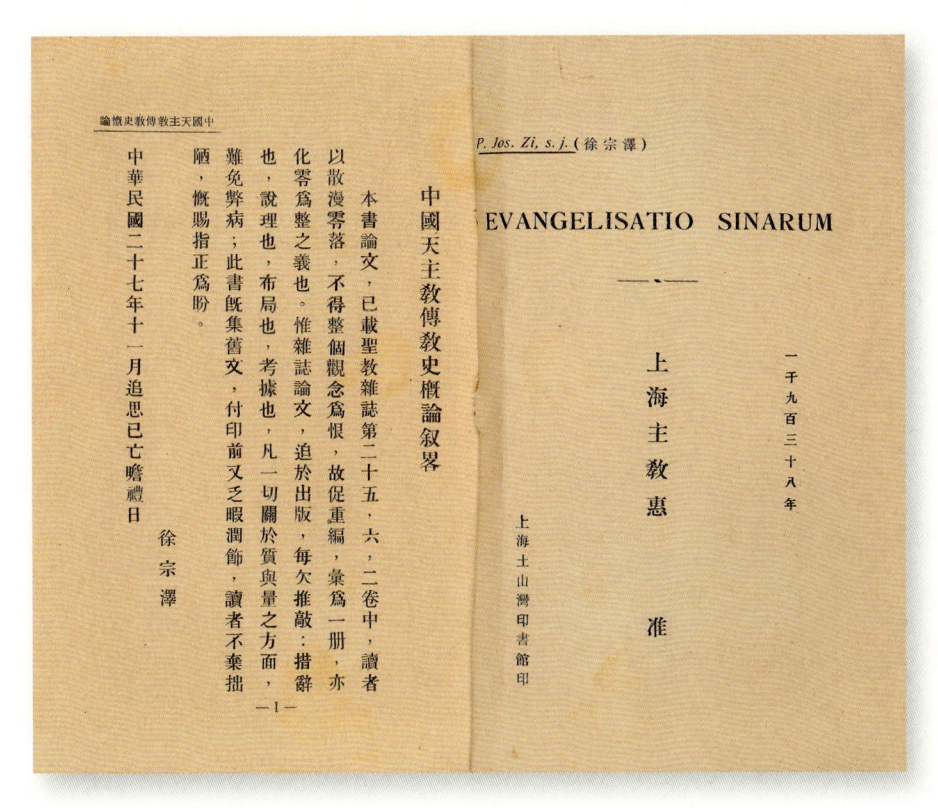

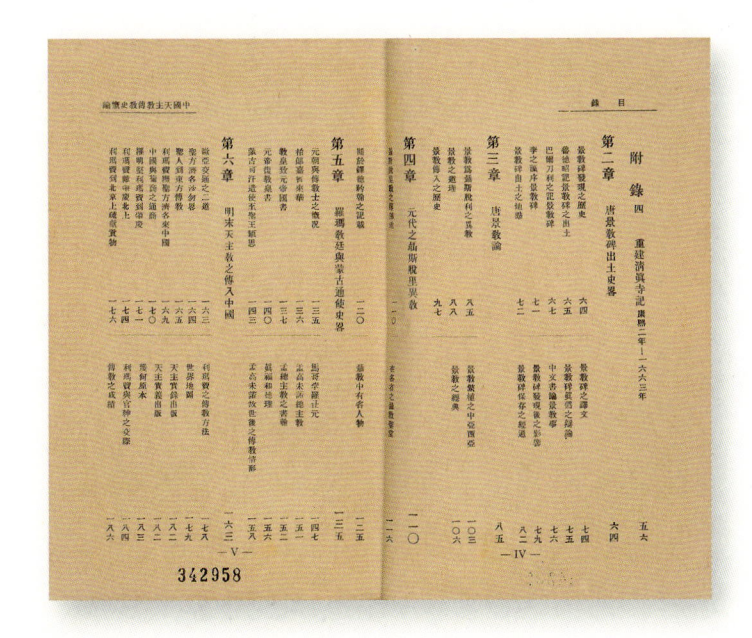

50
书介《马可孛罗：世界纪述》
《图书季刊（国立北平图书馆）》
1940

佚名，北京，中文
26×19 cm
上海图书馆

Book review on *Marco Polo: The Description of the World*,
Quarterly Journal of Book, 1940
Anonymous, Beijing, Chinese
26×19 cm
Shanghai Library

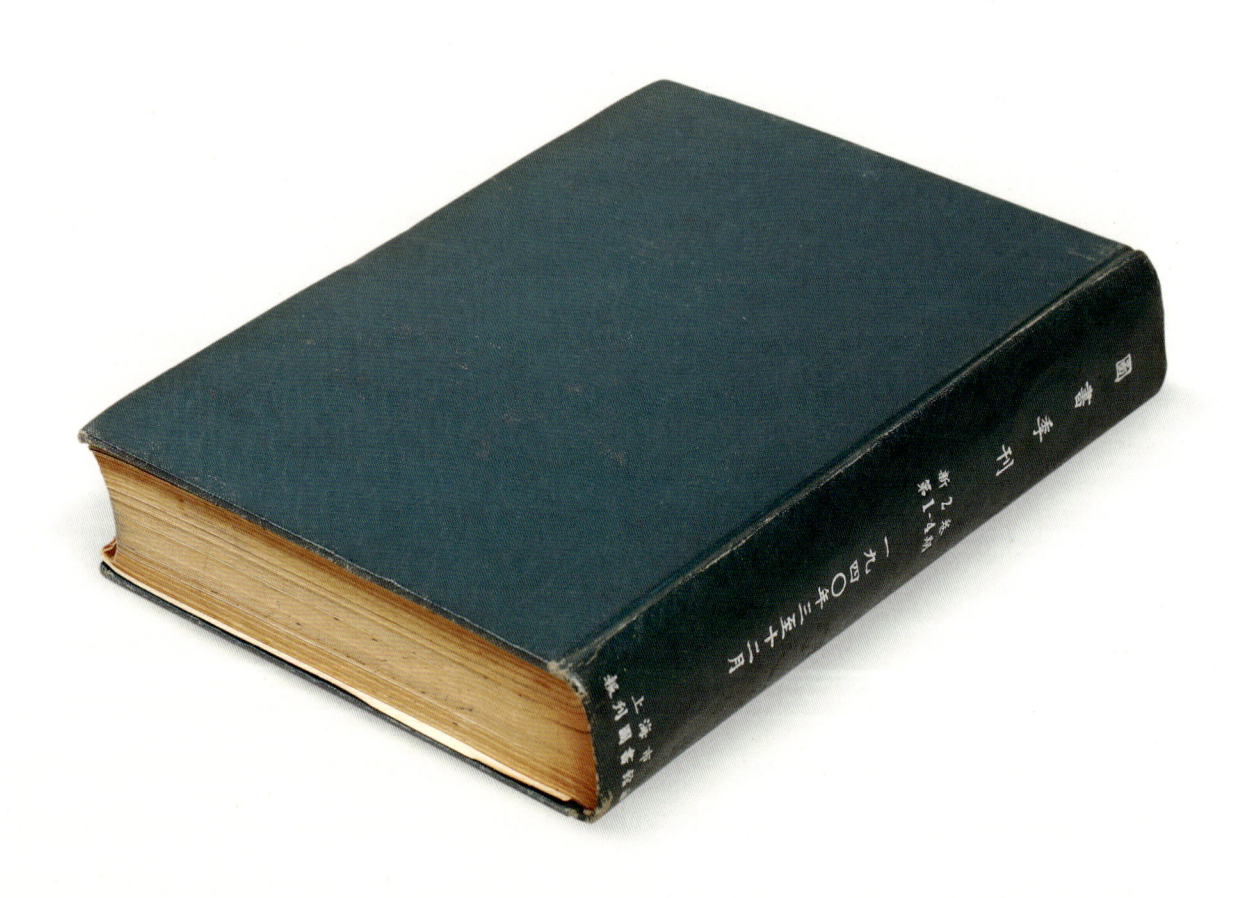

第三部分
日月有常

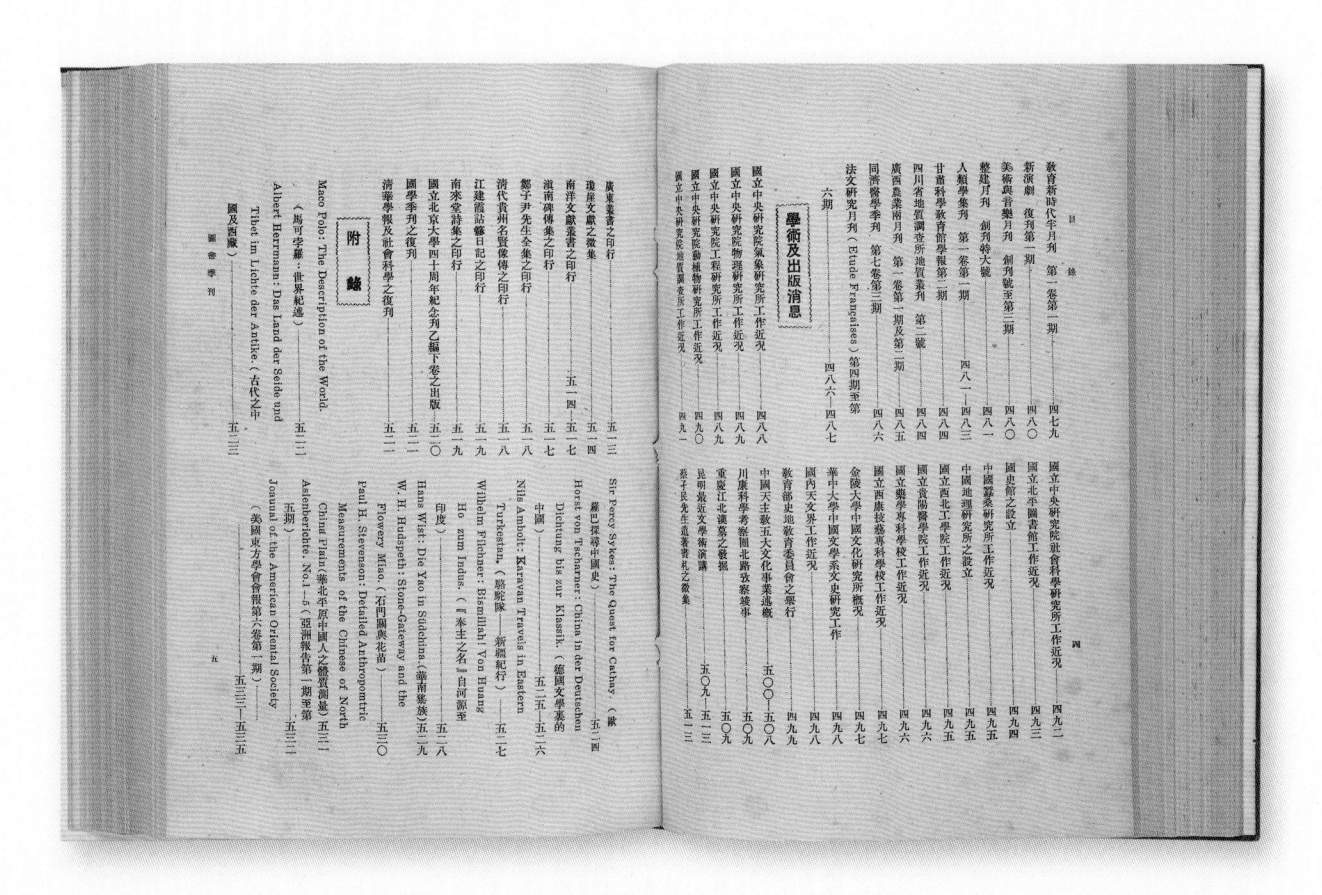

51
《西学考略》
1883

[美] 丁韪良（著），北京，中文
30×18 cm
上海图书馆

Brief introduction to Western culture, 1883
William Alexander Parsons Martin (au.), Beijing, Chinese
30×18 cm
Shanghai Library

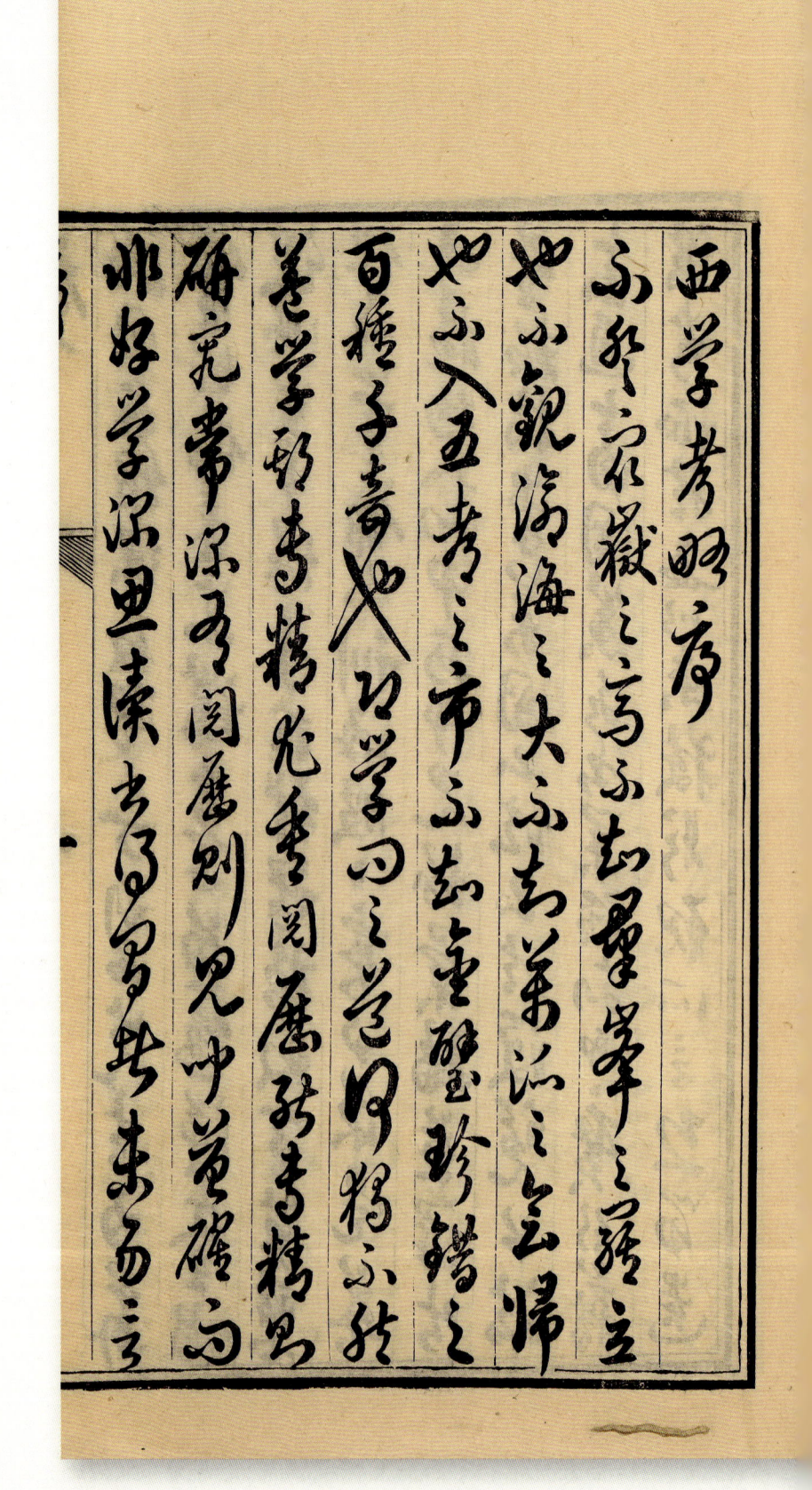

第三部分 日月有常

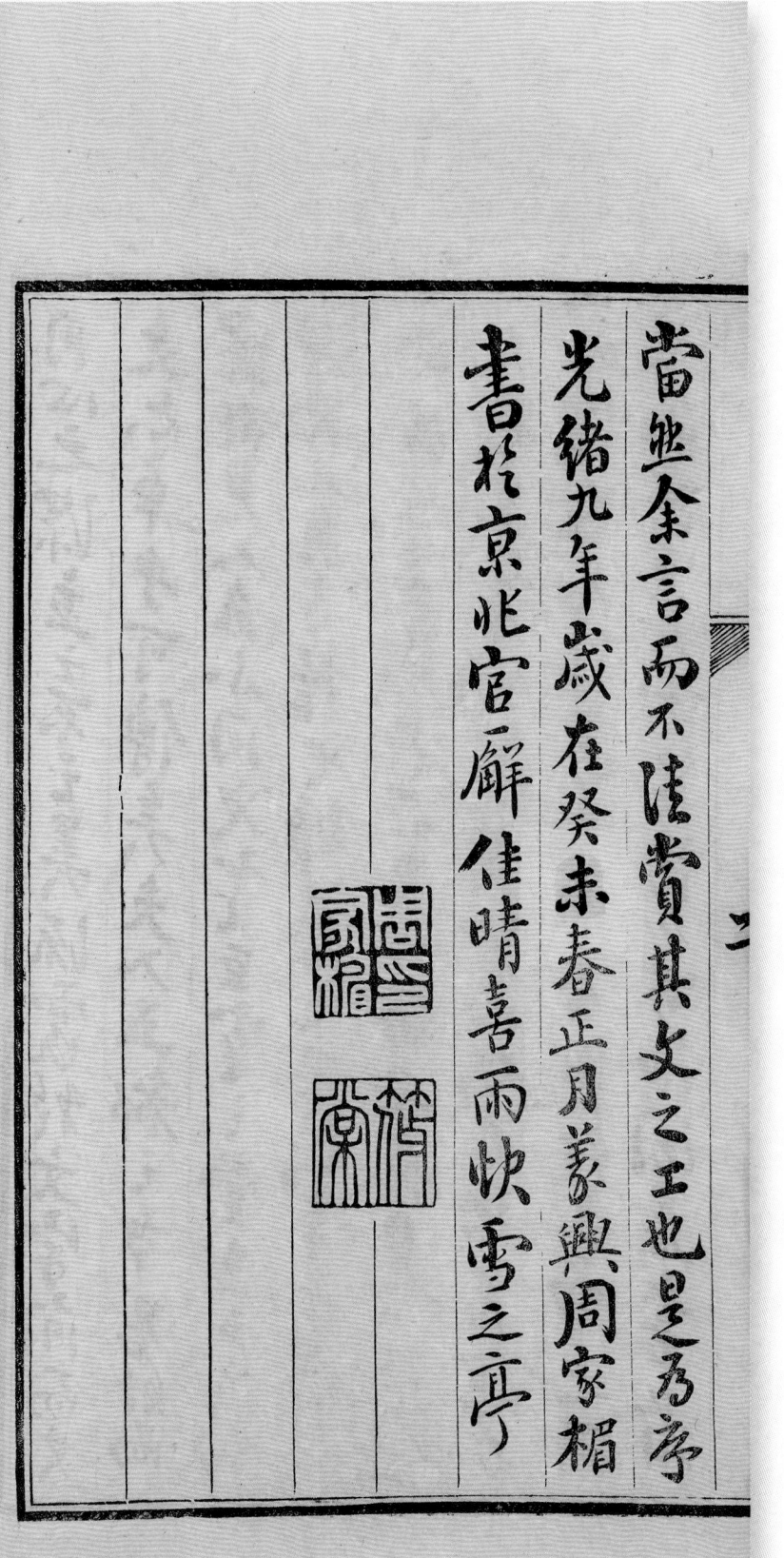

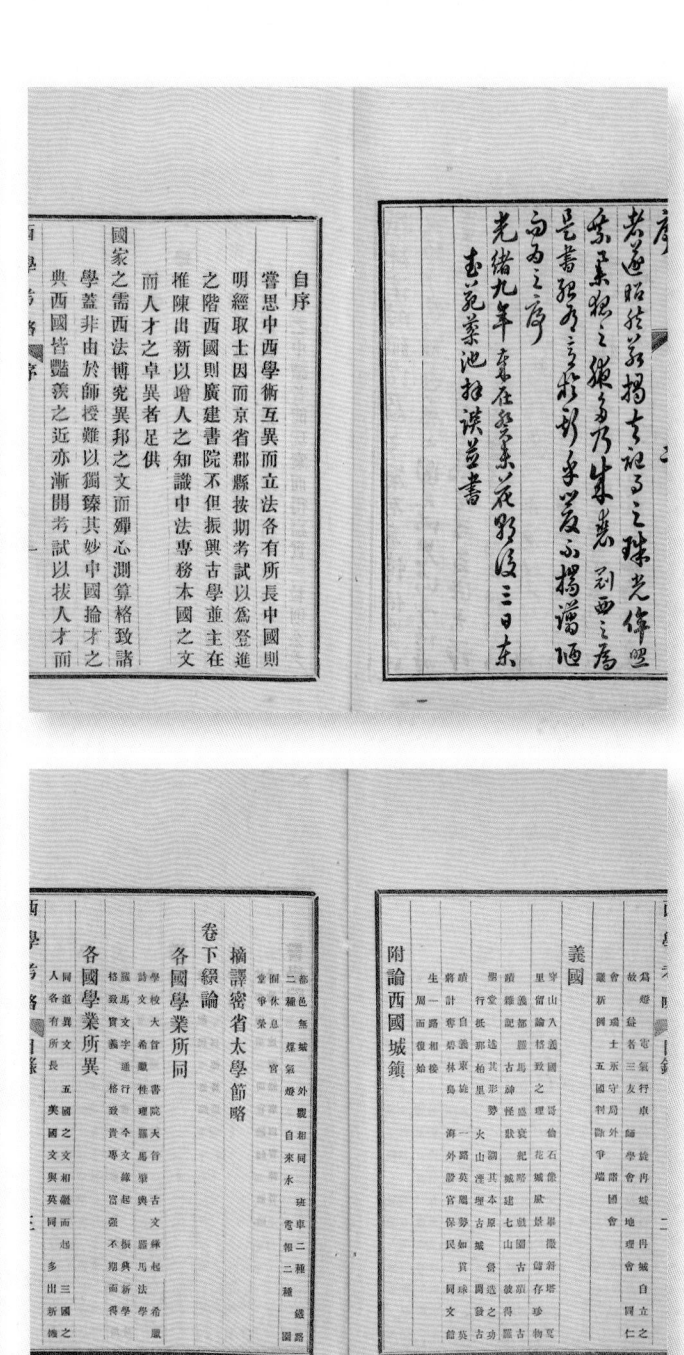

当思余言而不徒赏其文之工也是为序
光绪九年岁在癸未春正月蓂荚兴周家楣
书于京兆官廨佳晴喜雨䰟雪之亭

自序

尝思中西学术互异而立法各有所长中国则明经取士因而京省郡县按期考试以为登进之阶西国则广建书院不但振兴古学並主在推陈出新以增人之知识中法专务本国之文而人才之卓异者足供国家之需西法博究异邦之文而殚心测算格致诸学盖非由于师慢难以独臻其妙中国揣才之典西国皆艳羡之近亦渐开考试以拔人才面

摘译密省太学节略

卷下绿论
各国学业所同
各国学业所异
各国语文相离而有所长
五美国之文与英同多出新机三国之

附论西国城镇

[右侧表格内容略]

光绪九年岁在癸未花朝后三日东𦵔菜池托漠誌书

或就地行銷分別照章辦理再有來鹽均以新票爲憑若無新票其非底鹽堆積之私卽係灘地新買之私均應科罰 五現經本總局指定省城新民鐵嶺馬蜂溝三面船開原法庫門英守屯昌圖通江子錦州沙河營口各處爲准各商囤鹽之處其餘無論何處祗准落地不准囤鹽轉運如將來查有應添之處或由商民稟請再當酌量增添（內）

奉天財政總局試辦於勸加價章程 奉天

○一此次開辦菸絲係倣照直隸章程每勉加稅錢十六文合東錢一百文無論何省所產之菸每一勉卽收東錢一百文無論何菸葉菸絲亦無論何省所產之菸每一千枝收東錢一吊文吉成斗秤發給二聯票分別牌菸捲每一千枝收東錢一吊文吉成斗秤各局就近稽徵另案造報此項捐欵每兩個月彙解一次並由財政總局刊給二聯票分別塡川呈繳以備查核 一菸行菸棧售賣菸葉菸絲捲分別須先請領執照認納稅欵開張如未領照不准售賣違者准其同行舉發照應完稅從重罰辦嗣後有歇業者可將原領執照繳銷如執照失落情事准具同行保結呈補發凡請領執照及補照既不取分文 一行棧菸鋪旣已領照認稅自應暢其銷路所有菸攤菸挑凡零星售賣者統歸菸行菸鋪於小販購買時發給一菸行菸鋪應照各鋪隨時稽查以杜偷漏而裕嗣後有歇業者可將原領執照繳銷如有地痞及不肖書吏巡差向該商訛索情事由局指控嚴懲如有不貸貿易繁盛之區並可擇殷實菸商派爲董事郡同勸辦果有成效由局禀請督獎給功牌以示光寵（內）

札詢商董 松江（內）

○去歲典商林錫田運動商界中人令具名逕票商部舉爲商會董事商部恐有弊害特札上海商務總會轉行松江府查詢林某品望能否勝任府尊戚升淮太守遂札婁縣查訊聲覆費罄屈吉士大令以林董衆堂倉伜等詞備文申覆太守批稱詢之輿論未能一致果否堪勝商家之任總以商家能否爲斷頗得再詳細查覆旋得西門外某商董等聯名蓋印呈遞保單大令遂照此禀覆府署轉稟商部（後）

接商董一職關係頗重布非其人鮮有不敗事者戚太守批以商家能否公認僅憑聯名保單亦未必一無詢覆爲抱要惟公認斷頗爲抱要惟公認

來函

接意大利名人馬哥波羅事略 ○馬哥波羅時方十六歲亦偕行焉馬哥波羅年十二時卽隨其父叔至三人遵陸而行先經波斯海灣轉向東北經波斯土耳其斯坦輾行三百里世祖之消夏行宮在焉是役至三人遵陸而行先經波斯海灣轉向東北經波斯土耳其斯坦輾行三百里世祖之消夏行宮在焉是役古大道而行一千二百七十五年始抵長城之北三百里世祖之消夏行宮在焉是役也長途跋涉艱苦備當旣入境人民皆歡迎之而馬哥波羅又心傾蒙古王者之權勢回由是潛心學習波斯蒙古文字旁及漢文入贄樞機者凡二年旋奉使至大原府與安南古大道而行一千二百九十二年由中國南海古大道而行一千二百九十二年由中國南海至越南游覽馬哥波羅在元時服官於中國之事也至越南游覽馬哥波羅在元時服官於中國之事也者乘間攻擊晚節十七年官至高年深忍書與蒙古近族通婚世祖母因波羅父子叔至三人者乘間攻擊晚節十七年官至高年深忍書泛舟而往道經蘇門答臘遇颶風淹留半載內因泛舟而往道經蘇門答臘遇颶風淹留半載內因千二百九十五年抵波斯京城事畢一千二百九十五年抵波斯京城事畢其鄉建一宮室大書曰皆樓三處相距書即流傳京都成都府南至雲南西至大理府及西藏之邊界南至緬甸而盡者蓋取其尊重之意也世祖臨崩世祖兆謂馬哥波羅爲眞歐亞人所羨歸於尼斯眞歐亞畢露三處相距數十餘里爭起云馬哥波羅爲眞歐亞人所稱揚於是八省書亦亦其當日所入幸好問明寮之蒙古故事也其事也此意亦爲書即流傳京都成都府南至雲南西至大理府及西藏之邊界南至緬甸而盡者蓋取其尊重之意也世祖臨崩世祖兆謂馬哥波羅為眞歐亞人所羨歸於尼斯眞歐亞各國省有益於中國中外同八一堂共聚一堂其時去今已六百年矣然而彼之名文者十數年也謂馬哥波羅開鴻道路於歐洲迄今巳六百年矣然而彼之名其鄉建一宮室大書曰皆樓三處相距書即流傳京都成都府南至雲南西至大理府及西藏之邊界南至緬甸而盡者蓋取其尊重之意也世祖臨崩世祖兆謂馬哥波羅為眞歐亞人所羨歸於尼斯眞歐亞各國所傳揚漢視中國之政治謂中國之善政利未當謂中國應敬仰英人之耳目惟在中國者也自馬哥波羅傳可知其人樸矣夫馬哥波羅爲所著之馬哥波羅紀行叙述未竟其時中國聲名之播於歐洲為馬哥波羅之功大有造於中國也自馬各國省有益於中國中外同八一堂共聚一堂中國不可不追念之感謝可知其爲八雖其人表其景仰之意不獨意人李君演說之題卽馬哥波羅足跡所不到是泰東西各國景仰馬哥波羅之盛意亦可知也中國人亦從而知其人亦有功於中國當種道勿替也李君至之地府經彼曾畢步其風云聲同聲欲仰固不獨我資所作故中國人今日詳事演說之題卽馬哥波羅八雖其人之八省同聲欽仰固不獨我賓所作波羅未華歐洲人始悉歷海遣使至遠東救百年後歐洲人始悉亞洲倘有故中國於今日執事演說之題亦必詳考其地之名凡八省歐洲之人皆知欽仰尤如馬波羅如昆然如一相親相愛如昆季然相愛如昆季然大種族馬哥波羅爲眞歐洲人雖其人表其景仰之意不獨意人李君演說之題卽國君與梵蒂遣使至遠東救百年後歐洲人始悉歷史倘有君與教皇咸遣使至遠東救百年後歐洲人始悉亞洲倘有大種族馬哥波羅足跡所不到是泰東西各國景仰馬哥波羅之盛意亦可知也中國人亦從而知其人亦有功於中國當種道勿替也李君至之地府經彼曾畢步其風云聲同聲欽仰固不獨我賓所作故中國於今日執事演說之題亦必詳考其地之名凡八省歐洲之人皆知欽仰尤如馬波羅如昆然如一相親相愛如昆季然道謝曰今日執事演說之題卽馬哥波羅八雖其人之八省同聲欽仰固不獨我賓所作署迷馬哥波羅之路彼曾畢步其風云聲同聲欽仰固不獨我賓所作官於海軍不亦演說於此地府經彼曾畢步其風云聲同聲欽仰固不獨我賓所作謀公益李佳白君端果生之精力以圖之其成效可拭目而俟也所爲可感也我儕深盼將來東西聯合爲一相親相愛如昆季然

第三張閱者注意
今日尚有各省新聞及本埠新聞均列入

小腸氣永遠斷根

天下馳名廣東宏仁堂大藥局兌記仙傳萬分奇效異法郎
愈耳陰核偏墜諸症醫東手痛者萬分但將膏藥貼上立刻腎囊縮小小腸氣消除奇妙在將膏藥貼上立刻腎囊縮小小腸氣消除神效每服一元另有內服藥力奏效之速製煉之精雖數十年老症三日包能斷根愈後永不再發患一切耳內

此二張輕者一張包愈重患者一盒愈一盒一元○本堂仙傳異法郎愈耳聾丸此九專治耳聾此耳痛耳響耳脹百發百中效若仙丹無論陰囊腫脹奇方秘製不惟本堂獨得奇方秘製不惟本堂獨得奇方秘製在將膏藥七種神效無論男女老幼兩耳由毛孔拔出一掃而空刻愈斷根愈後永不再發患一切耳內

52

来函：意大利名人马哥波罗事略
《申报》
1906

[美]李佳白，上海，中文
30×28 cm
上海图书馆

Correspondence: Marco Polo, an Italian Celebrity,
Shun Pao, 1906
Gilbert Reid, Shanghai, Chinese
30×28 cm
Shanghai Library

申報

第五伯四十二號

附本館書

求知子論意國馬君之事某等學問譾陋於元史不能記憶於浙江通志亦未蒐閱有辱其謙虛下問厚意弟棘實有其事細查兩書必有錄載惟未知此書何名曾否傳于中國倘中國已知其書即令未傳於世而兩書藝文志亦必已列其書名矣夫西學之傳於中國者自明徐文定公厳後徵聘西士南湯諸君至京修歷而西學遂盛南湯諸君奉朝尚存故中國學士大夫尚有見而知之者亦有聞而知之者若馬君事在元初為時較遠且其姓名頗類蒙古諸人若非細心詳檢必至誤為蒙古之人矣做館書緒不多無從考究故特錄此兩件以呈覽倘著藏書之家淵博之士務祈代查蘭書詳示同人以為考據之助不徒求知子與敝館之幸實中西各學士之幸也昌勝禱跂之至

情死

語曰牡丹花下死做鬼也風流此王伯倫為情而死也然苟非其人則等一死如鴻毛矣前日閱香港新報載有梁某與某妓戀姦情密為妓所賣迫使其盤桓不去赴政務司衛門控其見惡達提質訊憤極自戕一案亦為情而死不想無獨有偶揆隔數千里竟有遙遙相對者如法租界豐里街有吳人名阿桂者失其姒同在寶興戲館門前擺水果攤度日者也拼識阿鄉某婦迄今九歲鰥夫寡婦已同結髪皆圖唱隨偕老計豈料婦女水性楊花近日竟別有情人從前恩愛一勾消婦之視夫早若眼中之釘矣初尚稍知避嫌繼則毫無顧忌前日阿桂因事外出野鴛正當變頸之際為阿桂檢熊家中所有牢被某婦運之一盡雖屬小本經營而數年之積蓄一旦棄之他人未免憤鬱難舒遂自閉戶服紫霞膏畢命嗚呼哀哉作不醒之黃梁矣其死也不動聲色先早剃頭洗浴衣服亦皆穿整故莫之能防可謂視死如歸可惜死非其所亦愚矣哉噫

寧波府試信息

府考題目 有斐君子 引詩第八句 次題夷考其行 詩題虛白光裏誦黃庭

鄞孫頭場

53
询意国马君事
《申报》
1874

（清）求知子（撰），上海，中文
26.5×25 cm
上海图书馆

Question about Ser Marco Polo from Italy,
Shun Pao, 1874
Qiuzhizi (au.), Shanghai, Chinese
26.5×25 cm
Shanghai Library

54
欧人游历中国之先登者马可波罗遗像
《新民丛报》
1905

佚名（撰），横滨，中文
22×14 cm
上海图书馆

Statue of Marco Polo, a European pioneer traveling to China,
Sein Min Choong Bou, 1905
Anonymous (au.), Yokohama, Chinese
22×14 cm
Shanghai Library

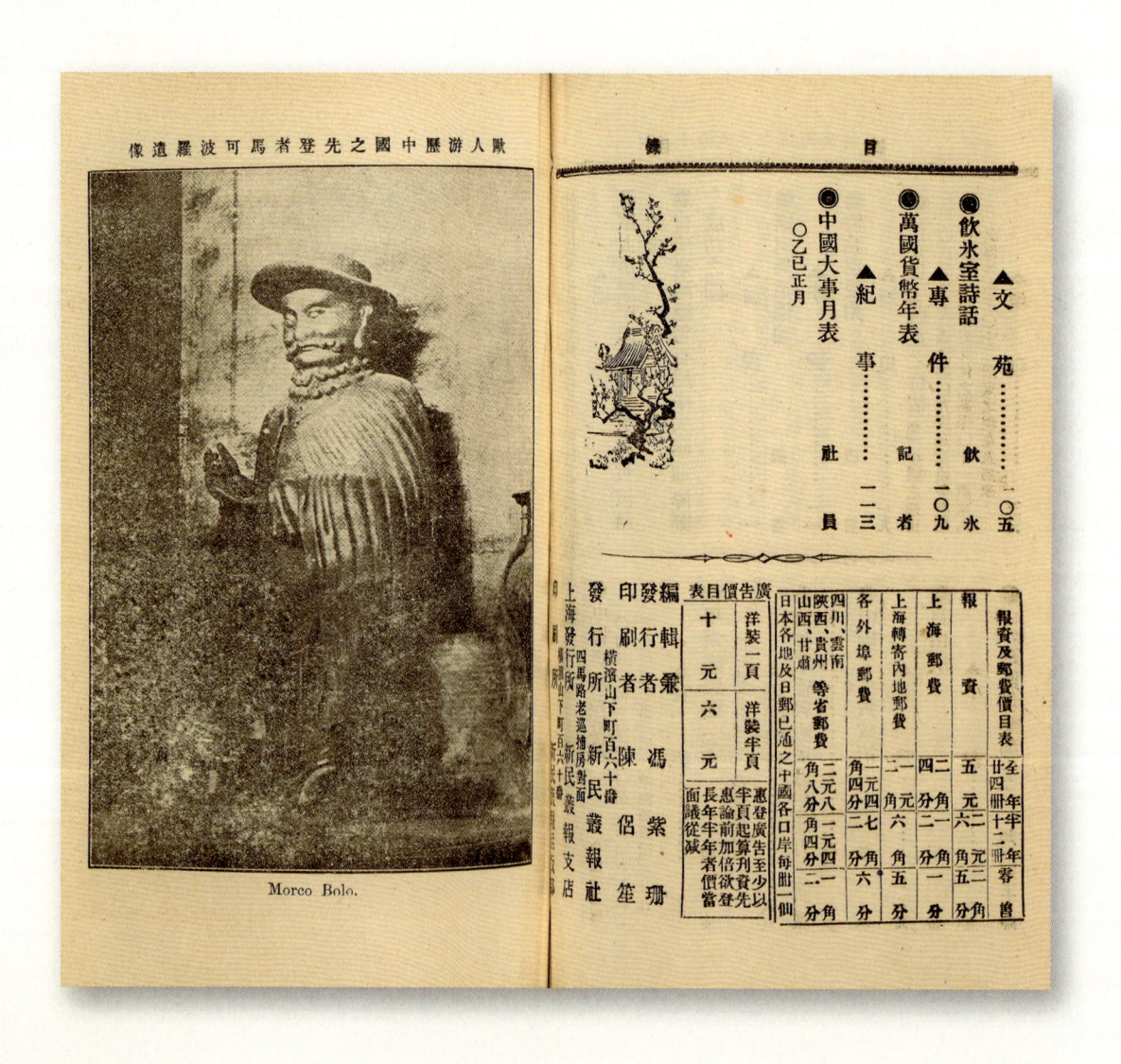

第三部分
日月有常

55

《归潜记》
1909

（清）钱恂（著），中文
29×17 cm
上海图书馆

Gui Qian Ji, 1909
Qian Xun (au.), Chinese
29×17 cm
Shanghai Library

始達上都。由布哈爾、羗和闐、拜城、哈喇沙爾、布淖爾、喀什噶爾、葉爾羗蔥嶺、歷喀什等處。又紆迴而達和林。未至前十一日、世祖已遣官候迎於道。旣見、備述數年中往返事、幷呈景宗書及所取耶穌墓鐙油。世祖大悅。更嘉馬哥博羅聰穎、畱待任使、築館居三人焉。

以上爲馬哥博羅父若叔事

馬哥博羅敏悟絕倫、本通波斯亞剌伯語言文字、旣東、又通中國蒙古語言文字。世祖愛之、信之、置左右、無專職、而頗預聞國政。所著書述中國事頗詳、凡所聞見所行事、多可與元史相印證。蓋世祖嘗遣赴各省路核錢穀事、朝頻有是使。馬哥又出使占城獅子等國、書敘占城事極詳。至元十四年七一二出使海外、歷六月程、或揣當使安南。是年安南王陳光昺从子……

（左頁）

馬哥博羅足本書始知之、或馬哥不願當世知之、故先不傳播歟。

羅按其獄、旋暴阿哈瑪特罪狀、明嘉靖間、五一五西人續得九年八一二、左相阿哈瑪特爲益都千戸王著所殺。馬哥博羅曾爲揚州路官、或是達魯花赤。大吏當指此、封畺言路凡二十七城。此至元十年元年十四年二月奉使……

元立遣使來朝、逾年、禮部尚書柴椿等奉使往……

博羅爲西人、據元史密副大夫宣慰使……

安兼博羅十四年二月奉使……

中名博羅十年……

知赤亦不知何人、馬哥博羅言元取襄陽得力於機發、其父……

第三部分
日月有常

56
马哥博罗游记之言苏州
《青年进步》
1918

佚名（撰），上海，中文
26×18 cm
上海图书馆

Suzhou in *The Travels of Marco Polo*,
Qingnian Jinbu, 1918
Anonymous (au.), Shanghai, Chinese
26×18 cm
Shanghai Library

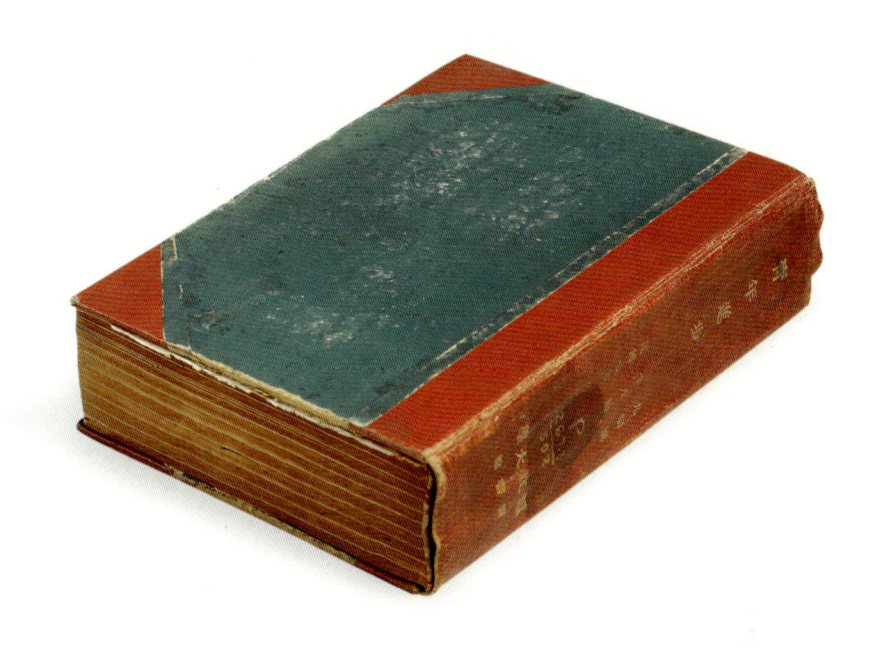

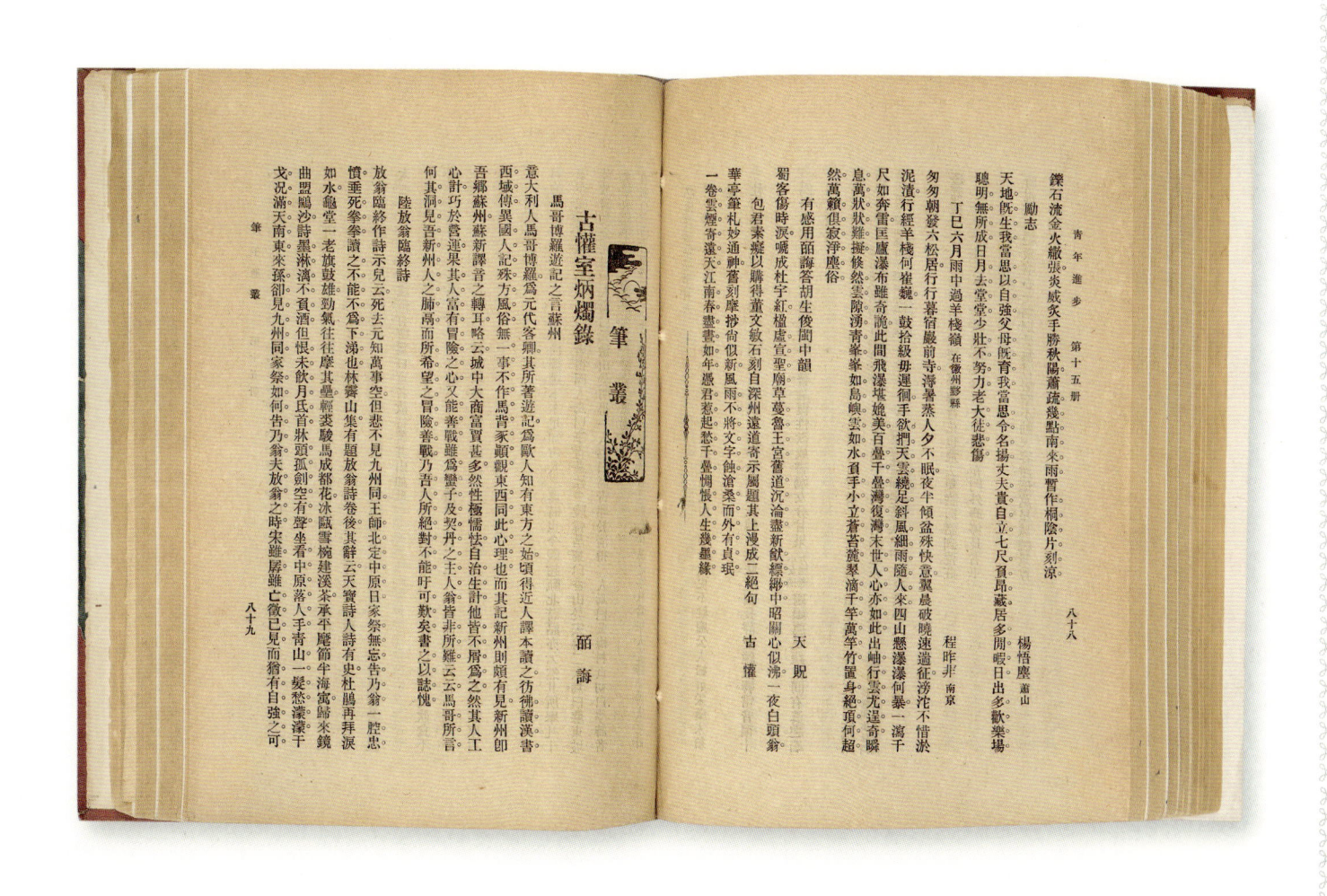

57

马哥孛罗游踪之追寻
《科学》
1925

君达（撰），上海，中文
26×19 cm
上海图书馆

Tracing Marco Polo,
Sciences, 1925
Junda (au.), Shanghai, Chinese
26×19 cm
Shanghai Library

科學第九卷第十期地質號目錄

插圖　東吳大學科學館攝影一幀　青島觀象臺攝影一幀

中國山脈考······翁文灝 1179－1214
太陽斑點與雨量之關係······高　魯 1215－1231
甘肅北部地形地質簡說······謝家榮 1232－1244
青島氣候之大概······蔣丙然 1245－1260
周代合金成分考······梁　津 1261－1278
美國天產博物院調查蒙古地質之成績
······奧斯朋 1279－1284

瑣聞　山東發見世界最古之金蟲化石
　　　中國鐵礦儲量之最新的統計
　　　請政府印行詳細地圖之提議
　　　喜馬拉那最高峯之探險
　　　馬哥孛羅游蹤之追尋
　　　西藏之新調查
　　　中國最古之地球儀
　　　全球災變圖之計劃
　　　水力生電
　　　中英兩國礦產之比較
　　　喀喇崑崙之新調查······君達編 1285－1292

雜俎　研究中國煤礦之新書
　　　中俄劃界之研究
　　　黃土之化學成分
　　　中國北方泉水成分之研究······君達編 1293－1296

科學名詞審查會　物理學名詞　電學······1297－1303

日用必備參考之書

購有諸君正編添應備補編

▼商務印書館出版

日用百科全書補編

發售預約

定價四元
約二元四角

一布面一巨冊
約一千九百頁
四月底截止
五月出書

郵費 國內二分
　　合購正編補編
　　(正編六元)
　　寄價六元

本書爲正編特付性質屬於社會經社會經濟訊，惟常用之材料器物名詞略載於正編特加入（中多物分類明顯顯時名日日用百科全書補編）約計二十四萬言。其內容仍依正編分十四編凡類屬亦屬日用之重要者，乃由遠頓(Norton) 將應用科目，詳細修改，每編自十萬言至二十萬言不等，皆以最新材料，詳細精繁，比較此編同時增加新國語詞調之新語，及新興藝術之新語。諸如教育文藝建築，交通郵傳水運語，冠軍陸軍，郵政航空及電機門等，社會學上之注意要者。

樣本　郵資須函索　三分冊

天(813)

1288　　科　學　　第九卷

人直發其巔，更求爲科學的調查。近年來英國地學家選次試探，以以以種種困難，未遂其極。本年(一九二四年)復由英國勃盧斯(Bruce)將軍率領專門學者十三人，於三月二十六日起程試登，定四月六日升至高度四千四百公尺(卽約一萬四千尺)，勃盧斯將軍因重病不能續進，乃由遠頓(Norton)將代爲首領繼續登行，并先派馬洛利及歐文(Mallory and Irvine)二君先行探路，至龍芳克(Rongbuk)冰川氣候嚴寒，風雪交作。馬歐二氏又死於人類與自然之戰爭，未達目的面逝。此已第三次矣，現聞一九二五年試探之計畫已在精極進行，仍當於春間再行試登云。

馬哥孛羅游蹤之追尋

近有美國人組織團體，擬探馬哥孛羅在中亞及中國經行之路線，幷沿途攝取活動電影，此團體名曰 Photo-Scientific Expedition, 其主任名 Tangier Smith, 於本年(一九二四)春間卽往河套前往甘肅，本稅卽可行由甘肅再往新疆，惟因經費不濟，或計畫變更，但已改道他行或於明年再舉云。

西藏之新調查

英國華德(F. Kingdom Ward) 及考道 (Cawdor) 二君調查西藏之植物人種及地質，於本年(一九二四)四月達 Chetang, (在雅魯藏布江谷中)沿江東行。又有谷斯洛夫(Kozlov)君亦在西藏某地方發見古墓，爲中國貴爵深埋惟十四公尺之下。

中國最古之地球儀

中國天球之製，導源甚古。面地球之說，則知之甚遲。因中不深信地爲球形也，卽今觀象臺所存淸初天主敎士所製之儀器，亦並無地球儀一物，惟庚子

第十期　　瑣　聞　　1289

擊價亂時，奧國遣任公使羅宋(Rosthorn)君曾在北京古物儲中，購得地球儀一具，現存維也納博物院中，此球儀係出自淸室宮中球係銀製，直徑長二十二公分，有橫軸二特軸架腳木製有中國式雕刻，球上有中文圖例，就其所記世界之地理製之，當在 Abel Tasman 及 Cook 旅行時代之間，卽其製作時代當在一五八二至一六二○年之間，則其時猶在利馬竇 (Matteo Ricci, 1580-1610) 在中國之後。據利氏遺書(曾於一九一一至一九一三年在意大利發見印行)，內記南京天文儀器甚詳，但未言有地球儀，惟謂當時有一中國大員名 Lingozuon (譯音)，對於西學熱心研究，曾自製天球儀，則當時殆已有地球儀歟。(據奧國 Oberhummer 著 The History of Globes)。

全球災變圖之計畫

去年六月瑞士檢內弗萬國紅十字會提議繪製全球災變圖，調查各國已往及現在之災禍，如地震火山風災海嘯水災旱災大水災蟲荒瘟疫等種種災象各就其地點範圍及程度表之於圖，以便一目了然。可以分別緩急設法救濟，亦可以精細研究設法預防。議決後卽由該會函致各國學術團體，實行，現已由檢內弗地學會會長孟當同(Raoul Montandon)君著有一文，載於紅十字會第五會會誌，附有各種災象圖多幅，可爲此類研究之初步。記者按吾國天災無歲無有，而科學的調查研究向極缺乏，官書報告不盡可恐，私家記載又多掛漏，卽有材料亦多散失，因統計之不確，比較爲難，救濟亦多失效。今國內不乏熱心救濟者於此類事業盍亦留之意乎。

水力生電

原動力之所出，除煤及搾油埋藏有限探勘堪虞之外，厥惟水力一項最爲重要。本年夏間英京倫敦舉行國際力源會議 (International Conference of

58
《世界著名探险家》
1925

陈家骥、陈克文（编译），上海，中文
19×13 cm
上海图书馆

Famous adventurers of the world, 1925
Chen Jiaji & Chen Kewen (eds. & tr.), Shanghai, Chinese
19×13 cm
Shanghai Library

第三部分
日月有常

世界著名探險家 上冊

四

魅之所居，往往出而為祟以屬行人，故死亡者相繼……於是聯羣結伍，始敢首途餘鈴於駝馬之頸，欲休止者則鳴號以相約焉。」

大汗睹故友重來欣喜無量，留此少年之馬哥波羅以官位焉。彼輩留中國凡十七年，時奉大汗之命遠使四方，足跡所屦奇開逸事多列載於其書中也。「每發馬哥波羅之驚奇者，則北京大城也。城門十二，綠以周牆厖長六英里。其自逃云「每城門執戟護衞之士千人，非以總寇也不過以為皇帝之所居，非是不足以示其威嚴且備賓小耳。」其他尚有更華美於此者，『城牆周圍百英里，石橋萬有二千其大者多可容大舟出入其下』此揚州城地（Han-chan）或稱為Kinsai。蓋馬哥波羅所稱之名也。在馬哥波羅逃中國地理種種逸出於大汗及其人民嘉會饗樂之事尤饒與趣。

歲月不居，時節如流，飄然異域，已有多年。威尼斯之鄉園時縈懷想，烏倦飛而知返，遊子思念故鄉，人情大抵然也波羅等將作歸計，但大汗倚畀方隆不肯遽令歸去，適有波斯王者大汗之近戚也，與汗之貴胄之女聯婚，之子歸道經海道，飢阻長途人護送舉國英能膺其任唯波羅等實能，於是使之護送以一二九二年（元世祖至元二十九年）乘四桅大舟十四艘每艘將事者二百五十人，自楊建揚帆逾海而遠颺，當時大汗賜波羅等人實已各一袋，一顆之價值等連城。可謂厚實矣。航行兩載矣已至波斯，已航行兩載矣日代諸人事無常，彼波斯王末睹新人之面而身已入故鬼矣，螺綿長很，天道寧論，而破衣裝百里浪而來之新人將可以處之亦薄命離憐矣。利行舟留五月始能啟椗於是與人將別，而幸前王之子繼父而立，固與成婚事乃無識波羅等之使命已終於是將西歸。既察威尼斯之岸郷園無志風景不殊環顧鄉等我行抵家門，即親之戚屬亦莫能察威尼斯之岸郷園無志風景不殊環顧鄉等我行抵家門，即親之戚屬亦莫能此詩埠為波羅等所詠也。波羅等始知波羅奇怪偉之事以相證然後人始信之斯時威尼斯人之不肯相信於中土大汗之朝者凡十有七年，今日始重歸故里也。波羅乃大張盛筵邀相信者赴宴，盛服麗衣絢爛耀客歷時既開出，破衣搖搖褸垢光乃其途故事者也。舉以示客客皆愕然不知其故波羅於是手持利刃而衣之縫緩處處自上而下劃之，裂口方開而燦爛光采之無價珠寶如飛泉迸落——其美富為威尼斯人所未夢見者於是波羅之名震於威尼斯矣。

馬哥波羅後不得壽終蓋尼斯人與其敵熱那亞人（Genoa）戰，馬哥波羅率戰艦以禦之戰敗被俘，終身為囚虜於熱那亞獄中，無聊因追憶羈書旅行故事為逃斯之干奴

一 馬哥波羅之旅行

五

世界著名探險家 上冊

二

記，其所稱逃東亞者尤為翔實而饒異味，實非常之傑作也。馬哥波羅之大陸遠征，其震駭一時之耳目，蓋不減於其後二百年之哥倫布云。

中華（Land of Far Cathay）之奇蹟及大汗（Great Khan）（稔元朝）之強盛豐富，早已由商人及僧侶之會至亞洲者遍傳於歐洲，而常是時復睹有見悍之亞洲韃靼，馬菲阿與匿哥羅波羅逑洪計探險入亞洲中部一去十有五年始歸啟程時為一二五四年（宋理宗祐二年）自威尼斯逑海而東抵君士坦丁陸行過小亞細亞（Asia Minor）直達布哈拉（Bokhara）韃靼中之一域也，於其後往元朝謁中國皇帝忽必烈汗（Kublai Khan）招與同行欣然從之路阻且長辛跋沙嶮峨高山運亙不絕雪凌峯镶若披白帽偶渡寒風凄凛則飄飄飛雪隨身撲襲可謂險阻艱難備嘗之矣，比其得立於覲謁之庭瞻拜大汗顏色已逾一載矣。千里鎔金爍石炎漠迫人或涉大江滔滔波濤一葉驚渡或遇寒風凄凛則飄飄飛雪隨身撲襲可謂險阻艱難備嘗之矣，比其得立於覲謁之庭瞻拜大汗顏色已逾一載矣。當是時也，大汗久已聞有西方之化此波羅之至即請其命使於羅馬教皇請遣博學之士百

59

名人小史：游历家马哥孛罗
《小朋友》
1927

陈季昂（撰），上海，中文
19×13 cm
上海图书馆

The traveler Marco Polo,
The Little Friend, 1927
Chen Ji'ang (au.), Shanghai, Chinese
19×13 cm
Shanghai Library

第三部分
日 月 有 常

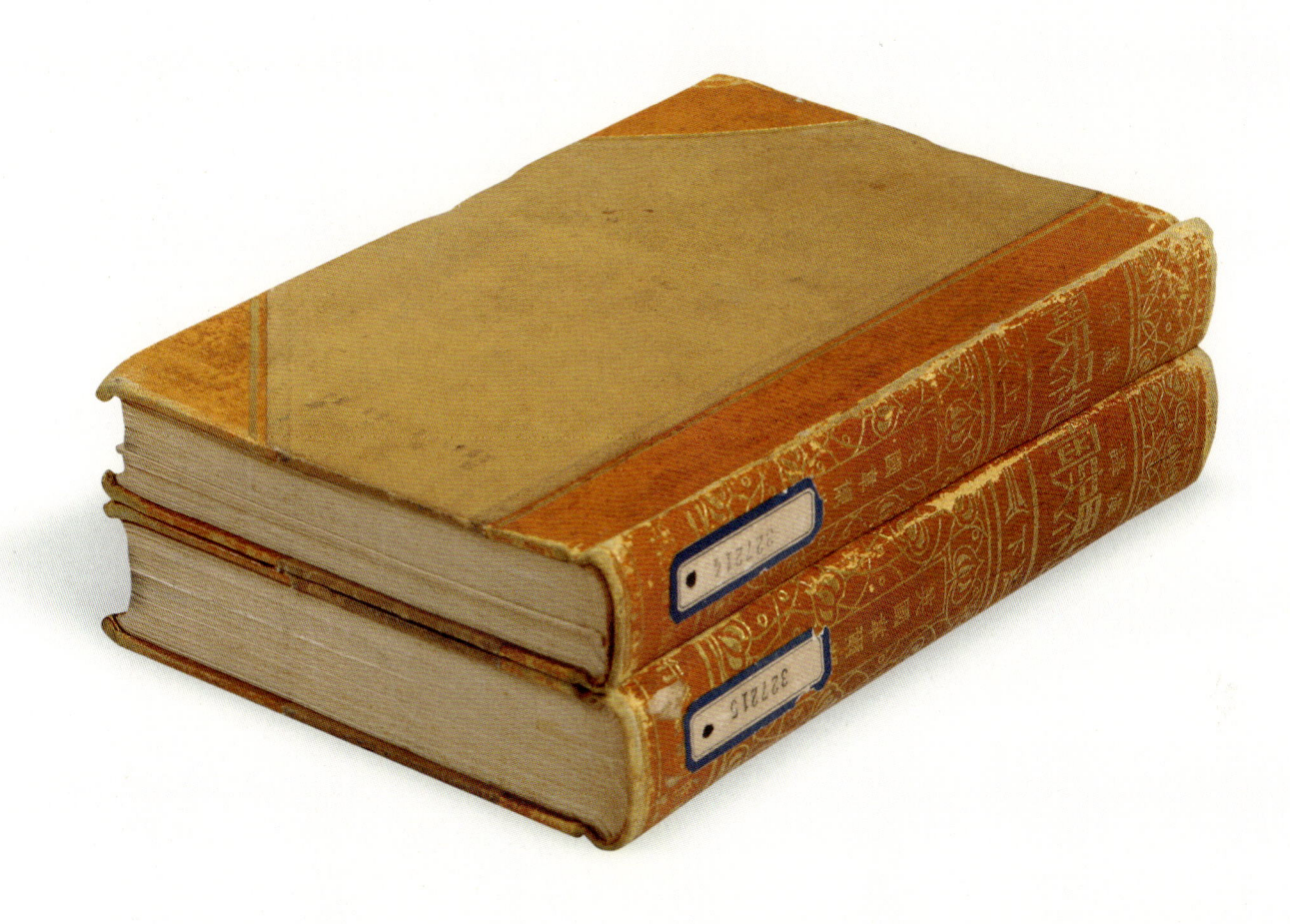

60
《世界史纲（第7册）》
1927

[英] 韦尔斯（著），梁思成（译），上海，中文
23×16 cm
上海图书馆

The outline of history, 1927
Herbert George Wells (au.), Liang Sicheng (tr.),
Shanghai, Chinese
23×16 cm
Shanghai Library

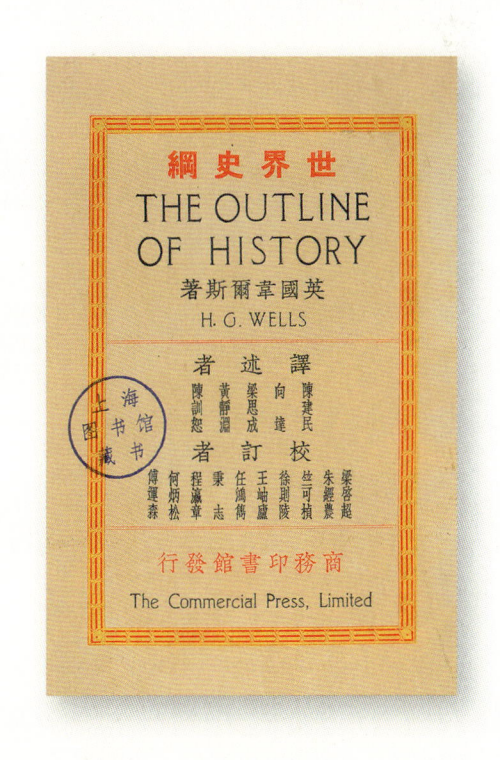

155

61

《艺术三家言》
1927

傅彦长、朱应鹏、张若谷（著），上海，中文
21.5×16 cm
上海图书馆

Talks from three Artists, 1927
Fu Yanchang, Zhu Yingpeng & Zhang Ruogu (au.),
Shanghai, Chinese
21.5×16 cm
Shanghai Library

第三部分
日月有常

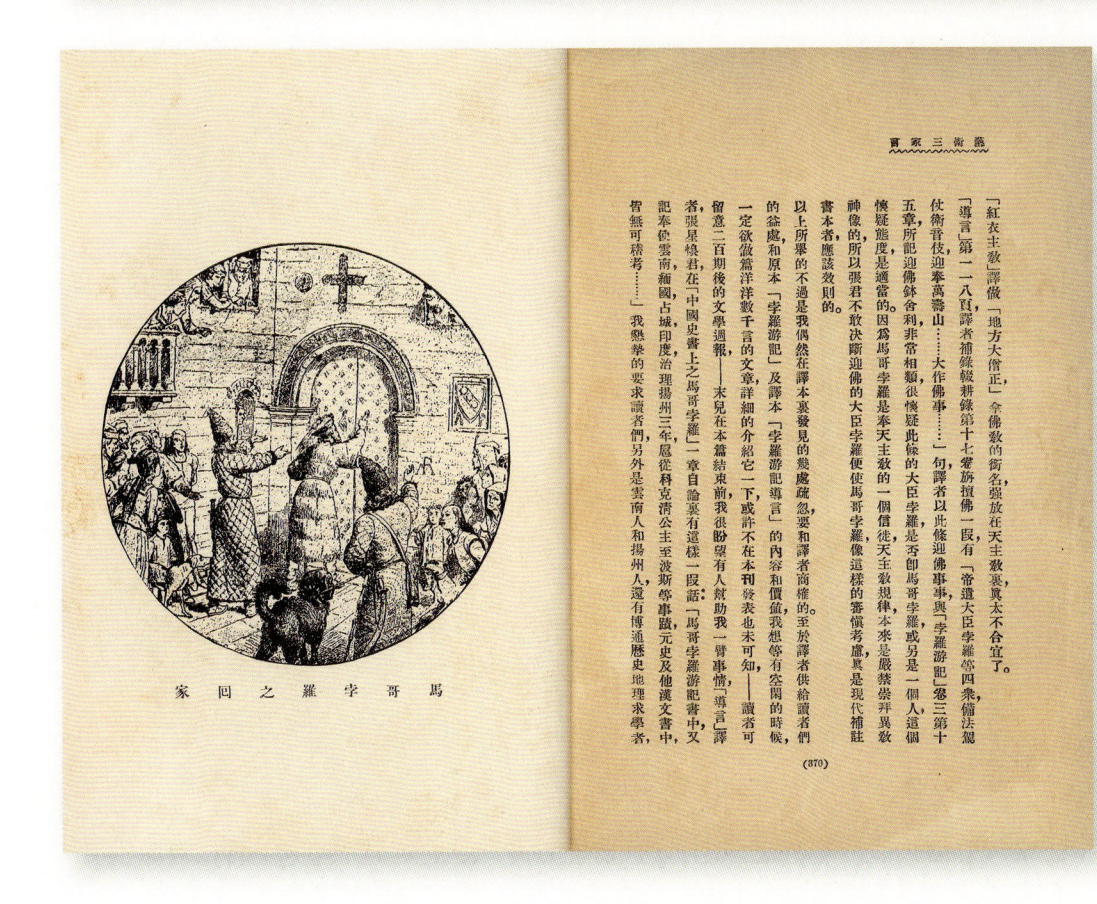

「馬哥孛羅游記」

在去年八月的某天，偶然一時高興，約了幾個不會繪畫而有藝術嗜好的朋友，到蒲柏路藝大二院，參觀晨光美術會第四屆展覽會場，拿到特刊一份，當時見有傅逢長君的「努力進行的藝術思想」一文裏面有這樣一段話：「哥侖布因為讀了馬哥孛羅游記之後，才有關拓新土的野心。」這段文章後，馬哥孛羅游記是勞動的有誘惑性的在藝術思想方面說真是偉大而有趣的作品了。看了這樣看來，「馬哥孛羅游記」六字途深印在我的腦筋中常隨處留意寬訪，總想拿來一睹為快，後來在去年第四期聖敎雜誌上，又看見一他在揚州到關於馬哥孛羅的記載說元朝時有一個意國底商人，名做馬爾谷保羅——卽馬哥孛羅——他在揚州到關於知府，後來問到歐洲很想揚書樓查本有原版的老法文者時我要看「馬哥孛羅游記」的欲望更增熱了，途往徐家滙書樓借到一本張星烺君譯的「馬哥孛羅游記」，起來很感謝辛苦於這部譯本，我會經途扶幾句和譯者商榷文字刊在時事新報附刊「鑑賞週刊」第二十三兩期後來又寫一篇東西專介紹游記的內容論書中主人翁馬哥孛羅並說明此書受當代文學上的

羅孛哥馬

「紅衣主敎」譯做「地方大僧正」余佛敎的銜名強放在天主敎裏竟太不合宜。「導言」第一二八頁譯者補偉耨耕錄第十七零旃揎佛一段有「帝遣大臣孛羅等四衆備法器仗衛晉伐迎奉高鬍山」「大作佛事……」句譯者以此條迎奉佛事與孛羅游記「五章所記迎奉佛鉢舍利非常相類很疑馬哥孛羅是奉天主敎的大臣孛羅便使其一個信徒天主敎的大臣孛羅像這樣的審慎考慮本來是嚴謹謹譽異敎神像的所以張君不敢決斷迎佛的大臣孛羅或另是一個人道懷疑態度是適當的因為馬哥孛羅是奉天主敎的一個信徒天主敎規律本來是嚴謹譽異敎書本者應該說效則的。以上所舉的不過是我偶然在譯本裏發見的幾處疏漏要和譯者商榷的益處和原本「孛羅游記」及譯本「孛羅游記導言」的內容和價值我想在空閒的時候一定欲做篇詳詳細細千言的文章評述它一下或許不在本刊發表也未可知——讀者們留意和原本後期的文學週報，末見在本篇結束前我很盼望有人幫助我一臂專情，「導言」譯者張星烺君在「中國史書上之馬哥孛羅」一章自論裏有這樣一段話：「馬哥孛羅游記上之馬哥孛羅跟元史及他漢文書中記奉使雲南緬國占城印度治理揚州三年歷從科克靑公主至波斯等事皆無可稽考……」
我懇摯的要求讀者們另外是雲南人和揚州人還有傳通歷史地理求學者。

馬哥孛羅之囘家

62
横贯中亚：马可波罗谓喀什噶尔乃新疆最大之城
《时兆月报》
1929

佚名（撰），上海，中文
26×19 cm
上海图书馆

Marco Polo's comments on cities in Xinjiang,
Signs of the Times, 1929
Anonymous (au.), Shanghai, Chinese
26×19 cm
Shanghai Library

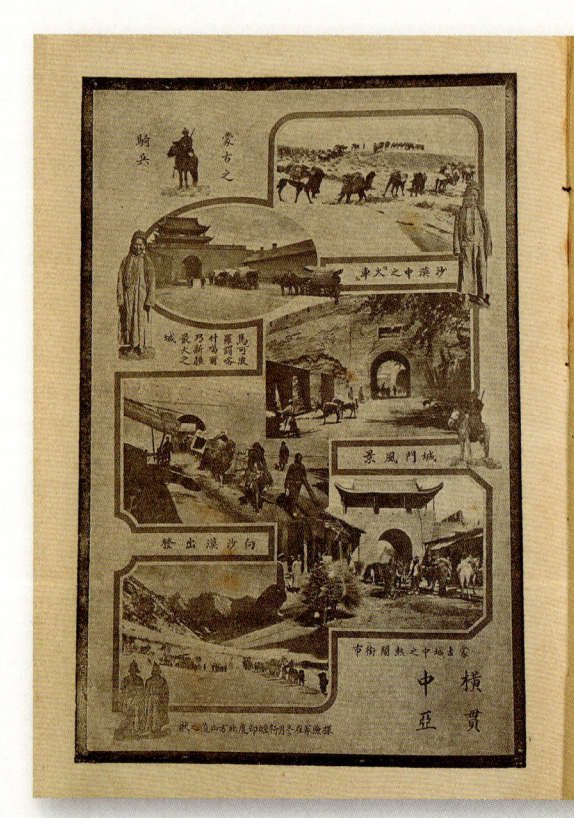

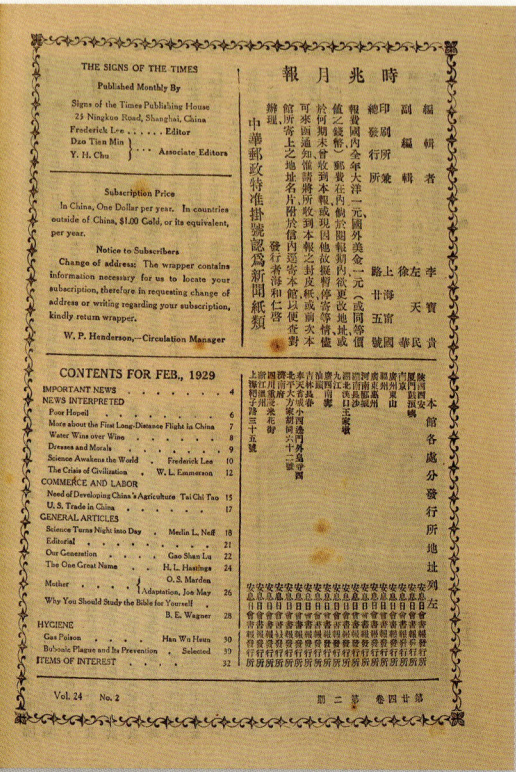

第三部分
日月有常

63
《马哥孛罗》
1931

张星烺（著），上海，中文
17.5×12 cm
上海图书馆

Marco Polo, 1931
Zhang Xinglang (au.), Shanghai, Chinese
17.5×12 cm
Shanghai Library

虚实之界：奇迹之书
《马可·波罗游记》主题文献图录

第一章　马哥学罗郯

第二节　蒙古大帝国情况

蒙古人為遊牧民族，居中國長城以北內外蒙古之地，其地自古即為強悍民族所居；秦漢時，有無語言不通，國際障礙之苦，而反有軍隊保護供給飲食之便者，則為古今未有之蒙古大帝國之樹立也。蒙古大帝國疆宇，東起太平洋，西迄地中海、多腦河、波羅的海南，起印度洋，北至北冰洋，在此廣漠區域內，無蒙古人之許可，雞不得鳴，犬不敢吠。驛站遍於全國兵隊布滿要津，維持秩序，保護行旅，蒙古人不得用驛站即可利用室內，也。自不相交通之中歐，至是乃成一家。共尊蒙古可汗為世界共主。觀極東之北京政治中心焉。有此不相通之東西往來如是其便，而馬哥孛羅乃利用之此遊世界，鮑其眼福，成其盛名。使一部書演成今日面貌之理想。中乘客利用機匠所造飛機航達火星，歸報地球上人類之此交通機會之蒙古大帝國不可不有數語述之，用以表明時代與人物之關係，兼以明孛羅書中所述也。

蒙古人為遊牧民族，居中國長城以北內外蒙古之地，其地自古即為強悍民族所居；秦漢時，有

toninus）於桓帝延熹九年來獻唐書記貞觀十七年拂菻王波多力遣使來獻中國以後歷高宗武后玄宗諸朝皆有使來獻羅馬史家佛羅得斯（Florus）記奧右斯都皇帝時四漢末時中國有使臣朝賀帝之威德達被以上見冊作中西上記載皆糊模影響片斷之辭而所謂使臣或為商販冒充回國以後毫無記載所傳口碑大約卽上方各書所留之記載也以即為真使而古代航海學未精舶船不堅或為洋海中風濤所破斃身魚腹或旅行沙漠中道渴死也各種原因故古以來迄於元初東西皆無直接交通真確詳細記載其情形狷也之代天文家以望遠鏡窺測火星中有黑影狷而搖測其人文明程度之高使人欲往一遊也設有人能親往一遊而何詳言空中航路者何可作後人航空之指南焉探險之飛達火星歸報其中真況者何飛行機中之乘客得達火星久不朽者蓋以能引起今日世界交通故馬哥孛羅狷之飛機其速率千萬倍於今之飛機及造飛機之人乎馬哥孛羅能有此便利由歐洲直達中國沿途豈可忘其飛機及造飛機之人乎馬哥孛羅能有此便利由歐洲直達中國沿途者完全風雲際會使之也造此風雲際會者蒙古人也馬哥孛羅

第三部分
日月有常

64
马可孛罗游记所纪的中国女俗
《妇女杂志》
1931

黄石（撰），上海，中文
26×19 cm
上海图书馆

Culture related to Chinese female in the travelogue of Marco Polo, *The Ladies Journal*, 1931
Huang Shi (au.), Shanghai, Chinese
26×19 cm
Shanghai Library

161

65
马可勃罗东游
《少年时代》
1931

心南、彭芳草（编），上海，中文
19×13 cm
上海图书馆

Marco Polo's Travel to the East,
Youth Magazine, 1931
Xinnan & Peng Fangcao (eds.), Shanghai, Chinese
19×13 cm
Shanghai Library

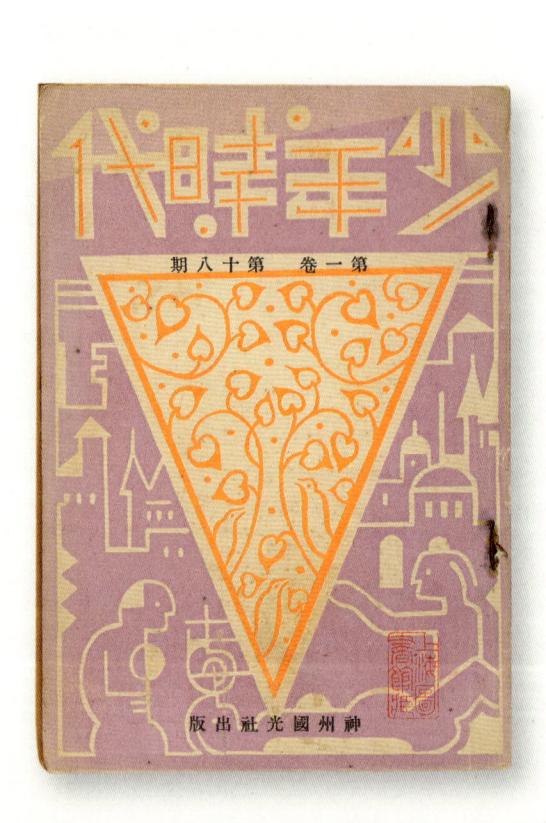

忽必烈像

彼此和靄地致候，友誼地訪問；到渾圓的月亮高懸頭頂的時候，那些遊客便坐於他們的帳篷的陰影之下，談講些怪人異獸的奇事。然而又有時，仇敵的軍隊或兇殘的匪黨來刼掠這些旅行隊。於是徒手打起仗來，甚或全隊都被殺掉，貨物與駱駝均被刼走。除了被野蠻民族攻擊的危險之外，還有在沙漠中迷路的，或因高熱而死的種種時機。

馬可勃羅的父親和叔父就是走到遠東而首先將那富饒的中華帝國之消息傳給威里市的人。但是，只有親聽他們口說，與間接聽見傳說的人，知道他們的大旅行的經歷，很早，他們所說的已經被忘記掉了。馬可勃羅回到家四年以後，於熱那亞威里市的海戰中被俘。他當了熱那亞的俘虜，對同居的囚犯談

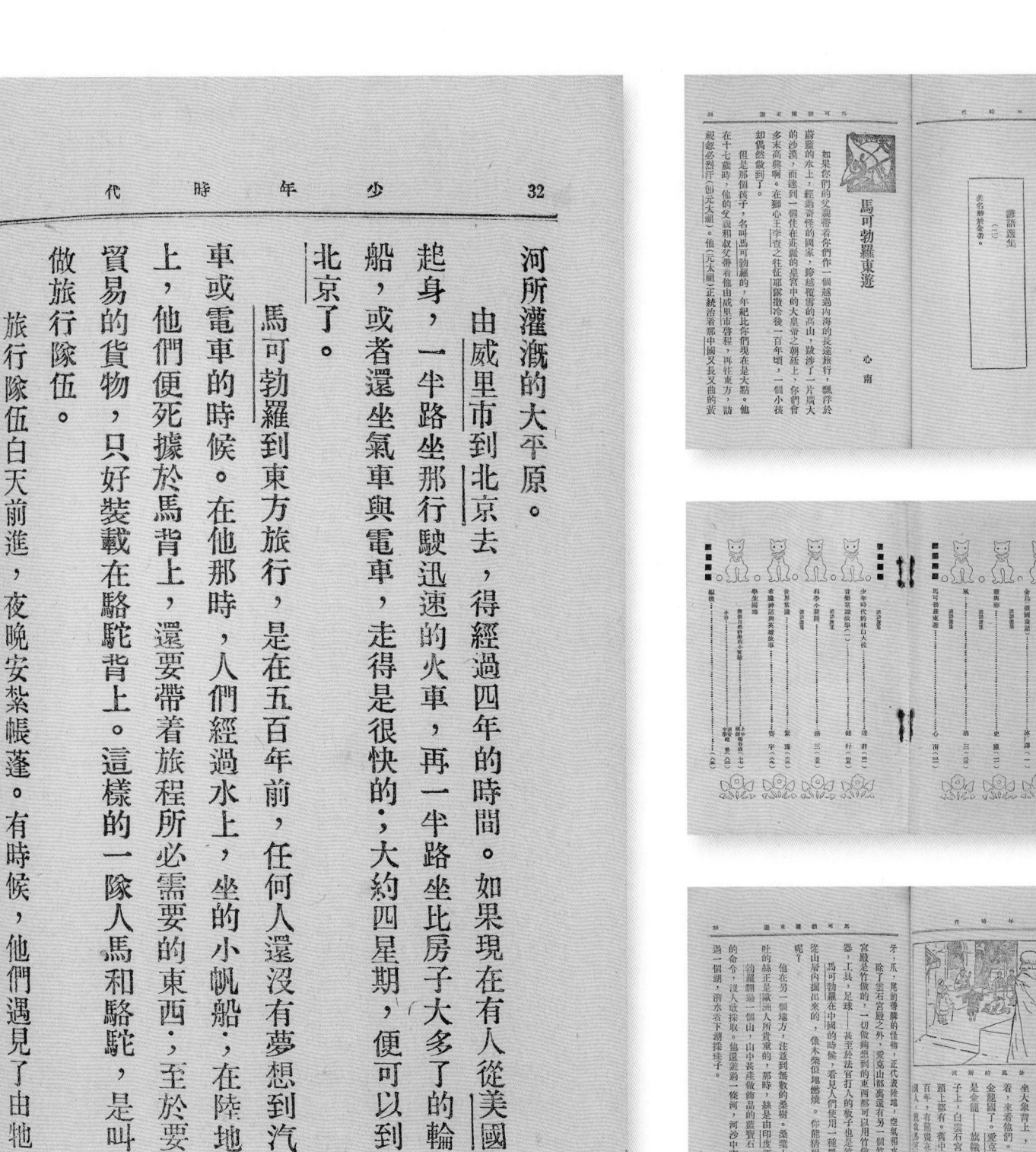

第三部分 日月有常

32 河所灌溉的大平原。

由威里市到北京去，得經過四年的時間。如果現在有人從美國起身，一半路坐那行駛迅速的火車，再一半路坐比房子大多了的輪船，或者還坐氣車與電車，走得是很快的，大約四星期，便可以到北京了。

馬可勃羅到東方旅行，是在五百年前，任何人還沒有夢想到汽車或電車的時候。在他那時，人們經過水上，坐的小帆船；在陸地上，他們便死據於馬背上，還要帶着旅程所必需要的東西；至於要貿易的貨物，只好裝載在駱駝背上。這樣的一隊人馬和駱駝，是叫做旅行隊伍。

旅行隊伍白天前進，夜晚安紮帳蓬。有時候，他們遇見了由地

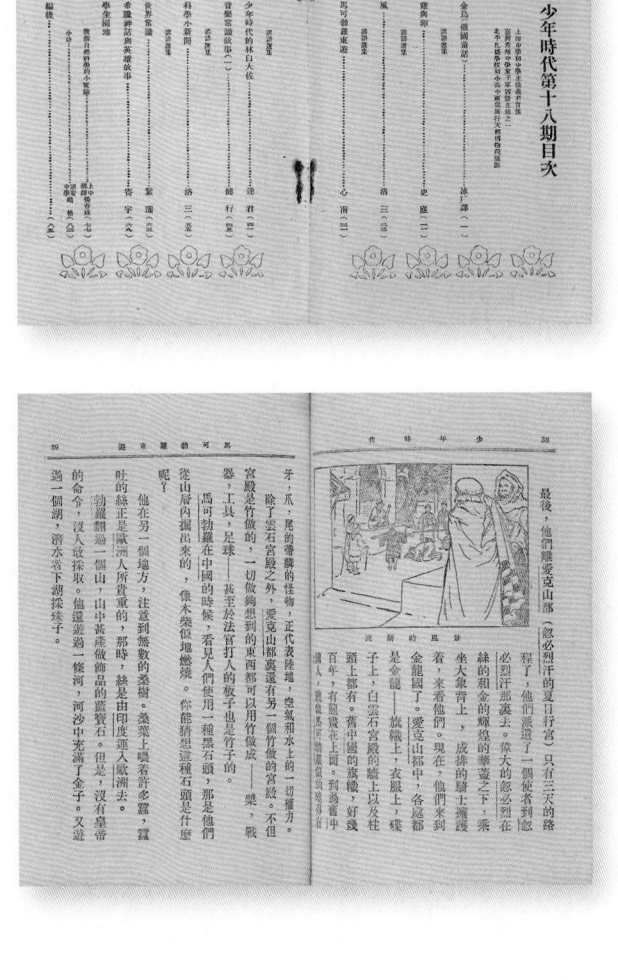

66
《马可波罗（小学生文库本）》
1933

束云逵（著），上海，中文
19×13 cm
上海图书馆

Marco Polo, 1933
Shu Yunkui (au.), Shanghai, Chinese
19×13 cm
Shanghai Library

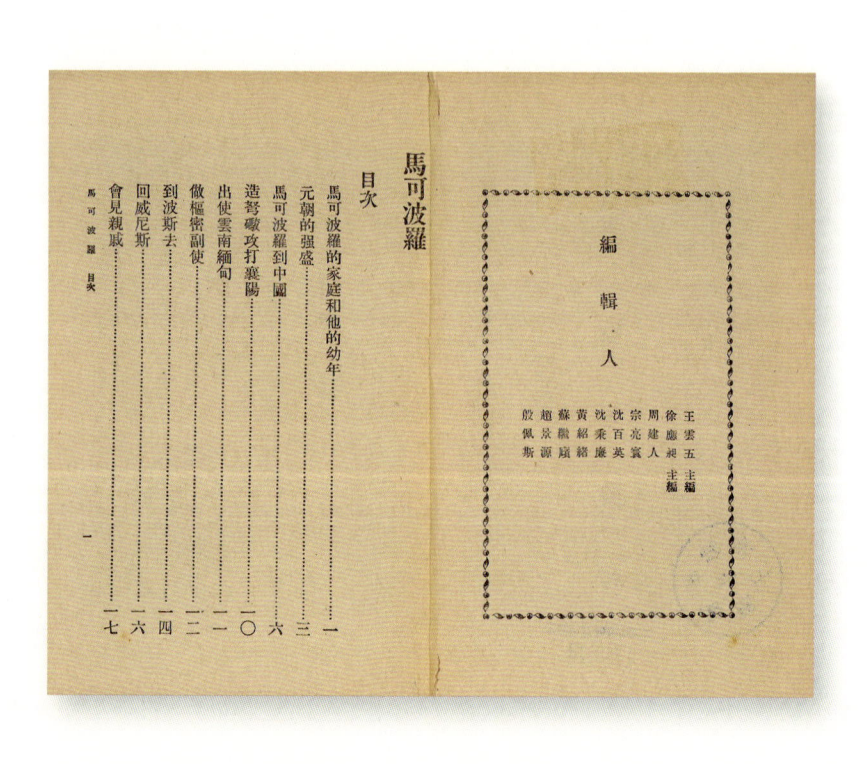

第三部分
日月有常

馬可波羅 目次

熱那亞和威尼斯戰爭 ………………………… 二〇
獄中著書 ……………………………………… 二二
出獄後事蹟 …………………………………… 二三
遊記的內容 …………………………………… 二五
遊記的價值和影響 …………………………… 三〇

馬可波羅

▲**馬可波羅的家庭和他的幼年**

馬可波羅（Marco Polo）是歐洲意大利國人家住在北方的威尼斯市（Venice），生於公元一千二百五十四年。他的祖父名叫安得利亞（Andrea）生了三個兒子：大的叫馬可（Marco，第二個叫尼哥羅（Nicolo），（就是馬可波羅的父親）小的叫馬飛（Maffeo），弟兄三人都善經商。

馬可波羅著了一本遊記，叫做東方見聞錄，書中的內容，大概記載他一生的經歷，尤其以中國元朝的事實為最多因此我們要了解馬可波羅必須先把元朝研究一下。

元朝是蒙古人建立的。他們本來住在中國的北邊（現在外蒙古東北一帶地方。）起初不過是幾個小小的部落，專門以遊牧為生人民很強悍，善於騎馬射箭所以很喜歡同人家打仗後來出了一個很利害的酋長名叫鐵木真，一號成吉斯汗，把幾個散漫的部落通通征服了，成了一個強大的部落先侵略金國又摧滅了印度和波斯。再用兵向西困花刺子模國主穆罕默德（Mohammed）於裏海的孤島上後來又越過高加索山侵入俄國南部公元一千二百二十三年的夏天大敗欽察和俄羅斯的聯軍這是蒙古人第一次的侵入歐洲。

後來成吉斯汗死了，他的兒子窩闊台繼續他的遺志第二次遠征歐洲。

67
《初中本国史》
1934

姚绍华（编），上海，中文
20.5×14 cm
上海图书馆

National history for junior high school, 1934
Yao Shaohua (ed.), Shanghai, Chinese
20.5×14 cm
Shanghai Library

第三部分
日月有常

四　蒙哥派甚麼人督兵西征？和甚麼人來攻南宋？當時南宋是甚麼人當國？他怎樣對付這緊張的局面？

五　蒙古在甚麼時候纔改稱國號為元？當元兵南逼時，南宋出了那幾個民族英雄？試略述他們抵抗元兵的經過。

六　試略述蒙古帝國的版圖？試略述蒙古帝國分治的情形。

第二十一章　中國文化之西漸

元代跨著歐亞兩洲，建立空前大帝國，東西水路交通，因而大盛：

元代之東西交通

在陸路方面，自拔都西征後，東西交通之路已開，後因太宗窩闊臺的提議，各汗國境內，都設立驛站，增置守備，於是從東亞以至東歐，彼此商販互通，行旅無阻。當時陸地重要的通路有二：一經天山北路出西伯利亞南部，一經俄國境南路出中央亞細亞，經亞剌伯以至歐洲，是為

南道。

至海路方面，則自元世祖招徠互市後，一時南洋諸國，甚至沿印度洋以至波斯灣等地居民，都相率來中國貿易。當時杭州上海澉浦溫州慶元（今寧波）廣東泉州等七港，均設有市舶司，以檢查輸出輸入的貨物；而泉州一港，尤當時世界上最著名的一個大商埠。

東西交通既開，歐洲人也有來中國的。教士有柏朗嘉賓[一]和羅伯魯[二]，商人則有馬哥孛羅[三]。馬哥孛羅曾在元朝做了十七年的官。歸國後，著書傳示歐人，極稱中國的富盛，實開後此歐人欣羨東方、發見新航路的動機。

註　[一]柏朗嘉賓，意大利人。他於一二四五年四月，奉敎皇英諾森四世(Innocent IV)之命，由里昂起程，來東方傳敎，直至翌年七月二十二日纔由拔都道入和林，時蒙古定宗貴由新卽大汗位，於傳敎事來常措意，柏氏不得要領而歸。

[二]羅伯魯，英名爲 William of Rubruick，一名巴爾多祿茂 (Bartholomew of Cremona)。他和他隨員三人，先由海道至彼都駐節處，於一二五二年十一月自其地到達和林，見蒙哥大汗，無結果而歸。[三]馬哥孛羅，英

名爲 Marco Polo，意大利威尼斯人。幼隨其父由陸路來中國，從他到上都的一二七五年起，至一二九二年止，馬哥孛羅任大汗親信，備顧問者歷十七年，且曾過印度。任揚州樞密副使三年，一二九二年由海路歸國，一二九五年纔囘抵威尼斯故鄉。

羅盤火藥印刷輸入歐洲

現在世界上所用的羅盤、火藥、印刷三種利器，都由我漢民族首先發明，逐漸傳入歐洲去的。大約這三種利器的應用，却都已很完備。現將這三種利器的發明，可是到了宋代，四川雲南和林均有其足跡，歷及西傳的情形，略述於下：

一、羅盤　羅盤的製造，是利用磁針的指極性。磁針的作用，我國在戰國時候，就已有人發明[四]。到北宋時，看風水的和航海的，每用他來定方向[五]。後來西人便利用他來發展航海貿易。據他們自己說，是由亞剌伯人從中國傳過去的[六]。

二、火藥　火藥的製造，雖不知道起源於甚麼時候，但在北宋的官書上，已經載有製造火藥的方法[七]。到了南宋虞允文，用紙包裹硫磺石炭，做成

68
中西文化交通史上重要史料：
马哥孛罗同时代人真福和德理游记
《我存杂志》
1934

卢伽（译），杭州，中文
25×18 cm
上海图书馆

The Travel of the Blessed Odorico da Pordenone, a contemporary of Marco Polo,
Wocun, 1934
Lu Jia (tr.), Hangzhou, Chinese
25×18 cm
Shanghai Library

聖教歷史欄

中西文化交通史上重要史料

馬哥孛羅同時代人

盧伽譯

真福和德理遊記

在三十年前，梁任公先生論廣州一文，就提到這一部著名的遊記，原文發表在新民叢報中；或許因為見過郭棟臣先生在光緒戊子年的譯本，嫌近英國倫敦 Jonathan Cape 出版的遊書中，於一九二八年刊行了一部馬哥孛羅同時代人的遊記，是由 Manuel Komroff 君編的。我現在試將其中的一分，卽真福和德理遊記重譯成為現代語體文。題前先說幾句話。

因為前年是真福和德理逝世六百年的紀念，我曾受了同志的敦促，為宣傳計，重譯此書。去年六月六日，宗座駐華代表，泰來到羅瑪聖禮部五月十八日公文，通令中國教會每年正月十四日，舉行慶祝真福和德理體禮。我以前讀每一個研究中西文化史的，愛讀這一部遊記。現在我努力研究文化史，愛讀這一部遊記，頌揚教會敬禮的聖人！

六百年前，這位聖人，沐九萬里的風霜，歷十六年的經營，非商業上的經營，非政治上的企圖，非軍事上的野心險圖，來華宣傳福音！有這一部遊記留給我們，正可供我們紀念和敬禮他呢！

本叢書的編者介紹：「和德理生於一二八六年，卽元朝至元二十三年，青年時卽入芳濟會，住在他們的修院中。不久他的聲譽也傳遠廣了。他是馬哥孛羅後第一個大旅行家，描寫這一部分的世界，尤其是奔於觀察人情風俗，是他長途中。曾經作伴的，一個愛爾蘭人 Irishman，名雅各伯 James 者，由運河來北平。時時，穿行大陸，到亞洲，經西藏，波斯，及著名的 Assassius 的地方。他死於一三三一年正月，在五丁修院中目的，是虔敬的高尚者。」訪麗州。

（?）及波羅洲 Borneo，抵馬建，杭州，經西藏，波斯，及著名的 Assassius 的地方。他是馬哥孛羅後第一個大旅行家，描寫這一部分的世界，尤其是奔於觀察人情風俗，包，喝的是清水，赤足無履，身穿「苦衣」（

所謂「苦衣」，是某種鐵絲作成，而有刺的，為宗教家克己苦身的用品！）在他未出發旅行以前，就有了許多奇行奇蹟云。約至一三一八年，和德理已抵印度西境，為擴大傳教運動。一三三一年前，卽抵印度西境，為擴大傳教運動。一三三一年前，卽抵廣華，而留駐者，凡經三年。在他的行程中，他嘗調多默聖宗徒的地方，又航行至蘇門答剌島 Sumatra 爪哇 Java（?）及波羅洲 Borneo，抵馬建，杭州，經西藏，波斯，及著名的 Assassius 的地方。他是馬哥孛羅後第一個大旅行家，描寫這一部分的世界，尤其是奔於觀察人情風俗，不久他的聲譽也傳遠廣了。他死於一三三一年正月，在五丁修院 Udine 地方。

後人研究此種舊俗而努力改也；卽此對於研究民俗學的，亦有偉大精神的貢獻！凡我同志學友請追隨而努力！

一九三三年春聖後學盧伽謹譯並序

芳濟會士傳教東來
聖和德理口授行程

第一章

話說世界風土民俗，已有各種專家記載，故事奇聞，五花六門；可是我，兄弟和德理，福樂儒利人，為願往見那未奉教的違反國去了，也頗耳聞目睹那些好些奇異的事情，那些我能忠實的報告。

最初，我從比拉起程，經君士坦丁，那麼得加以更正後再付梓！

至於遊記中關於風俗人情的記載，乃六百年前的民俗，雖有如此鄰愚難以理喻者，正可。

便到了德必索 Trebizond 。這地方是佔便利的位置，對於波斯人和欺地亞人，同海外的別國

馬哥孛羅省略未詳的，他描寫了。據說有過一位爵士 Sir John Mandevile 如果他不是所謂烏有先生的話，他抄襲了和德理的記事，做成了他的虛偽的遊記呢！

以上譯述本叢書編者的引言。譯者需要附加下列的幾點聲明：

（一）本譯文，和郭譯的章節不同，本譯祗十八章，郭譯分為七十四章，續有二章，追遺一章，且多若干關於教事的記載，後將錄出，另成附編。

（二）本譯文，據其譯者所知，附註若干新考證。

（三）重譯者自誌庸才，容有疏陋的缺點，敬祈專家，不客指正，「悼將來欲衷印一冊時，得加以更正後再付梓！

至於遊記中關於風俗人情的記載，乃六百年前的民俗，雖有如此鄙愚難以理喻者，正可

69

横贯欧亚旅行之马哥波罗
《交通职工月报》
1934

伟公（撰），上海，中文
26×19 cm
上海图书馆

Marco Polo, a traveler across Euro-Asia,
Monthly Magazine of Traffic Employees, 1934
Weigong (au.), Shanghai, Chinese
26×19 cm
Shanghai Library

第三部分
日月有常

70
介绍欧人来华的一个先驱：马哥波罗 《国际贸易导报》
1934

佚名（撰），上海，中文
26×19 cm
上海图书馆

Marco Polo, a pioneer of Europe in China, *International Trade Herald*,
1934
Anonymous (au.), Shanghai, Chinese
26×19 cm
Shanghai Library

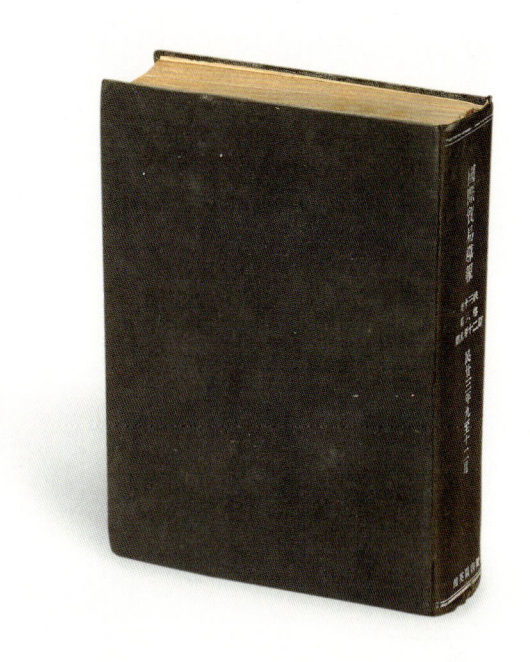

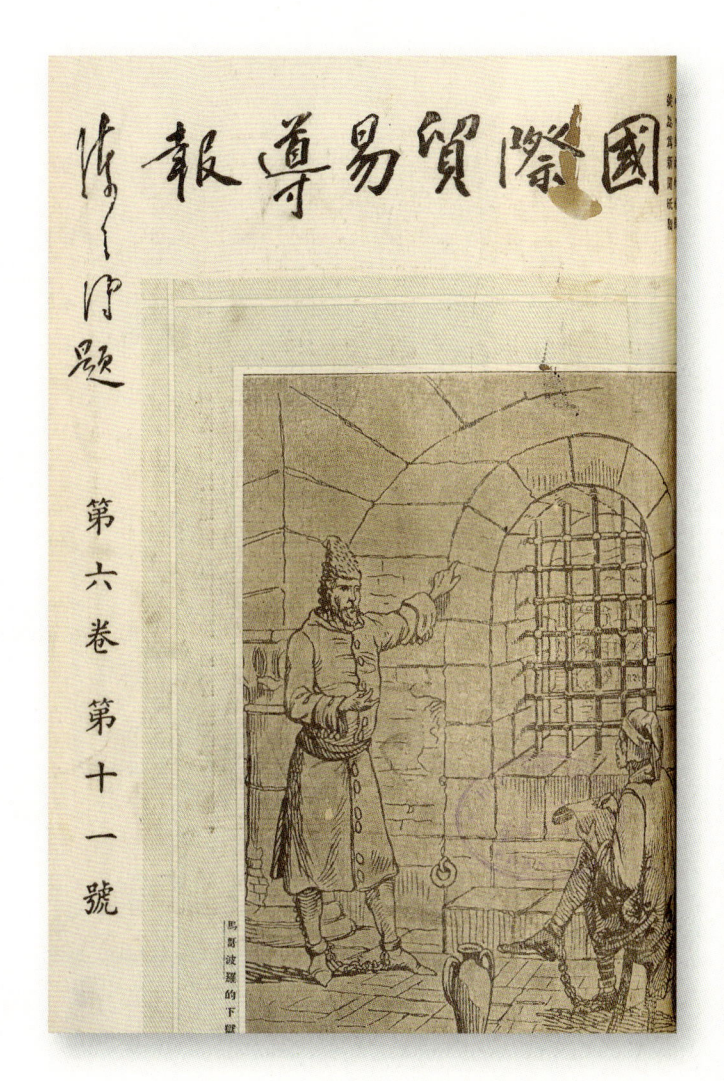

171

71
元代的西方客人
——读《元代客卿马可波罗游记》
《文化建设》
1935

学敏（撰），上海，中文
26×19 cm
上海图书馆

A Western guest in Yuan Dynasty: review of *The Travels of Marco Polo*, *Wennhwa Kiensheh Monthly*, 1935
Xuemin (au.), Shanghai, Chinese
26×19 cm
Shanghai Library

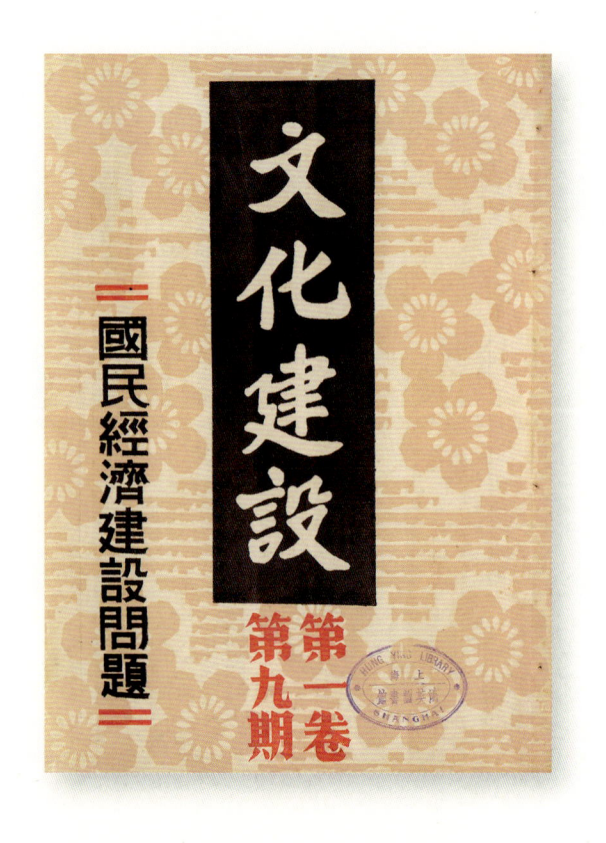

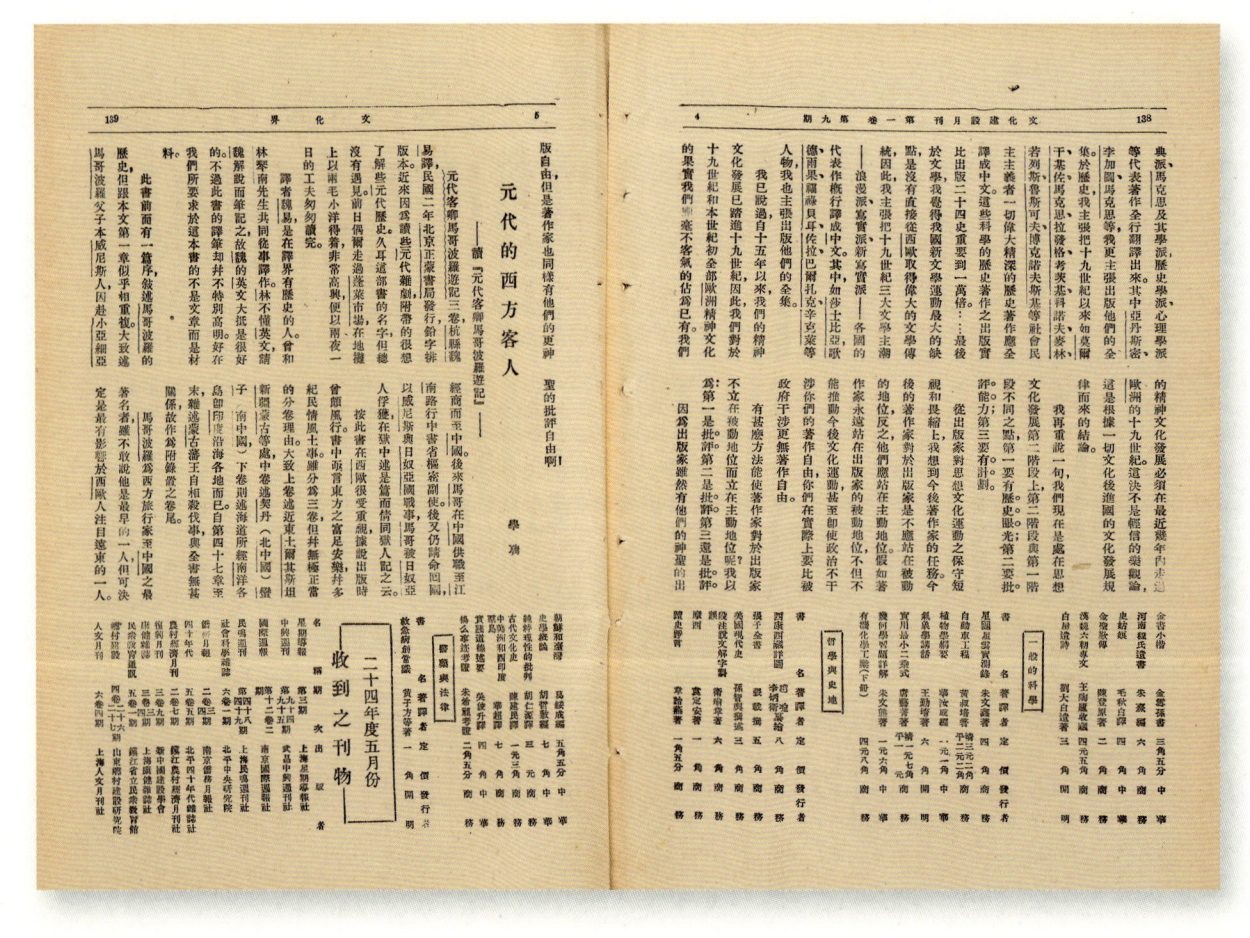

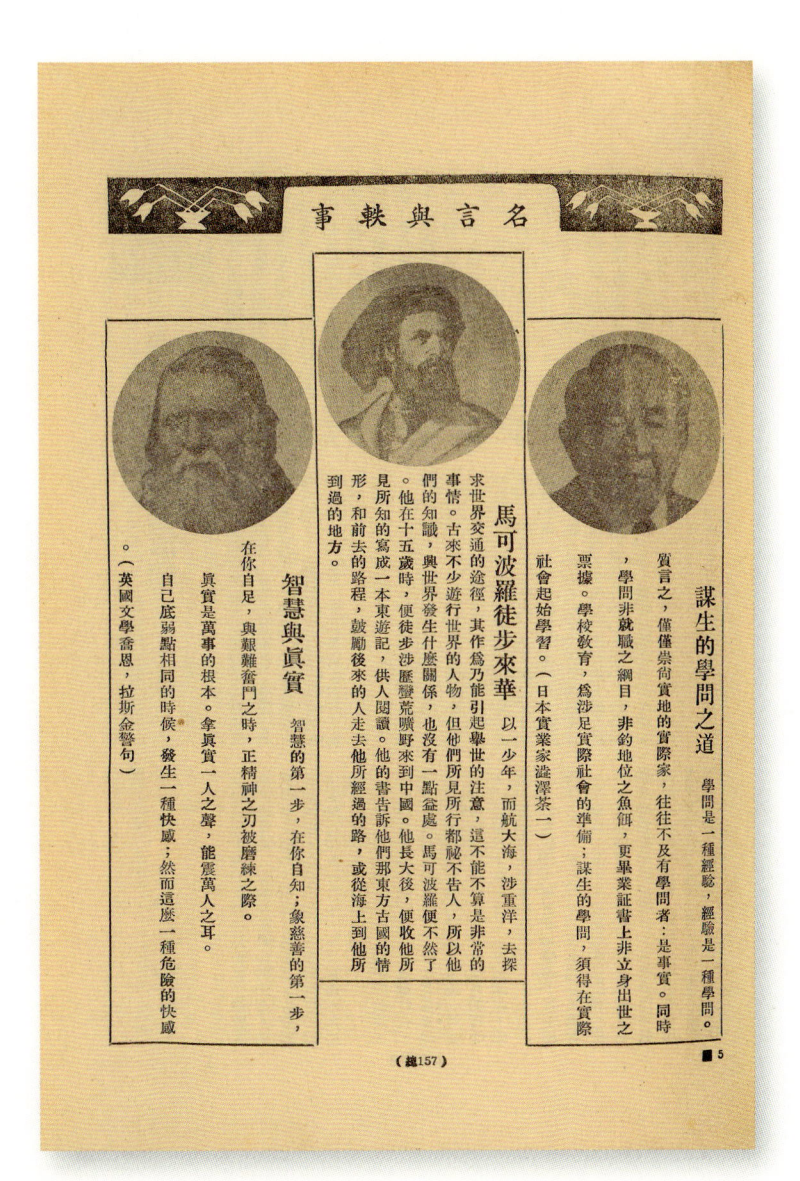

第三部分
日月有常

72

名言与轶事：马可波罗徒步来华
《现代青年半月刊》
1936

佚名（撰），北京，中文
26×19 cm
上海图书馆

Anecdote: Marco Polo's journey to China on foot,
Modern Youth Fortnightly, 1936
Anonymous (au.), Beijing, Chinese
26×19 cm
Shanghai Library

73

东西两大旅行家
——马哥波罗和徐霞客
《家庭星期》
1937

尤怀皋（著），上海，中文
26×19 cm
上海图书馆

Marco Polo and Xu Xiake, two great travelers,
Family Weekly, 1937
You Huaigao (au.), Shanghai, Chinese
26×19 cm
Shanghai Library

哥波羅的出世。

他們到了北京，其時元帝已是一個老年人，但是他的威力卻是非常偉大。因為他喜歡馬哥波羅，他就叫他學中國的文字，居然能說許多中國各地的方言，後來元帝又派他做專使，到中國內地各處去遊歷和考察，一次到過西藏，他把各處的民風物景寫成一書。據說他還做了三年杭州總督啦。

這一次他們三個人在中國竟住了長長的二十年。他們屢次想囘祖國，可是總得不到元帝的允許。後來因為元帝要送一個某王的公主嫁與一位皇孫到波斯去，忽必烈就給了很多的財物，叫他順道向歐洲各國的君主，傳達元帝的好意。於一二九二年，他又離開中國出發到波斯去了。

此次到波斯國，走的是海路，經過了兩年的航程，始行到達，當時的困苦艱難可以想見了，隨從的人死去很多。後來他們再從波斯囘到意國去，從此就沒有囘到中國，那時他年齡已很大了。他很受本國人的敬仰，因為他是第一個人把亞細亞洲全部路綫規劃出來的。他的足跡走遍了中國，印度，日本，爪哇，蘇門達臘及波斯，可以算是一個空前絶後的旅行家了。

作第二次的遊歷，這一次所經多的旅行，人——馬哥波羅，也可說是我們的主要人物馬

號，江陰人，生於明萬曆十四年，西曆一五八一生的游程搞成一表，可以知道他游踪的普遍和年月的攸久了。

廿二歲　始游太湖，登東西洞庭兩山，訪雲威丈人遺跡，母王夫人為製遠遊冠，以壯其行。

廿四歲　游齊，魯，燕，冀間，上泰岱，拜孔林，謁孟廟三遷故里，嶧山吊枯桐。

廿八歲　入浙，獨走甯波，渡海游落迦山，返趨天台，雁宕。

廿九歲　冬游金陵。

卅一歲　游安徽之白岳，黃山，武夷，九曲。

卅三歲　游廬山，再游黃山。

卅五歲　游福建仙游縣之九鯉湖。

卅八歲　游河南嵩山少林寺，出潼關入陝，返游嵩山。

卅九歲　游華山。

四三歲　游閩後入粵邊，游浮羅，經建甌延平，間至漳州。

四四歲　游京師，游盤山。

四五歲　再游閩。

四七歲　再游浙之天台，雁宕；游能仁寺，重游太湖之洞庭。

四八歲　游山西之五台山及恆山，同年再赴

，一生他是早年喪父，在父喪之後，被羣豪所欺，但是他喜受了些閑氣。在他幼年的時候，他喜歡讀奇書，已能「博覽古今書籍，及輿地表，山海圖經，喜搜古人逸事。」他生來清高，所以不屑趨豪貴，博名高。他事母最孝，替他母親到過西藏，王夫人建了一所晴山堂。母親死後，他是三年不遠游，在家守孝。他家裏很富有，所以他能「以布衣而得交當時名士，多藏奇書，出游四方，自給旅費，未嘗有求於人。」

當時在明末的時代，魏忠賢當權，殺害忠良，正是國難日急，國家最黑暗的時代，所以他絕意功名，決意向自然界去求真知識，他不是一個普通的旅行者。吳江潘次耕先生的舊序裏說來最透明，他說：「霞客一遊，在中州者，無大過人；其奇絕者：闐粵楚蜀滇黔，百蠻荒徼之區，皆往返再四，其行不從官道，輒迂迴屈曲以尋之；先審視山脈如何去來，水脈如何分合，既得大勢後，一丘一壑，支搜節討。登不必有徑，荒榛密箐，無不穿也；涉不必有津，衝溫惡瀧，無不絕也。峯極危者，必躍而踞其巔，洞極遙者，必猿掛蛇行，窮其旁出之竇。途窮不憂，行悞不悔。瞑則寢樹石之間，飢則嚙花木之實。不避風雨，

第三部分 日月有常

東西兩大旅行家——馬哥波羅和徐霞客

尤懷皋

一、馬哥波羅 Marco Polo

在西曆一二九五年,大約六百四十二年前的一天,有三個飽經風霜,滿面鬍子的怪人,回到意大利的凡尼斯城來(Venice)。他們都穿了破舊不堪的外國式衣服,樣子很奇怪。他們自己說一個叫做尼格羅波羅 Necolo Polo,一個叫摩非波羅 Matfeo Polo,還有一個摩非的兒子馬哥波羅 Marco Polo。他們是新從中國回來,據說在中國居住了二十多年,現在回到本國來,甚至他們的親屬都不認識他們,以為他們早已都死去了。

這三位波羅先生,開了一個大宴會,邀集了全城的紳士和領袖。當宴會的時候,他們好像演戲一樣的換了三次中國帶去的錦繡衣服,先生們也隨同到了中國。當時派去的幾個專使,因這班專使先生必須同到元朝大皇帝派去的幾個專使,因這班專使先生必須同到元朝大皇帝那地方遇見元朝大皇帝忽必烈已在一個大城叫白克里來Bokhara在那地方遇見元朝大皇帝派去的幾個專使,因這班專使先生必須同到元朝大皇帝那裡,二位波羅先生也隨同到了中國。當時忽必烈已在一二六七年做了中國的皇帝了。這個皇帝雖然雄踞了亞洲大部份的土地

以後就把這衣服分割給與來賓以作紀念。在乘客人驚異之中,波羅先生就把他們途中所穿的三件破棉衣取來,當眾把他割開,取出來很多很多的寶貝——有寶石、青玉、金鋼鑽等,都是無價之寶,這種寶物是元朝皇帝賜給他們的。金銀笨重,攜帶不便,所以換取了寶石帶回來的。這班凡尼斯人

貴的待遇。

先前馬哥波羅還是一個嬰孩,他的父親和他的叔父冒了大險到克利米(Cremia)去販買貨物,後來愈走愈遠竟到達了中亞西亞,在中國新疆的西,一個大城叫阿富汗的北,一

九六六年,那時尼格羅的妻子已經死了,摩格波羅已是十五歲了。他們費了很多的困難才把元帝的意思達到了教皇,可是並沒有什麼效果。

因此他們二人就囘到凡尼斯去,時在一二

到過歐洲人,現在聽了這白種人的一番陳述,引起了很大的興趣,所以元帝忽必烈就派他們囘到義大利去見教皇,名義是中國的專使,希望教皇派一百個教師到中國來傳道及溝通文化

74
马哥孛罗（冒险家故事连载）
《少年读物（创刊号）》
1938

[美] 凯兹（著），一知（译），上海，中文
20.5×15 cm
上海图书馆

Marco Polo (serial of an adventurer),
Teen Magazine, 1938
Keltz (au.), Yizhi (tr.), Shanghai, Chinese
20.5×15 cm
Shanghai Library

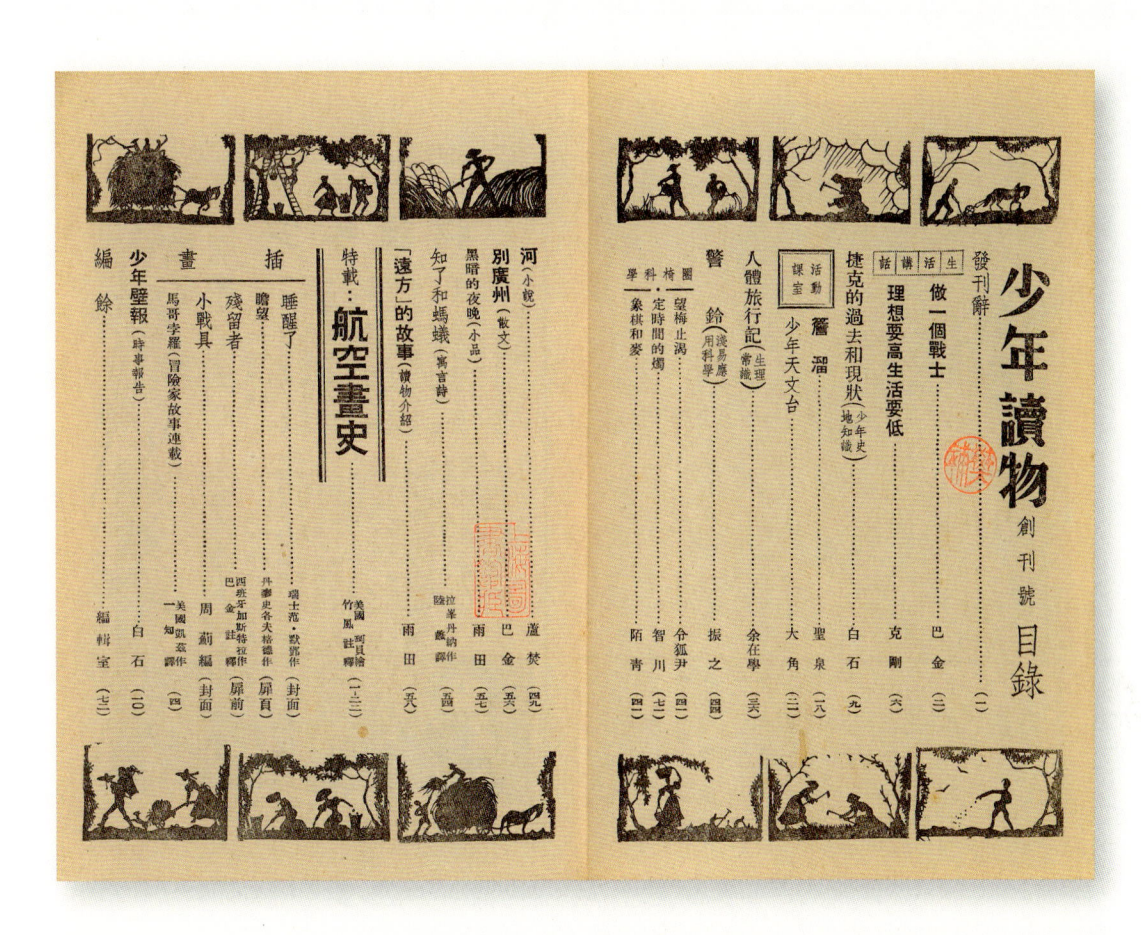

第三部分
日月有常

《少年讀物》創刊號 目錄

發刊辭 .... 巴金（1）

生活講話
做一個戰士 .... 巴金（3）
理想要高生活要低 .... 克剛（6）
捷克的過去和現狀（少年史地知識）......... 白石（9）

活動課室
篁 溜 .... 少年天文台
人體旅行記（生理）........................... 余在學（18）
籐椅（常識）................................. 大角（22）
警 鈴（遠易廢用科學）....................... 令狐尹（七）
望梅止渴（定時間的燭）..................... 振之圓（七）
科學定時間的燭 .... 智川（七）
象棋和麥 .... 陌青（四）

特載：航空畫史

插畫
睡醒了 .... 瑞士克·歐駕作（封面）
瞻望 .... 丹麥·阿貝納作（扉頁）
殘留者 .... 四班牙加斯夫精編作（扉前）
小戰具 .... 巴金註釋（四）
知了和螞蟻（寓言詩）....... 拉峰丹納作 陸蠡譯（四）
「遠方」的故事（讀物介紹）................. 雨田（英）
別廣州（散文）............................. 雨田（五）
河（小說）................................. 巴金（六）
馬哥孛羅（冒險家故事連載）............... 周蘇編 周石（封面）
少年壁報（時事報告）....................... 一知（10）
編 餘 .... 編輯室（七）

馬哥·孛羅 第一個來華的西方人

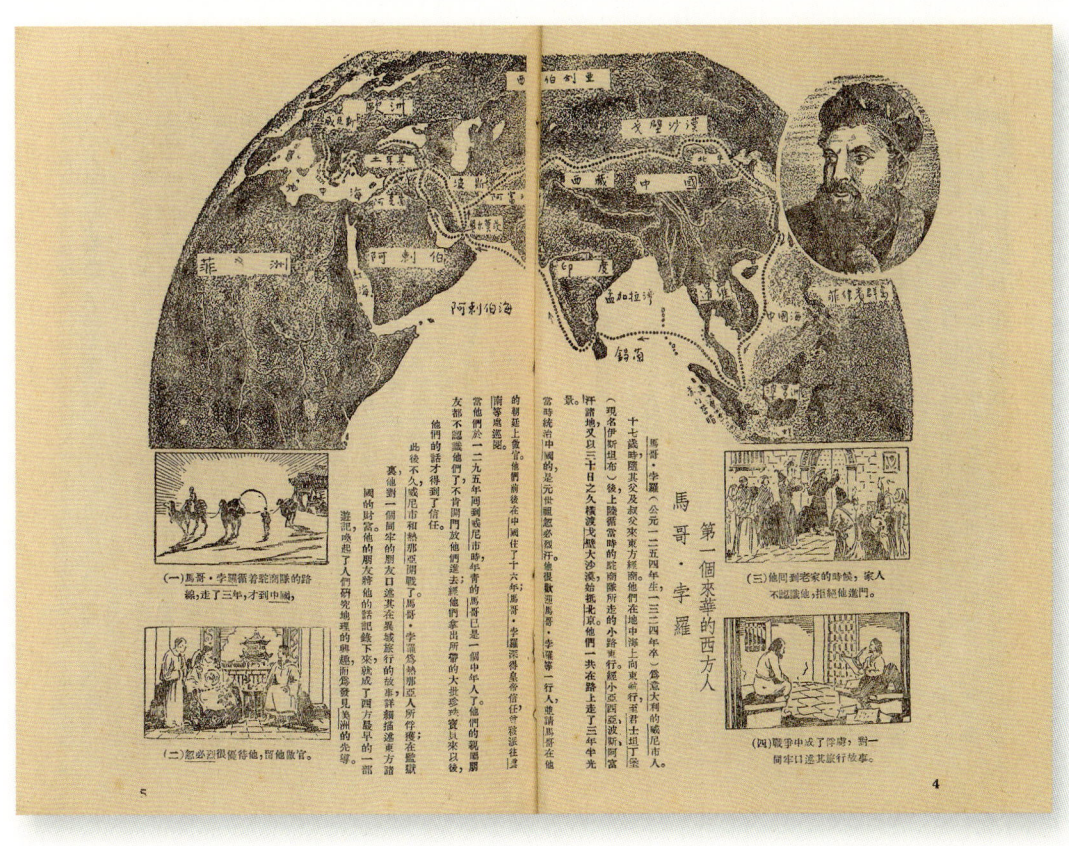

馬哥·孛羅（公元一二五四年生，一三二四年卒）是意大利威尼斯市人。
（一）馬哥·孛羅著著商隊的踪跡，走了三年，才到中國。
（二）起必烈很待他，留他旅行。
（三）他回到老家的時候，家人不認識他，指認他叫門。
（四）戰爭中成了俘虜，對一個牢囚述其旅行故事。

75

马可波罗云南行纪笺证
《西南边疆》
1939

方国瑜（撰），昆明，中文
26×19 cm
上海图书馆

Notes on Marco Polo's travel in Yunnan,
Southwest Frontier Research, 1939
Fang Guoyu (au.), Kunming, Chinese
26×19 cm
Shanghai Library

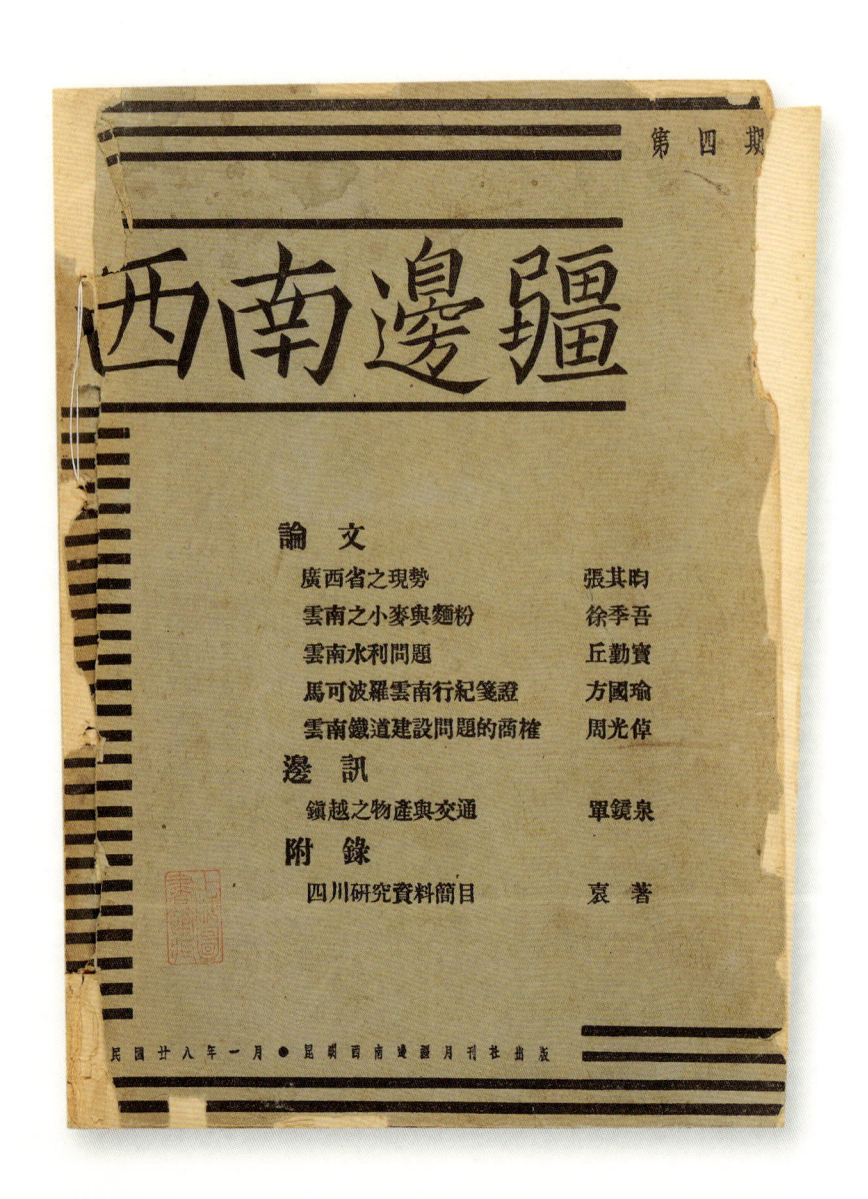

第三部分
日 月 有 常

76

马可波罗之歌（长诗）
《改进》
1939

[美] 贝奈（著），周学普（译），福建永安，中文
25×18.5 cm
上海图书馆

A Song for Marco Polo,
Improvement, 1939
Stephen Vincent Benét (au.), Zhou Xuepu (tr.), Yong'an, Fujian,
Chinese
25×18.5 cm
Shanghai Library

第三部分
日月有常

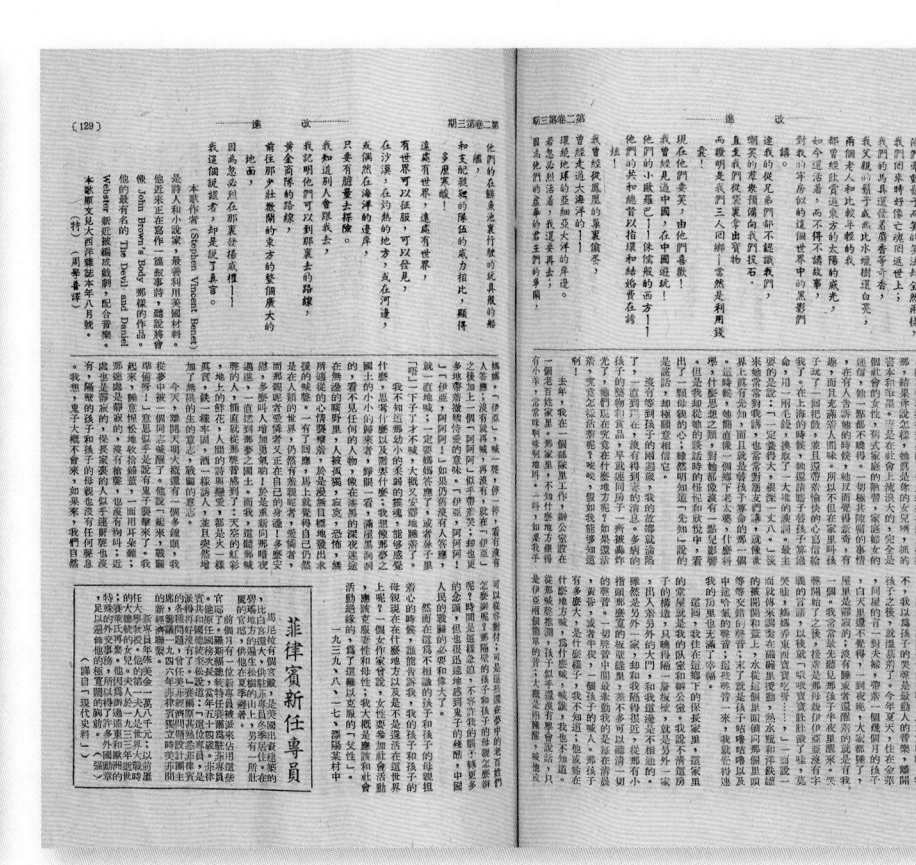

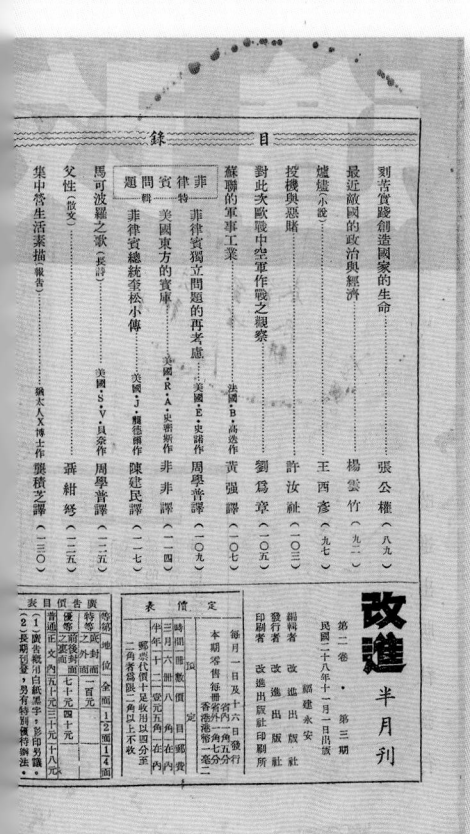

77

影迷信箱：马哥孛罗片中的布景
《好莱坞（上海）》
1939

电影周刊社（编），上海，中文
26×18.5 cm
上海图书馆

Fans correspondence: scenes in the film Marco Polo,
Hollywood (Shanghai), 1939
Film Weekly (ed.), Shanghai, Chinese
26×18.5 cm
Shanghai Library

第三部分
日月有常

78
麦高包禄之几个镜头
《好莱坞（上海）》
1939

电影周刊社（编），上海，中文
26×18.5 cm
上海图书馆

A few scenes from "The Adventure of Marco Polo",
Hollywood (Shanghai), 1939
Film Weekly (ed.), Shanghai, Chinese
26×18.5 cm
Shanghai Library

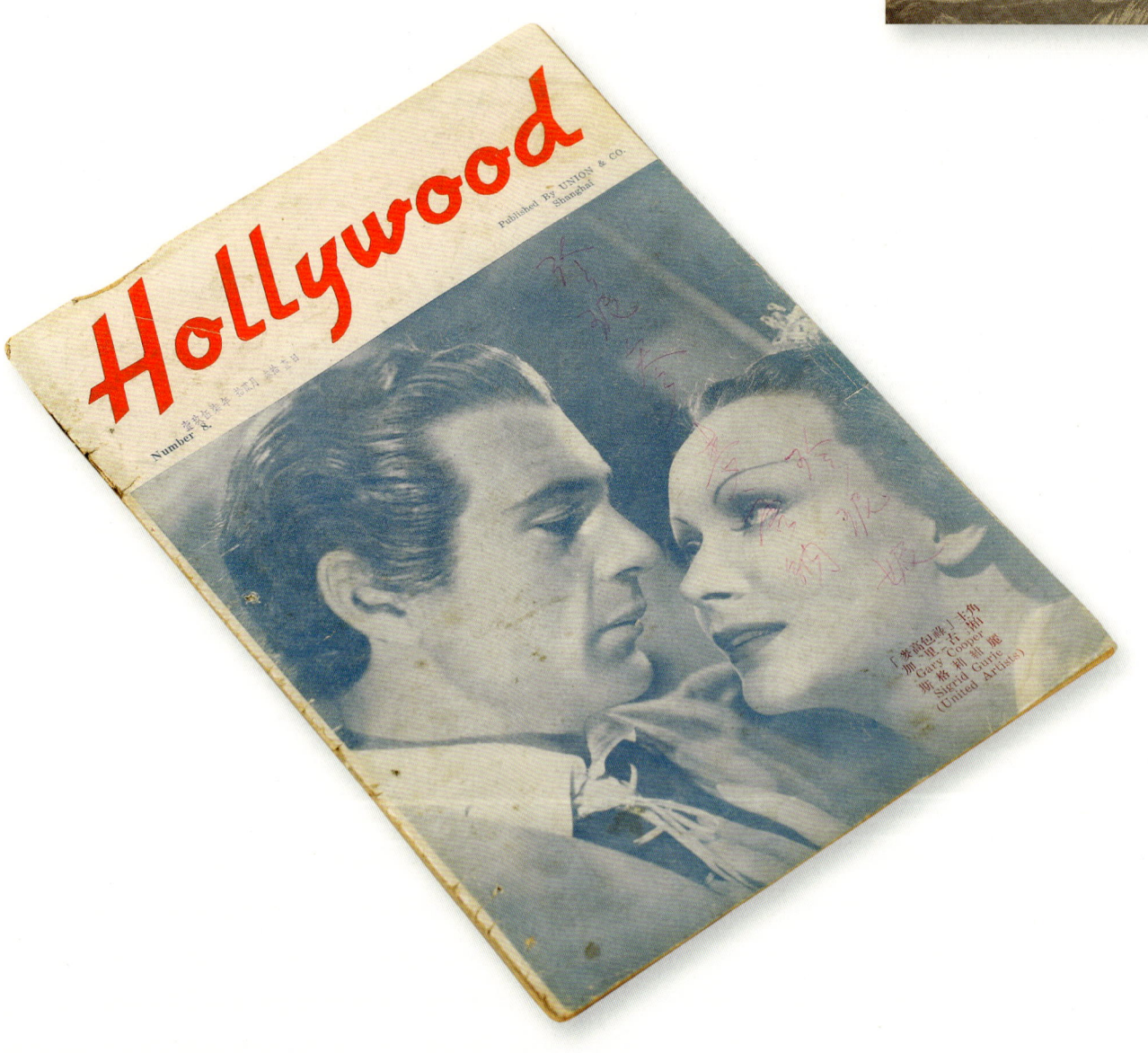

第三部分
日月有常

79
马可孛罗游记中之驿运
《交通文摘》
1941

张孟令（译），重庆，中文
22×15 cm
上海图书馆

Stage transportation in *The Book of Ser Marco Polo, Communications Digest*,
1941
Zhang Mengling (tr.). Chongqing, Chinese
22×15 cm
Shanghai Library

80

马哥波罗游记海南诸国新注
《真知学报》
1942

李长傅（撰），南京，中文
26×18 cm
上海图书馆

New notes on Southeast Asian countries in *The Travelogue of Marco Polo*,
Zhenzhi Xuebao, 1942
Li Changfu (au.), Nanjing, Chinese
26×18 cm
Shanghai Library

81

马哥孛罗的爱情故事
《时与潮副刊》
1948

[美]科姆罗夫(著),张素(译),上海,中文
20×15 cm
上海图书馆

Love story of Marco Polo,
Supplement of Time and Tide, 1948
Manuel Komroff (au.), Zhang Su (tr.), Shanghai, Chinese
20×15 cm
Shanghai Library

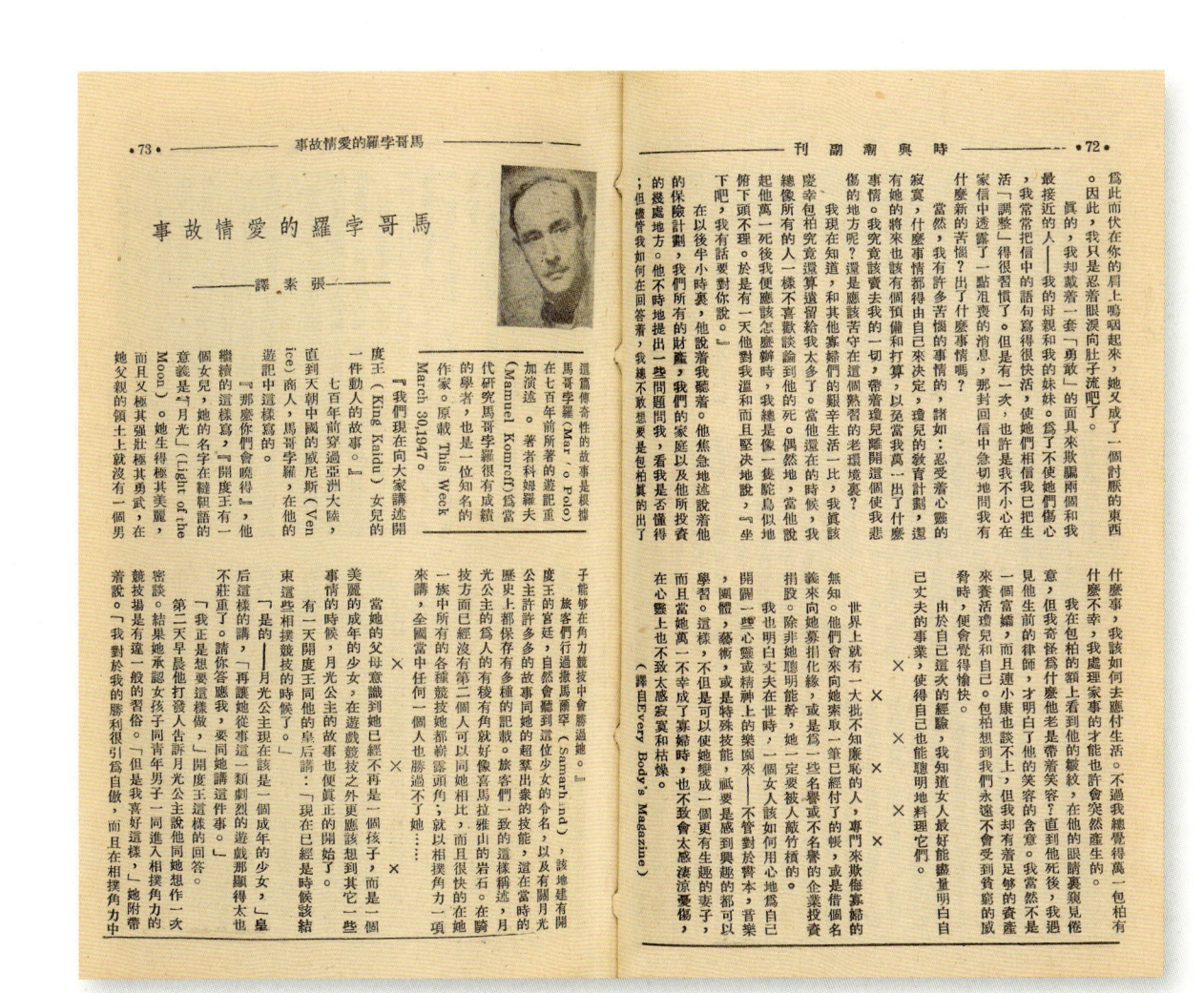

82

马可波罗和他的游记
《中华少年》
1948

王耕云（撰），上海，中文
18×13 cm
上海图书馆

Marco Polo and his travelogue,
Chinese Juvenile, 1948
Wang Gengyun (au.), Shanghai, Chinese
18×13 cm
Shanghai Library

第三部分
日月有常

中華少年 第五卷 第七期

馬可波羅和他的遊記

王耕雲

一、父親回來了

所裏。有一天，主人馬可波羅走了出來，可是僕人不認得他，那時馬可波羅剛好十五歲，這兩個人對那出來開門的僕人說，他們乃是這家的主人，突然有兩個陌生人來敲他家的大門，那兩個陌生人中的一個，一手放在小波羅的肩上，說道：「呵，你就是我的兒子馬可，我真高興！」

原來他的父親和叔父自從十五年來沒有音信。現在，好像是這十五年來沒有出生之前，曾因經商，而違到過白種人所到的地方，從各方面情形，證明那人果然是他的父親尼古拉，此刻正從那遠得令人不敢想像的東方大國回來。他們非常喜歡這洪濤約兼營商業，尚還有一位同來的旅伴，說他還有一個叔父，另一個是他的叔父馬太。

他的父親，一向談了文親臨終前的話，他父親告訴小波羅，說他還有另一個叔父，此刻在君士坦丁經商，不久也要回到家鄉來和他相談。從談話中，小波羅知道他的父親和叔父到過中國，他們爲中國的皇帝貴賓遇，大利爲最盛。他們很嚮往中國去。他們帶那不渡尼古拉，他們的馬可波羅，十五歲的。

二、萬里長征

馬可波羅，便從此開始了其他諸地和危險。尼古拉一家的計劃雖定，可是約了兩年的工夫，才約集了三個人的旅行準備，只是尼古拉險而經過高原，也紹過高山，又約過兩個老命送回到原。有時，地方上的靈柩搬回，大家聽說馬可波羅因為在沙漠中得下了大病，飽一頓，餓一頓，再加上十七歲的少年馬可，不蹤諸地取道向東，經過兩年的靈險而退回原，也沒有白過。這艱因為在沙漠中不顧意和他們同行。但是就這兩個叫做阿富汗的地方，他們一路上說說不盡的困難，結果，這六拉花了兩年的光景，同時休息了一年之久。他們毫不疲倦地向東，有時侯東方風俗，沒有一個不仲伸否則，教士和他們同行。因此，他們自動提議要跟着他們同行到中國去。再三，他們回到了意大利人要去訪問這大利國。

元一二七五年到達中國了，那時終於又恢復元氣，就在當常遭東方進行，有許多少年馬可，在驢背中時，他世祖召見他們得很好，重文老查人情風俗，同時也會了一，詳細地寫着當時中國的盛大光景，有時又遇着許多困難；波羅認爲這就是他們旅行上的目的。那時正是中國皇帝忽必烈元世祖。他招待他們十分隆重，在宮殿裏招待得很好，當時波羅他們曾在元世祖中見，也不願意把他們十分恭敬，對中國文明，接受當時中國的一切服裝、中國樂器，詳細地寫着當時中國的盛大光景，乃是歐洲人的第一次認識中國文物。而是那當時中國的皇帝——元世祖的慇懃招待，遠山歐洲各國，這因爲當時中國業已統一，不過正在戰火不能各種不人道以後在中國的「中國遊記」裏將要開化的國家，安居樂業，到處污穢，而西藏污穢，馬可波羅和他的遊記

一四

189

虚实之界：奇迹之书
《马可·波罗游记》主题文献图录

马可波罗和他的遊記

街示衆。同時又有黑死病的疫厲流行着。反過來看當時中國的情形，街道整潔，樹木遍街都是，橋樑也修得偉大美觀。這些，他一一都記在遊記裏，準備作為歐洲的示範。

那時，歐洲尚沒有印刷，而在中國，馬可波羅就看見人民們從山洞裏掘出一些「黑顏色的石頭來……其燃燒的力量，較諸歐洲所用的木材更佳。」他又看見中國人製造的耐火布。這些東西，威尼斯人在兩百年後才有，當時自然是做夢也沒想到。

馬可波羅在中國時，曾經去過許多地方。他曾到過一個港口，他的遊記裏說，「這裏所有的店鋪，都是滿載着從印度運來的商品。大門敞開，從不會失落一小點東西。至於來往客人，無論日夜，都可自由行走，毫無一些麻煩和危險。」

又曾到過一個省會，看見元世祖每年都要派人去到各地視查，看看水旱災荒。假如有些地方發生災情，農人們即可不必納糧，而且由官家賙濟與糧食。

馬可波羅又看見了運河制度，看見了銅壺滴漏，消防組織，公共浴場等。這一切都是他在歐洲從來沒有聽見說的。

三、他作了中國的官了

馬可波羅以一個不滿二十歲的青年，處處都在歐洲之上。因此，他覺得中國當時的文明，最使他驚異的，要算看見人民使用一種「紙錢」，這是今日的紙幣了。但在那些時候，除了中國而外，世界各國尚沒有這種東西。他又看見中國的驛馬制度，傳遞公文信件，這是彼時歐洲所無。還有叫他更感仰慕的，便是元世祖每年都要派人去到各地視查。他每到一個地方，都是他所不了解中國青年不只誠實可靠，而且頭腦明晰。作為一個大國統治者的他，於是馬可波羅便成為了他的使臣，被派到遠方視查。他每到一個地方，有些邊遠土地的情形，都是他所不了解的。有些新鮮而熱心的眼光去觀察，決不為偏見所左右。每當視查完畢，回來報告的時候，他又能說得鮮活動聽。他不單只報告稅收情形，並及於民間風俗習慣，這使得元世祖十分高興。

有一次，據報有一個邊遠的地方，住得有一族侏儒。從那裏回來的客人，都證明這報告是確實的，因為他們就帶得有這種侏儒的醃過的屍體。元朝派馬可波羅去查看。他查看的結果，原來他所發現的並不是侏儒，而是一些猴子，土人們把猴子捉來殺了之後，把毛剃掉，又把肢體醃過，異象大白，土人們的假人貢不出去，這殘酷的買賣就從此停止了。馬可波羅到了元朝之後，因他會到過交趾，到過印度，到過緬甸和日本。他作了幾年使臣之後，叫他去作一個地方的地方長官。他在那裏，一共作了三年的地方長官。

四、父子還鄉

正當馬可波羅受元世祖的知遇的時候，他的父親和叔父的商人，在中國作了多年生意，似乎錢已賺得很夠，便想到回到家鄉的威尼斯去。他們都是非常能幹的商人，自然不敢隨便離開中國家。但是當馬可提出回國的話時，世祖卻不答允。馬可波羅因為世祖一再慰留不許，自然不敢違背提出回國，湊巧元朝發生了一椿大事，幫他們解決了這個困難問題。

原來波斯國王會和元朝有婚姻之約，元朝公主嫁給波斯王子；此刻波斯王來信請元朝把公主護送到波斯。此時值疆境中戰事頻仍，從陸路護送，非常危險。波斯使者建議請走海路。馬可波羅父子便提議如果世祖肯讓他們回去，他們可以護送公主，盡保護之責。世祖欣然答允，並下令把波羅父子的財產，都換成可以攜帶的珠寶，並賜以許多金銀。

於是，一二九二年，馬可波羅和他的父親，從海上取道波斯，再轉回故鄉威尼斯。一路上遇着暴風，幾經危險，走了兩年之久，他們才走到波斯。到時，那要和公主結婚的王子已經病死了。結果，這公主又另嫁給另一個王子的兒子，以了此一椿公案。

波羅父子又從波斯出發以來，歲月如流，他們足足在外經了二十四載星霜。他們於一二九五年到達故鄉威尼斯。計自從威尼斯出發以來，二十四年前到東方的波羅一家人。但是他們回到威尼斯時，誰也不相信這就是二十四年前到東方的波羅一家人。大家才相信果有此事。

馬可波羅又參加過去，領着威尼斯的一隻戰艦去攻擊日內瓦的艦隊。一二九六年九月七日，寇佐拉一戰，馬可波羅失利被擒，給日內瓦關在牢裏，受了三年監禁。

馬可波羅的最大不幸，可說是一件大幸事。因為馬可在獄中無事，每每和囚人們談論他在東方的經歷，同囚者聽得津津有味，就慫恿他把這些故事寫了出來。（下接第二六頁）

第三十一次懸獎徵答

連長的難題

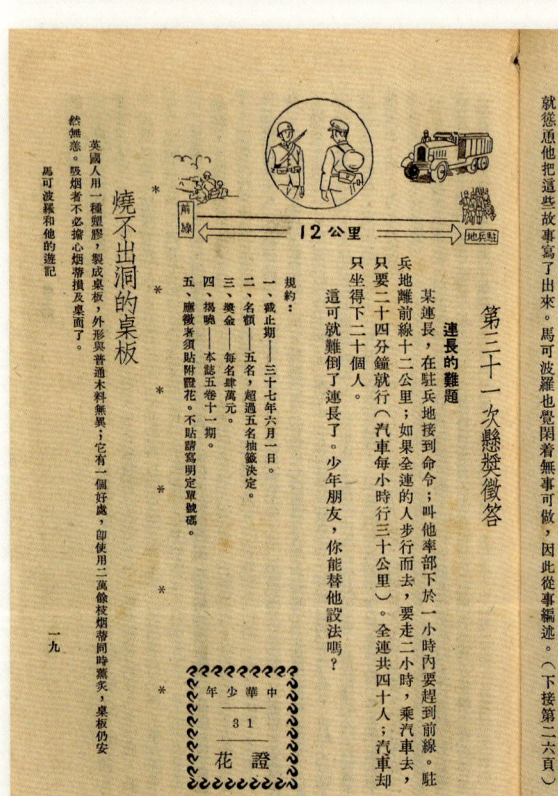

某連長，在駐兵地接到命令，叫他率部下在一小時內要趕到前線。駐兵地離前線十二公里；如果全連的人步行而去，要走二小時，乘汽車去，只要得下二十四分鐘就行（汽車每小時行三十公里）。全連共四十個人，汽車卻坐得下二十個人。少年朋友，你能替他設法嗎？這可就難倒了連長了。

規約：
一、截止期——三十七年六月一日。
二、名額——五名，超過五名抽籤決定。
三、獎金——各得萬元。
四、獎品——本期五卷十一期。
五、應徵者須貼足郵費，不貼郵寫明定單號碼。

*　　　*　　　*

燒不出洞的桌板

英國人用一種塑膠，製成桌板，外形與普通木料無異，它有一個好處，即使用二萬磅枝煙等同時薰灸，桌板仍安然無恙。吸煙者不必擔心煙蒂燒及桌面了。

第三部分
日月有常

83
《马可波罗·哥伦布》
1948

谭正璧（编），上海，中文
12.5×17 cm
上海图书馆

Marco Polo and Columbus, 1948
Tan Zhengbi (ed.), Shanghai, Chinese
12.5×17 cm
Shanghai Library

馬可波羅

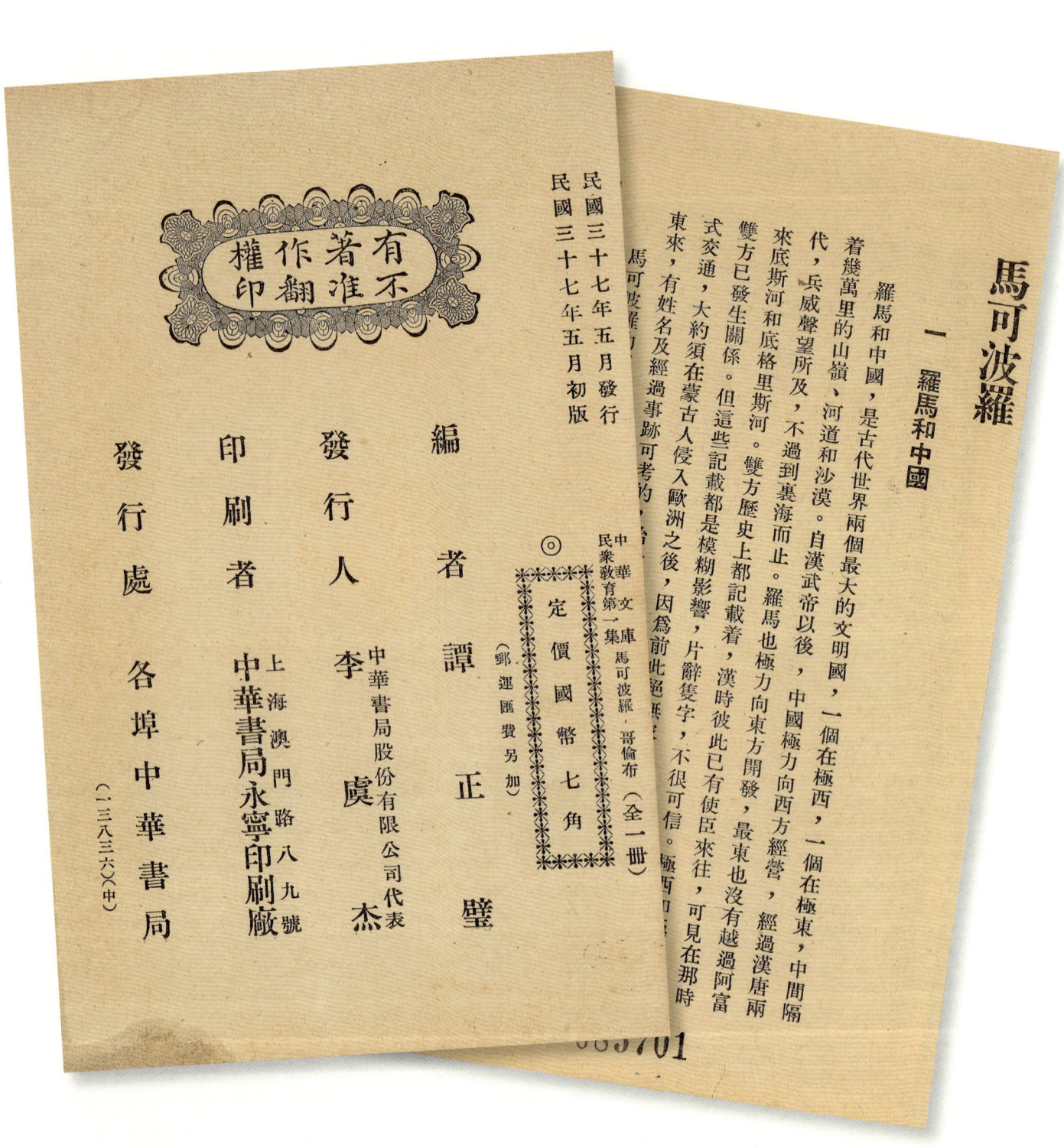

一 羅馬和中國

羅馬和中國，是古代世界兩個最大的文明國，一個在極西，一個在極東，中間隔着幾萬里的山嶺、河道和沙漠。自漢武帝以後，兵威聲望所及，不過到裏海而止。羅馬也極力向東方開發，最東也沒有越過阿富汗，大約須在蒙古人侵入歐洲之後，雙方歷史上都記載着，漢時彼此已有使臣來往，片辭隻字，不很可信。來底斯河和底格里斯河。雙方已發生關係。但這些記載都是模糊影響，式交通，有姓名及經過事跡可考的，東來，因為前此絕無

馬可波羅……

民國三十七年五月發行
民國三十七年五月初版

有著作權 不准翻印

中華文庫第一集 馬可波羅·哥倫布（全一冊）
◎ 定價國幣七角
（郵運匯費另加）

編者	譚 正 璧
發行人	中華書局股份有限公司代表 李 虞 杰
印刷者	上海澳門路八九號 中華書局永寧印刷廠
發行處	各埠中華書局

民衆教育第一集
（二三八三六〇）（中）

SECTION 4

烂然星陈

Bright Interconnections

中意两国的文化交流源远流长。远在古罗马时代，远隔万里的两大文明互相已有耳闻，汉代的中国人就听说罗马人高大端正，与我们相似；普林尼（23—79）相信中国人身材高大、性情温和。很有意思的是，双方都用"秦"来称呼对方，这或许是中亚诸国的中介作用所致。南宋（1127—1279）时海关官员赵汝适（1170—1231）的著作，在传闻和想象之上多少增添了一些更为可信的记述。明（1368—1644）末，以意大利人利玛窦（1552—1610）为代表的来华传教士们真正开启了两个古老文明之间的直接接触，把一个真实的中国形象传回了西方。清朝（1644—1912）末年，一批有幸远渡重洋的中国官员和知识分子，用自身的游历所得，使中国对西方有了更清晰的了解。直到今天，这种不断加深的相互交流从未停歇。

随着元朝的覆灭，明朝迎来了以利玛窦为代表的新一批意大利传教士，自此而后至清朝，从利玛窦、艾儒略（1582—1649）、卫匡国（1614—1661）、马国贤（1682—1746）到郎世宁（1688—1766），他们取汉姓、说汉语，用自己的脚步丈量中国的土地，将西方的科学技术引入中国，用文字记录下自己的亲身经历。如果说马可·波罗让西方认识了中国，那么以利玛窦为首的传教士们则让当时的中国认识了西方。到了中国近代，随着"开眼看世界"浪潮的兴起，介绍外国风土人情的著作不胜枚举，一批批曾经出使国外的中国官员亦留下了不少出访游记，这些作品从另一个视角展示了当时中国人对西方的认识。

在这里，你将会看到两个古老文明的碰撞与融合，了解当时的西方是如何看待中国，中国又是如何认识西方世界的，每一位读者都是中西文化交流历史的见证者。

作为中意文化交流重要的一环，马可·波罗的故事早已成为一门"显学"。从19世纪末20世纪初，中文世界开始认识马可·波罗以来，学术界就开始了对马可·波罗的研究，他们在浩如烟海的原始史料中挖掘关于马可·波罗的一切，找寻他来过中国的证据。关于马可·波罗的文献与研究论著多如牛毛，这些作品从各个角度解读马可·波罗，探求他背后的故事。直到现在，中国学界对马可·波罗以及《马可·波罗游记》的研究仍在继续。

在这里，我们将向大家展示现当代中国学者、作家的相关论著及手稿，这些作品体现了在新的历史背景下，学界对马可·波罗研究的新方向，是中意文化交流重要的组成部分。

Encounters and exchanges between Italy and China date back to the time of ancient Rome, when two of the greatest civilizations and empires on earth were already aware of each other, despite being thousands of miles apart. In the Han Dynasty (202 BCE-220 CE), Chinese people had heard that Romans were tall and upright, similar to us, while Pliny (23 -79) believed that the Chinese were tall and gentle in nature. It is interesting to note that both sides referred to each other as "Qin," possibly due to the intermediation of Central Asian nations. In the Southern Song Dynasty (1127-1279), a customs official, Zhao Rukuo (1170-1231), added with his writings further credible accounts beyond rumors and imagination. At the end of the Ming Dynasty (1368-1644), the Italian missionary Matteo Ricci (1552-1610) initiated and promoted the direct contact between these two ancient civilizations, contributing to the formation of the real image and understanding of China in the West. Towards the end of the Qing Dynasty (1644-1912), a group of Chinese officials and intellectuals who had the opportunity to travel abroad carried back their expertise and clearer knowledge of the West. Even today, the rooted-in-history and profound mutual exchange is continuing.

With the fall of the Yuan Dynasty, a wave of Italian missionaries, primarily led by Matteo Ricci (1552-1610), arrived and lived in the China of the Ming and Qing Dynasties. Ricci, Giulio Aleni (1582-1649), Martino Martini (1614-1661), Matteo Ripa (1682-1746), and Giuseppe Castiglione (1688-1766) were some of the missionaries who adopted Chinese names and became proficient in Chinese language. Through their work, they spread notions of Western science and technology to China, while recorded local experiences in their writings. If Marco Polo introduced China to the West, Matteo Ricci and his fellow missionaries introduced the West to China. Along the process of cultural exchanges and within the modernization of the Chinese empire, numerous books and travelogues were written by Chinese officials who had travelled abroad to disclose and further introduce foreign countries to the Chinese readers. These publications present a new perspective from which the Chinese looked at the West.

This part of the exhibition displays the encounter and integration of two ancient civilizations and aims to show how the West viewed China and how China perceived the Western world.

As a crucial node of the cultural exchanges between Italy and China, the story of Marco Polo has long been a prominent field of research. Marco Polo and his travels have been rediscovered in China in the late 19th and early 20th centuries, which led to a great deal of researches. Scholars have pored over primary historical sources, looking for everything available about Marco Polo and for evidence of his arrival in China. The result is a great deal of literature on Marco Polo. These publications examine the figure and the experience of Marco Polo from all perspectives and explore the historical background in which he lived. Until now, the study of Marco Polo and of *The Travels of Marco Polo* continues in China.

This part of the exhibition displays relevant treatises and manuscripts by contemporary Chinese scholars and writers and how these works are significant contributions to the contemporary cultural exchanges between China and Italy. Furthermore, a selection of books and articles show the new direction of scholarly research on Marco Polo in a new historical context.

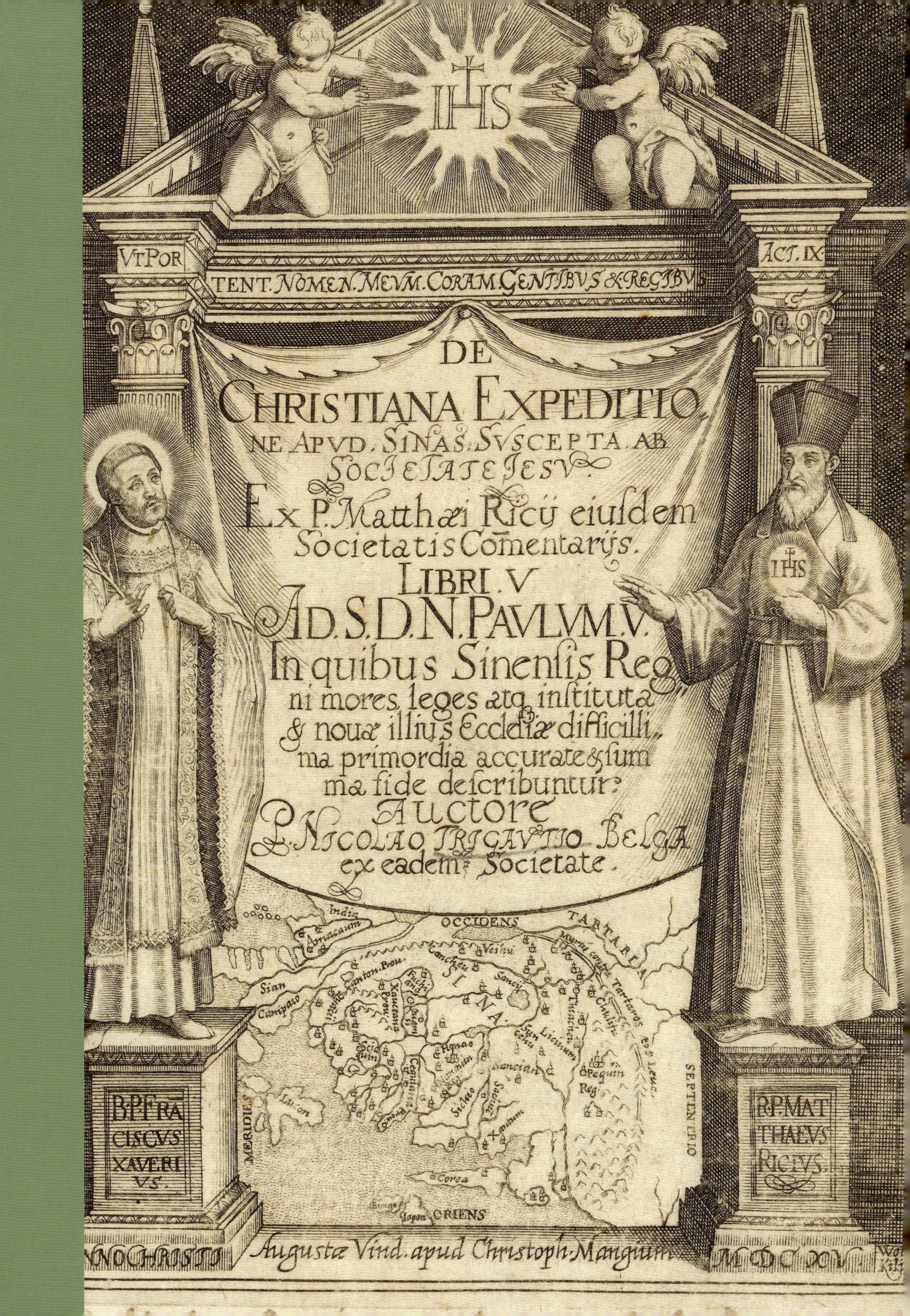

UT PORTENT NOMEN MEUM CORAM GENTIBUS & REGIBUS — ACT. IX

DE
CHRISTIANA EXPEDITIO
NE APUD SINAS SUSCEPTA AB
SOCIETATE JESU.
Ex P. Matthæi Riccii eiusdem
Societatis Comentarijs
LIBRI V.
Ad S.D.N. PAULUM V.
In quibus Sinensis Regni mores, leges atq; instituta
& nouæ illius Ecclesiæ difficillima primordia accurate & summa fide describuntur.
Auctore
P. NICOLAO TRIGAUTIO BELGA
ex eadem Societate.

B. P. FRACISCUS XAVERIUS

R. P. MATTHAEUS RICCIUS

ANNO CHRISTI Augustæ Vind. apud Christoph. Mangium M. DC. XV.

上段（書影）

羌胡大擾貪二千餘人寇武威張掖酒泉三郡[...]延光二年敦煌太守張璫上書陳三策以為北虜呼衍王常展轉蒲類秦海之間專制西域共為冦鈔今以酒泉屬國吏士二千餘人集崑崙塞先擊呼衍王絶其根本因發鄯善兵五千人脅車師後部此上計也若不能出兵可置軍司馬將士五百人四郡供其犁牛穀食出據柳中此中計也如又不能[...]

下段（開かれた本）

中國遂絶並復役屬矣匈奴歛稅重刻諸國不堪命建武中皆遣使求内屬願請都護光武以天下初定未遑外事竟不許之會匈奴衰弱且末為鄯善所并小宛精絶戎盧王賢滅諸國賢死之後遂更相攻奪小宛精絶戎盧且末為鄯善所并其地鄯善復立其國復役屬匈奴會北虜衰弱胡桓大人會廣譽死于此明帝乃命將帥北征匈奴取伊吾盧地置宜禾都尉以屯田遂通西域于寘諸國皆遣子入侍西域自絶六十五載乃復通焉明年始置都護戊巳校尉及明帝崩焉者龜茲攻沒都護陳睦覆其眾匈奴及車師圍戊巳校尉河西郡縣城門晝閉建初元年酒泉太守段彭大破車師於交河城章帝不欲疲敝中國遂迎還戊巳校尉不復遣都護二年復罷屯田伊吾盧地伊吾復為匈奴所䕃遂令出復置之[...]

第四部分
烂然星陈

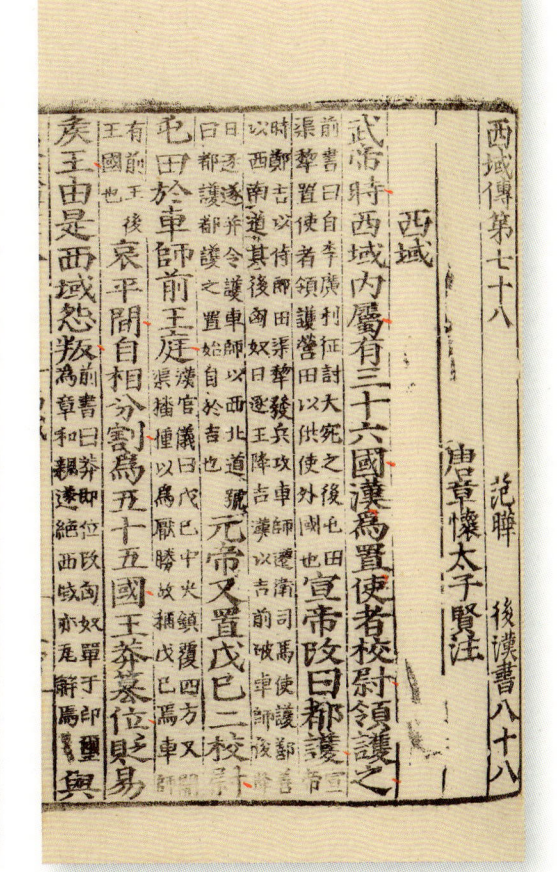

84

《后汉书》
嘉靖十六年刻本

（南北朝）范晔，中文
25.5×17 cm
上海图书馆

Book of the Later Han, 1537
Fan Ye (au.), Chinese
25.5×17 cm
Shanghai Library

虚实之界：奇迹之书
《马可·波罗游记》主题文献图录

85

《旧唐书》
嘉靖十七年刻本

（后晋）刘昫（撰），江苏苏州，中文
27×18 cm
上海图书馆

Old Book of Tang, 1538
Liu Xu (au.), Suzhou, Jiangsu, Chinese
27×18 cm
Shanghai Library

第四部分
烂然星陈

86
《元史》
乾隆四年刻本

(明) 宋濂，北京，中文
28×18 cm
上海图书馆

History of Yuan, 1739
Song Lian (au.), Beijing, Chinese
28×18 cm
Shanghai Library

元史卷三十六

明翰林學士亞中大夫知制誥兼修國史宋濂等修

本紀第三十六

文宗五

三年春正月辛未朔高麗國王王燾遣其臣元忠奉表稱賀貢方物癸酉命高麗國王王禎襲王爵仍為高麗國王賜金印初燾有疾命其子禎襲王爵至是燾疾愈故復位甲戌賜燕鐵木兒妻公主月魯金五百兩銀五千兩丁丑禁冒哀敘復者賑糶米五萬石濟京師貧民己卯特享太廟罷諸建造工役惟城郭河渠橋道倉庫勿禁廣

乾隆四年校刊

元史卷四十

明翰林學士亞中大夫知制誥兼修國史宋濂等修

本紀第四十

順帝三

五年春正月癸亥禁蠱子僧人名爾者庚午大陰犯井宿乙亥熒惑犯天江濮州鄆城范縣饑賑鈔二千一百八十錠冀寧路交城等縣饑賑米七千石桓州饑賑鈔二千錠雲需府饑賑鈔五千錠開平縣饑賑米兩月興和寶昌等處饑賑鈔萬五千錠二月庚寅信州雨土甲午太陰犯昴宿戊戌祭社稷庚子免廣海添辦鹽課萬五

乾隆四年校刊

千引止辦元額壬寅太陰犯靈臺三月辛酉八管剌思千戶所民被災遣太禧宗禋院斷事官塔海發米賑之戊辰灤河住冬怯憐口民饑每戶賑糧一石鈔二十兩夏四月辛卯草興州興安縣癸巳立伯顏南口過街塔二碑乙未加封孝女曹娥為慧感靈孝昭順純懿夫人壬寅太陰犯日星及房宿己酉申漢人南人高麗人不得執軍器弓矢之禁是月車駕時巡上都五月己未朔晃火兒不刺賽禿不刺紐阿迷列孫等卜刺等處六愛馬大風雪民饑發米賑之庚午太陰犯心宿壬申太陰犯斗宿丙子太白犯昴宿丙戌加封瀏陽州道吾山龍

87
《诸蕃志》
（重印本）
1914

（南宋）赵汝适（撰），东京，中文
26.5×19 cm
上海图书馆

Chu-fan-chi (reprint), 1914
Zhao Rukuo (au.), Tokyo, Chinese
26.5×19 cm
Shanghai Library

第四部分
烂然星陈

諸蕃志

諸蕃志序

禹貢載島夷卉服厥篚織貝蠻夷通貨於中國古矣
籛漢而後貢珍不絕至唐市舶有使招徠懷遷之道
自是益廣國朝列聖相傳以仁儉爲寶聲敎所曁累
譯奉琛於是置官於泉廣以司互市蓋欲寬民力而
助國朝其與貴異物窮侈心者烏可同日而語汝适
被命此來暇日閱諸蕃圖有所謂石牀長沙之險交
洋竺嶼之限問其志則無有廼詢諸買胡俾列其
國名道其風土與夫道里之聯屬山澤之蓄產譯以
華言刪其穢渫存其事實名曰諸蕃志海外環水而

POSTFACE.

The Chu-fan-chï (諸蕃志) of Chau Ju-kua, Superintendent for merchant shipping for the province of Fu-kién during the latter part of the Southern Sung dynasty, was written, as stated by the author in his Preface, in A. D. 1225. It was extensively made use of by the famous thirteenth century encyclopedist Ma Tuan-lin in his Wên-hién-t'ung-k'au (文獻通考), and in the next century by the compilers of the History of the Sung dynasry (宋史).

The book may have been printed in the lifetime of the author, at all events, it figures in the catalogue of the books of the family library of Ch'ên Chên-sun (陳振孫), who wrote about the middle of the thirteenth century. It was incorporated in the great collection called the Yung-lo-ta-tién (永樂大典), which was brought to a conclusion in the year 1407. The next reference to it is in the catalogue of the library of a famous writer of the 16th century, Ch'ên Ti (陳第), published in 1616 under the title of Shï-shan-t'ang ts'ang shu-mu (世善堂藏書目). The earliest edition which has reached us, for the text as given in the Yung-lo-ta-tién is practically inaccessible, is that published in 1783 by Li T'iau-yüan (李調元) in the 11th section (函) of his collection of miscellaneous works bearing the title of Han-haï (函海). A reprint of this text was made in 1805 by Chang Haï-p'êng (張海鵬) in his miscellaneous collection entitled Hiau-tsin-t'au-yüan (學津討原).

Both Li T'iau-yüan's edition of the Chu-fan-chï and that of Chang Haï-p'êng omitted the original preface by Chau Ju-kua. This has fortunately been copied from the Ta-tién by a contemporary Chinese scholar, Miu Ts'üan-sun (繆荃孫),

and published by him in his work entitled I-fêng-ts'ang-shu-ki (藝風藏書記), with the statement that the Chu-fan-chï, with its original preface, is found in the 4,262d volume of the Yung-lo ta-tién, under the character 番.

The text published in the present volume is that of Li T'iau-yüan, to which has been added the text of Chau Ju-kua's Preface as given by Miu Ts'üan-sun. The divisions of the text are those found in earlier editions, and the pagination is the same. A few obvious corrections are given in small characters in brackets.

A translation of the Chu-fan-chï, under the title of "Chau Ju-kua: His work on the Chinese and Arab Trade in the Twelfth and Thirteenth Centuries," was prepared by Professor Friedrich Hirth and the present editor, and published in 1912 by the Imperial Academy of Sciences of St. Petersburg (1 vol. 4. London Agent for the Imperial Academy, Luzac and Co.)

W. W. Rockhill.

Peking. April. 1. 1914

---

* I-fêng-ts'ang-shu-ki, 3. fol. 12. The author's preface is dated 1901. The work is in 8 chapters forming two volumes 8°. I am indebted to Monsieur Paul Pelliot, Professor at the Collège de France, for my first knowledge of this work.

88
《三才图会》
万历三十七年刻本

(明) 王圻、王思义（撰），中文
26×16 cm
上海图书馆

Illustrated descriptions of the world, 1609
Wang Qi & Wang Siyi (au.), Chinese
26×16 cm
Shanghai Library

第四部分
烂然星陈

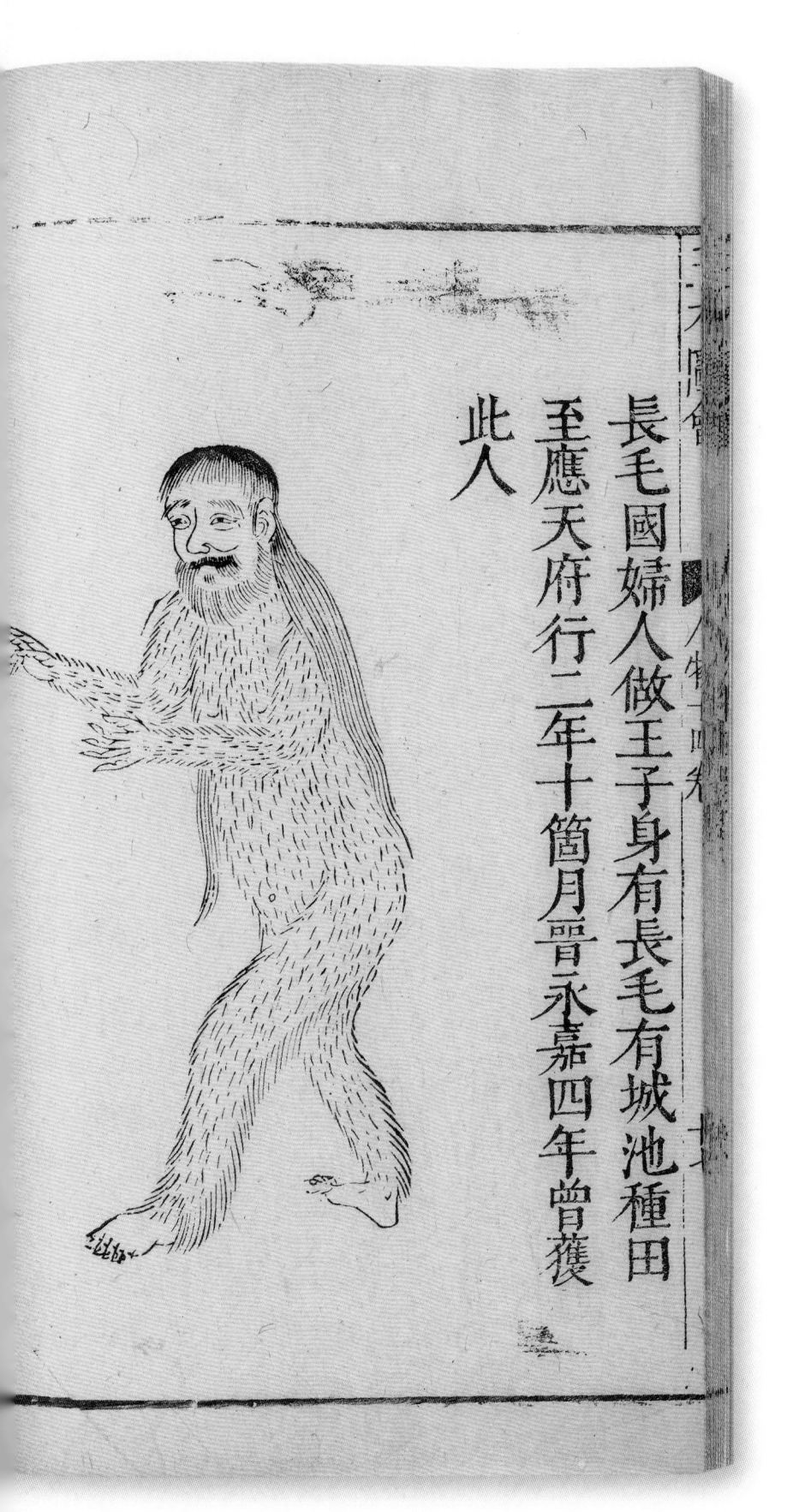

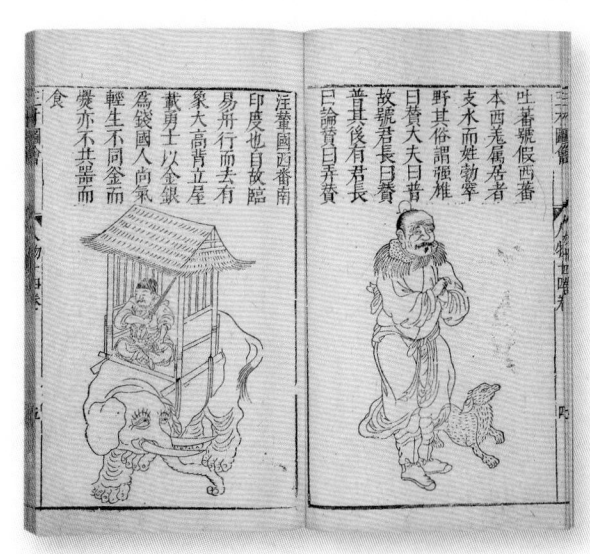

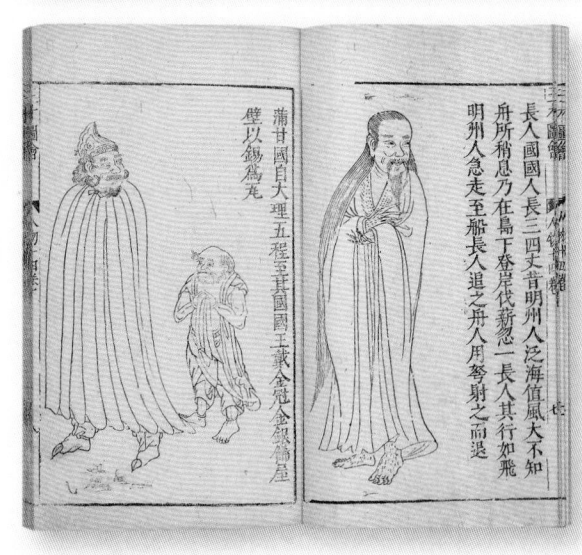

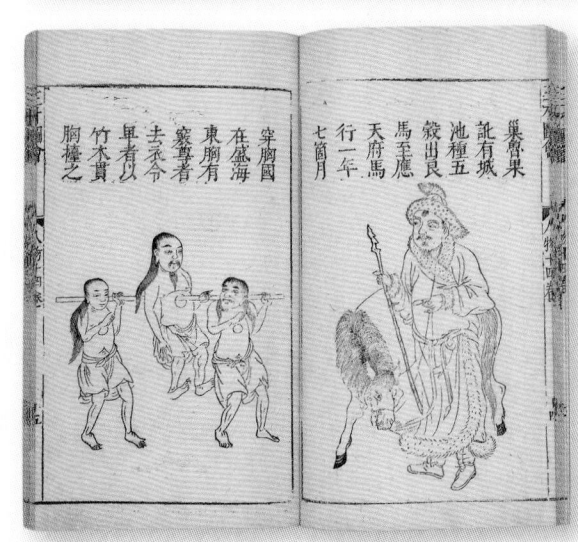

長毛國婦人做王子身有長毛有城池種田至應天府行二年十箇月晉永嘉四年曾獲此人

89

《瀛環志略》
道光二十八年刻本

（清）徐继畬（撰），福建福州，中文
29.5×20.5 cm
上海图书馆

Yinghuan Zhilüe: A Short Account of the World, 1848
Xu Jiyu (au.), Fuzhou, Fujian, Chinese
29.5×20.5 cm
Shanghai Library

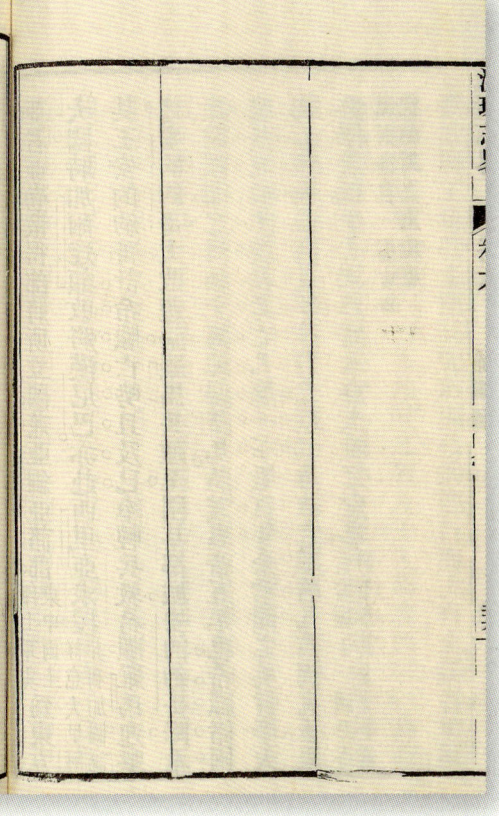

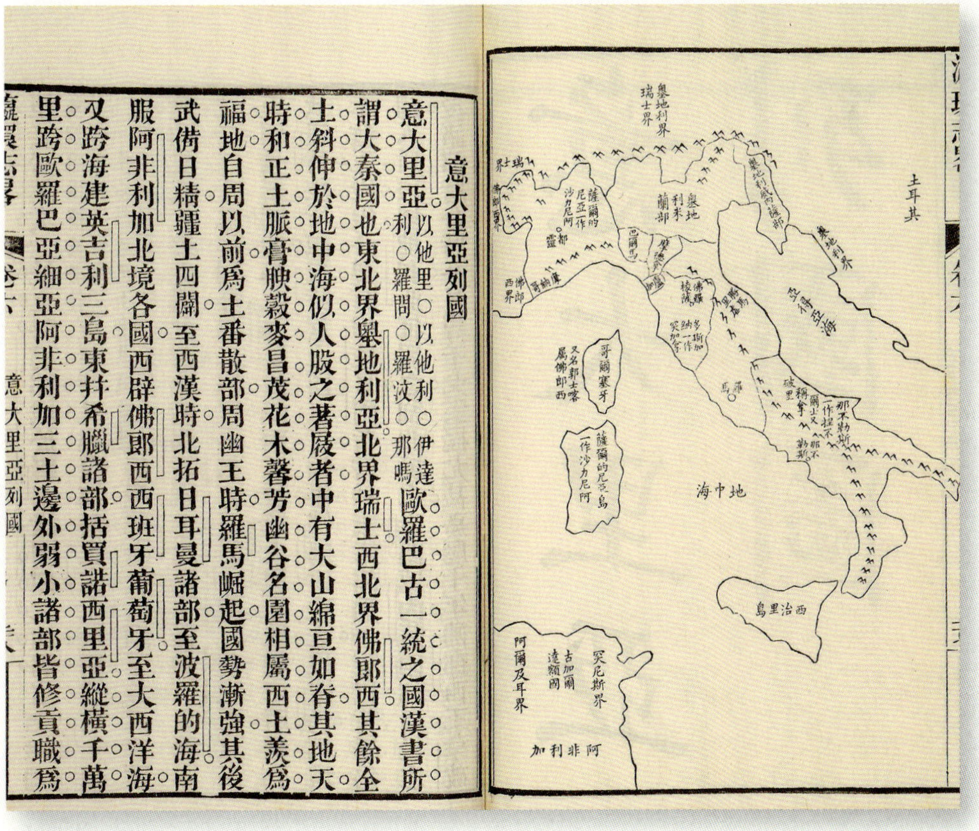

意大里亞列國圖

意大里亞列國

意大里亞以他利○羅問○羅汶○那嗎歐羅巴古一統之國漢書所謂大秦國也東北界奧地利亞北界瑞士西北界佛郎西其餘全土斜伸於地中海似人股之著屨者中有大山綿亘如脊其地天時和正土脈膏腴穀麥昌茂花木馨芳幽谷名園相屬西土羨為福地自周以前為土番散部周幽王時羅馬崛起國勢漸強其後武備日精疆土四闢至西漢時北拓日耳曼諸部至波羅的海南服阿非利加北境各國西辟佛郎西班牙葡萄牙至大西洋海又跨海建英吉利三島東并希臘諸部括買諾西里亞縱橫千萬里跨歐羅巴細亞阿非利加三土邊外弱小諸部皆修貢職為

瀛環志畧

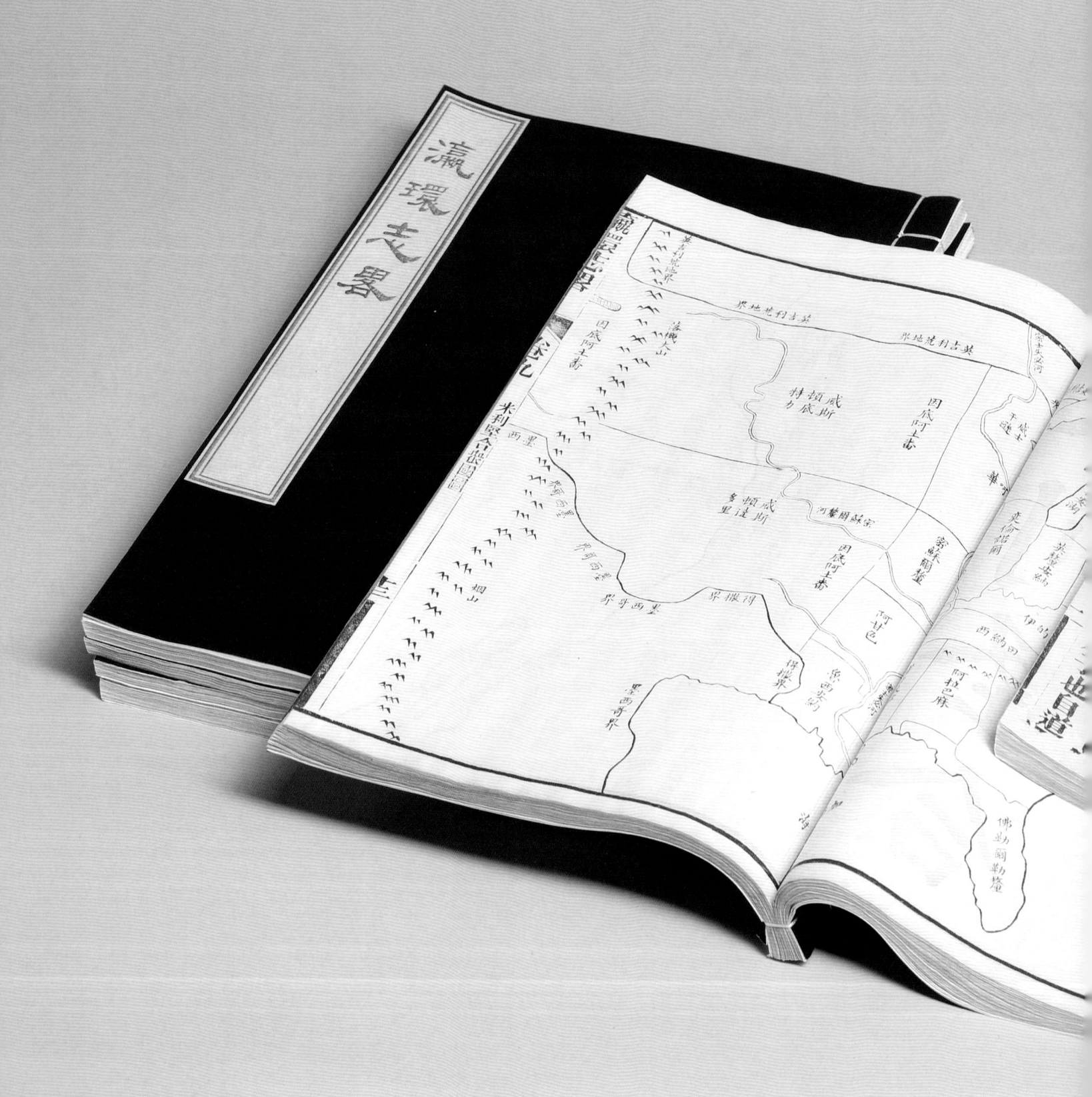

序

嘗聞康熙年間西洋懷仁珅輿全圖周圍九萬里宇中
曰海乃水之溢出于地者地盡處復有大瀛環則無八十一州或
地球乃天平之一今以圖考則不止
說入一度二千五百里較小于地球能容先必照長日下迪則太安易
詳則圖之所未詳全圖中亦本許山海經之奇怪全屬虛撰
近時海國志天下臆說即海國見錄與重圖俯未能
九圖中亦八千餘萬里日本見錄與重圖俯未能
馬嘗中亦之記或曰月地考處復有大瀛環則無止
海曰水之溢出于地者地盡處復有大瀛環則無止
九州乃水之溢出十地者海外更有九州
民物瞭如指掌古之言地球者海外全圖周圍九萬里
高聞康熙年間西洋懷仁珅輿全圖周圍

道
光
戊
申
年
鐫

璧星泉先生
劉玉坡先生鑒定

瀛環志畧

本署藏版

90

《八述奇》
光绪三十四年

（清）张德彝（撰），抄本，中文
23×15 cm
上海图书馆

My wonderful experiences, the 8th part, 1908
Zhang Deyi (au.), manuscript, Chinese
23×15 cm
Shanghai Library

第四部分 烂然星陈

光緒戊申 八述奇 袁樹勛拜題

敘

同光以來出使絕域者海上相望，橐筆萬里外言海外奇事犖犖可數然翔實資考鏡有名於時匪所易得郭曾薛洪尚矣其它爬梳皮毛盛誇外國所有無關宏惜者恆目眩而耳聾也張在初都護往年銜

必聞其政其必有異乎人之求之者與又豈第如斯篇所謂述奇已也
宣統元年己酉春萊陽王塽拜撰

八述奇自序

瀛寰五洲邦國數百欲盡知其國政民風豈云難
美小國之邨鎮風氣尚有此疆爾界之異同矧大國

虚实之界：奇迹之书

《马可·波罗游记》主题文献图录

91

《使西纪程》
1875—1908

（清）郭嵩焘（撰），北京，中文
24×15 cm
上海图书馆

Account of an mission to the West, 1875-1908
Guo Songtao (au.), Beijing, Chinese
24×15 cm
Shanghai Library

212

第四部分
烂然星陈

92
《游历闻见录》
光绪十六年

（清）洪勋（撰），抄本，中文
17×11 cm
上海图书馆

My travel in Europe, 1890
Hong Xun (au.), manuscript, Chinese
17×11 cm
Shanghai Library

第四部分
烂然星陈

案司馬溫公作切韻指掌圖辨字母次第例有云今之以五音運之若四時故始於牙音為角其行木次曰舌音舌音夏之象也其音徵次曰唇音唇音季夏之象也其音商其行金次曰齒音齒音秋之象也其音商其行金次曰喉音喉音冬之象也其音羽其行水蓋字母之次如此然勤幼時所誦者少有更改以舌上音少删知徹澄娘句或附於舌頭音端透定泥句影曉匣喻作曉匣影喻如天籟遙有韻天有也此句之下列非敷奉微輕唇音句讀之似較為順適始取其便於記誦茲譜從之

法字母審音辨氣計二十五字

A 喉音也音挨有時讀入聲如阿若ba陪挨音排或作拔da臺挨音大平聲或作達之類是也

B 重唇氣也讀如陪其轉如勒

C 齒頭氣也讀如綏其轉如克

D 舌頭氣也讀如臺其轉如特

E 喉音也惡寒切音安本音之外有二音以記號別之e安字上有撇向右者音安其聲巳止, ê安字上有撇向左者音良其聲勃愛特之類

F 輕唇氣也讀如愛夫其轉如弗并音重在夫字其

字母之音五加之以ê衷ê愛二音得七音俱系喉音影字一母其氣則散見於各母無與音同母之字可知聲音之發由於天籟有不期然而然者又有an盎.in俺on翁ou烏a挨i衣o啞u紆ê衷ê愛e安十一音此外無同母他音而乃以氣配此十一音而得各母之音惟乙禪特之氣并音則禪母日母an盎.in俺on翁ou烏a四音亦系影字母之則為哀切之氣相同壬愛夫之氣并音巳非敷母下皆有∨物下其音相同壬愛夫之氣并音巳非敷母下皆有∨物一格斯丫一格而來格雖可歸母不復列入也

字母合譜

昔曾見音韻譜橫行疊韻直行雙聲曰張真中珠招齋茲遮專占鑽十一字於法音為最合因作譜

見 kan kin kon kou ka ki ko kê ku
    kaŋ kiŋ koŋ kok kak kik kok kêk kuk

溪 guan guin guon guou gua gui guo guê gu
    guaŋ guiŋ guoŋ guok guak guik guok guêk guk

疑

端 tan tin ton tou ta ti to tê tu
    taŋ tiŋ toŋ tou tat tit tot têt tut

透 tlan tlin tlon tlou tla tli tlo tlê tlu

定 dan din don dou da di do dê du

虚实之界：奇迹之书
《马可·波罗游记》主题文献图录

93
《出使英法意比四国日记》
光绪十八年石印本

（清）薛福成（撰），上海，中文
24×15.5 cm
上海图书馆

Diary during a mission to four countries, 1892
Xue Fucheng (au.), Shanghai, Chinese
24×15.5 cm
Shanghai Library

第四部分
烂然星陈

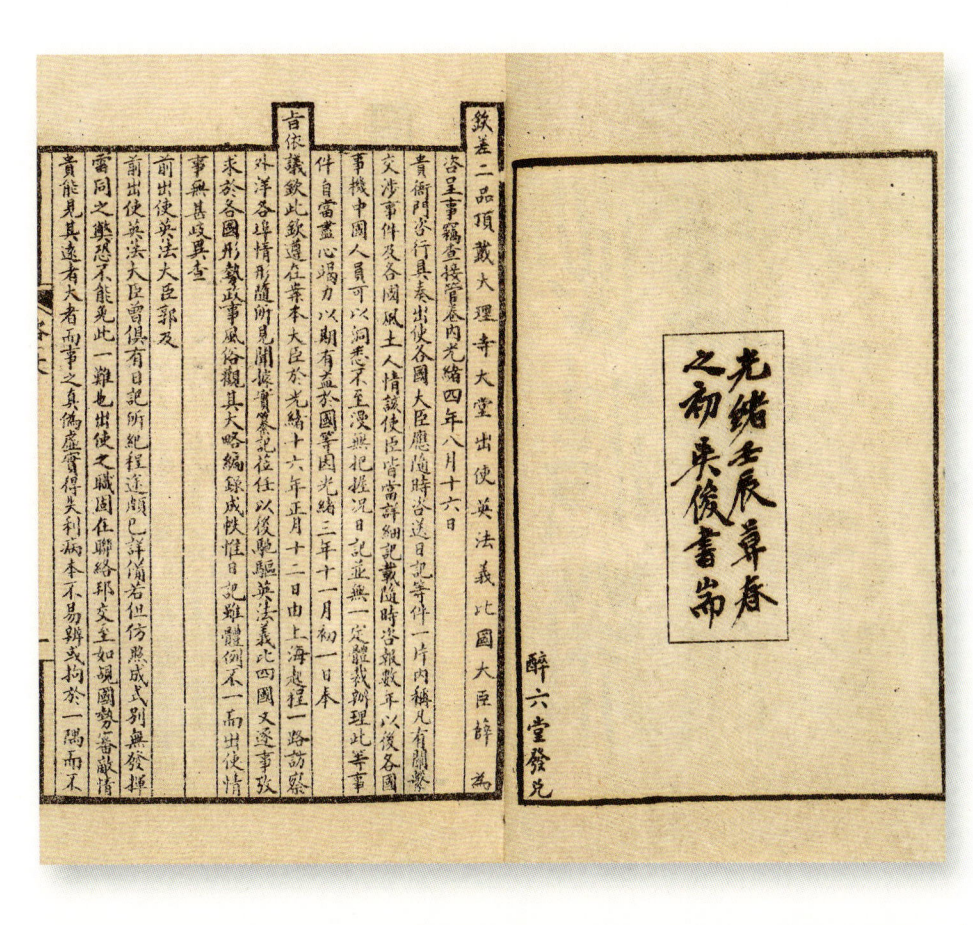

光绪壬辰季春之初东俊书耑

醉六堂发兑

钦差二品顶戴大理寺大堂出使英法义此国大臣薛为

吉依议钦此钦遵在案本大臣于光绪十六年正月十二日由上海起程一路访察交涉事件及各国风土人情诚使臣官员详细记载随时咨报数年以后此等事件自当尽心竭力以期有益于国等因光绪三年十一月初一日本贵衙门给有片表出使各国大臣应随时咨送日记等件一片内称凡有关系事机中国人员可以洞悉不至漫无把握况日记亦无一定体裁办理此等各件随查接管卷内光绪四年八月十六日

前出使英大臣曾纪泽有日记所纪程途已详悉但仿照成式别无发挥

外洋各埠情形随所见闻撰编纪录铁惟日记虽体例不一而出使事务于各国形势政事风俗观其大略编录铁惟日记虽体例不一而出使

前出使英大臣郭嵩焘

事无甚可观其志

贵能见其逸才者而举之身伪虚实得失利病本不易辨或拘于一隅而不需同之势然不能死此一难也出使之职固在联络邦交至如观国势之善败清

综必至蓉前报赛又日承人或写福作苜始知前史称徐市者乃苜之误偶胎

苇头耳盖福苴本同音也

十七日记

英国驻俄公使报外部云中俄通商向由陆路往来俄人独擅利益自咸丰壬河间通商后中俄商务年年递减去年俄商由恰克图运入中国货均由海道运入中国故也近来恰克图贸易便奋俄英人刻下所估俄商之利益东边铁路会在重兴恰克图贸易便奋俄英人刻下所佔俄商之利益前禁烟会英国官绅人会者甚多至捐距甚巨以英为最大宗

十八日记

秦哈士报福英之陷米尔属土兴俄之边界相距不过三日路程中间仅隔以中国之哈拉库尔夫湖及一游牧族名为局外之地照未能久据局外也盖英俄交界相近之故由堪故十归印度复奋据帕米尔地于是辣时斡大利亚沃土盖为英人所有惟其东北之朝衣都拉碱麦为中国喀什噶尔兵所戍守近日此处并无一人英人甚愿中国之守而勿弃兒为俄人所据处

十九日记

乐会在不罢且非英不休嗣因中英制中国而强之以必受洋烟也况闽中国自种罢来日甚一日自是会绅禀者太半

左必禁以毒物贻害中国致资不义之名因相约设法挽回勷其国家勉罢斯

不应以此毒物贻害中国致资不义之名因相约设法挽回勷其国家勉罢斯

大臣西九月二十三日照会英廷文内开

接英国外部尚书侯沙力斯伯里照会云照会等义本部堂接准咨告知贵大臣愿领沙廷照会事已经由本署领事派员事照详领亦愿领相应照鐟贵大臣驻紥英廷事照鐟相应照鐟贵大臣驻紥英廷

申朝欲派领事官驻紥英廷与中国所派之领事官同样查看情景定复办理但间有审紥地方情形有重要刻下或有不能照给与外洋各邦之须领事官照会文凭贵大臣请烦查照须至照会者一千八百五十年十一月二十九日自外部衙门发

二十日记

余间马清臣外部照会所称间有审紥地方情形之处不能照给文凭者是否

94
《欧洲十一国游记》
1905

（清）康有为（撰），上海，中文
22×15 cm
上海图书馆

Travel in eleven European countries, 1905
Kang Youwei (au.), Shanghai, Chinese
22×15 cm
Shanghai Library

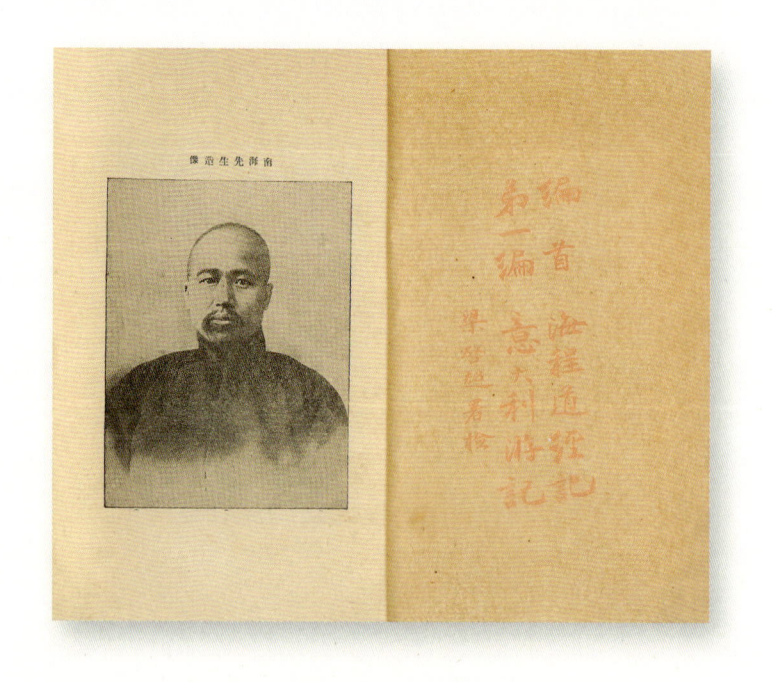

第四部分
烂然星陈

歐洲十一國游記

第一編 意大利游記

南海康有爲廣廈

先泊巴連的詩往奈波里道中

五月三日夜十二時。至意大利之巴連的詩距鉢隙九百三十英里爲中里凡三千一百八十九里。經五十小時而到。不及兩日半可謂迅速矣。此爲小埠人民不多然街道屋舍甚整。亦有來船紅歌者。警察者戴雞毛冠彈壓於埠頭。船客下船以序整淨不譁。自此登歐洲大陸矣。

時已一時矣。然船客皆登岸覓客舍宿。以船中運煤入艙太鬧故也。然實不甚鬧。吾在船酣寢竟夕。至凌晨六時乃登岸。凡一入客舍所費不貲。自房租食費外浴費一二餅金賞費自侍食鋪床守門運行李牽梯亭五六人皆須賞賜。虛糜無算然船客僅登岸宿四五時。乃無一留船者。可見歐人之俗求安而必不少節。彼此同不節。故客舍及馬車侍役得以分養華人則必節之。故客舍馬車難鬧美而侍役亦無以爲分養故

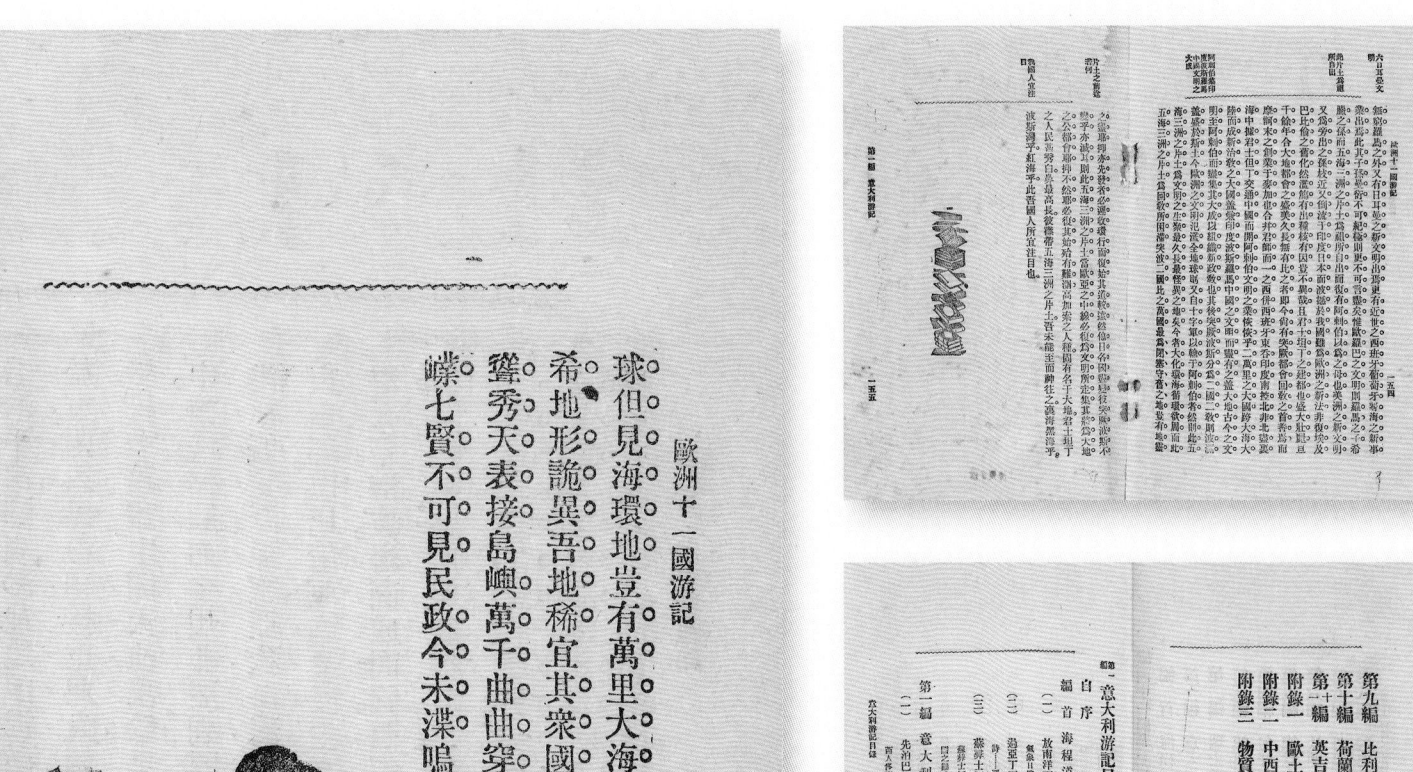

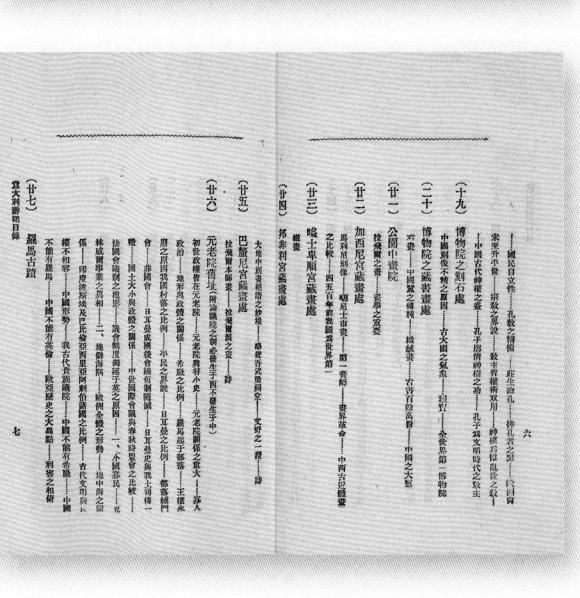

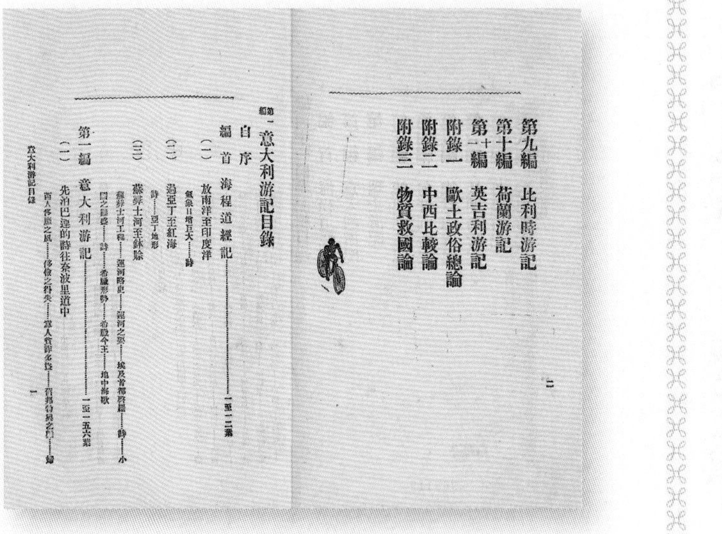

欧洲十一国游记

球但见海环地岂有万里大海在地中之怪奇不知木土火诸球地似此海者有几
希地形诡异吾地称宜其众国之竞峙而雄立日新而妙微昨日一日行希腊云峰
銮秀天表接岛屿万千曲曲穿澜漪绿碧翻翻涉遥望雅典哥林多岚霭溪濠岳巇
嵘七贤不可见民政今未渫呜呼文明出地形谁继天骄此泙渫

95
《出使九国日记》
1906

（清）戴鸿慈（撰），北京，中文
24×16 cm
上海图书馆

Diary during a mission to nine countries, 1906
Dai Hongci (au.), Beijing, Chinese
24×16 cm
Shanghai Library

第四部分
烂然星陈

(第三)考察政治大臣戴鸿慈 考察政治大臣端方

(第二)考察政治大臣礼部尚书戴鸿慈

第四十七图 罗马斗兽场(义)

第四十八图 奈波里丹脱庙(义)

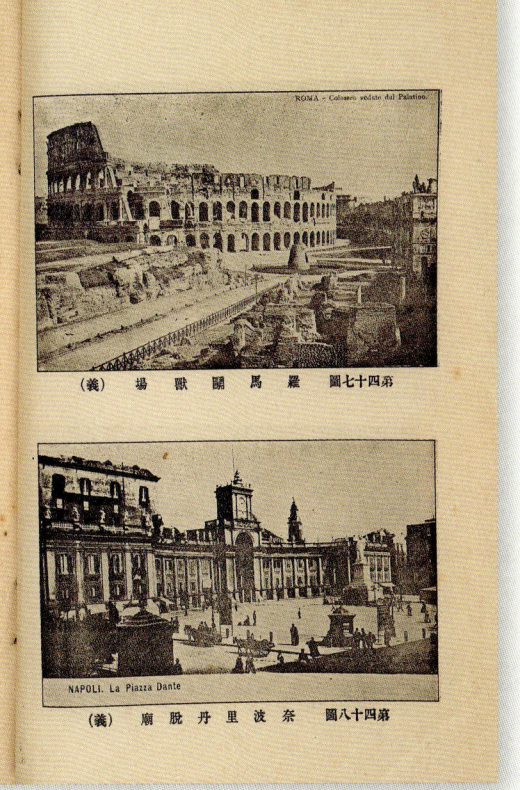

例言

一 是书分卷凡十有二自京启程道秦王岛至沪卷第一自沪放洋历日本渡太平洋而至美卷第二自旧金山横过大陆而至华盛顿纽约卷第三由纽约往费城各省游历卷第四渡大西洋西至英法卷第五到德居柏林卷第六游历南方西方各省卷第七游历丹麦瑞典那威卷第八游历撒克森巴延而至奥斯马加卷第九荷比卷第十瑞十义大利卷第十一渡印度洋而归入京卷第十二

一 从前日记地名人名译音纷歧为读者所苦今鉴其弊悉注本文俾易寻绎其不便者问以英文代之惟已沿用华字之名则多从略

一 此次出洋考察政治调查所及编辑斯详是书专就部人所亲历随时记录间及委细足以补其所未备故章程规法概不阑入体固宜尔也

一 每日往观各处足不停趾无一刻之暇夜归辑录所见信笔直书并未修饰

出使九国日记　例言

一

96
《真福和德理传》
1889

[意] 鄂多立克（著），（清）郭栋臣（译述），湖北武汉，
中文
24.4×14 cm
上海图书馆

Odoric and his travel, 1889
Odoric de Pordenone (au.), Guo Dongchen (tr. & comp.),
Wuhan, Hubei, Chinese
24.4×14 cm
Shanghai Library

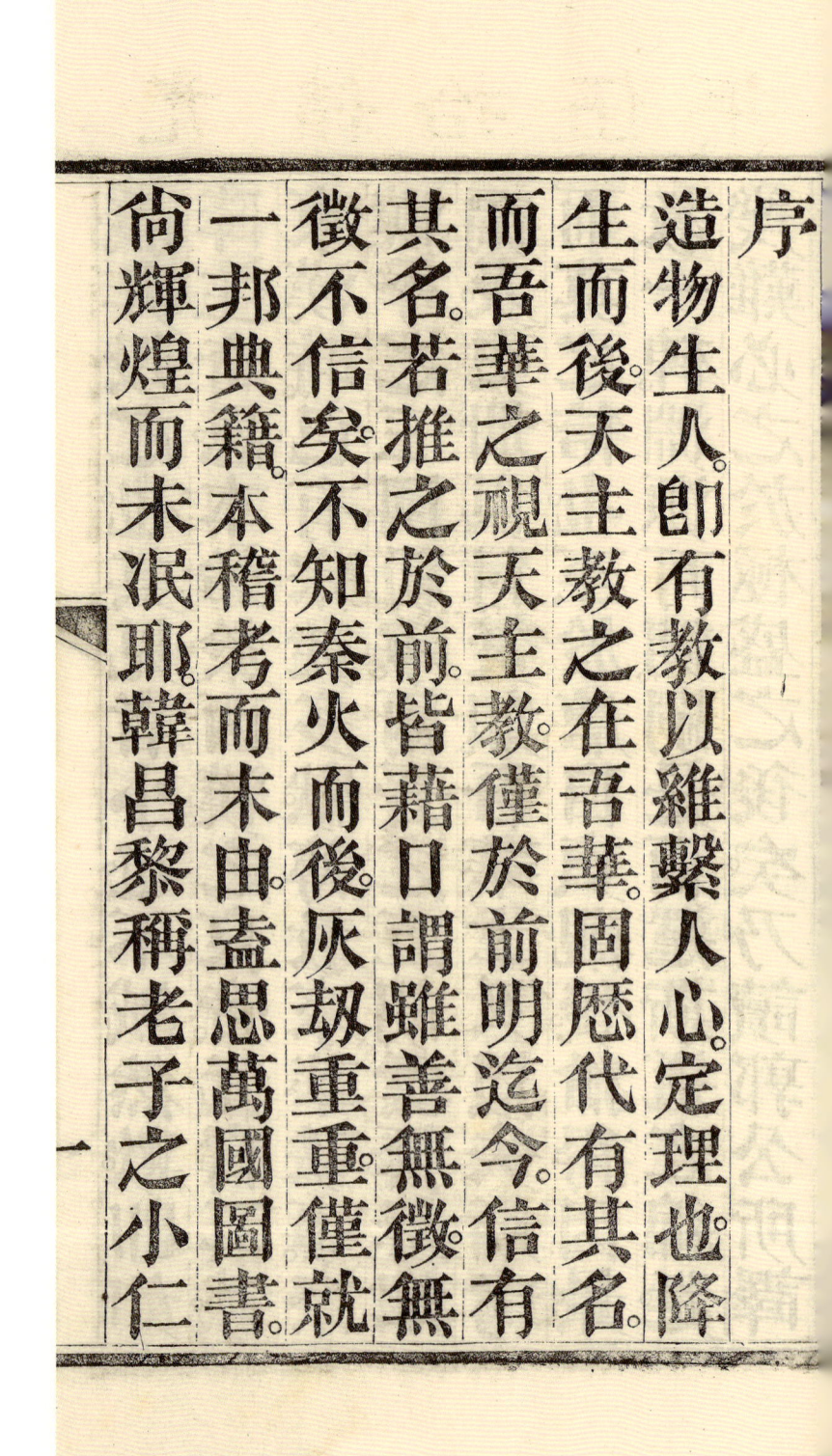

序

造物生人，即有教以維繫人心，定理也。降生而後天主教之在吾華，固歷代有其名，而吾華之視天主教，僅於前明迄今，信有其名。若推之於前，皆藉口謂雖善無徵無徵不信矣。不知秦火而後，灰刧重重，僅就一邦典籍，本稽考而未由。盍思萬國圖書，尚輝煌而未泯耶。韓昌黎稱老子之小仁

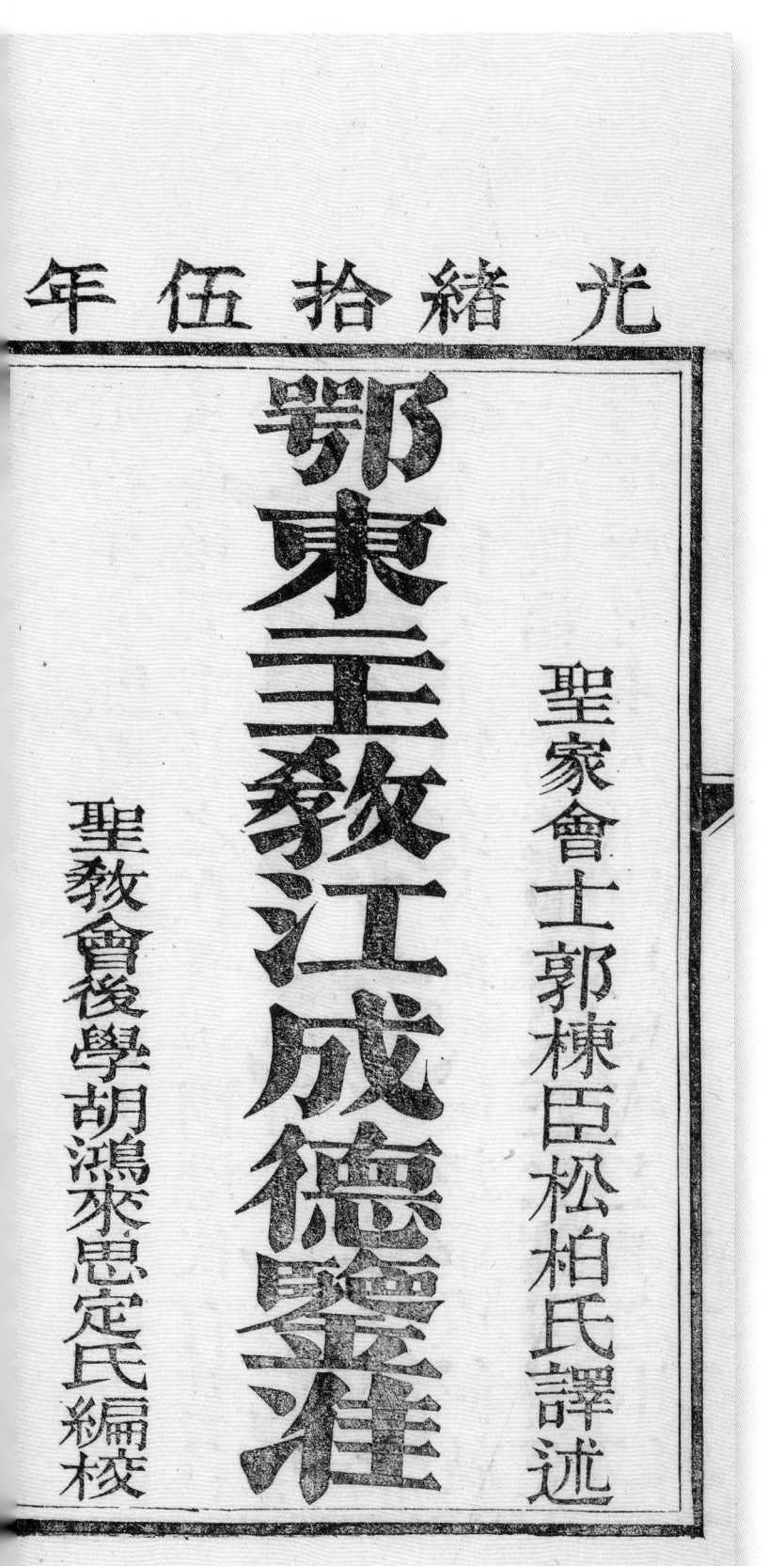

光緒拾伍年

鄂東主教江成德鑒准

聖家會士郭棟臣松柏氏譯述
聖教會後學胡鴻來思定氏編校

自序

溯自開闢以來疆宇常易始分五洲繼稱萬國或東西而阻鉅海或南北而隔流沙政令別風俗殊而交字語言因而各異夫華映之地猶覺溫文若蠻野之區不堪污陋當夫梯航未問不通各國一隅拘其俗尚誰復知有井外之天耶幸救世主降凡而後施救贖之奇功布福音於

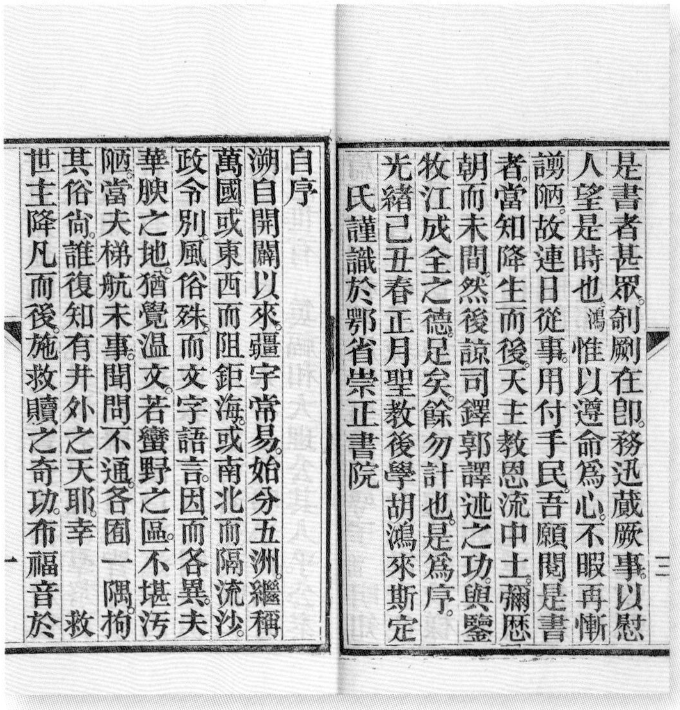

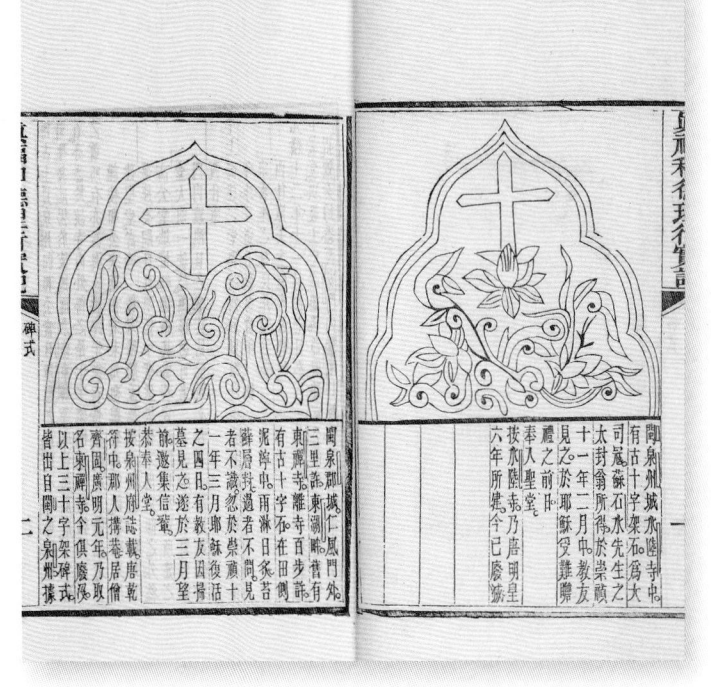

是書者甚眾剞劂在即務迅蔵厥事以慰人望是時也馮惟以遵命爲心不暇再慚謭陋故連日從事用付手民吾願問是書者當知降生而後天主教恩流中土彌歷朝而未間然而德足矣餘勿計也是爲序

牧江成全之德足矣餘勿計也是爲序
光緒己丑春正月聖教後學胡鴻來思定氏謹識於鄂省崇正書院

97
《东域纪程录丛》
1866

[英] 亨利·玉尔（著），伦敦，英文
23×15 cm
上海图书馆

Cathay and the way thither: being a collection of medieval notices of China, 1866
Henry Yule (au.), London, English
23×15 cm
Shanghai Library

第四部分
烂然星陈

CATHAY

AND THE WAY THITHER;

BEING A COLLECTION OF

MEDIEVAL NOTICES OF CHINA,

TRANSLATED AND EDITED
BY
COLONEL HENRY YULE, C.B.,
LATE OF THE ROYAL ENGINEERS (BENGAL).

WITH A

PRELIMINARY ESSAY

ON THE INTERCOURSE BETWEEN CHINA AND THE WESTERN NATIONS
PREVIOUS TO THE DISCOVERY OF THE CAPE ROUTE.

VOL. I.

LONDON:
PRINTED FOR THE HAKLUYT SOCIETY.

M.DCCC.LXVI.

Bas-relief of Odoric from the Shrine at Udine. See p. 16.

---

466   TRAVELS OF IBN BATTUA IN BENGAL, CHINA,

which was just going to sail for the country of JAVA, distant forty days' voyage.

On this junk he took his passage, and after fifteen days they touched at BARAHNAGAR, where the men had mouths like dogs, whilst the women extremely beautiful. He describes them as in a very uncivilised state, almost without an apology for clothing, but cultivating bananas, betel-nut, and pawn. Some Mahomedans from Bengal and Java were settled among them. The king of these people came down to see the foreigners, attended by some twenty others, all mounted on elephants. The chief wore a dress of goatskin with the hair on, and coloured silk handkerchiefs round his head, carrying a spear.[1]

the curious and half obliterated *Portulano Medico* of the Laurentian Library (A.D. 1351), and also in the Carta Catalana of 1375. By Fra Mauro *Bengalla* is shown in addition to Sonargauam and Satgauam (probably Chittagong). Its position in many later maps, including Blaeu's, has been detailed by Mr. Badger. But I may mention a curious passage in the travels of V. le Blanc, who says he came "au Royaume de Bengale, dont la principale ville est aussi appellée *Bengala* par les Portugais, et par les autres nations; mais ceux du païs l'appellent Batacouta." He adds, that ships ascend the Ganges to it, a distance of twenty miles by water, etc. Sir T. Herbert also speaks of "Bengala, anciently called *Baracura*," etc. (Fr. transl., p. 400). But on these authorities I must remark that Le Blanc is almost quite worthless, the greater part of his book being a mere concoction, with much pure fiction, whilst Herbert is here to be suspected of borrowing from Le Blanc; and there is reason to believe, I am sorry to say, that the bulk of Sir Thomas's travels *eastward of Persia* is factitious and hashed up from other books. One of the latest atlases containing the city of Bengala is that of *Coronelli* (Venice 1691); and he adds the judicious comment, "*creduta favolosa.*"

[1] Lee takes Barahnagar for the Nicobar Islands, Dulaurier for the Andamans. With the people of the latter there does not seem to have been intercourse at any time, but the Nicobars might be fairly identified with the place described by our traveller, were it not for the elephants which are so prominent in the picture. It is in the *highest* degree improbable that elephants were ever kept upon those islands. Hence, if this feature be a genuine one, the scene must be referred to the mainland, and probably to some part of the coast of Arakan or Pegu, where the settlements of the wilder races, such as the Khyens of the Arakan Yoma, might have extended down to the sea. Such a position might best be sought in the neighbourhood of the Island Negrais (NAGARIS of the Burmese), where the extremity of the Yoma Range does abut upon the sea. And it is worth noting that, the sea off Negrais is called by Cæsar Frederic and some other sixteenth century travellers, "the Sea of BARA." The combination of *Bara-Nagaris* is at least worthy of consider-

AND THE INDIAN ARCHIPELAGO.   467

In twenty-five days more they reached the island of Java, as he calls it, but in fact that which we call SUMATRA.[1]

ation. The coloured handkerchiefs on the head are quite a characteristic of the people in question; I cannot say as much for the goat-skins. Dulaurier, however, points out that *Barah Nagár* may represent the Malay *Bárat* "West," and *Nagári* "City or Country." This is the more worthy of notice as the crew of the junk were probably Malays, but the interpretation would be quite consistent with the position that I suggest. I take the dog's muzzle to be only a strong way of describing the protruding lips and coarse features of one common type of Indo-Chinese face. The story as regards the beautiful women of these dog-headed men is exactly as Jordanus had heard it (*Fr. Jord.,* p. 44; and compare *Odoric,* p. 97). This probably alludes to the fact that among some of these races, and the Burmese may be especially instanced, considerable elegance and refinement of feature is not unfrequently seen among the

women; there is one type of face almost Italian, of which I have seen repeated instances in Burmese *female* faces, never amongst the men. A like story existed amongst the Chinese and Tartars, but in it the men *were* dogs and not dog-faced merely; this story however probably had a similar origin (see *King Hethum's Narr.* in *Journ. As.,* ser. ii, tom. xii, p. 288, and *Plano Carpini,* p. 657). I give an example of the type of male face that I suppose to be alluded to; it represents however two heads of the *Sunda* peasantry in Java, as I have no Burmese heads available.

[1] The terms *Jawa, Jawi,* appear to have been applied by the Arabs to the islands and productions of the Archipelago generally (*Crawf. Dict. Ind. Islands,* p. 165), but certainly also at times to Sumatra specifically, as by Abulfeda and Marco Polo (*Java Minor*). There is evidence however that even in old times of Hindu influence in the islands Sumatra bore the name of Java or rather Yava (see Friedrich in the *Batavian Transactions,* vol. xxvi, p. 77, and preced.).

30²

98
《马国贤神父回忆录》
1844

［意］马国贤（著），［意］普兰蒂（选译），伦敦，英文
17.5×12 cm
上海图书馆

Memoirs of Father Ripa, 1844
Matteo Ripa (au.), Fortunato Pranti (tr.), London,
English
17.5×12 cm
Shanghai Library

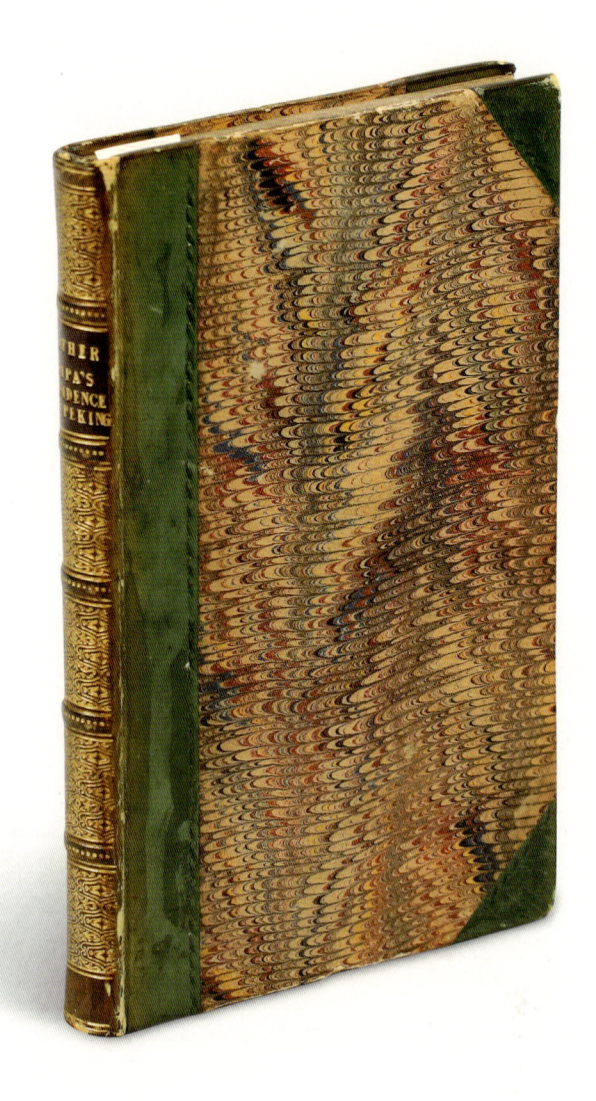

第四部分
烂然星陈

MEMOIRS

OF

FATHER RIPA,

DURING

THIRTEEN YEARS' RESIDENCE AT THE COURT OF PEKING
IN THE SERVICE OF THE EMPEROR OF CHINA;

WITH

AN ACCOUNT OF THE FOUNDATION OF THE COLLEGE FOR THE EDUCATION
OF YOUNG CHINESE AT NAPLES.

SELECTED AND TRANSLATED FROM THE ITALIAN,
By FORTUNATO PRANDI.

LONDON:
JOHN MURRAY, ALBEMARLE STREET.
1844.

(iii)

PREFACE.

The following pages are a condensation of the most interesting portions of Father Ripa's 'History of the Chinese College,' published at Naples in 1832, in three volumes octavo. For any amusement or instruction that the reader may derive from their perusal, he will be indebted to Sir Woodbine Parish. But for him, Father Ripa's work, like those of several other modern Italian historians, of far greater merit, would never, perhaps, have been known in this country. Sir Woodbine Parish had himself intended to publish it in English, connected with the map of Peking, which he obtained at the Chinese College at Naples. Other more important avocations having prevented him from executing his intention, the task has fallen to the share of the actual translator. The original title has not been retained, because the present abridgment is more intended to give the passages relating to China, than those concerning the institution to which the Italian work is especially devoted.

It may perhaps not be uninteresting to the English reader to know that it was from Father Ripa's foundation that Lord Macartney obtained two interpreters for his embassy.

CHAPTER VI.

Departure for Manilla—Miraculous Escape—Preaching in earnest—Cardinal de Tournon's Imprisonment in Macao—His Death—The Population of China—Order to Paint for the Emperor.

I might relate a great deal more respecting Bengal, but as my sojourn in this country was very short, I think it best to omit doing so, lest I should state anything inaccurate. On the 22nd of February we set out for Manilla, in the ship San Lorenzo, which, though very small, had fifty passengers on board, twenty-three of whom were Catholics, and the remainder Mahomedans and idolaters; but six of the latter were slaves, and had been bought with a view to their being instructed and baptized. On my arrival on board the San Lorenzo, I again put on my cassock, throwing off the lay dress I had worn ever since my departure from Cologne, and applied myself in good earnest to reclaim the Catholics on board, who were mostly relapsed sinners, entirely heedless of their religious duties. During some stay we made in Malay, I was requested by the captains of two other ships to assist their crews in their spiritual exercises, which I did with great pleasure, and I hope with some success.

I did not go from Malay to Manilla by the San Lorenzo, but in Our Lady of Guadaloupe, having been solicited by the captain to give his sailors some religious instructions. In the Strait of Malay, not far from Singapore, we were very nearly lost, the navigation of those seas being extremely dangerous, owing to a multitude of little islands which, opposing the waves in all directions, form a labyrinth of eddies and whirlpools. One day whilst I was at my morning devotions, I suddenly heard a dreadful noise under the ship, followed by a great uproar and confusion above my head; and almost at the same moment an American merchant burst into my cabin, and, without uttering one word, seized me by the arm and led me on deck, and I then perceived that the vessel had been driven upon a rock, and was near sinking. I immediately rushed back to my cabin, and taking the holy water, and a candle of the holy Father Innocent XI., I first blessed the sea, then broke the candle into pieces, and threw it to the waves, well knowing its miraculous powers in similar cases. Very soon after I had done this we were out of danger; and the means which God in his ineffable goodness employed to save us were, that the boat of another ship, taking one of our anchors, went and lowered it at a considerable distance, and enabled us to tow the vessel out of its fearful position.

At Manilla I was desired by the Governor to teach the principles of our faith to eight Dutch deserters who were confined in the fort; and to my great satisfaction, after forty days' exertions, they were brought to make a public abjuration of their heresy. Taking advantage of my free access to the fort, on Sundays I went about carrying the cross and singing hymns till I had collected a pretty numerous congregation, when I proceeded to teach them the Catechism, and to preach a sermon on some important point of our holy religion. After the sermon I again took the crucifix in my hand, and made a profession of repentance, imparting to each word all the warmth of my soul. Then, in order to make a deeper impression on my hearers, I untied my cassock, which for this express purpose I wore open behind, and I scourged myself till both my shoulders bled. For some time my companions ridiculed these inflictions; but when they perceived that a captain, who had never paid the least attention to my exhortations, was so touched by them that he resolved to reform, and live as a Christian, they no longer jested on the subject. Since my return to Naples I have not continued these practices—not that I should ever censure them in any one else, but merely because, in my old age, I came to understand that reasoning and prayer are the surest means of persuasion, whilst violence and exaggeration can produce at best but a blaze which no sooner appears than it vanishes.

As there was no ship at Manilla bound for China, the King of Spain having interdicted all intercourse between his subjects and the Celestial Empire, a small ship was fitted out by subscription, entirely for us, under the orders of Don Teodorico Pedrini, a missionary who had already been some years in these regions, and who for this purpose had disguised himself as a

99
《赵汝适和他的〈诸蕃志〉》
1911

［德］夏德、［美］柔克义（著），圣彼得堡，英文
29×23 cm
上海图书馆

Chau Ju-kua: his work on the Chinese and Arab trade in the twelfth and thirteenth centuries, entitled Chu-fan-chi, 1911
Friedrich Hirth & William Woodville Rockhill (au.),
St. Petersburg, English
29×23 cm
Shanghai Library

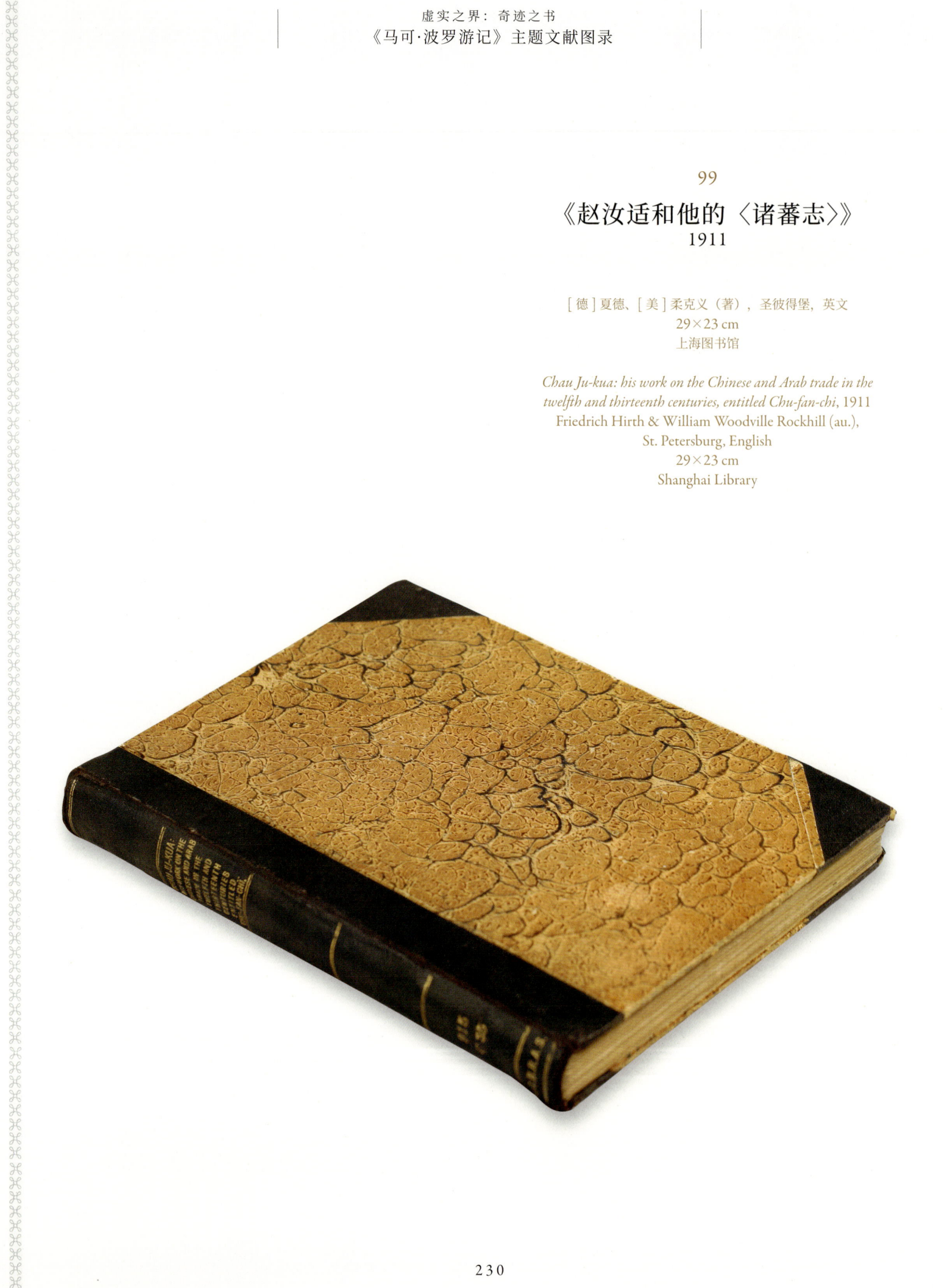

第四部分
烂然星陈

CHAU JU-KUA:

His Work on the Chinese and Arab Trade in the twelfth and thirteenth Centuries, entitled Chu-fan-chï.

Translated from the Chinese and Annotated

by

FRIEDRICH HIRTH

and

W. W. ROCKHILL.

ST. PETERSBURG.
Printing Office of the Imperial Academy of Sciences,
Vass. Ostr., 9th Line, 12.
1911.

Preface.

Chau Ju-kua (趙汝适), the author of the *Chu-fan-chï* (諸蕃志), i. e. «A Description of Barbarous Peoples», or «Records of Foreign Nations», deserves to be named among the most prominent writers on the ethnography and trade of his time. As throwing light on the mediaeval trade with the Far East, then in the hands of Arab or Persian merchants, his notes compete successfully with those of Marco Polo and the early Arab and Christian travellers. The authors of this volume have, therefore, endeavoured to furnish a translation, illustrated by notes derived from other sources, which it is hoped will place readers in the position to fully realize the value of this new Chinese source on an interesting historical subject.

The *Chu-fan-chï* is a rare and expensive work, obtainable only as part of certain voluminous collections of reprints. For the benefit of Sinological readers, therefore, Chinese characters and passages have been frequently added, and this has increased the difficulty of printing the book, credit for which is due to the Printing Office of the Imperial Academy of Sciences at St. Petersburg.

Friedrich Hirth. W. W. Rockhill.

100
《利玛窦中国札记》
1615

[意]利玛窦（著），[比]金尼阁（译），奥格斯堡，拉丁文
21×16.5 cm
上海图书馆

De Christiana Expeditione apud Sinas Suscepta ab Societate Jesu, 1615
Matteo Ricci S.J. (au.), Nicolas Trigault S.J. (tr.), Augsburg, Latin
21×16.5 cm
Shanghai Library

第四部分
烂然星陈

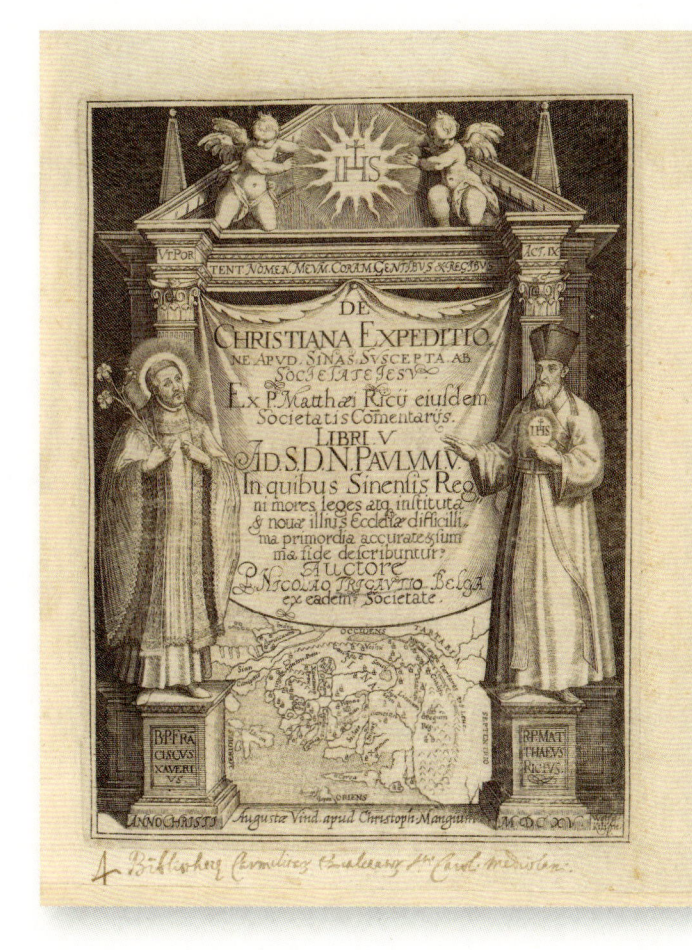

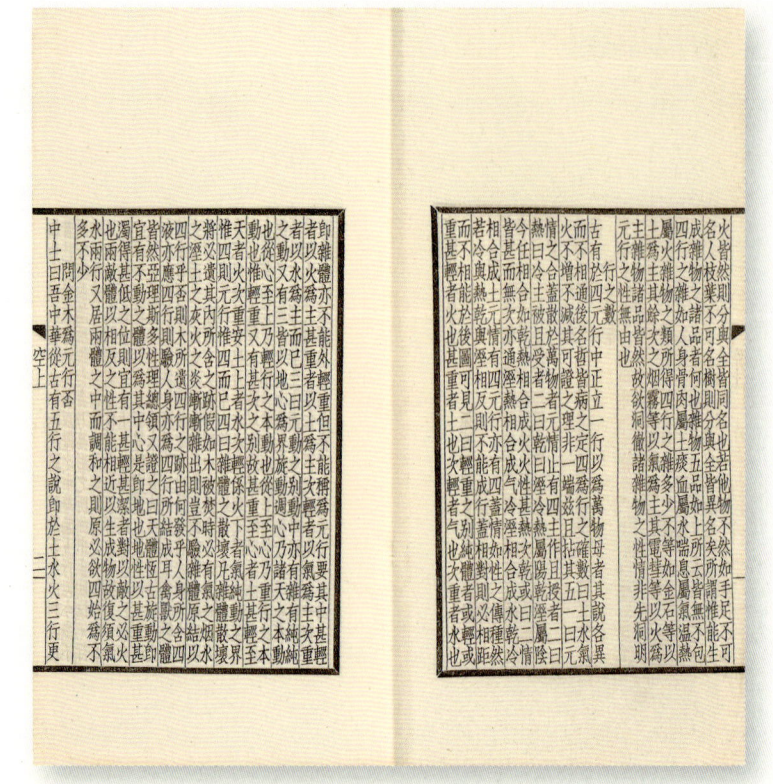

101
《空际格致》
1912—1949

[意] 高一志（著），上海，中文
27×15 cm
上海图书馆

Kongji gezhi, 1912-1949
Alfonso Vagnoni S.J. (au.), Shanghai, Chinese
27×15 cm
Shanghai Library

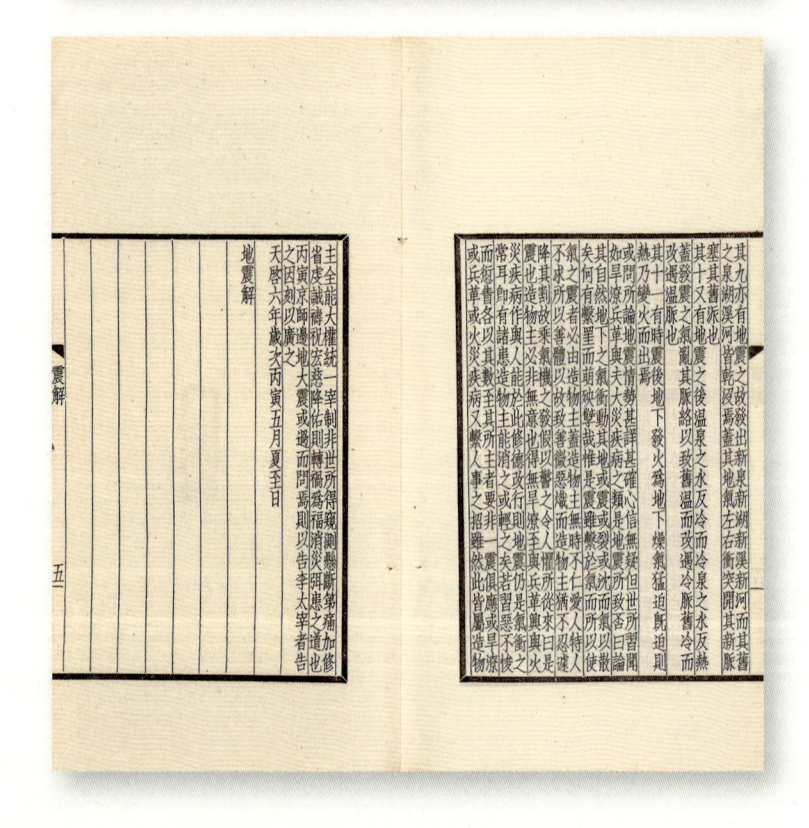

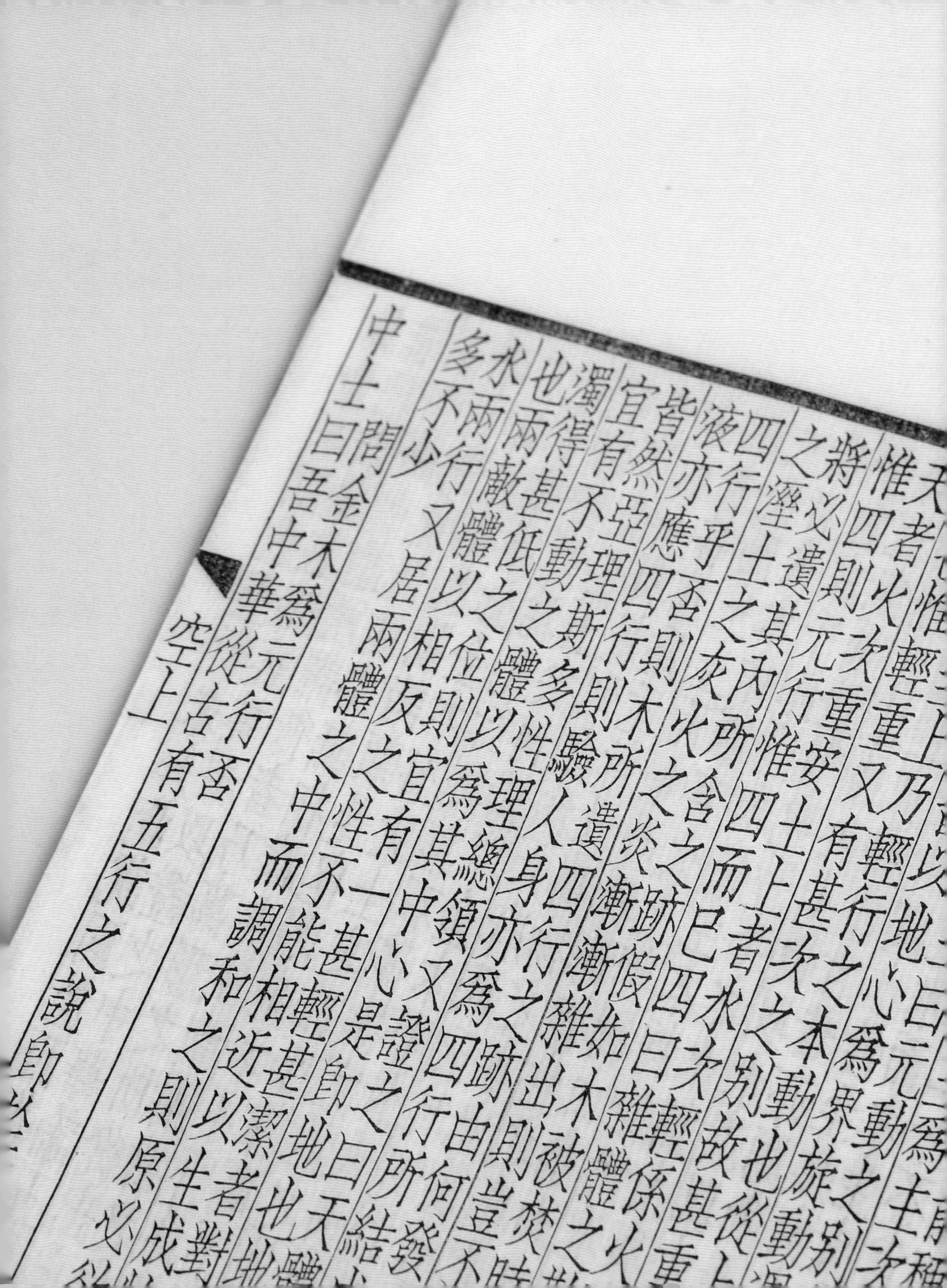

天者四行則元行次重行次之本動也故其從重之火
惟四行火次之乃又有其心為界旋動之主動
者火亦次重又輕又有心為別動也從重之
之將必遺其元則其元行之體係動之火
之墊四行則元行次其灰之所遺而已四者
宜皆有不亞乎土之灰則四日水曰木曰雜體
四行亦應否即則木火之炎漸漸雜出則被焚時
液亦不動斯所木火之舍炎漸雜體豈不
也濁得甚低之體以性理總領之四行所由所發
兩兩敵體以相位則宜為其中又之證四行之跡
水行少又居兩體之性有不甚即是之跡由
多不少又居兩體之中而
中土問金木為元行否
土曰吾中華從古行古有否
曰五金木華從古行否
空上有五行之說即以二

102
《灵言蠡勺》
1919

[意] 毕方济、[明] 徐光启（编著），北京，中文
26×16 cm
上海图书馆

Lingyan lishao, 1919
Francesco Sambiaso S.J. & Xu Guangqi (eds.), Beijing, Chinese
26×16 cm
Shanghai Library

第四部分
烂然星陈

四庫總目提要 子部雜家類存目二

靈言蠡勺二卷

明西洋人畢方濟撰而徐光啟編錄也書成於天啟甲子皆論亞尼瑪之學亞尼瑪者華言靈性也凡四篇一論亞尼瑪之體二論亞尼瑪之能三論亞尼瑪之尊四論亞尼瑪所向美好之情而總歸之於敬事天主以求福其說多誇誕迂怪輾轉敷衍以文其誕大抵為天主之學者慧黠巧辯能撮釋氏覺變幻之以明佛經而實剿其緒論西士行之盛性之說而歸之尊

103

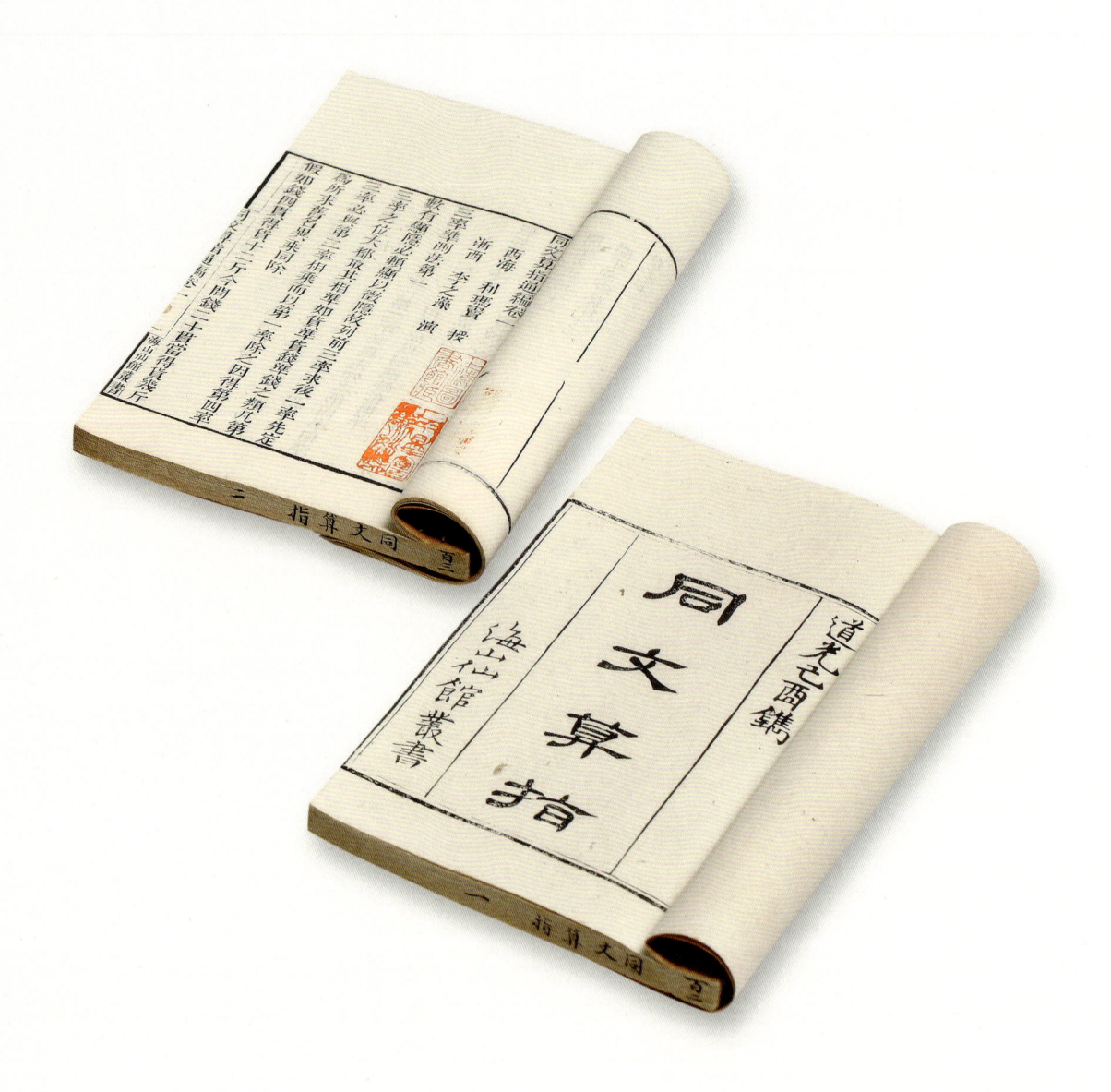

《同文算指》
道光二十九年刻本

[意]利玛窦、（明）李之藻（编译），广东广州，中文
18×12 cm
上海图书馆

Tongwen suanzhi, 1849
Matteo Ricci S.J. & Li Zhizao (eds.), Guangzhou, Guangdong, Chinese
18×12 cm
Shanghai Library

第四部分
烂然星陈

数致远恐泥尝试为之当亦贤于博奕矣乃自古学既远实用莫窥安定苏湖犹存告傿其在於今士占一经恥握从衡之示才高七步不嬾律度之宗无论河渠历象顯武其方尊思更治民生阴受其破吁可慨已往游金臺遇西儒利瑪竇先生精言天道旁及算指术弥假操觚弟资毛颖寻其便于日用退食译之久而成帙加减乘除总亦不殊中土至於奇零分合特自立暢昔贤未发之旨盈縮句股开方测圆舊法最難新译彌捷夫西方远人安所亲龙马龟畴之秘隶首商高之业历写字为算开元檳謂繁瑣遂致失傳視此異同今亦無從萊考若乃

而十九符其用書数共其宗精之入委微高之出意表良亦心同理同天地自然之数同歟普婆羅門有九執

聖明在有道方文献何嫌亞蓄兼收以昭九译同文之盛矧其獻琛輯瑞儻亦有不平乎僕性無他嗜自揆寡昧游心此道庶補幼學灑掃應對之闕復感存亡之永隔幸心期之尚存耆輯所聞纂為三種前編為上海山仙館叢書

（三）
四柒九
〇六捌玖六
一五三肆九六四
三一五貳九六六四
一六二五叁六六四
四六捌四
壹

復列四六九而四不能除三始變其位作〇於格右其下層四六以下層四六九陳其位又列四九四三看除數四六上變六除得總數五四九轉馬九則不足故馬作四十八九又因減之以〇六以下層四九陳其位又列四九四因得四六六九以三減之剩四九變四位以〇六以下層四陳其位又列一百二十六變二位以一百二十命之日以為母數注列〇二以〇〇六以下層一陳其位又列一百六十四又不盡四十九

右尾第二位變六作〇緣進位尚有一數須作〇以存其位此法切記

若上層除餘之數反多於下層除數者或上數與下數相等者定是除法有差只就除過木位上下相較亦不必另創第將差者抹去而另註所除數於上層另註除數於下層之下又另註除得之數於格右以從簡便

先以二除二十六常用五却誤用四是宜多一因多一與四因得四十八下首位六變一少者且如四因一以二因入减六少六以四因入得四八三一二

六
二八九五
除
四八三一二
上海山仙館叢書

104
《泰西水法》
万历四十年刻本

[意]熊三拔（译），（明）徐光启（笔记），北京，中文
27×17 cm
上海图书馆

Taixi shuifa, 1612
Sabbatino de Ursis S.J. (tr.), Xu Guangqi (ed.), Beijing, Chinese
27×17 cm
Shanghai Library

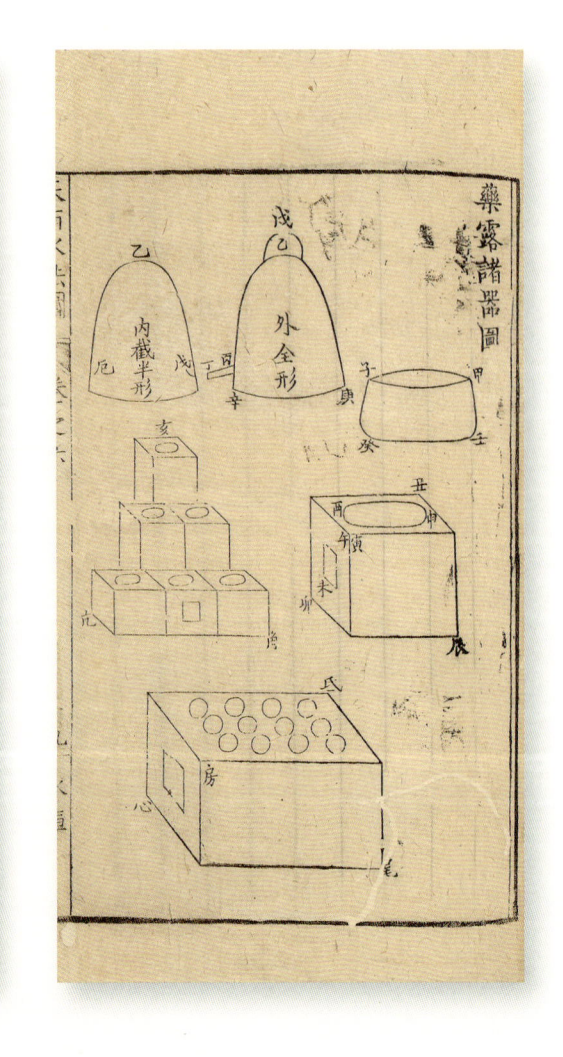

第四部分
烂然星陈

泰西水法

泰西水法序

惟

上帝好生既生人则为之生食食出於地

蓺秫人人有遗能地乃有遗利食亦

其不足恒以旱乾天泽既不可徼乃不吕

溉灘急焉顧亦宇所讲究甸西北之鄉允

曹遺利食乃则渠塘

西國熊有綱先生譯

北京原板

105
《进呈鹰论》
光绪十六年

[意] 乌利塞·阿特洛旺地（著），[意] 利类思（译），抄本，中文
28×16 cm
上海图书馆

Ornithologiae, 1890
Ulisse Aldrovandi (au.), Ludovico Buglio S.J. (tr.), manuscript, Chinese
28×16 cm
Shanghai Library

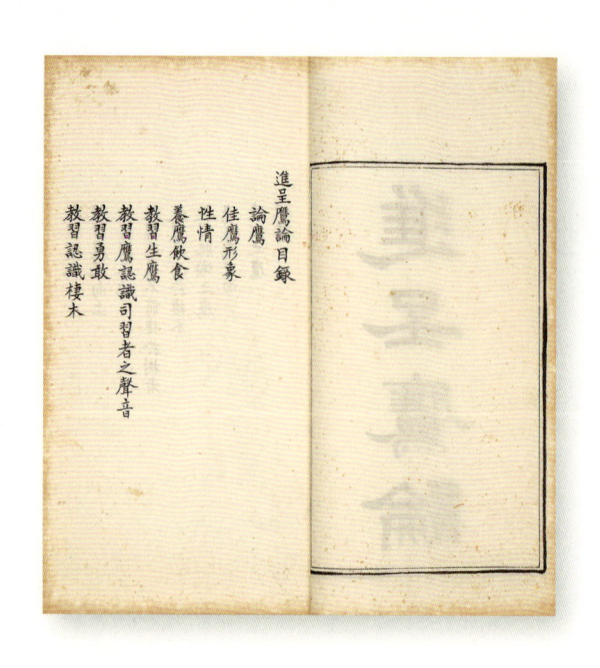

第四部分
烂然星陈

106

《视学》
乾隆十四年

（清）年希尧、[意] 郎世宁（编译），抄本，中文
36×27 cm
上海图书馆

Shixue, 1749
Nian Xiyao & Giuseppe Castiglione S.J. (eds.), manuscript, Chinese
36×27 cm
Shanghai Library

第四部分
烂然星陈

107
《几何原本》
咸丰八年刻本

[英]伟烈亚力、（清）李善兰（译），上海，中文
24×16 cm
上海图书馆

Euclidis Elementorum Libri XV, 1858
Alexander Wylie & Li Shanlan (tr.), Shanghai, Chinese
24×16 cm
Shanghai Library

第四部分
烂 然 星 陈

108
《汉字西译》
1723

[意] 叶尊孝（撰），抄本，拉丁文 / 中文
22×16 cm
上海图书馆

Han tsu si fan, 1723
Basile Brollo da Gemona O.F.M. (au.), Manuscript, Latin / Chinese
22×16 cm
Shanghai Library

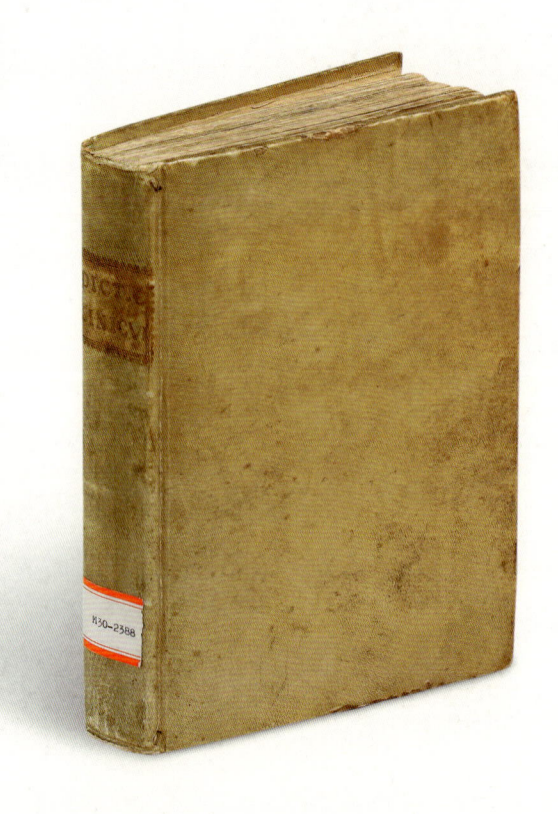

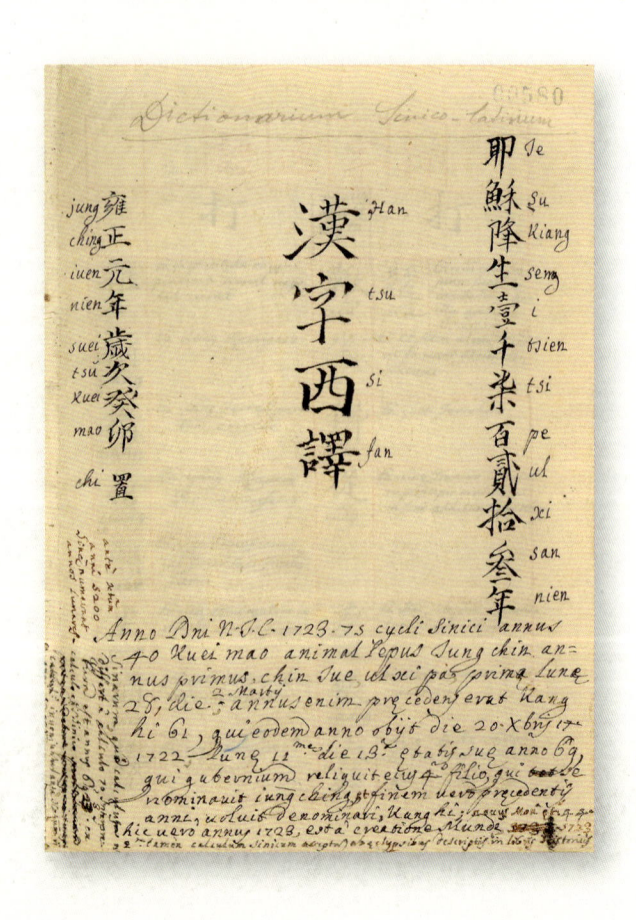

第四部分
烂然星陈

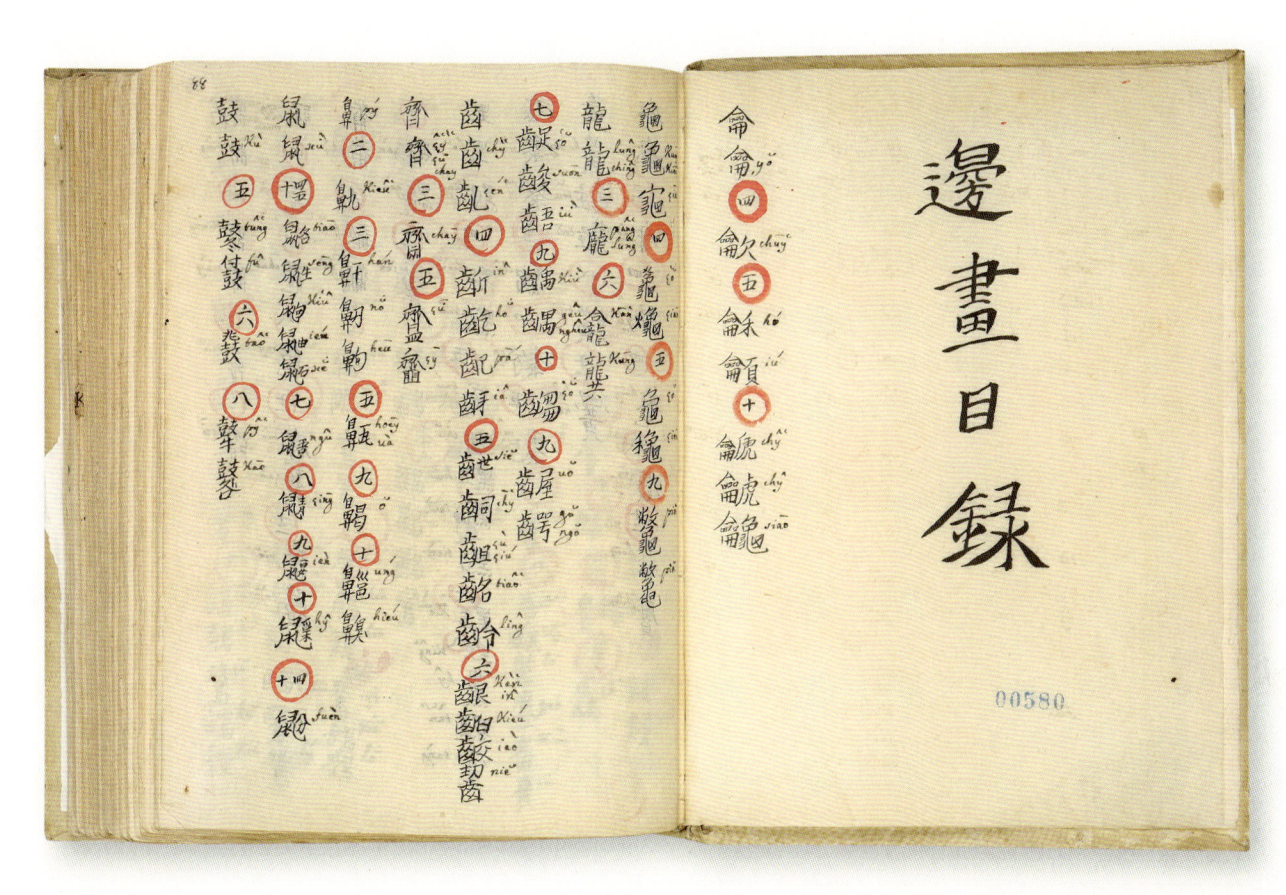

虚实之界：奇迹之书
《马可·波罗游记》主题文献图录

109

《中国文化教程》
1879—1883

［意］晁德莅（著），上海，拉丁文 / 中文
23×16 cm
上海图书馆

Cursus Literaturae Sinicae, 1879-1883
Angelo Zottoli S.J. (au.), Shanghai, Latin / Chinese
23×16 cm
Shanghai Library

第四部分
烂然星陈

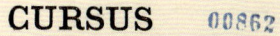

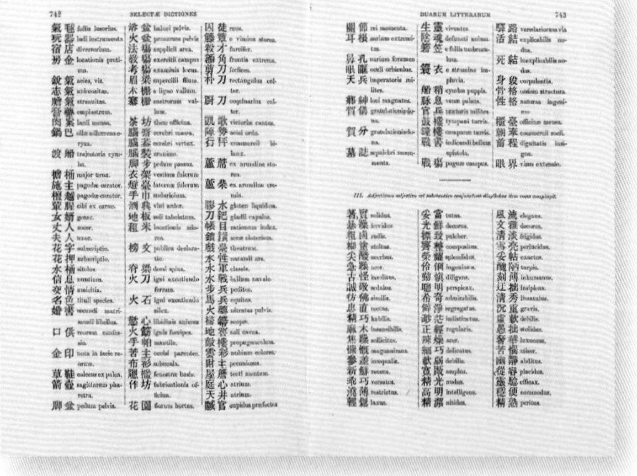

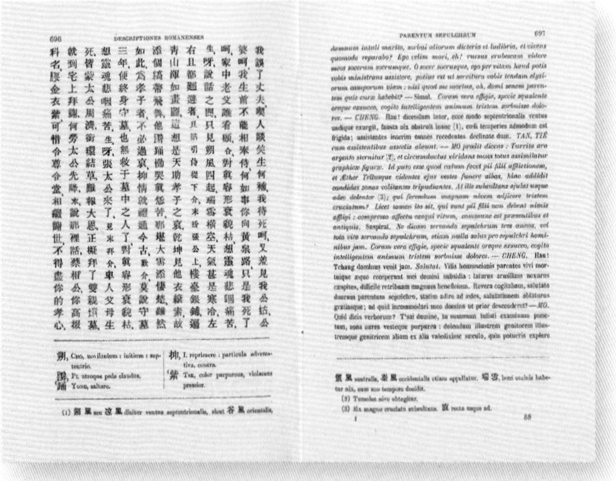

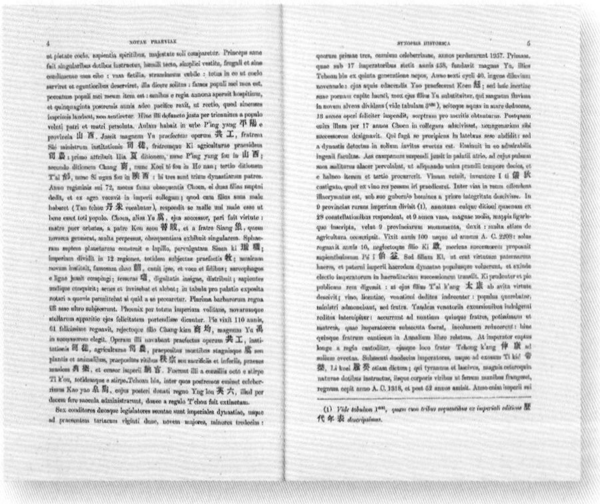

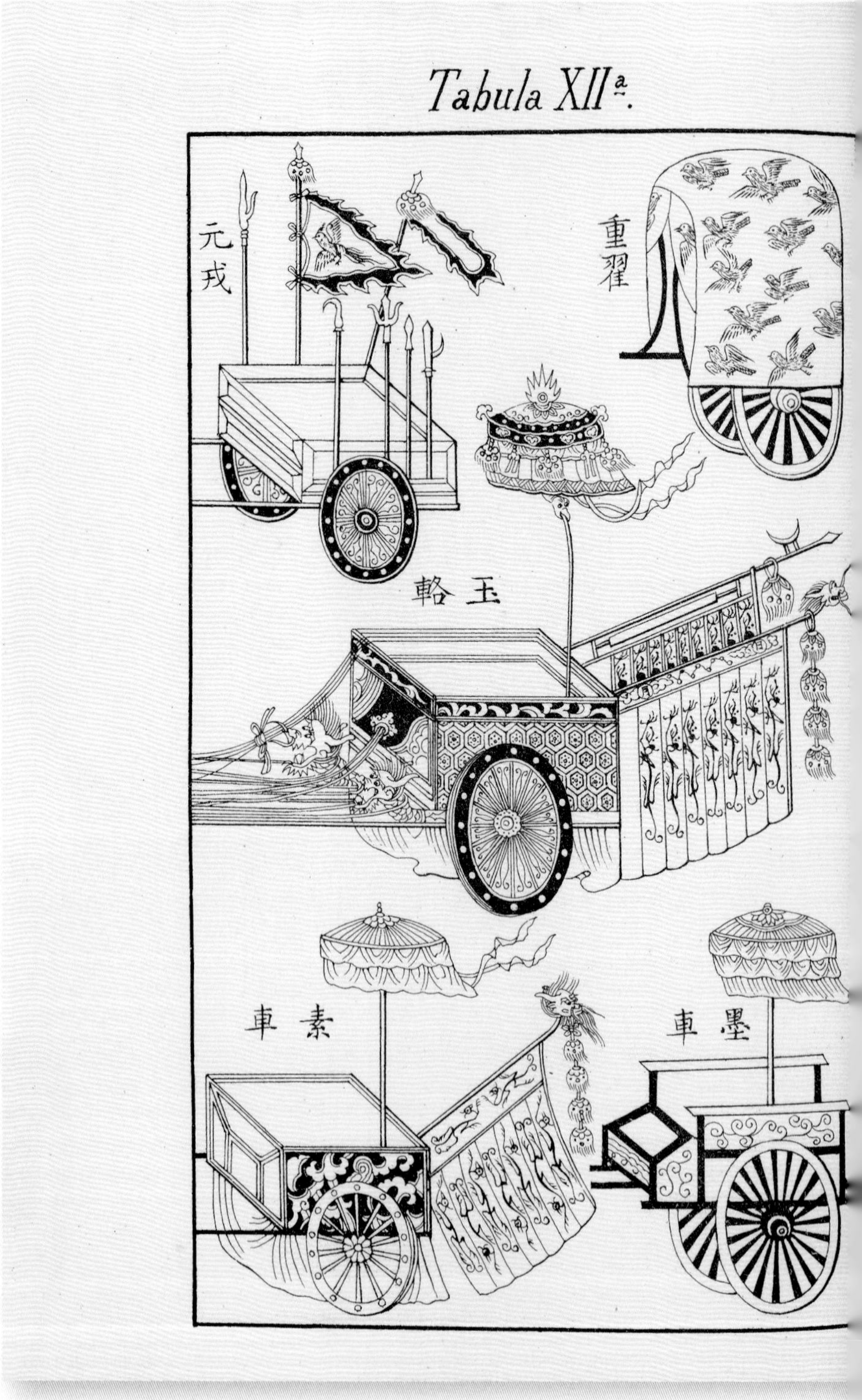
Tabula XIIa.
元戎
重翟
玉輅
素車
墨車

第四部分
烂然星陈

110
《博物进阶》
1862

[意] 晁德莅（撰），抄本，中文
23×13 cm
上海图书馆

Elements Scientifiques, 1862
Angelo Zottoli S.J. (au.), manuscript, Chinese
23×13 cm
Shanghai Library

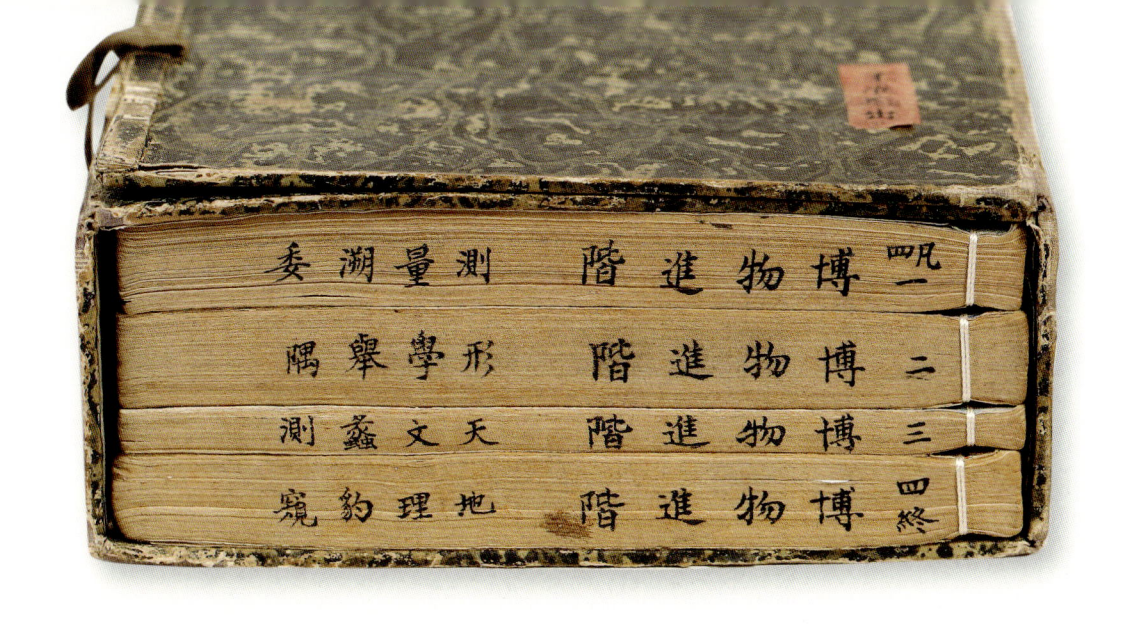

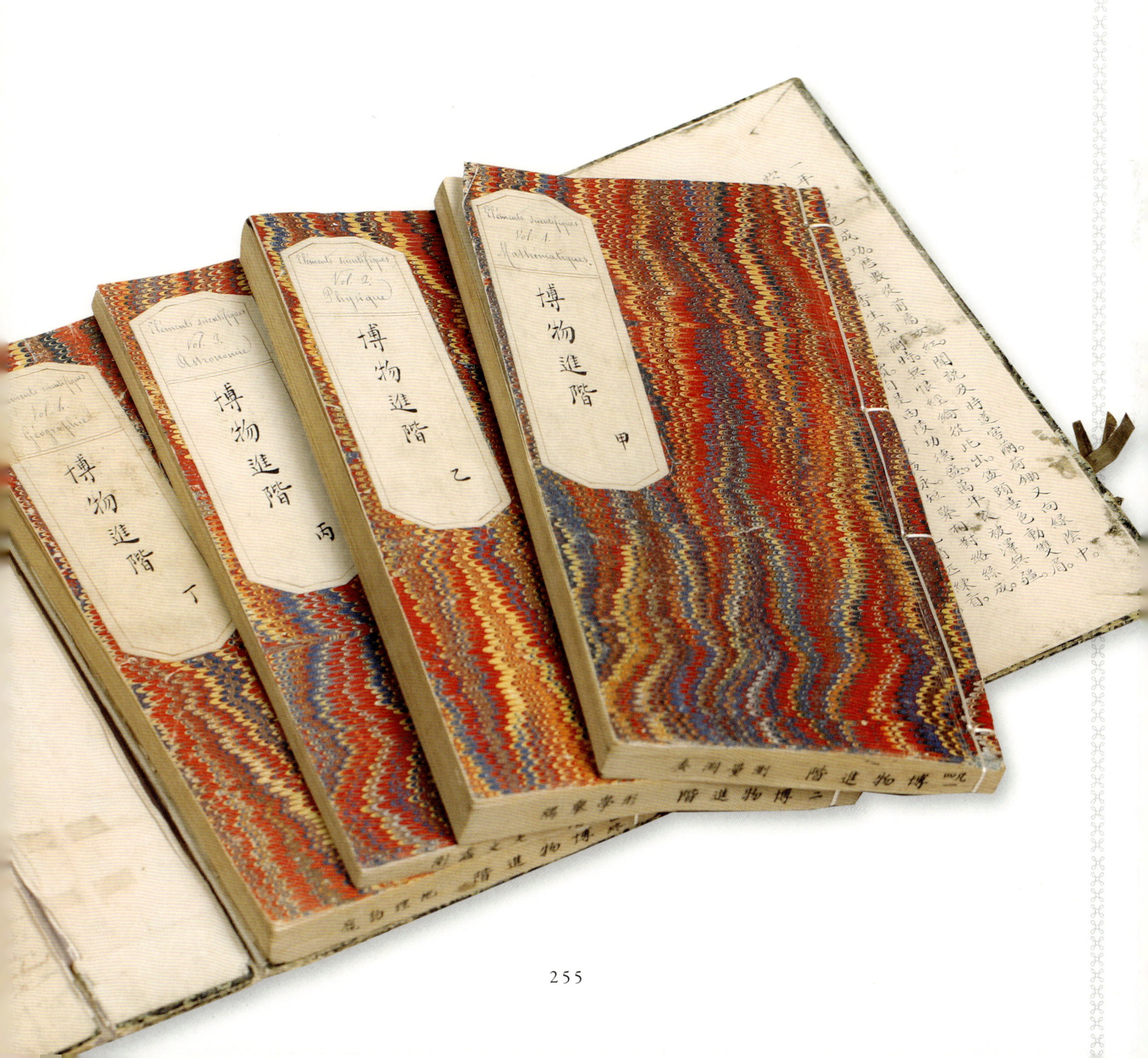

凡	博物進階	測量測溯委
二	博物進階	形學舉隅
三	博物進階	天文芻測
終	博物進階	地理豹窺

Éléments scientifiques, Vol. 1. Mathématiques — 博物進階 甲
Éléments scientifiques, Vol. 2. Physique — 博物進階 乙
Éléments scientifiques, Vol. 3. Astronomie — 博物進階 丙
Éléments scientifiques, Vol. 4. Géographie — 博物進階 丁

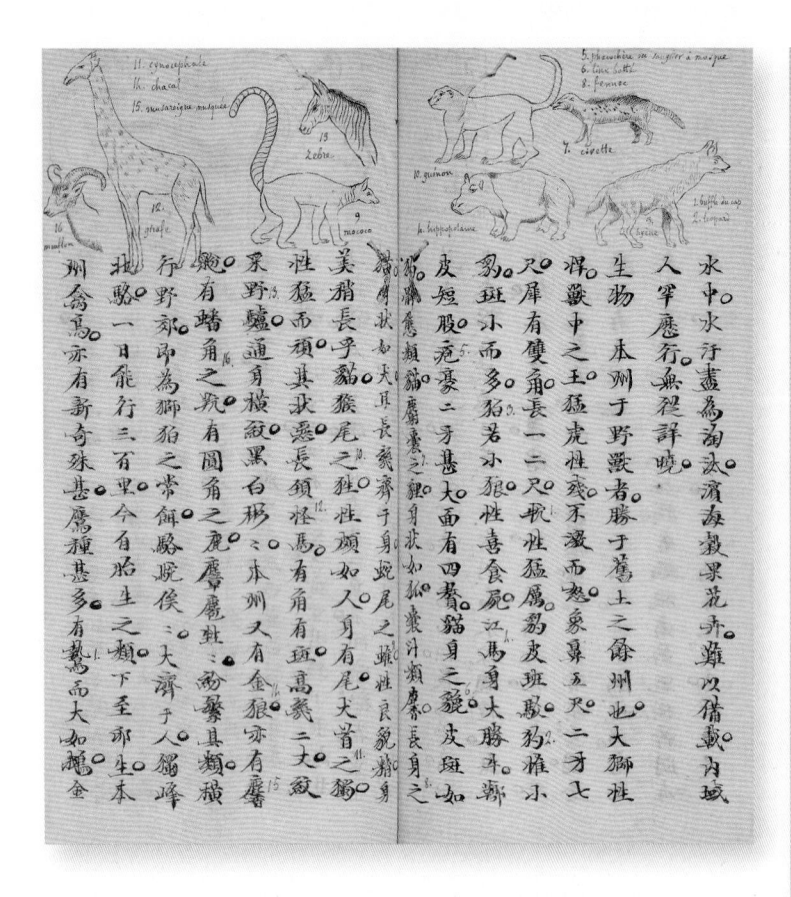

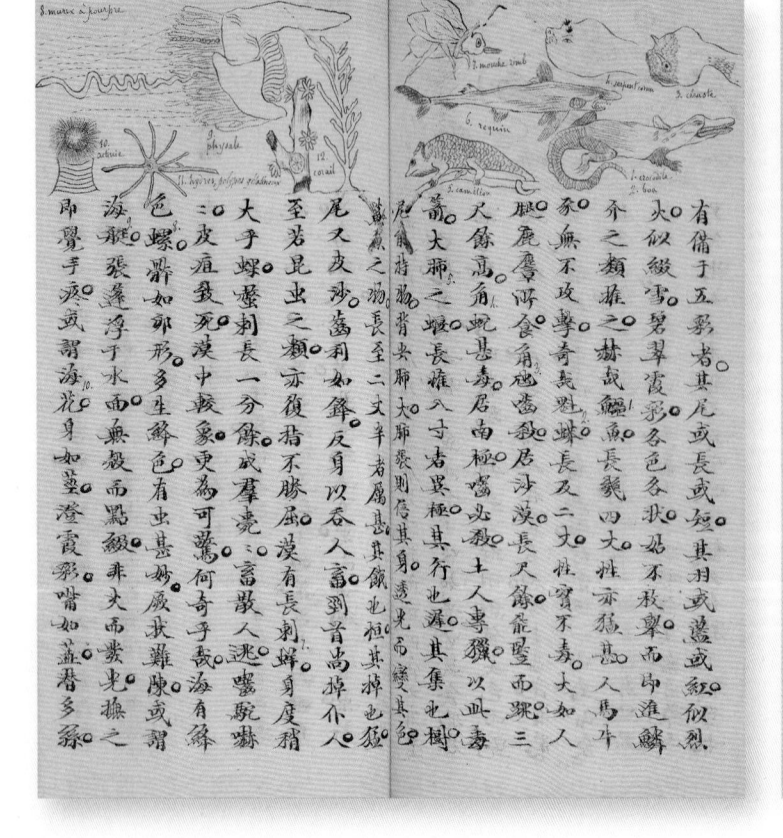

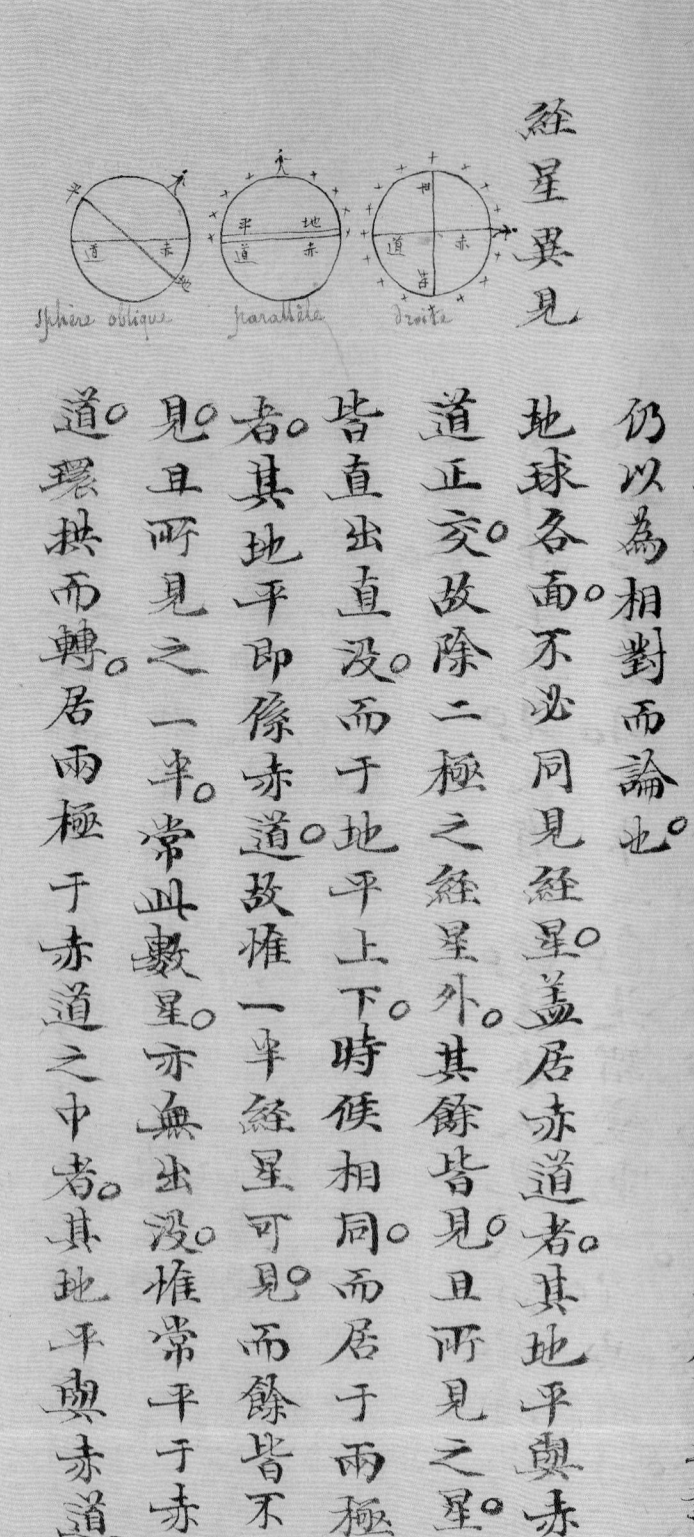

虚实之界：奇迹之书
《马可·波罗游记》主题文献图录

第四部分 烂然星陈

稠密併聚一處。但見其眾星之光不見其各列之位

耶昔有一名士用千里鏡窺天河一刻時間見有經

星之過約計十一萬六千又一次四十一分時見有

廿五萬八千今以無數之星合成為宿北宿三十有

六○南宿四十有六○黃道之中十有二○即曰巨蟹宮獅

子宮○室女宮○天秤宮○天蝎宮○人馬宮○磨羯宮○寶瓶宮

雙魚宮○白羊宮○金牛宮○雙兄宮○是也特因經星之動

亦自西之東故在黃道諸宮于天主降生前八百十

111
《大秦景教流行中国碑》
（拓片）
781

[伊] 景净（撰），陕西西安，叙利亚文 / 中文
27.5×177 cm
上海图书馆

Rubbing of the Nestorian Stele, 781
Jingjing (au.), Xi'an, Shaanxi, Syriac / Chinese
27.5×177 cm
Shanghai Library

第四部分
烂然星陈

大秦景教流行中国碑

虚实之界：奇迹之书
《马可·波罗游记》主题文献图录

景教流行中國碑頌并序

粵若常然真寂先先无元宵然靈虛後後而妙有惣玄摳而造化妙
二氣暗空易而天地開日月運而晝夜作匠成万物然立初人別賜良
此是之中陳其同於彼非之內是以三百六十五種肩隨結轍竟織法
有說之舊迫煎燒積昧二途之迷休復於是三一淨風無言之新教陶良用旡
朓以趣法理家國於於天敵設能事斯畢亭午昇真經留廿七部張元正施
礼心及登明宮含靈於是于既濟浮惟事所以削頂所以無內情不蓄臧貴賤
洗趣生荣之路存頋所以難名言以行削頂昭章强稱景教惟道非聖不弘聖
羅本占青雲而載真道經妙而難名言功用昭彰強稱景教惟道非聖不弘聖
年秋七月詔曰道無常名聖無常體随方設教密濟群生大秦國大德使聖
濟物利人宜行天下所司即於京義寧坊造大秦寺一所度僧廿一所大
景門聖跡騰祥永輝法界栞西域圖記及漢魏史策大秦國南統珊瑚
俗無寝盗人有樂康法非景不行主非德不立土宇廣闊文物昌明
道國冨元休玄宗至道皇帝令寧國等五王親臨福宇建立壇場法棟暫
絶紐傾頻家殷百城家給玄宗至道皇帝令寧國等五王親臨福宇建立壇場法棟
足奉慶睿圖龍髯雖遠弓劍可攀日角舒光天顏咫尺三載大秦國有
是天題寺牓額戴龍書寶裝璀翠灼爍丹霞睿扎宏空騰凌激日寵賞
青於靈武等五郡重立景寺元善資而福祚開大慶崑而皇業建

大秦寺僧景

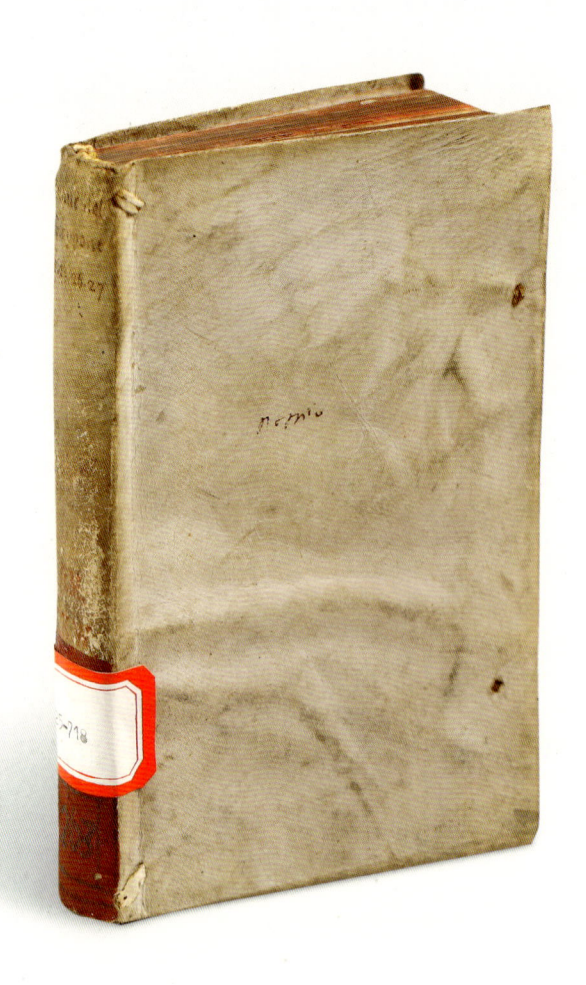

112
《日本年信1625，1626，1627》
1631

[意]弗朗西斯科·科贝莱蒂（编），罗马，意大利文
15.4×10.3 cm
上海图书馆

Lettere annue del Giappone de gl'anni 1625, 1626, 1627.
Al molto rev. in Christo P. Mutio Vitelleschi preposito generale della
Compagnia di Giesù, 1631
Francesco Corbelletti (ed.), Rome, Italian
15.4×10.3 cm
Shanghai Library

第四部分
烂然星陈

Queste Lettere annue di Giappone de gl'anni 1625. 1626. e 1627 si potranno stampare, se così parerà à Monsign. Reuerendiss. Vicegerente, & al Reuerendiss. P. Maestro del Sacro Palazzo. In Roma li 30. di Agosto 1631.

Mutio Vitelleschi Generale della Compagnia di GIESV.

Imprimatur, si videbitur Reuerendiss. P. Magistro Sacri Palatij Apostolici.

A. Episc. Bellicastren. Vicesg.

Imprimatur.
Fr. Nicolaus Riccardius Sacri Palatij Apostolici Magister, Ord. Præd.

Si protesta, che con la licenza hauuta di potersi stampare queste Lettere, non si pretende di contrauenire in niente alli Decreti fatti della Sacra Congregatione de' Riti, intorno alla Beatificatione, e dichiaratione de i Martiri, nè meno di fare scalino, con la semplice narratione delle cose contenute in esse, per venir alla proua, che quelli serui d'Iddio, la cui morte si racconta, siano veri Martiri, nè meno all'autentichezza de i Miracoli.

Molto Reu. in Christo Padre.

LA persecutione già tredici anni cominciata nel Giappone, seguita in quest'anno 1625. à porger materia di ragionare di tormenti, e di morti di varie persone, la cui costanza, e fortezza in tollerar per la fede supplicij diuersi, riferirò à V. P. dopo hauerle prima in breue, conforme al solito dato ragguaglio dello stato della Chiesa in questo Regno.

Dello Stato temporale del Giappone, e della Christianità di esso.

HA' commádato il nuouo Xogun quest'anno, che tutti li principali titolati del Regno, insieme con le mogli e figli habitino nella Città, doue egli risiede, ò per ingrandir la corte con la presenza di tanti Signori, ò per meglio dire per accrescere, & assicurare con quasi tanti ostaggi la regia Maestà, a' quali, perche non si solleuino a sperar più l'antica libertà, và sminuendo ogni giorno la potenza, e le forze in varie guise; ne solo serba di suo Padre, che anco viue, vn' odio crudele contro i Christiani, ma con l'istesse arti di regnare s'ingegna difendere, e propagare il suo impero, cercando ogni giorno nuoue

nuoue ragioni per essercitar la tirānia, dando ad intendere, che all'hora più teme, quando procura più di esser temuto da suoi vassalli. Non hà egli, sebene è crudelissimo nemico de' fedeli questi anno fatto morir veruno, ma dall'esempio di lui dell'anno passato mossi li Gouernatori hanno ferocemente proceduto contro i seguaci di Christo, de' quali cēto venti chi di ferro, e chi di fuoco sono morti in varij luoghi, ma particolarmente ne' Regni di Oxu, e Deua, per difesa della Santa Fede. Hà abbattuti, è vero, questa tempesta alcuni pochi neofiti, ma nè hà trouati molti apparecchiati talmēte, che la morte era loro più cara della vita; anzi de gli abbattuti si sono varij solleuati nel vedere la fortezza de' Compagni, e hanno ricomprato con varie dimostrationi di magnanimità quanto haueuano perduto nel discoprirsi fiacchi e debolo in difendere la religione Cattolica.

Nel rimanente del Giappone doue non è stata sì grande la persecutione, non solo si sono animati i Christiani antichi, ma con l'esempio di tanti generosi campioni, che hanno sparso il sangue per Christo molti di nuouo hāno riceuuto il santo Battesimo fin'al numero di mille cento e quattro adulti per opra de' nostri Padri, senza quelli, che si sono conuertiti con l'aiuto di altri Religiosi. Non è credibile con quanti bandi siano perseguitati quelli, che predicano la Santa Fede, nondimeno venti Sacerdoti, & quattro Fratelli Coadiutori, Religiosi nostri, trauestiti, hanno

hanno atteso con varie industrie senza perdonare à pericolo veruno a coltiuare, & accrescere la Christianità. Et in vero è sì grande lo sdegno del Xogun, che hormai non vi è più luogo ascoso doue si possino asscurare dal furore di lui.

Città, è distretto di Nangasacchi.

GRANDE è il numero de i Christiani, ma maggiore è l'ardore, che si scorge in tutti di conseruare la fede, che col latte molti di loro hāno beuuta: non si può negare, che dalle ruine dell'altre Chiese questa Christianità non sia cresciuta, perche nelle torbolenze, e calamità presenti non hanno i fedeli altro luogo più sicuro di questa Città. Sette della nostra Compagnia sono stati nascosti in essa, perche andar palesi non è concesso da gli ordini seueri, e dalla moltitudine di quelli, che vegliano per accusare i predicatori del Santo Euangelio. Con tutti i pericoli della vita, e della robba non sono però mai mancati Christiani, i quali à vicenda chi poco e chi molto tempo l'habbino alloggiati in casa per zelo di propagare la santa Fede. Hanno proceduto, con tutto ciò i nostri con gran cautela, di non prouocare à sdegno l'Imperatore, accioche per l'auidità di vn poco d'accrescimento non si perda quanto si è acquistato.

Haueua vno abbandonata la Santa Fede, quando oppresso da febre maligna mandò à chiamar' vn de' nostri Padri per accommodar l'anima

113
《科普特人与早期埃及人》
1636

［德］基歇尔（著），罗马，拉丁文
21.3×14.5 cm
上海图书馆

Prodromus coptus sive aegyptiacus, 1636
Athanasius Kircher S.J. (au.), Rome, Latin
21.3×14.5 cm
Shanghai Library

Imprimatur, si videbitur Reuerendiff. Patri Mag. Sacri Palatij Apostolici.

A. Torniellus Vicesg.

Iussu Reuerendissimi Patris F. Nicolai Riccardij S. Palatij Apostolici Magistri; librum P. Athanasij Kircheri Societatis Iesu, qui Prodromus Coptus, seu AEgyptiacus, notatur, ritè & ordine censui; In eo, non solum nihil offendi Religioni Catholicæ & bonis moribus pugnans, sed contra, quàm plurima ex abditis sacræ vetustatis, & mysticis AEgyptiorum penetralibus, ingeniosè eruta argumenta, quæ cum ob genuinam multarum linguarum cognitionem, tum ob reconditam rerum peregrinarum eruditionem ex ipsis fontibus haustam, orthodoxæ veritati robur & firmamentum sufficiunt, errores & hæreses labefactant. Dignum initium, vnde cætera æstimentur. Vigebit que diu, repertitium felicitate laboris & ingenij studium, nulli non eruditioni Sacræ & profanæ, lampada (quod dicitur) tradens. Ita censeo. Romæ, ex Domo professa, Iunij 15. An. 1636.

Melchior Inchofer . Soc. Iesu.

Imprimatur.
Fr. Nicolaus Riccardius S.P.A.M.

DOCTORVM ORIENTALIVM
De Prodromo Copto
Testimonia Encomiastica.

第四部分
烂然星陈

Isaaci Sciadrensis Maronitæ Archiepiscopi Tripolitani Syriæ ad Admodum R. P. Patrem sibi amantissimum Athanasium Kircherium è Soc: Iesu

Rhythmus Syriacus cantu Iacobitico

ATHANASII KIRCHERI
FVLDENSIS BVCHONII
E SOC. IESV.

PRODROMVS
COPTVS SIVE ÆGYPTIACVS.

Ad
Eminentiss: Principem S.R.E. Cardinalem
FRANCISCVM BARBERINVM.
in quo
Cùm linguæ Coptæ, siue AEgyptiacæ, quondam Pharaonicæ, origo, ætas, vicissitudo, inclinatio; tùm hieroglyphicæ literaturæ instauratio, vti per varia variarum eruditionum, interpretationumque difficillimarum specimina, ita noua quoque & insolita methodo exhibentur.

Romæ. Typis S. Cong: de propag: Fide. 1636.
Superiorum permissu.

Eminentissimo Principi
FRANCISCO
CARD: BARBERINO
S.R.E. Vicecancellario

ATHANASIVS KIRCHERVS
è Soc: *IESV*
perpetuam felicitatem.

Iacienda est, Eminentissime Princeps, mihi penè dixerim inuito, existimationis alea; dum hasce Coptæ, seu AEgyptiacæ linguæ primitias, sub Eminentissimi Nominis tui splendore mentis oculorumque arbitrio committo, æqua atque iniqua variorum iudicia non iniquo animo præstolaturus. Et latuissent illa sanè cum suo Authore, sicuti reliqua omnia, quæ de prisca, atque hucusque incognita AEgyptiorum symbolica sapiētia indefesso studio, conatu pertinaci, iam compararam supellectilia; nisi officiosa amicorum importunitas, armata deprecatio & amica quædam vis, quotidiana penè expostulatione de manibus extorsisset. Quorum ego, si authoritatē æque ac rationes eneruare valuissem, animum meum procul dubio

74　*Cap. III. De Copt. Aethiop. Colon.*　　　*Cap. III. De Copt-Aethiop. Colon.*　75

Inscriptio Syriaca ad Euangelij in China prædicati testificationem lapidi incisa, & postmodum in China singulari folio impressa.

Hi Chatacteres sinenses nōmi, & officia significant.

K 2

288　*Cap. III. De varia diuisione Literarum.*

radices dentium affixa, & inde ad inferiore, relabente pronunciantur. suntque sequentes.

Χ Θ Λ Ν Τ Ϯ Ϯ

Palati siue Palatinæ, aere ad palatum oris protruso pronunciantur. vt

Γ Κ Χ Ϧ Ϫ

Dentium siue dentales, quæ dentibus anterioribus lingua pulsatis efferuntur. vt

Ζ Ϛ Ρ Ϲ Ϣ Ϭ

Labiorum siue Labiales, quæ è labijs compressis erumpunt. vt

Β Π Φ Ψ Ϥ

CAPVT QVARTVM.

De particulis seu literis quibusdam genus dictionum distinguentibus.

Notandum hic primò in Coptis dictionibus seu nominibus genus nequaquam ex fine, quemadmodum apud Latinos, Græcos, & Hebræos, aut per articulos, dignosci; sed ex præfixis quibusdam literis seu signis vt ipsi vocant, quæ articulorum ad instar sunt, totam nominum generis distinctio-

C. IIII. De partic: genus dict: distinguentibus.　289

ctionem desumendam esse vt in exemplo.

1. Omnis dictio quæ præfixum habuerit signum Π₁, indicat nomen masculinum singulare determinatum articulo, quod Arabes cognoscunt per ا & ال. vt Exem:C

ⲡⲣⲱⲙⲉ Vir.　ⲡⲥⲱⲧⲏⲣ Saluat or.
ⲡⲙⲱⲓⲧ Semita.　ⲡⲙⲁⲣⲧⲩⲣⲟⲥ. Testis.

Exceptio.

Nomina propria hoc signo carent. vti etiam apud Latinos, Græcos. vt

Ⲙⲁⲣⲕⲟⲥ　Marcus.　(ⲡⲙⲁⲣⲕⲟⲥ
Ⲥⲓⲙⲱⲛ　Simon.　non (ⲡⲥⲓⲙⲱⲛ
Ⲥⲁⲩⲗⲟⲥ　Saulus.　(ⲡⲥⲁⲩⲗⲟⲥ
Ⲡⲁⲩⲗⲟⲥ　Paulus.　(ⲡⲡⲁⲩⲗⲟⲥ

2. Omnis dictio quæ habuerit præfixum signum Ϯ significat nomen fæmininum determinatum, quod Arabes per ا & ال cognoscunt.

Ϯⲉⲕⲕⲗⲏⲥⲓⲁ Ecclesiâ.　Ϯⲡⲁⲣⲑⲉⲛⲟⲥ Virgo.
Ϯⲇⲓⲁⲑⲏⲕⲏ Testamentuū.　Ϯⲉⲓⲣⲏⲛⲏ Pax.

Signum Ϯ quoque indicat hominem (vt iuxta Arabum idioma loquar) de se ipso loquētem in prima persona singulari.

Ϯⲛⲁⲕⲁϫⲓ loquar.　Ϯⲛⲁⲉⲣϩⲏⲧⲥ incipiam.
Ϯⲛⲁⲧⲱⲟⲩⲛ surgam.　Ϯⲛⲁⲉⲣϩⲉⲗⲡⲓⲥ sperabo.

Omnis dictio quæ initio habuerit præfixum signum Ⲛ̄, indicat pluralitatem nominum, vel fæmininorum vel

O o　　ma-

第四部分
烂 然 星 陈

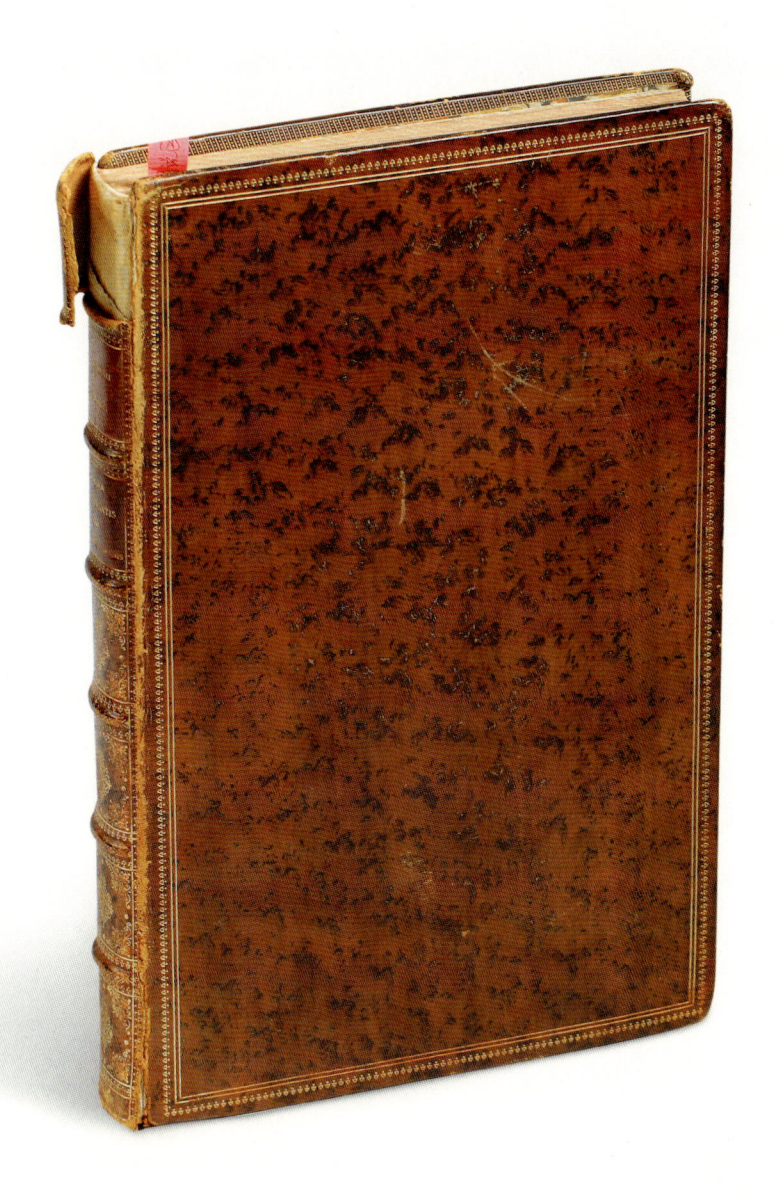

114
《中国图说》
1667

[德] 基歇尔（撰），阿姆斯特丹，拉丁文
39.3×25.4 cm
上海图书馆

China Monumentis, 1667
Athanasius Kircher S.J. (au.), Amsterdam, Latin
39.3×25.4 cm
Shanghai Library

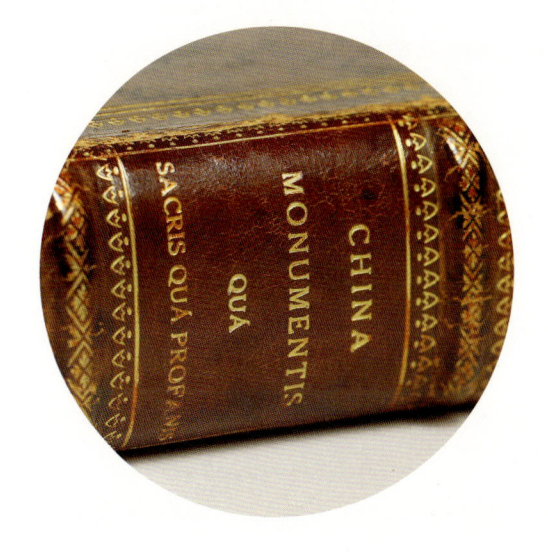

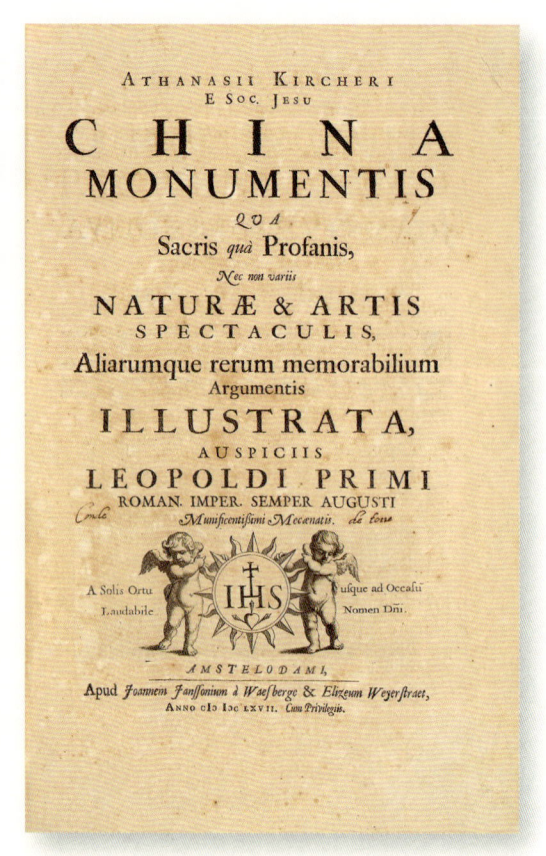

虚实之界：奇迹之书
《马可·波罗游记》主题文献图录

第四部分
烂然星陈

115
《中国上古史》
1658

[意] 卫匡国（撰），慕尼黑，拉丁文
20.5×16.7 cm
上海图书馆

Sinicae historiae decas prima, 1658
Martino Martini S.J. (au.), Munich, Latin
20.5×16.7 cm
Shanghai Library

第四部分
烂然星陈

116
《中国新图志》
1655

［意］卫匡国（编），阿姆斯特丹，拉丁文
52.5×36 cm
上海图书馆

Novus atlas sinensis, 1655
Martino Martini S.J. (ed.), Amsterdam, Latin
52.5×36 cm
Shanghai Library

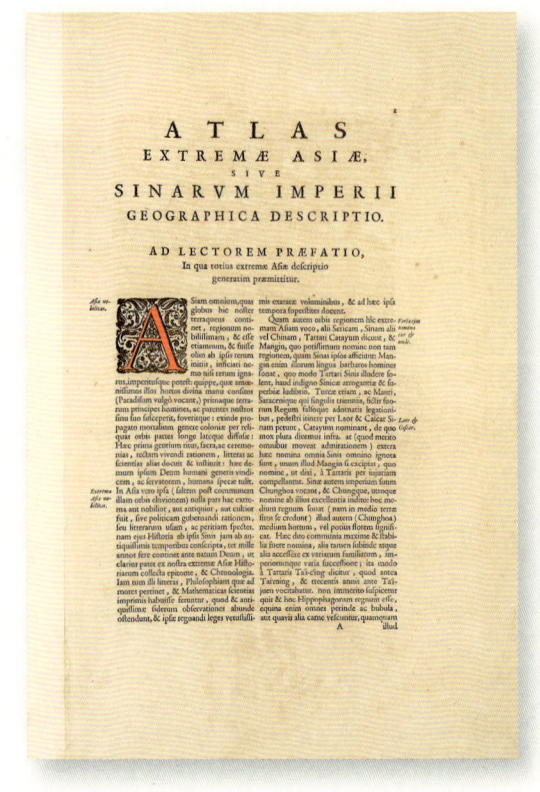

第四部分
烂然星陈

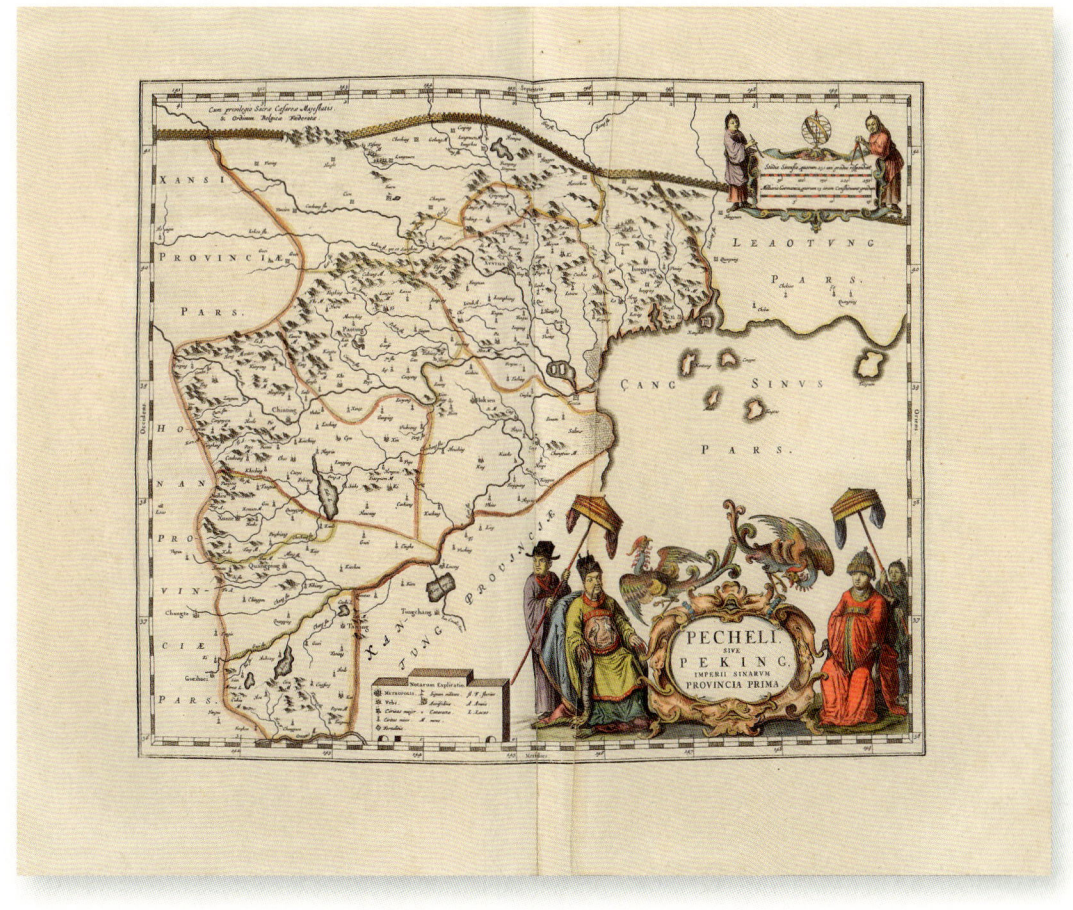

117
《广舆图》
万历十七年刻本

（明）罗洪先（撰），江苏常熟，中文
35×23 cm
上海图书馆

Guangyu tu, 1579
Luo Hongxian (au.), Changshu, Jiangsu, Chinese
35×23 cm
Shanghai Library

第四部分
烂然星陈

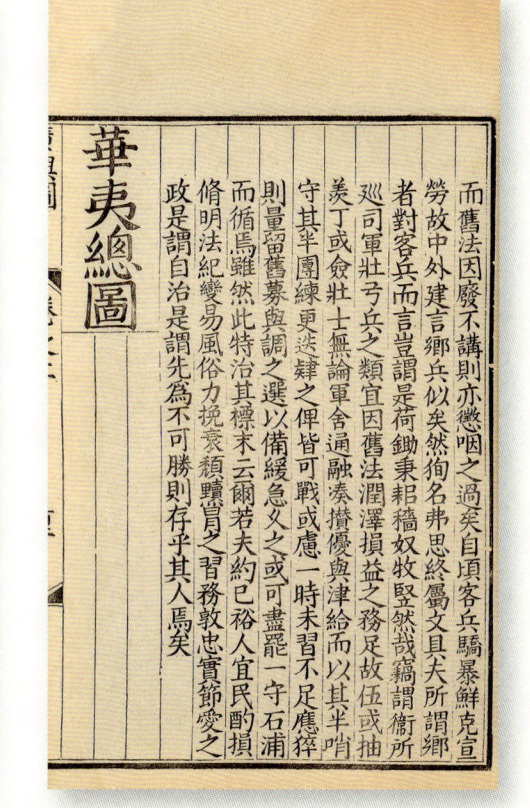

九邊輿圖總論

或有問於論者曰今天下之患何居論者曰北方最可憂餘無忠焉此莫強於遼金元莫弱於我

朝而始盛於今日蓋自我

太祖高皇帝三犁其庭窮荒餘落僅存喘息是以九邊戍率

成祖文皇帝迅掃之後元裔半留中國入遜沙漠者無幾不過四十萬其視宋人備西夏一路而屯戍七十萬盖倍蓰矣百餘年來生聚既蕃浸淫近開平與和東勝河套之地皆為所據不過依險結營以防衝突僅能守禦之不能持久每一大舉即為萬全絕無堂堂一戰者盖眾寡之勢殊強弱之形不亂耳幸擾掠之外無有他志計日數程異隴肉瞭馬頗亦勞費若得志眼眼惟無已是以邊境

華夷總圖

而舊法因廢不講則亦懲咽之過矣自項客兵驕暴鮮克宣勞故中外建言鄉兵似矣然狗名弗思終屬文具夫所謂鄉者對客兵而言豈謂是荷鋤秉耒耡名弗思屬文具夫所謂鄉巡司軍壯弓兵之類宜因舊法潤澤損益之務足哉鄉所美丁或僉兵無論軍舍通融奏攢優與津給而以其半啃守其半團練更迭番之俾皆可戰或慮一時未習不足應猝則量留舊募與調之選以備緩急父之或可盡罷一守石浦而循焉雖然此特治其標末云爾若夫約已裕民酌損脩明法紀變易風俗力挽衰頹嘗之習務敦忠實節愛之政是謂自治是謂光為不可勝則存乎其人馬矣

118

《中国智慧》
（《论语》部分）
康熙元年刻本

［葡］郭纳爵、［意］殷铎泽（译），江西建昌，拉丁文／中文
18×27.6 cm
上海图书馆

Sapientia Sinica, 1662
Ignace da Costa S.J. & Prospero Intorcetta S.J. (tr.), Jianchang, Jiangxi,
Latin / Chinese
18×27.6 cm
Shanghai Library

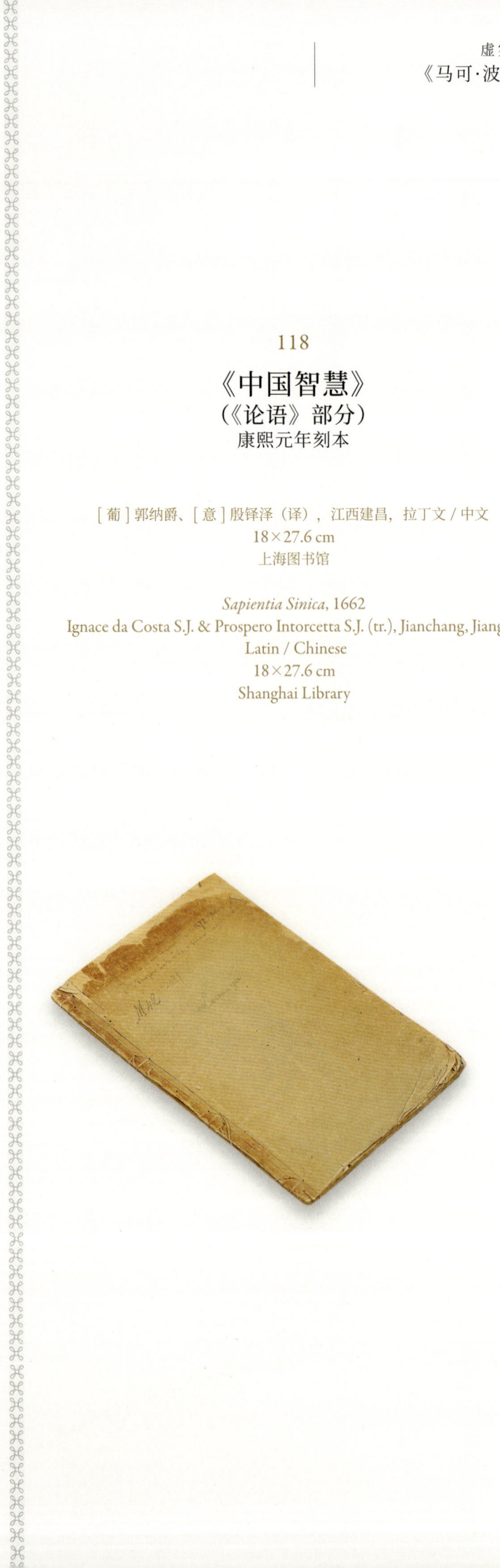

第四部分
烂然星陈

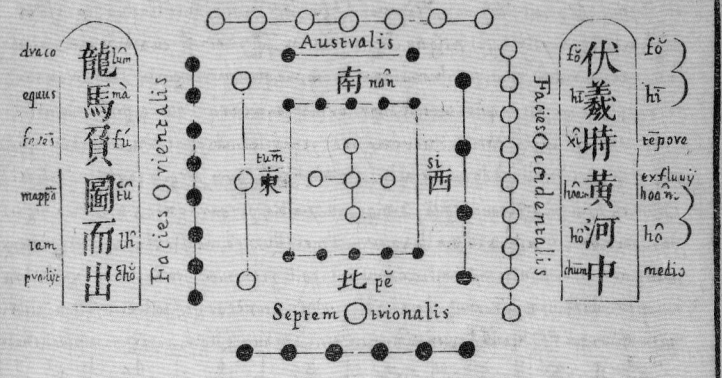

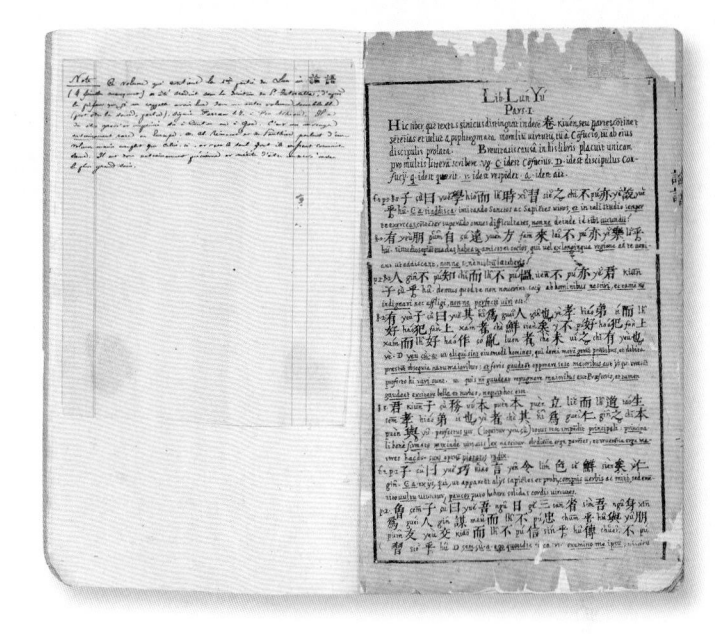

119
《中国政治道德学说》
（仿真件）
1669/2016

［意］殷铎泽（译），果阿，拉丁文/中文
34×28 cm
意大利西西里大区中央图书馆 / 私人收藏

Sinarum scientia politico-moralis (facsimile edition)
1669/2016
Prospero Intorcetta S.J. (tr.), Goa, Latin / Chinese
34×28 cm
Biblioteca Centrale della Regione Siciliana / Private collection

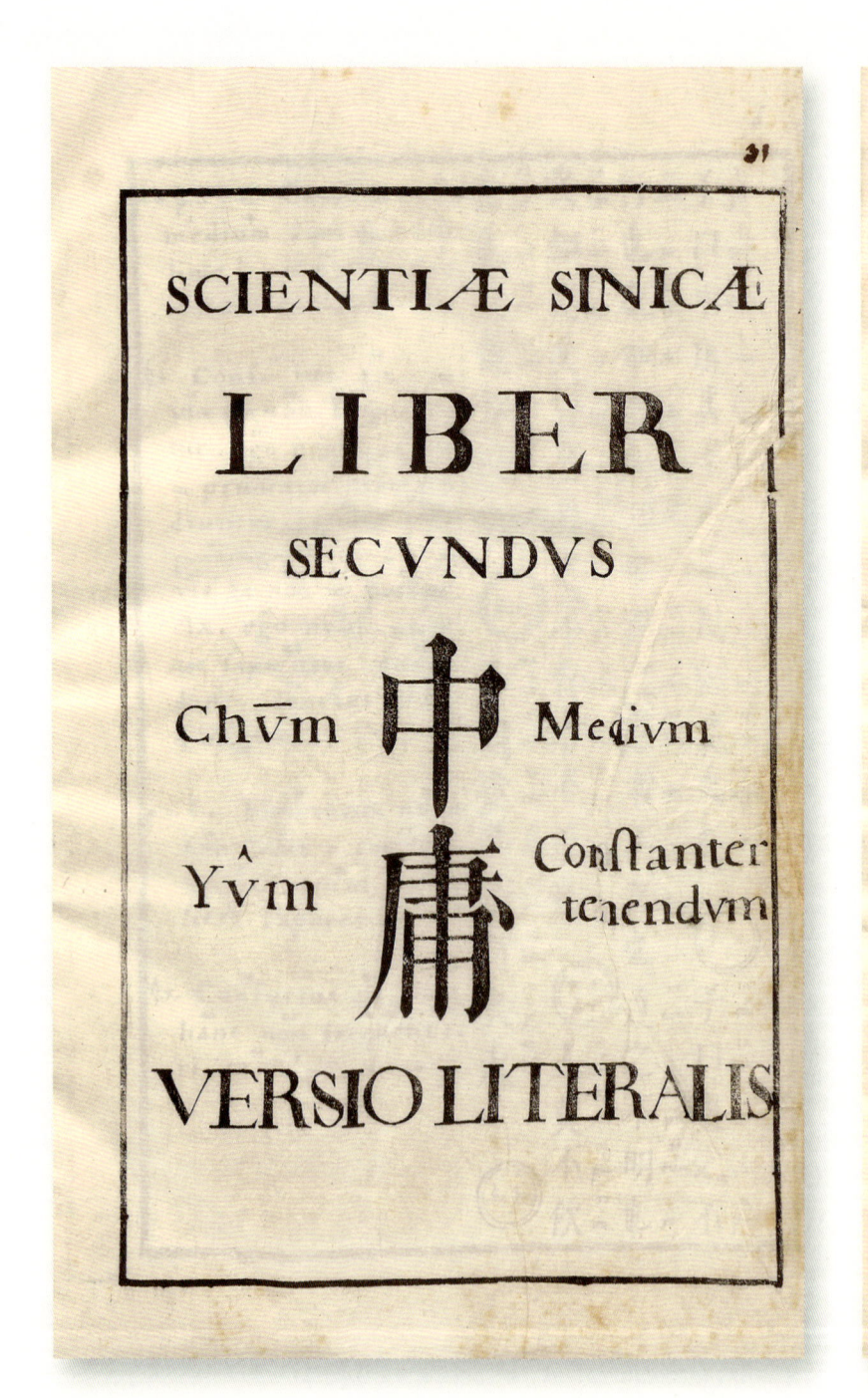

第四部分
烂然星陈

---

4. p. 1. §. 1. Confucius ait: medium ò quàm illud sublime! quod è vulgo pauci illud teneant, iam diu est.

2. Confucius ait : cur via hæc non frequentetur, ego noui ; quia scilicet prudentes transgrediuntur ; rudes non pertingunt. Cur item vid. hæc non sit perspecta, ego noui ; quia scilicet sapientes excedunt ; inertes non attingunt.

§. 1. Hominum nullus non bibit et comedit: at pauci valent dignoscere sapores.

2. Confucius ait. viam hanc non frequentari, proh! quàm dolendum!

CONFVCII VITA

Cum 孔 kum 夫子 fu çu, siue Confucius, quem Sinenses vti Principem Philosophiæ suæ sequuntur et colunt, vulgari, uel domestico potius nomine 丘 Kieu dictus; cognomento 仲 chum 尼 nhi; natalem habuit sedem in Regno 魯 lu (quod Regnum in Prouinciam deinde, quæ hodie 山 xan 東 tum dicitur, redactum fuit) in pago 陬 çeu 邑 ye territorij 昌 cham 平 pim, quod ad ciuitatem 曲 Kio 阜 feu pertinet; hæc autem ciuitas paret vrbi 兗 yen 州 cheu dictæ. Natus est anno 21 Imperatoris 靈 lim 王 uam (fuit hic tertius et uigesimus e familia, seu domo Imperatoria 周 cheu dicta) Anni nomen 庚 Kem 戌 sio; secundo item et uigesimo anno 襄 siam 公 cum Regis, qui eá tempestate Regnum lu obtinebat; die 13 undecima lunæ 庚 Kem 子 çu dicta, sub horam noctis secundam, anno ante Christi ortum 551. Mater ei fuit 徵 chim, e familia prænobili 顏 yen oriunda; Pater 叔 xo 梁 leam 紇 he, qui non solum primi ordinis magistratu quem gessit in Regno 宋 fum, sed generis quoque nobilitate fuit illustris; stirpem quippe duxit 宋 (uti Chronica sinensium testantur, et tabula genealogica, quæ prologomenis ad annales sinicos inseritur, perspicue docet) ex uigesimo septimo, siue penultimo Imperatore 帝 ti 乙 ye dicto. Porro natus est Confucius Patri iam septuagenario, quem adeò trienis infans mox amisit; sed Mater pupillo deinde superstes fuit per annos unum et uiginti, coiuge in monte tum 防 fam Regni lu sepulto. Puer iam sexenis præmaturá quadam maturitate, uiro, quàm puero similior, cum æqualibus nunquam uisus est lusitare. Oblata edulia non ante delibabat, quàm prisco ritu, qui 祖 çu 豆 teu nuncupatur, cælo uenerabundus obtulisset. Annorum quindecim adolescens totum se dedere cœpit Priscorum libris euoluendis, et reiectis ijs, quæ minús utilia uidebantur, optima quæque documenta selegit, primúm expressurus ea suis ipse moribus, deinde alijs quoque ad imitandum propositurus. Non multo post uná cum 孟 mem 懿 y 子 çu

120
《马可·波罗圣经》
（仿真件）
13世纪/2012

巴黎 / 罗马，拉丁文
27.5×17.6 cm
佛罗伦萨老楞佐图书馆 / 意大利特雷卡尼百科全书研究院

Bible of Marco Polo (facsimile), 13th century/2012
Paris / Rome, Latin
27.5×17.6 cm
Biblioteca Medicea Laurenziana / Istituto della
Enciclopedia Italiana Treccani

第四部分
烂然星陈

121
《漫游七百年前的中国——〈马可波罗游记〉》
年代不详

叶永烈（撰），手稿，中文
27×20 cm
上海图书馆

Wandering in China 700 years ago——"The Travels of Marco Polo", [s.d.]
Ye Yonglie (au.), manuscript, Chinese
27×20 cm
Shanghai Library

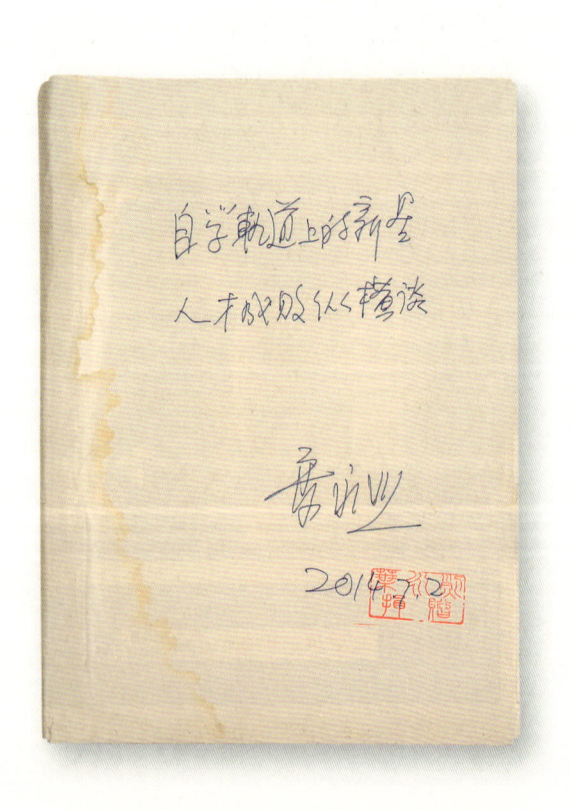

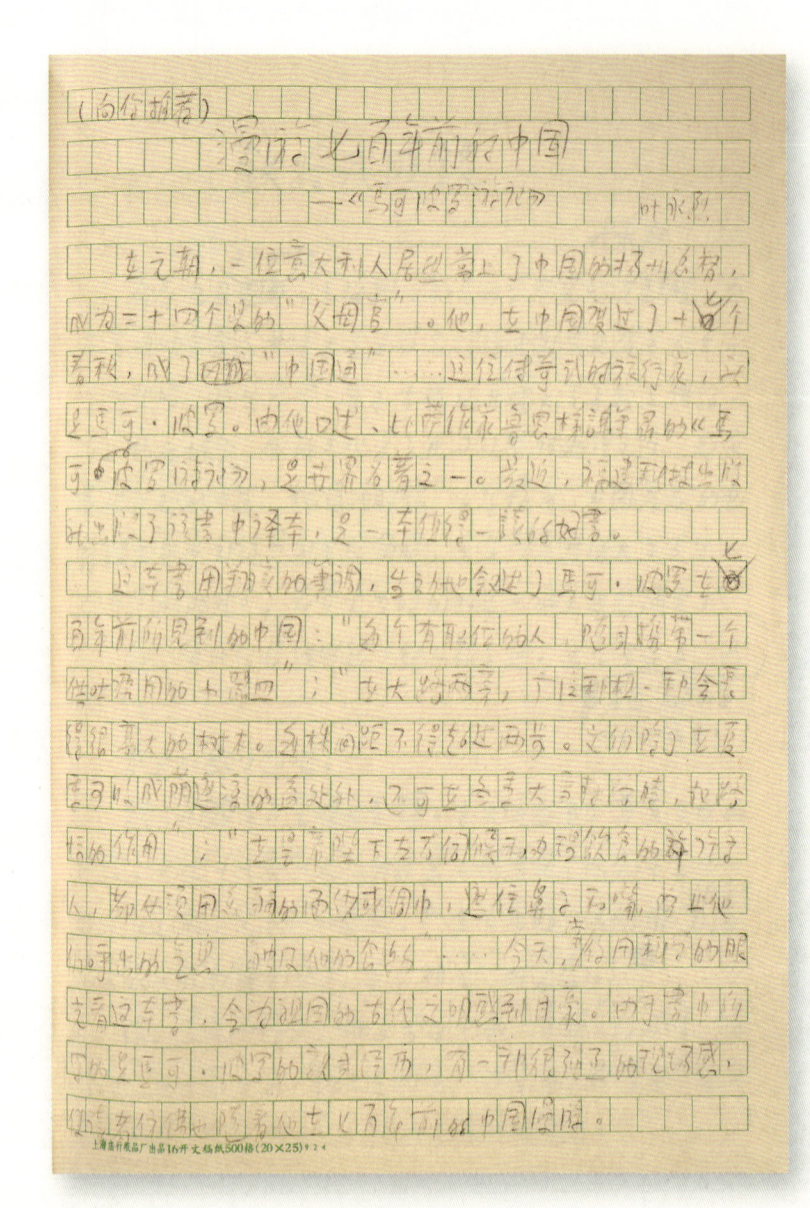

第四部分
烂然星陈

122
《文艺复兴的先驱
——但丁（1265—1321）》
年代不详

高莽（撰），手稿，中文
43.9×21 cm
上海图书馆

Dante, a pioneer of Renaissance, [s.d.]
Gao Mang (au.), manuscript, Chinese
43.9×21 cm
Shanghai Library

123
《夜访但丁故居》
年代不详

许淇（撰），手稿，中文
26×18.8 cm
上海图书馆

A visit to the house of Dante at night, [s.d.]
Xu Qi (au.), manuscript, Chinese
26×18.8 cm
Shanghai Library

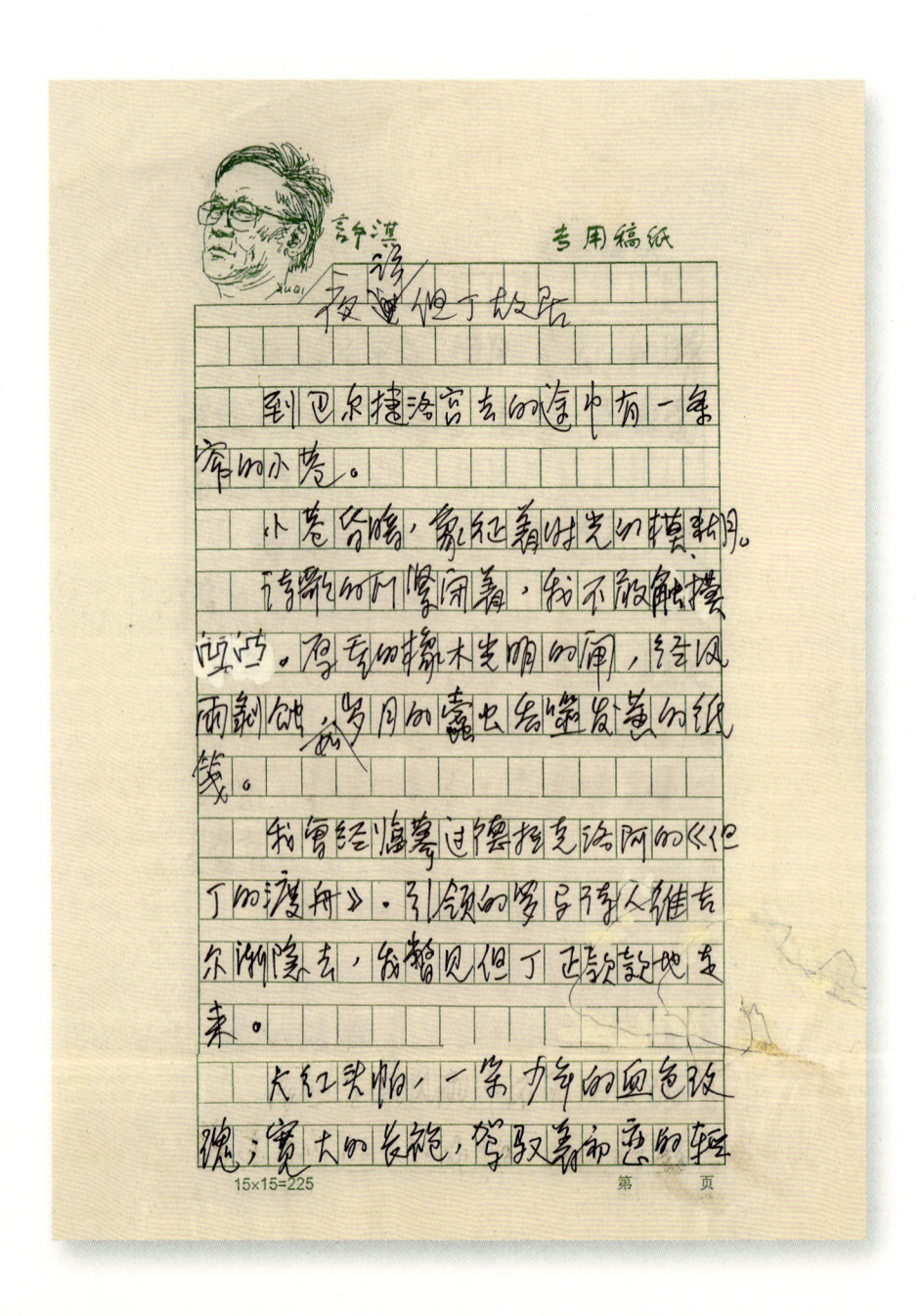

第四部分
烂 然 星 陈

124
《但丁故居》
1988

沈柔坚（绘），油画
80×64.5 cm
上海图书馆

The house of Dante, 1988
Shen Roujian (paint), oil painting
80×64.5 cm
Shanghai Library

125

点名号在吹响……衰老的但丁
《普希金抒情诗全集》
2009

[俄]普希金（著），冯春（译），中文
29.7×21.1 cm
上海图书馆

Bugle call is blowing...Aged Dante,
Pushkin's lyric poetry, 2009
Aleksandr Sergeyevich Pushkin (au.), Feng Chun (tr.), Chinese
29.7×21.1 cm
Shanghai Library

点名号在吹响……衰老的但丁
从我的手中掉落在地上，
刚在唇边读出的诗行
没有读完便归于沉静。
我的思绪已飞向远方。
多熟悉的声音，多悦耳的声音，
在久远的往昔，我曾悄悄
成长的地方，你常常响起，
在我的耳边萦回缭绕。

第四部分
烂然星陈

126
《马可·波罗研究论文选粹（中文编）（外文编）》
（荣新江签名）
2021

荣新江、党宝海（编），上海，中文
24×17 cm
上海图书馆

Chinese Scholars on Marco Polo: Selected Essays;
Foreign Scholars on Marco Polo: Selected Traslations
(with signature), 2021
Rong Xinjiang & Dang Baohai (eds.), Shanghai, Chinese
24×17 cm
Shanghai Library

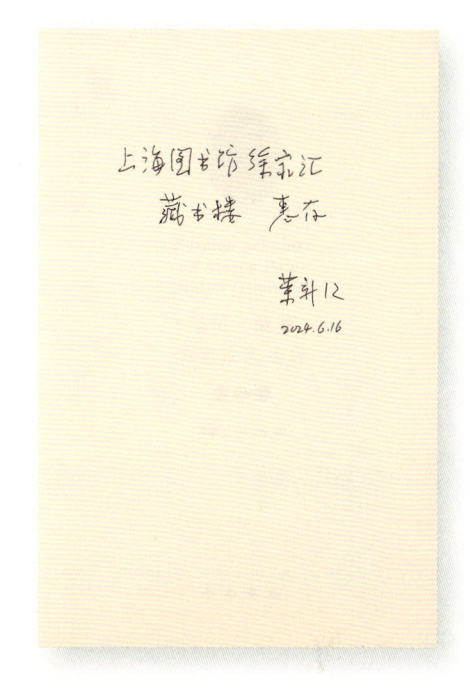

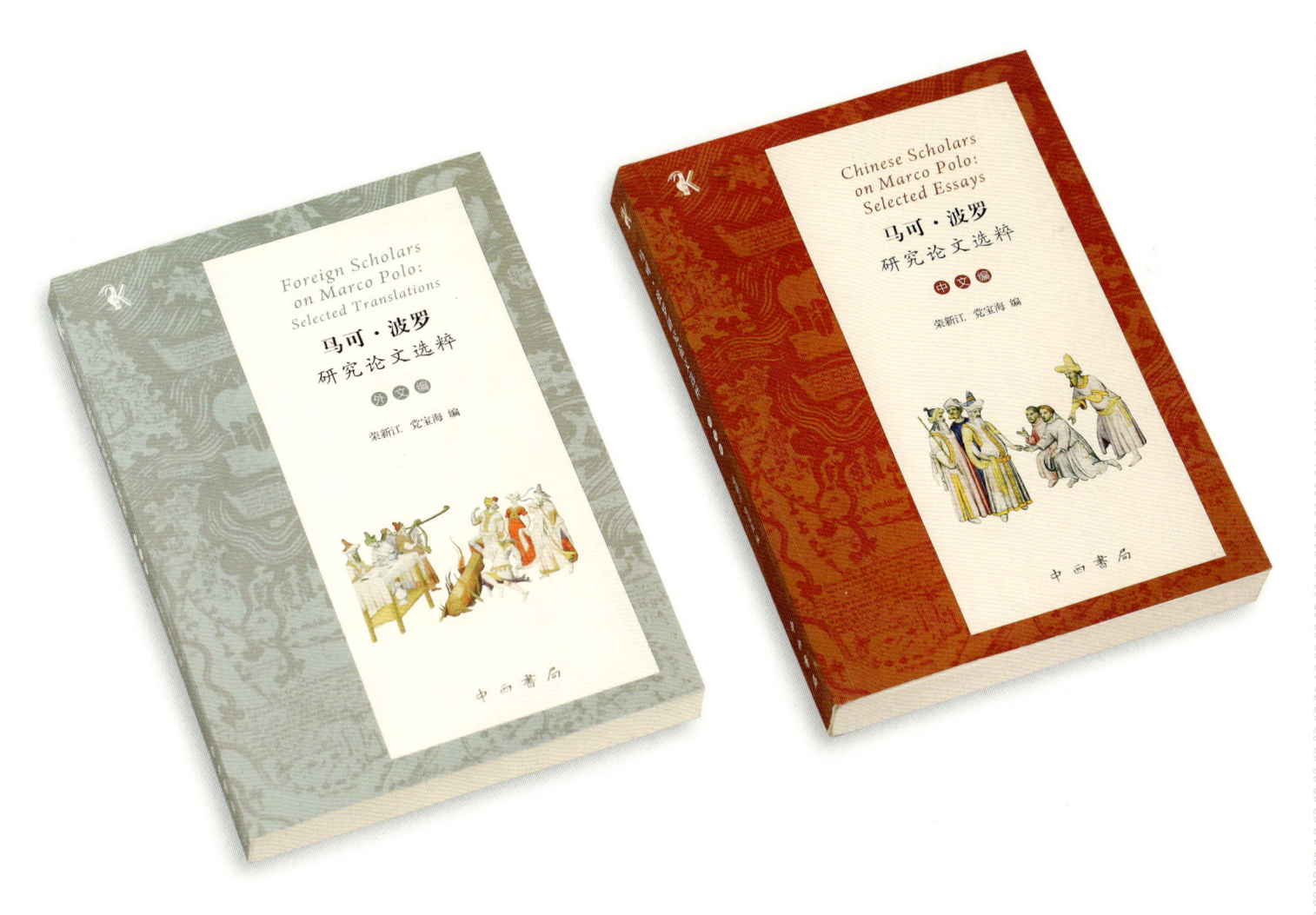

虚实之界：奇迹之书
《马可·波罗游记》主题文献图录

第四部分
烂 然 星 陈

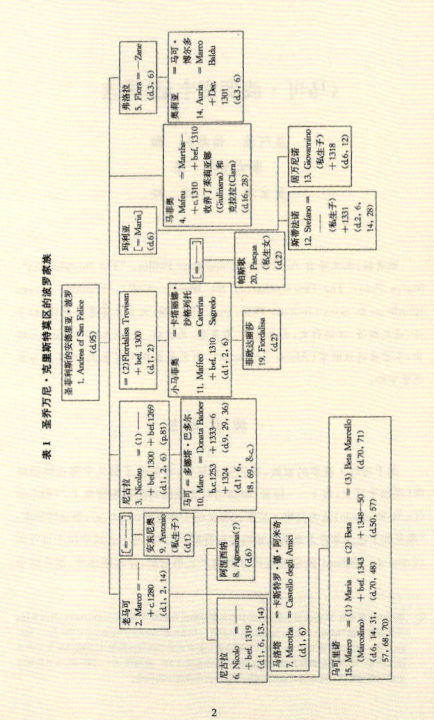

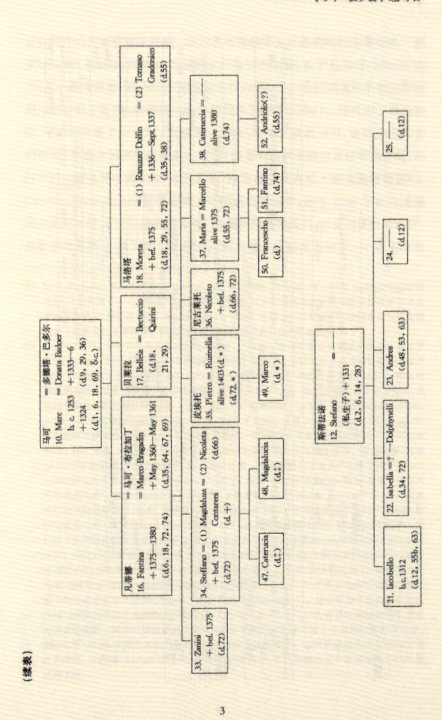

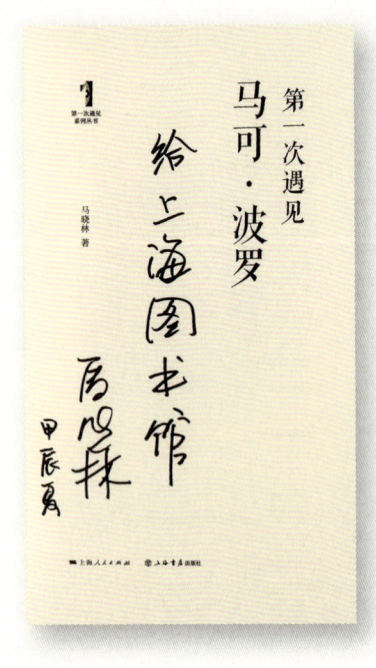

127
《第一次遇见马可·波罗》
（马晓林签名）
2024

马晓林（著），上海，中文
18×11.5 cm
上海图书馆

Meeting Marco Polo (with signature), 2024
Ma Xiaolin (au.), Shanghai, Chinese
18×11.5 cm
Shanghai Library

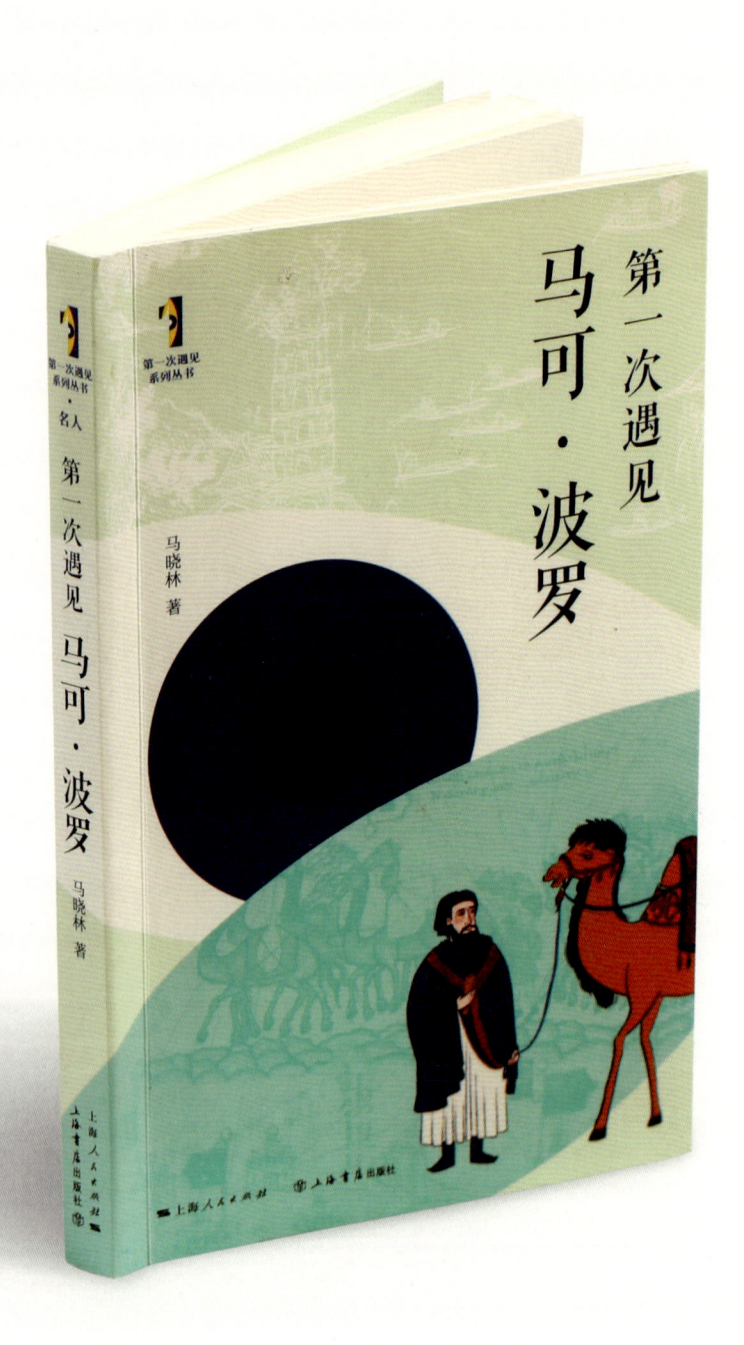

第四部分

烂 然 星 陈

图书在版编目(CIP)数据

第一次遇见马可·波罗/马晓林著.—上海：上海书店出版社，2024.5
("第一次遇见"系列丛书)
ISBN 978-7-5458-2370-7

Ⅰ.①第… Ⅱ.①马… Ⅲ.①马可·波罗(Marco Polo 1254—1324)-传记-通俗读物 Ⅳ.
①K835.465.89-49

中国国家版本馆CIP数据核字(2024)第071689号

策划编辑　徐如梦
出版统筹　杨英姿
责任编辑　张　冉　胡美娟
封面设计　周伟伟

第一次遇见马可·波罗

马晓林 著

出　版　上海人民出版社
　　　　　上海书店出版社
　　　　　(201101　上海市闵行区号景路159弄C座)
发　行　上海人民出版社发行中心
印　刷　上海商务联西印刷有限公司
开　本　787×1092　1/32
印　张　6.875
版　次　2024年5月第1版
印　次　2024年5月第1次印刷
ISBN 978-7-5458-2370-7/K·495
定　价　49.00元

他的模样

十七岁的马可·波罗（Marco Polo）乘着贡多拉小舟，离开威尼斯的家，划过曲折的水道、弯弯的石桥，眼前终于豁然开朗。亚得里亚海，是地中海的一个大海湾，也将是马可·波罗一生中渡过的第一片海。在这里，他换乘大船，远航东方。

马可·波罗的传奇故事，从此启航。

马可·波罗的容貌是怎样的呢？

我们在动画片、影视剧和电子游戏里，能看到平面的或者立体的马可·波罗形象；在杭州、扬州、张掖等城市的街头，能遇到他的塑像；在历史课本或者《马可·波罗行纪》的插图中，能看到他的画像。这些形象虽有差异，但气质大体一致——这是一位精神奕奕的意大利人，而且常常留着一副络腮胡子。他穿着的长袍，不中不西，让人觉得就是丝绸之路旅行家该有的款式。他步履矫健，风尘仆仆，仿佛随时都要踏

3

马可·波罗肖像
（收藏于巴蒂亚亲王旧藏画馆）

法国国家图书馆藏
《加泰罗尼亚地图集》细节：马可·波罗商队

128
《马可·波罗寰宇记》
2017

[英]慕阿德、[法]伯希和（译），上海，英文
25×17.5 cm
上海图书馆

Marco Polo: The Description of the World, 2017
Arthur Christopher Moule & Paul Pelliot (tr.),
Shanghai, English
25×17.5 cm
Shanghai Library

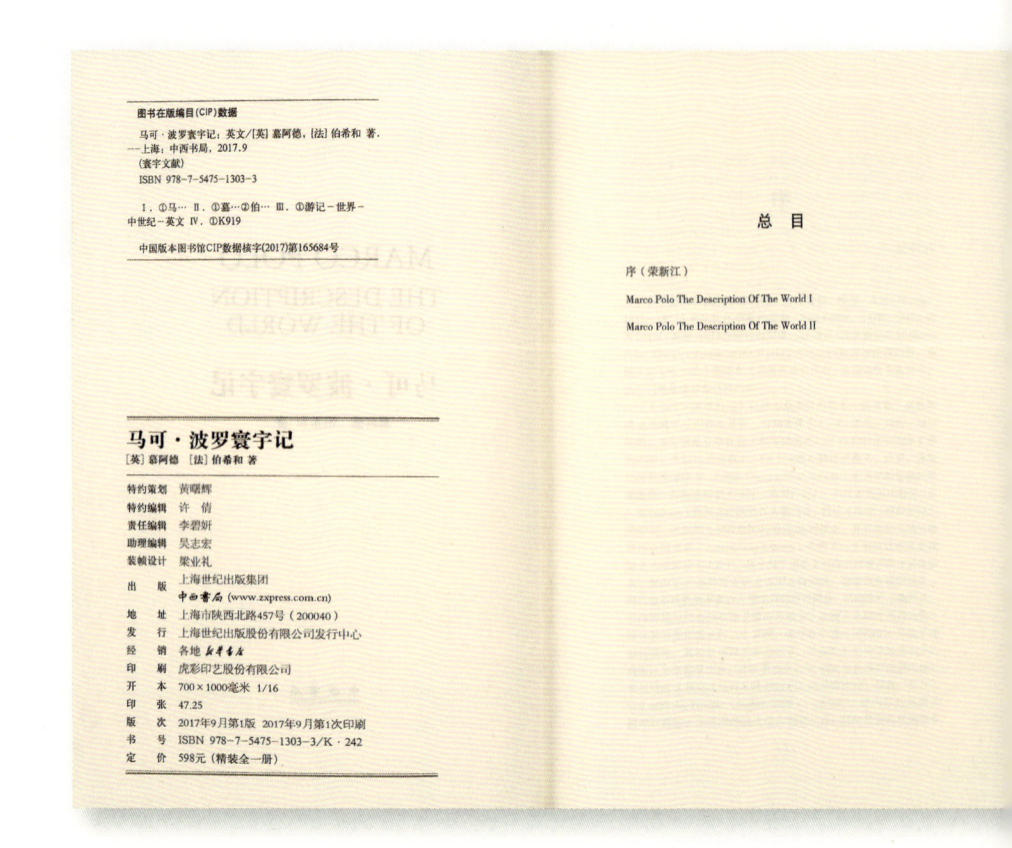

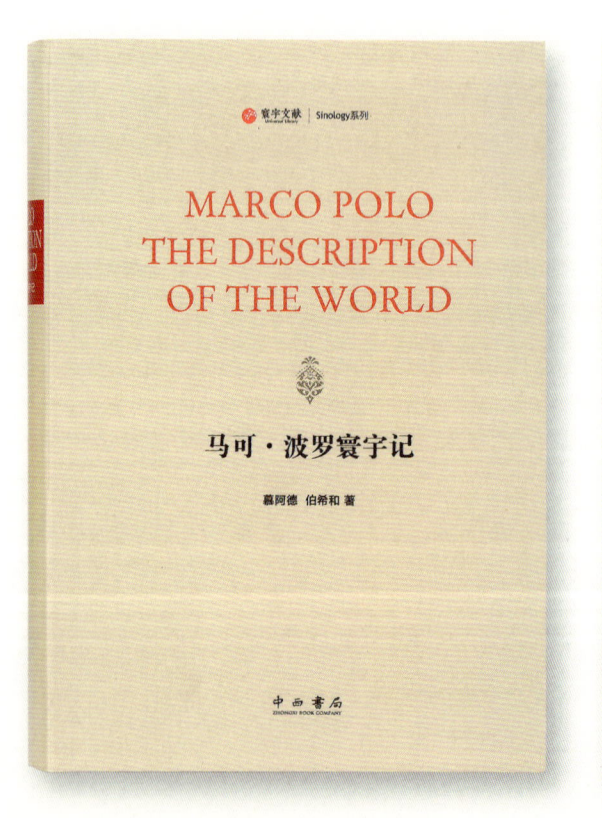

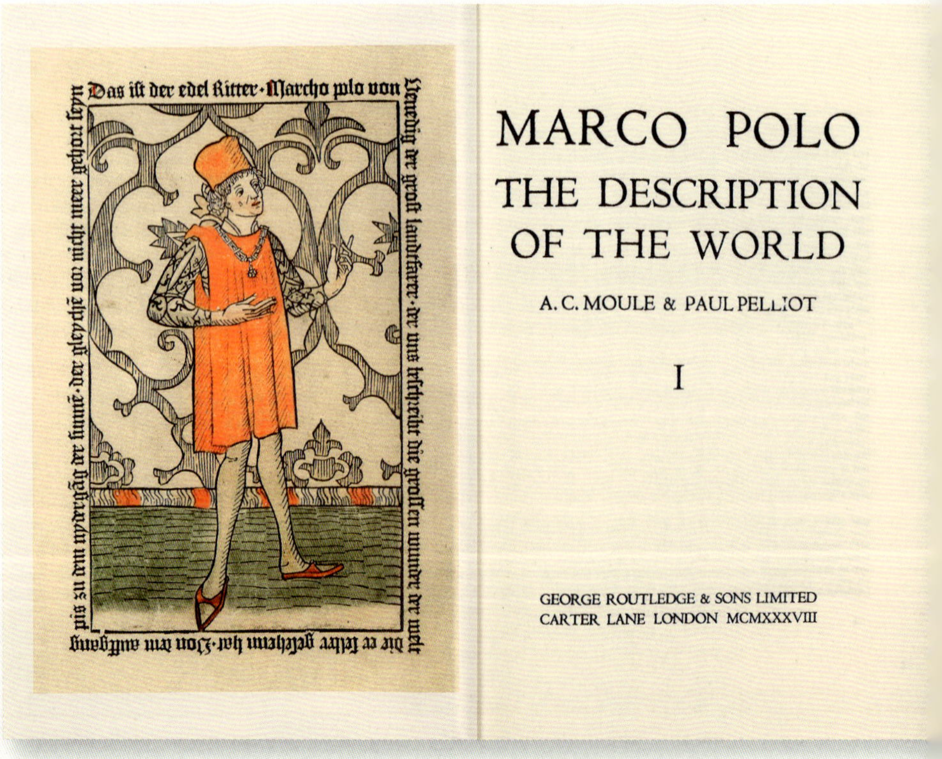

第四部分
烂然星陈

序

荣新江

本书是英国汉学家慕阿德（又译穆勒、穆尔，A. C. Moule，1873—1957）和法国汉学家伯希和（Paul Pelliot，1878—1945）合著的《马可·波罗行记》的研究和翻译，以《马可·波罗寰宇记》（*Marco Polo: The Description of the World*）之名，1938 年在伦敦出版，是继玉尔（H. Yule）英译本之后最权威的译本，也是最学术的译本，迄今仍然是学界最信赖的本子。

《马可·波罗行记》以抄本众多且内容不一致著称，现已知道主要分属于三个抄本系统，分别简称为 F、R、Z 本。1862—1870 年间，玉尔曾经长年在意大利等地调查，以 75 种抄本和刊本汇校为四类，而以宫廷法语本（FA）为底本翻译成英文。此后，意大利国家地理学会（Italian Geographical Society）和威尼斯市政府希望纂修一部国家版的《马可·波罗行记》，所以委托贝内带托（L. F. Benedetto）教授访察欧洲各大图书馆，搜访《马可·波罗行记》的抄本。他发现玉尔没有见过的约 60 种抄本，并且在米兰的安布罗西亚图书馆（Ambrosiana Library）找到了一个当时还没有发现的 Z 本的转抄本（Z'）。这个拉丁语本上有许多内容不见于其他抄本，但由于 Z' 抄写者缺乏古写本的知识，致使该本错误较多，而且他不理解原本页边大量注释种的缩写等语，因此没有正确细读。贝内带托对所有抄本做了精心的校对，并做了比较合理的分类，即今天学界所遵从的三个系统，在导言中他对每种抄本都做了详细的描述。其校订本以 F 本为底本，并在页下把见于其他本子的内容以小字校录出来，并注明出处，于 1928 年在佛罗伦萨出版，书名用意大利对《马可·波罗行记》的习惯称呼，题作《百万》（*Il milione*, Firenze: Olschki, 1928）。1932 年，贝内带托出版了据校订后的 F 本译成的现代意大利语文本，其中包含有其他抄本

中重要段落的增补，但为方便阅读，没有标注出处，还对原本的一些明显错误做了改订（*Il libro di messer Marco Polo, cittadino di Venezia, detto Milione, dove si raccontano le meraviglie del mondo*, Milano-Roma: Treves-Treccani-Tumminelli, 1932）。意大利人里奇（Aldo Ricci）根据贝内带托提供的意大利语文本译成英文，末及出版而亡故。丹尼森·罗斯（E. Denison Ross）与贝内带托对其译稿做了校订，完善了这个英译本，出于谨慎的考虑，罗斯对贝内带托校改订的部分改回为原状。此英译本题"马可·波罗游记"，提前于 1931 年在伦敦出版（Aldo Ricci, *The Travels of Marco Polo, translated from the text of L.F. Benedetto, with an introduction and index by Sir E. Denison Ross*, London: G. Routledge & Sons, 1931）。此本颇受好评，被译成多种语言。我国张星烺先生所译《马哥孛罗游记》（上海商务印书馆，1937 年）即据此本，但删掉绝大多数注释。日本学者青木一夫、爱宕松男先后据以译成日语，均载《东方见闻录》（前者东京校仓书房，1960 年；后者东京平凡社刊本东洋文库丛刊，1978 年）。

然而，贝内带托的校本虽好，但只印了三百部，流通不广；里奇的英译本十分准确流畅，但却没有译出处。与此同时在做《马可·波罗行记》整理研究的慕阿德，对此有所不满，他先后撰写书评，除对其成就给予充分肯定之外，还指出贝内带托校本的一些错误和现代语体本的出处问题（刊 *BSOS*, 5/1, 1928, pp. 173-175；*JRAS*, 3, 1932, pp. 603-625）。然而，促使慕阿德重新翻译《马可·波罗行记》的更大动力，是 Z 本的发现。

1924 年贝内带托在安布罗西亚图书馆找到的 Z 本转抄本 Z' 本的口文中说，这个拉丁文的本子是 1795 年受朱塞佩·图阿多（Giuseppe Toaldo）之命根据中世纪的一个托莱多（Toledo）抄本复制的，朱塞佩·图阿多为此特意感谢泽拉达（Cardinal Zelada）主教借给他这个抄本。1932 年 12 月，英国的大维德爵士（Sir Percival David, 1892—1964）在西班牙托莱多天主教大教堂分会图书馆（Chapter Library of the Cathedral）找到了这个抄本，并于 1933 年 1 月得到了抄本的照片。Z 本的前面部分有大量删节，但后面越来越多的内容完全不见于其他抄本，因此价值连城。这个本子由大维德爵士交给慕阿德和伯希和，促成了新译本的产生。

根据最先于 1935 年 3 月出版的《马可·波罗寰宇记》第 2 卷后面的一个简要目录，这部由大维德爵士设计、由慕阿德和伯希和合作的新著的完整计划是：第 1 卷约 580 页，包括导言、翻译、章节对照表、抄本目录和各种文书档案；第 2 卷 135 页，为大维德爵士找到的泽拉达拉丁文本（Z 本）的校订排印本；第 3 卷约 580 页，是不同作者的专题研究论文、专有名词和东方语言文字的考释、参考文献目录、索引；第 4 卷是大约 80 幅地图和图版。显然，慕阿德主要负责第 1 卷和第 2 卷，即抄本整理、校勘和英译；而伯希和主要负责第 3 卷和第 4 卷，即专有名词考释、研究论文整理、图版的准备和地图的绘制。据说有 60 页图版和 20 幅地图，其中有些地图是伯希和专门为此绘制的（此据戴闻达/Jan Julius Lodevijk Duyvendak 的书评，载 *T'oung Pao*, 34/3, 1938, pp. 246-248）。

慕阿德正是按照这个计划工作的，继 1935 年出版《马可·波罗寰宇记》第 2 卷后，Z 本拉丁文校订排印本之后，1938 年又出版了本书第 1 卷，包含上述计划中的所有内容。根据慕阿德撰写的长篇导言，他在玉尔、贝内带托等前人工作的基础上，总共收集到 143 种《马可·波罗行记》的抄本和刊本，其中 119 种为抄本，并以 F 本为底本，对绝大多数本子据原件和照片做了校对，甄别异同，辑录诸本多出的文字。在整理工作的基础上，慕阿德把 F 本全文译成英文，把同一词句的不同异文放到脚注当中，同时把不同本子上多出的词句，用斜体字插入 F 本的正文当中，如果有两个不同的增补，则中间用分隔号区分开来，在页边注明插入文本的缩写符号，如 R、Z 等等。这种有如中国"百衲本"的方式，既可以让读者阅读连贯的 F 本的原貌，而且还可以看到主要来自 17 种多出来的文字 Z 本多出来的文字。他知道它们原本应当是分离的，但迄今为止，这种"百衲本"仍然是最为学术、包含各本信息最全的本子。慕阿德费尽心力，把不同文本的句子揉入 F 本，同时保持了英语语法的正确，我们在使用中也能感受到他的这种苦心。与底本较差的玉尔本、无注出处的贝内带托/里奇译本相比，慕阿德把 F 本为主、汇集所各种本子的异文，学术价值最高，而用英语翻译，也便于一般读者阅览，因此可以说，

这是到目前为止最好的本子。因为译者认为马可·波罗这本书并不是一个旅行故事，而是对世界奇闻逸事的描述，所以采用 F 本的题目 *Le divisiment dou monde* 作为书名，英译为 *The Description of the World*，直译就是"对世界的描述"，也有人译作更典雅一些的"寰宇记"，因此这个影印本的中文名字，就定名为"马可·波罗寰宇记"。

在第 1 卷的长篇导言中，慕阿德依次讨论了有关波罗家族、马可·波罗的生平和旅行、波罗家族的宅邸、《马可·波罗寰宇记》的抄本和刊本、本书的译本等问题，书后附有《寰宇记》7 种版本的章节对照表、各种抄本的分类目录，以及关于波罗家族及马可·波罗墓志的文书档案全文，其中有些是首次发表。

1957 年，慕阿德又出版了《行在及其他有关马可·波罗的注释》（*Quinsai, with other Notes on Marco Polo*, New York: Cambridge University Press, 1957），主要是根据东方史料，对《寰宇记》中最后的一章加以专门的研究，涉及杭州历史、地理的一些问题。书后也对《马可·波罗寰宇记》的勘误表，读者在使用这个权威的译本时应当注意。

虽然第 1—2 卷《马可·波罗寰宇记》由慕阿德和伯希和共同著名，但无疑主要工作为慕阿德所做。慕阿德 1873 年 5 月 18 日出生在中国杭州，父亲慕稼谷（George Evans Moule）是英国安立甘会华中区主教。1898 年慕阿德从剑桥大学毕业，回到中国，作为建筑工程师在中国的教会工作。1904 年在山东传教。1909 年回到国，从事汉学研究。1933 年接替翟理斯（Herbert A. Giles）任剑桥大学中国语言和中国历史教授，1938 年退休，职位由哈隆（Gustav Haloun）接任。慕阿德在汉学方面没有多少建树，他主要的研究领域是中西交通史，大概是他家族或本人的传教士背景，他最关心的是基督教入华史，陆续发表《早期基督教入华传教的失败》（The Failure of Early Christian Missions to China, *The East and the West*, 12, 1914, pp. 383-410）、《十字架在中国景教徒中的使用》（The Use of Cross among the Nestorians in China, *T'oung Pao*, 28, 1931, pp. 78-86）、《中国的景教徒》（The Nestorians in China, *JRAS*, 1933, pp. 116-120）等论文，著有《1550 年前的中国基督教史》（*Christians in China before the year 1550*, London: Society for

Promoting Christian Knowledge, 1930）；有郝镇华汉译本，中华书局，1984 年）、《中国的景教徒》（*Nestorians In China*, London: Stephen Austin & Sons LTD, 1940）等。这样的学术背景，对于慕阿德整理研究《马可·波罗寰宇记》一定是有帮助的，而他在杭州的生活经历，无疑更有利于他理解马可·波罗的记述，大概也是由此之故，他还专门把马可·波罗有关杭州的记载写成一本专著——《行在》。1957 年 6 月 5 日，慕阿德在英国与世长辞，他没有等到伯希和的注释卷的出版，那是他去世两年后的事情了。

《马可·波罗寰宇记》的另一作者伯希和，没有按期完成庞大的任务，他的著作在其身后才得以出版，对于他的介绍见笔者给《马可·波罗行记》影印本所写的序。

慕阿德与伯希和合著的《马可·波罗寰宇记》无疑是玉尔《马可·波罗之书》出版以后，最好的《马可·波罗行记》的英译本，因为涵盖了一百多个本子的信息，所以学术性也最强。多年来，这本书成为学者们利用《马可·波罗行记》时的依据。1955 年，伯希和的弟子韩百诗（Louis Hambis）曾根据本书翻译成典雅的法语，前有导言，后有简要的注释、索引和地图（*La description du monde, Texte intégral en français moderne avec introduction et notes par Louis Hambis*, Paris: Library C. Klincksieck, 1955），颇受法语读者看好评。但遗憾的是，中国学者一直没有人翻译此书，大多数读者还是在使用 1936 年出版的冯承钧译《马可·波罗行记》。近年来，我和党宝海副教授组织马可·波罗读书班，会读并翻译《马可·波罗寰宇记》，将来有望出版一个准确的中文本。在本书本已经很少流通、而中译本还没有出版的情况下，中西书局拟影印原本，以飨中外读者，这真是一个好想法，故乐为之序。

2017 年 4 月 28 日完稿于北大朗润园

129
《马可·波罗之书》
2017

[英]玉尔（译注）、[法]考狄（补注），上海，英文
25×17.5 cm
上海图书馆

The Book of Ser Marco Polo, 2017
Henry Yule (ed. & tr.), Henri Cordier (revised),
Shanghai, English
25×17.5 cm
Shanghai Library

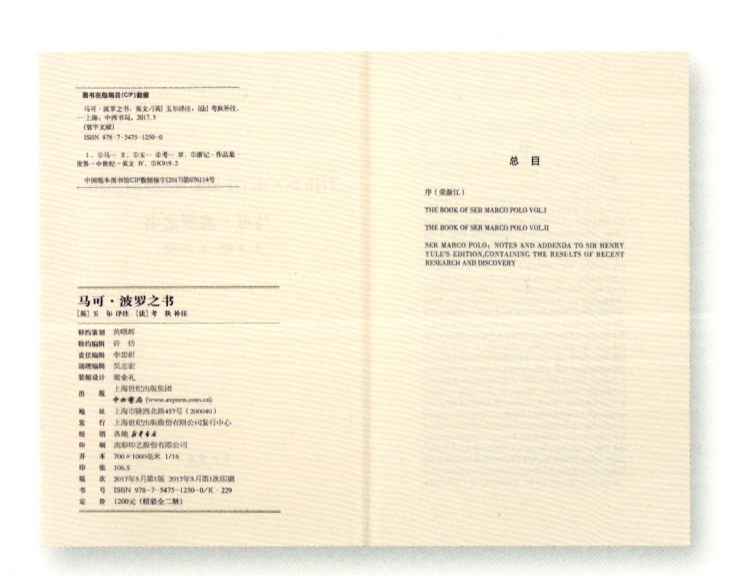

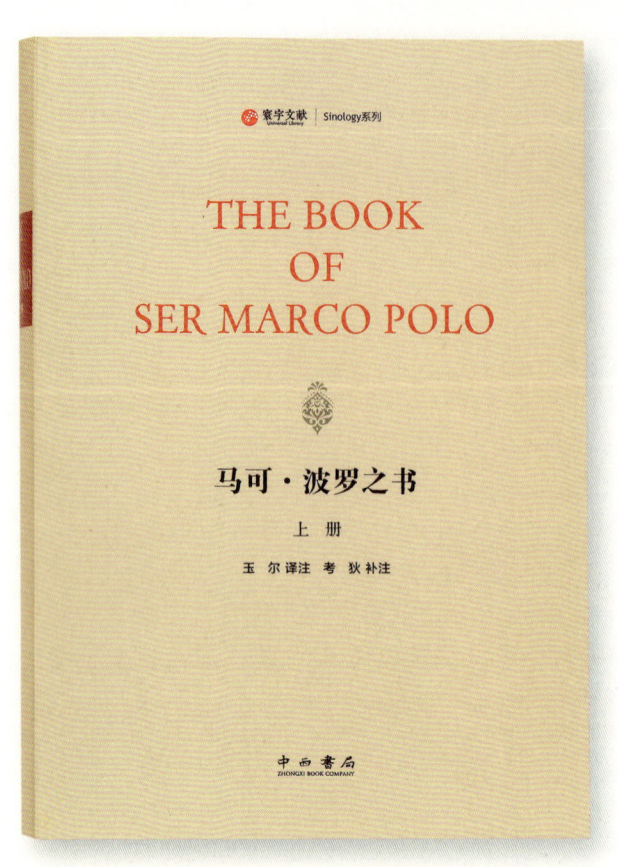

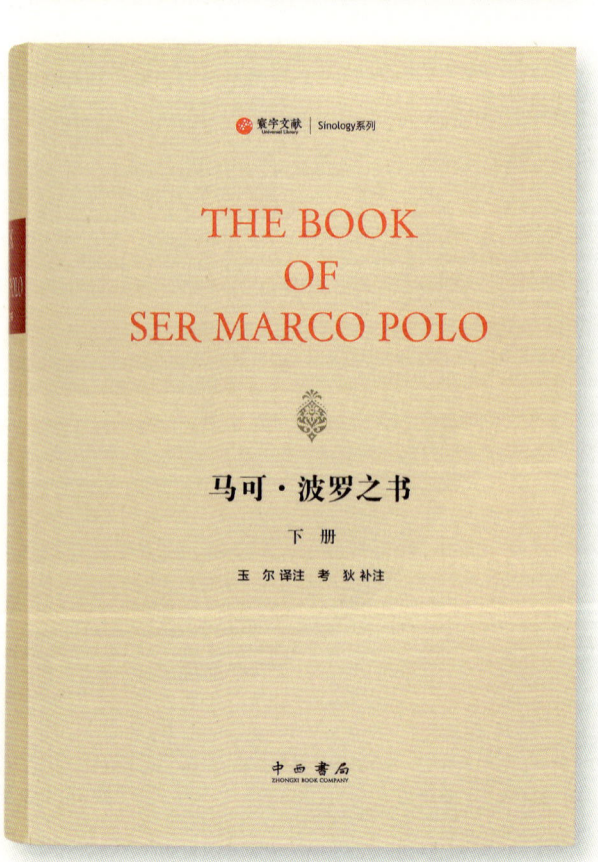

第四部分
烂 然 星 陈

130
《马可·波罗注》
2017

[法]伯希和（著），上海，英文
25×17.5 cm
上海图书馆

Notes on Marco Polo, 2017
Paul Pelliot (au.), Shanghai, English
25×17.5 cm
Shanghai Library

第四部分
烂然星陈

虚实之界：奇迹之书
《马可·波罗游记》主题文献图录

第四部分
烂 然 星 陈

序

蒙新江

本书是法国汉学家伯希和（Paul Pelliot, 1878—1945）对《马可·波罗寰宇记》中出现的专有名词所做的注释和研究，作为伯希和的遗著之一，由其弟子韩百诗（Louis Hambis）整理出版，第1—2卷为注释，第3卷为索引，分别在1959、1963、1973年陆续出版。

伯希和的《马可·波罗注》（Notes on Marco Polo），原本是他与英国汉学家慕阿德（A. C. Moule, 1873—1957）合作的《马可·波罗寰宇记》（The Description of the World）的第3卷，这本在《寰宇记》第2卷的后面有明确的记录，其中部分稿于在1939—1940年间已经交到伦敦。但伯希和多才多艺，属意的事情实在太多，所以直到1945年去世为止，也未撰完成。伯希和最初对此做了详细的规划，首先是把本书中所有的专有名词抽取出来，通过各种写本、印本的拼法，找出《寰宇记》笔录者鲁斯蒂谦（Rustichello）所使用的正确格式，以便于在维打的校译本中使用最正确的拼法。然后按照字母顺序，对这些专有名词做详细的解释，包括对这些专名的语源考证、找出专名在各种语言中的转译以及异写的原因。根据东西方史料对人名、地名、官名等追本溯源而做考证，并加以阐述。由于工作量太大，即使有有天本事的伯希和，也未去来颠沛先死，生前只写了从A字头的Abacan到C字头的Culificar，两未完成C字头的最后条目比较简单。在伯希和去世后，对蒙古史也有很高造诣的弟子韩百诗将他留下的笔记整理成两卷本《马可·波罗注》，并包括D到Z字头的注释稿，又编制详细的索引，作为本书第3卷。正是出于这样的原因，第1卷所收的A至C字头专有名词的注释稿共1—203页，计611页；第2卷所收的D至Z字头专有名词的注释稿有204—386页，计613—885页；前者三个字母有六百多页，后者24个字母只有272页。

可见是一部未完成的《马可·波罗注》。作为伯希和与慕阿德合著的《马可·波罗寰宇记》的续编，这部在巴黎出版的著作用宽体大16开的开本、咖啡色的封面，都和前者保持一致。

在已写就的A至C字头的条目中，我们可以看到伯希和才华横溢的篇章。我们不能用一般的"注释"词义来理解伯希和的《马可·波罗注》，在那个注释越长越是显示学问的时代，有些条目早已超出一般的注释，而成为一篇系统论述该主题的文章。这里一本书哩！我们不妨看看一些条目的页数，比如Alains "阿兰"，也就是古代的奄蔡，是16—25页，Caragian "哈刺章"，云南，169—181页；Caraunas "哈邓兀纳思"，183—196页；Cascar "喀什噶尔"，汉唐的疏勒，196—214页；Catai "契丹"，216—229页；Cin "秦"，中国，264—278页；Ciorcia "主儿拍"，即女真，上溯到靺鞨、柔然，366—390页；Cotan "新哉"，于阗，408—425页；Cowries "贝币"，531—563页；Cublai "忽必烈"，565—569页；Curmos "忽鲁谟斯"，576—582页；Caiton "刺桐"，泉州，583—597弧等等都有着小标题，加扁者论了人昌印等，中亚军棉花的记录，以及如何进入中国的问题，两者都是一本书的规模。这就是伯希和的风格；他生前完成的正式著作并不多，大多数是论文、札记、书评。马可·波罗的书本来是最能让伯希和展现其才华的场域，可惜他做的过头了。在他去世后，我们看到这部未完的《马可·波罗注》成为一座尼重翻的倒金字塔。

伯希和于1878年5月28日出生在巴黎，毕业于巴黎自由政治和东方语言学院，师从沙畹（E. Chavannes）、考狄（H. Cordier）和列维（S. Lévi），在汉学、佛学方面受到良好的训练。1900年，伯希和在北京进上与幕阿德会识。随后几年负责的远东学院任职，主要研究印度佛教。1906—1908年，他率领法国中亚考察队，发掘巴楚、库车等古代佛教遗址，并深入敦煌，搜索大量敦煌写本和附画。敦煌的巨大收获虽然引起争议，但最终止不年33岁的伯希和在1911

年登上法兰西学院讲座教授的席位。但因为第一次世界大战爆发，伯希和应征入伍，又一直宣身份于1912—1919年间再次来到北京，公务之余，兼做顾问。1919年回到巴黎后，伯希和进入学术研究的最佳境界，在《通报》、《亚洲学报》、《法国远东学院刊》等杂志上，连篇累牍地发表论文、书评；1921年，伯希和人选为法国金石与美文学院院士。1932年，他代表法国教育部，到印度支那巡视法国远东学院工作。然后前往中国和日本访问，均受到热烈欢迎。第二次世界大战的爆发，显然影响了这位学术巨人的正常发挥，而此时的一项重要工作，正是《马可·波罗注》的撰写。1945年10月26日，刚刚迎来德国投降的波兰和国际汉学界，却失去了年仅67岁的伯希和教授。

作为一位欧洲的汉学家或东方学家，伯希和承其老师学狄的衣钵，很早就关注马可·波罗《寰宇记》了。1904年撰写《交广印度两道考》（Deux itinéraires de Chine enIndé à la fin du VIIIe siècle, BEFEO, 4, 1904年）时，就引用了《马可·波罗》对中国南方的描述。韩百诗忆说，伯希和在1918—1930年和1936—1939年间度在法兰西学院授课期间，曾多次讲述马可·波罗之书。除了与慕阿德合作出版《马可·波罗寰宇记》外，伯希和独发表的有关《寰宇记》的专题文章不多，但他几乎与一种新的《马可·波罗行记》的整理本或译本，都撰写了书评：1904年发表尔（Henry Yule）译注、考狄补注的《马可·波罗之书》（The Book of Ser Marco Polo, The Venation, Concerning the Kingdoms and Marvels of the East）第三版的书评（BEFEO, 4, 768—772页）；1928年发表沙海昂（A.J.H. Charignon）现代法文译本（Le Livre de Marco Polo citoyen de Venise）的书评（T'oung Pao, 25, 156—169页）；1932年发表里奇（Aldo Ricci）英译本《马可·波罗行记》（The Travels of Marco Polo）的书评（T'oung Pao, 29, 233—235页）。因此，伯希和虽然没有对马可·波罗的书有专题论文，但主在跟踪马可·波罗书的最新研究成果。伯希和学术抱负和对《马可·波罗寰宇记》的长期关注，使他成为解释这部书中有名物最佳人选，但一个人的学术生命是有限的，他没有计算好自己学术生命的时间。最后没有完成他的《马可·波罗注》之类。他的这部遗著出是在他去世多年后，在戴密微（P. Demiéville）院士的推动下，经

过弟子韩百诗的努力，加上突厥学家哈密屯（J. Hamilton）、藏学家麦克唐纳（A.W. Macdonald）的帮助，才得以出版。至于从学术角度看伯希和对马可·波罗研究的贡献，则可以参考法国当今马可·波罗研究的泰斗菲利普·梅纳尔（Philippe Ménard）的专文（Paul Pelliot et les études sur Marco Polo, Paul Pelliot (1878—1945), De l'histoire à la légende, Actes de colloque, Paris, Académie des Inscriptions et Belles-Lettres, 2013, pp. 493-525）。

伯希和大概是中国读者最熟悉的一位汉学家了，这不仅仅是因为他在敦煌盗宝的故事，还缘于冯承钧先生翻译了他的大量西域南海史地论著，耿昇先生则翻译了他的许多西域敦煌考察探险记录。但他用英文撰写的《马可·波罗注》，一直没有中文译本。之前曾听说龚方震先生曾组织人员翻译，但书稿"文革"中遗失而未能重新再译。在中华书局成立汉学编辑室座谈会上，一位资深专业翻译家说想翻译这部著作，但苦于手边无书。我随后复印一套寄上，迄今未见出版。这部书的原本现在同样已经很难寻觅，中西书局打算将其影印出版，对于学界无疑是个喜讯。我近年来关注马可·波罗及其《寰宇记》的研究，应邀撰序，因略述伯希和研究马可·波罗之原委，以便读者使用其详略不一的注释时参考。

2017年4月30日完稿于东京旅次

NOTES ON MARCO POLO

图书在版编目（CIP）数据

虚实之界：奇迹之书《马可·波罗游记》主题文献图录 / 上海图书馆编. -- 上海：上海书画出版社，2025.2. -- ISBN 978-7-5479-3544-6

Ⅰ. K919.2-64

中国国家版本馆CIP数据核字第2025Q0V072号

虚实之界：
奇迹之书《马可·波罗游记》主题文献图录
上海图书馆　编

责任编辑	孙　晖　袁　媛
审　　读	陈家红
英文审读	张　颖
责任校对	田程雨
装帧设计	陈绿竞
技术编辑	吴　金

出版发行	上海世纪出版集团 上海书画出版社
地址	上海市闵行区号景路159弄A座4楼
邮政编码	201101
网址	www.shshuhua.com
E-mail	shuhua@shshuhua.com
制版印刷	上海雅昌艺术印刷有限公司
经销	各地新华书店
开本	965×635　1/8
印张	37.5
版次	2025年2月第1版　2025年2月第1次印刷
书号	ISBN 978-7-5479-3544-6
定价	480.00元

若有印刷、装订质量问题，请与承印厂联系